Inventing the "American Way"

Inventing the "American Way"

The Politics of Consensus from the New Deal to the Civil Rights Movement

WENDY L. WALL

OXFORD
UNIVERSITY PRESS

Oxford University Press, Inc., publishes works that further
Oxford University's objective of excellence
in research, scholarship, and education.

Oxford   New York
Auckland   Cape Town   Dar es Salaam   Hong Kong   Karachi
Kuala Lumpur   Madrid   Melbourne   Mexico City   Nairobi
New Delhi   Shanghai   Taipei   Toronto

With offices in
Argentina   Austria   Brazil   Chile   Czech Republic   France   Greece
Guatemala   Hungary   Italy   Japan   Poland   Portugal   Singapore
South Korea   Switzerland   Thailand   Turkey   Ukraine   Vietnam

Published by Oxford University Press, Inc.
198 Madison Avenue, New York, NY 10016

www.oup.com

First issued as an Oxford University Press paperback, 2009

Oxford is a registered trademark of Oxford University Press

Library of Congress Cataloging-in-Publication Data
Wall, Wendy, 1962–
Inventing the American way : the politics of consensus from the New Deal to the civil rights movement /
Wendy L. Wall.
p. cm.
Includes bibliographical references and index.
ISBN 978-0-19-539240-1 (pbk.)
1. United States—Politics and government—1933–1945. 2. United States—Politics and government—
1945–1989. 3. Political culture—United States—History—20th century. 4. Nationalism—United States—
History—20th century. 5. Businessmen—United States—Political activity—History—20th century. 6. United
States—Officials and employees—Political activity—History—20th century. 7. Elite (Social sciences)—United
States—Political activity—History—20th century. 8. Political activists—United States—History—20th
century. 9. Intellectuals—United States—Political activity—History—20th century. 10. United States—Social
conditions—20th century.
I. Title.
E743.W355 2008
973.917—dc22   2007010975

9 8 7 6 5 4 3 2 1

Printed in the United States of America
on acid-free paper

To my parents
John Kliewer Wall and
Joyce Brickman Wall

Acknowledgments

When a project takes as long as this one has one accumulates many debts—to colleagues, institutions, friends, and family. To those named below, and many others here unnamed, I am immeasurably grateful.

The insightful comments, criticisms, and suggestions of various mentors helped shape this project from its inception. David Kennedy offered enthusiastic support (occasionally balanced by judicious skepticism), and prompted me to think even more broadly about the topics addressed here than I was inclined to do on my own. Meetings with George Frederickson left me both reenergized and intellectually inspired; the interest with which he read my accounts of people and events he'd sometimes experienced firsthand persuaded me that I was on the right track. Steven Zipperstein's quiet generosity of spirit always made his office seem like an ocean of calm. Daniel Kevles and Nancy Hewitt offered me invaluable support and sage counsel at various stages in the process. As meticulous scholars committed to nurturing younger historians and to reaching a broader public, all offered wonderful models of the best that academia has to offer. Although she does not know it, my high school history teacher Tassie Hadlock Piltz first sparked my interest in America's national identity.

My thinking has benefited enormously over the years from the insights of seminar and panel participants, manuscript reviewers, and colleagues at Stanford, Caltech, Duke, and Colgate. Susan Thorne and Faye Dudden read the entire manuscript at different stages; both offered helpful editorial advice and a gentle nudge to "send it off." The comments of Kevin Kruse, David Hollinger, and two anonymous readers helped guide my thinking at various stages in the revision process. I am also grateful to Eric and Jessica Allina-Pisano, Antonio Barrera, David Bennett, Robert Cherny, Estelle Freedman, Chris Henke, Carolyn Hsu, Glenn Loury, Robert Nemes, David Robinson, Andy Rotter, Camilla

Townsend and Judith Weisenfeld for their comments on ideas or langauge in this book.

Audience members at professional conferences and other forums responded graciously and thoughtfully to my work. I am particularly thankful to the following institutions for giving me the opportunity to discuss my findings: the American Historical Association, the American Studies Association, the Organization of American Historians, the Research Triangle's Intellectual History Seminar, the Research Triangle's Feminist Women in History Group, the research workshop of B.U.'s Institute on Race and Social Division, and the University of Wisconsin's History Department. Special thanks to Ragnhild Fiebig-von Hase who provided my earliest model of a professional historian and later arranged for me to present some preliminary thoughts to the annual conference of historians in the German Association of American Studies.

Stanford University provided financial support for this project in its earliest stages. The National Endowment for the Humanities generously awarded me a dissertation fellowship. I began thinking about this project while a predoctoral fellow at the Stanford Humanities Center, and launched my revisions while a research associate at Boston University's Institute on Race and Social Division. Both centers offered not only financial support, but wonderful colleagues who helped to sharpen my thinking. A Clarke Chambers Travel Fellowship from the Social Welfare History Archives at the University of Minnesota, a Gilder Lehrman Fellowship at Columbia University's Rare Book and Manuscript Library, and research grants from the Hagley Museum and Library, the Rockefeller Archive Center, and the Harry S. Truman Library Institute allowed me to do extensive work in those archives. Colgate University's Research Council funded further travel, translating help, and the acquisition of many of the images found in this book.

Archivists and librarians provided vital assistance at various stages along the way. I am indebted to the staffs of the research libraries and archives mentioned above, as well as to those at the National Archives in Washington, D.C. and College Park, Maryland; the National Records Center in Suitland, Maryland; the Library of Congress; the Wisconsin State Historical Society; the Harvard University archives; Baker Library at Harvard Business School; the New York Public Library; the American Jewish Committee's Blaustein Library; the YIVO Institute for Jewish Research; the Advertising Council Archives at the University of Illinois; the Immigration History Research Center; the Hoover Institution's library and archives; and the university libraries at Stanford, the California Institute of Technology, Duke, and Colgate. David Klaassen at the

Social Welfare History Archives deserves special thanks for alerting me to the papers of the Child Study Association of America, a discovery that made Superman a part of this story. Special thanks also to Ann Ackerson, Karen Forni Austin, and others on the circulation and interlibrary loan staffs at Colgate; their creativity and persistence allowed me to complete this book at a time when the college's main library was closed for renovation and much of the collection relevant to my project was in long-term storage.

Irving Elichirigoity and Anthony Cashman helped me translate articles from the Italian-American press. Linda Hallberg translated portions of Gunnar and Alva Myrdal's *Kontakt med Amerika* from Swedish. Cindy Ryan spent weeks restoring research files that became garbled when I translated them from WordPerfect to Word. Ray Nardelli and Carolyn Hsu helped me prepare some of the illustrations for this volume.

Both the 1942 and 1965 editions of Margaret Mead's national character study *And Keep Your Powder Dry* are quoted courtesy of the Institute for Intercultural Studies, Inc. in New York, New York. Parts of chapters 3 and 5 previously appeared in altered form in "'Our Enemies Within': Nazism, National Unity and America's Wartime Discourse on Tolerance," in *Enemy Images in American History*, eds. Ragnhild Fiebig-von Hase and Ursula Lehmkuhl (Providence, R.I.: Berghahn Books, 1997), 209–229. A portion of Chapter 8 appeared as "America's 'Best Propagandists': Italian Americans and the 1948 'Letters to Italy' Campaign," in *Cold War Constructions: The Political Culture of United States Imperialism, 1945–1966*, ed. Christian Appy (Amherst: University of Massachusetts Press, 2000), 89–109. Thanks to both presses for permission to reprint this material.

At Oxford University Press, Susan Ferber shepherded this project through the approval process with lightning speed. Armed with her ever-present Blackberry, she answered questions from hotel rooms in Texas and a highway in Virginia. Many thanks also to my production editor Gwendolyn T. Colvin for all her work on the final stages of the book.

Friends and family members unstintingly offered emotional support, a sounding board for my ideas, lodging, emergency childcare, and last-minute computer assistance. Although any list would be incomplete, I am particularly indebted to Johnny Wall, Kimberly and Chris Wall Overton, Michael Wall and Wendy Feng, Rochelle and Ari Zak, Paul Engelmayer and Emily Mandelstam, Inés Salazar and Jeff Ungar, Thomas and Friedemarie Farrar, Scott Kilman, Katherine Jolluck, Jehanne Gheith, Andy Rotter and Padma Kaimal, Carolyn Hsu and Chris Henke, Kären Wigen, Pilar Mejia Barrera, Regina Conti, Astrid

Helfant, and Elizabeth Marlowe. This project could never have been completed without the cheerful staff of the Chenango Nursery School and a host of exceptional babysitters. In the final decade of his life, the late Eugene Robertson shared with me his love of Paul Robeson and much more; he embodied for me the humane and progressive patriotism that marked much of the American left during the 1930s.

A handful of individuals deserve special thanks for sustaining my faith in myself and this project. For the better part of three decades, Amy Schwartz has been a close friend and soul mate. She allowed me to camp in her tiny apartment for weeks at a time, was intellectual midwife to this project in its early stages, and brought her journalist's ear and eye to the completed manuscript. Alison Tucher has also listened patiently and cheered me on since this book's inception; she and her husband, Chuck Dyke, established the "Tucher-Dyke Fund for Mothers in Academia" to help me pay for some additional childcare during the book's final stages. On my journey through graduate school and beyond, I have been blessed with the company of a wonderful and evolving group of fellow sojourners: Karen Dunn-Haley, Ariela Gross, Leslie M. Harris, Alice Yang Murray, Wendy Lynch and Renee Romano. Over the years, we shared meals, laughs, sorrows and confidences; practiced job talks and lectures; and swapped writing at regular reading group "retreats." They have all read multiple versions of this manuscript, and they inevitably had more confidence in me than I had in myself. For this, and for their criticisms and companionship, I am deeply grateful.

My greatest debts are to my immediate family. Andrew W. Robertson has experienced both the joys and perils of being married to a fellow historian. Over the years, our wide-ranging discussions of my topic have never failed to restore my enthusiasm, and his love, support and sense of humor have lighted my path in the darkest times. Our dogs, Beau and Nimh, accompanied me on numerous restorative beach walks and hikes. Laura Joyce Robertson and Thaddeus Daniel Wall Robertson both arrived while I was turning my dissertation into a book and they were forced to share their mother with that project. They constantly reminded me that there are more important things than manuscripts, and they invariably kept me laughing, even in the final grueling stretch.

My love of history was born at my parents' dinner table and in their living room. When I was eleven or twelve, we would gather by the fireplace while my father read chapters from a lengthy history of the Revolutionary War; later we would replay battles over dinner with the carton of milk standing in for the Continental Army and the peas representing their British foes. Family vacations took me to California missions and Colorado mining camps, Civil War battlefields and Mississippi river towns, and through nearly forty states. I first heard about the original Freedom Train from my parents, as we waited to board its more limited reincarnation in 1976. Without my mother and father's interest in history and their faith in America, I would never have gone to graduate school, let alone tackled this project. Without their enduring love and support—not to mention a certain degree of inherited stubbornness—I would never have seen it through to fruition. With love and gratitude, I dedicate it to them.

Permissions

Contents

Inventing the "American Way"

Introduction

In May 1947, an illustrious group of business and advertising executives, Hollywood moguls, labor leaders, and heads of religious, civic, and civil rights organizations gathered at the White House to put their stamp of approval on one of the most ambitious ideological campaigns ever undertaken in the United States: the Freedom Train. Later that year, a train carrying over one hundred *original* documents—among them, Jefferson's draft of the Declaration of Independence, Washington's copy of the Constitution, and Lincoln's scrawled Gettysburg Address—left on a sixteen-month journey through 322 cities in all forty-eight states. The Freedom Train's passage was coordinated with hundreds of local celebrations, dubbed patriotic "revival meetings," and a nationwide media blitz. Newsreels, newspapers, and national magazines gave the train extensive coverage; Freedom Train messages were worked into popular radio programs such as *Fibber McGee and Molly*; Irving Berlin composed a song in the train's honor; and four million schoolchildren received copies of the comic book *Captain Marvel and the Freedom Train!* An estimated 3.5 million Americans boarded the train during its travels, and as many as one in three participated in Freedom Rallies, Freedom Fashion Shows, and other events staged to celebrate the train's arrival in their towns.[1]

Both the train and the media barrage were ostensibly designed to remind Americans of their shared heritage and values. Comments made by the train's organizers, however, suggested that the project was designed to instill, rather than simply reflect, those common mores. Attorney General Tom Clark, whose office originated the idea, argued that "indoctrination in democracy is the essential catalytic agent needed to blend our varying groups into one American family."[2] Paramount Pictures president Barney Balaban, the son of Russian Jewish immigrants and the man who helped transform the train into a major extravaganza, saw in the Freedom Train "a wonderful vehicle for creating good will among various racial and religious groups."[3] Thomas

D'Arcy Brophy, the advertising executive who ultimately orchestrated the entire project, hoped to defuse class tensions and head off "state socialism" in the U.S. by "re-selling Americanism to Americans."[4]

Each of these individuals had a slightly different agenda, and their voices were not the only ones shaping the project. Indeed, the façade of consensus surrounding the Freedom Train concealed an ongoing contest involving many different groups. Behind the scenes and occasionally in public, corporate and advertising executives, Truman administration officials, civil servants with New Deal loyalties, Communists, pacifists, ardent segregationists, and southern blacks fighting to end Jim Crow vied to control the message and meaning of the train. Controversy erupted over the documents that would be included in the exhibit and over the interpretation ascribed to each: Were the Fourteenth and Fifteenth amendments to the Constitution—those guaranteeing "due process" and the right to vote—really the "*common* heritage of *all* Americans"?[5] Were pictures of immigrants, artifacts documenting the rise of the labor movement, or even FDR's 1940 speech declaring America to be the "arsenal of democracy" sufficiently noncontroversial to be displayed aboard the Freedom Train? How much attention should be paid to Alexander Hamilton, a favorite of economic conservatives, as compared to Thomas Jefferson, the founding father beloved by New Deal Democrats? The issue of race—specifically, whether whites and blacks should board the train and view the documents together—proved particularly troublesome when the train headed into the South. Indeed, the controversy over segregation became so heated that train organizers instructed advance workers operating below the Mason-Dixon Line to refer to it in telegrams simply as "Problem D." In this charged environment, even a word as seemingly central to America's national identity as "democracy" was ultimately deemed too controversial to be used in slogans and press materials. Under the banner of "freedom," Americans with widely divergent interests used the Freedom Train to reinforce the corporate order, shore up support for the cold war, and campaign for religious tolerance and civil rights.

The story of the Freedom Train highlights the politics of consensus in America in the middle decades of the twentieth century. At first glance, these two notions—"politics" and "consensus"—may seem at odds. After all, "consensus" suggests a fundamental agreement on values—in the words of the *Oxford English Dictionary,* "the collective unanimous opinion of a number of persons."[6] Certainly, American pundits and scholars writing in the two decades following World War II tended to downplay political battles and to stress the values their fellow citizens shared. In 1949, Arthur M. Schlesinger Jr., optimistically declared that most Americans, in the North and South, accepted the basic tenets of civil rights, while "liberals have values in common with most members of the business community."[7] Eleven years later, the political scientist Clinton Rossiter agreed: "In this favored country we have almost always found more things on which to agree than to disagree," he wrote in a report commissioned by President Eisenhower. The early 1960s, he added, "appear to be a time of broad consensus on fundamentals."[8]

Our view looking back has been strongly shaped by such pronouncements. For nearly half a century, both scholarly and popular commentators have depicted the postwar years, and especially the 1950s and early 1960s, as a time of unusually deep and well-grounded national unity, a time when postwar affluence and the cold war combined to produce a remarkable level of agreement about the nation's core values.[9] Observers on both the left and the right compare the fractiousness and polarization of politics today to the presumed harmony of those earlier decades.

In recent years, some scholars have challenged this picture of ideological cohesion, pointing to evidence of grassroots resistance on both the left and the right.[10] Their approach, however, begs a central question: If Americans remained divided on many issues in the postwar years, why did a tone of unity and accord so pervade the writing and politics of the era? Why did a "veneer of consensus and civility" reign?[11] After all, the combined effects of affluence and anti-communism did not produce even the appearance of consensus in other epochs of U.S. history—the 1920s or the 1980s, for example. What made the postwar decades different?

This book tackles that question. It begins with the premise that America's mid-century "consensus" can best be understood not as a "natural" development but as a political project. Broad societal trends may have contributed to the "centripetal impulse" of postwar political culture, but that culture was strongly shaped by the conscious activities of multiple groups.[12] Business and advertising executives, interfaith activists, government officials, and other cultural elites seized on the notion of a unifying and distinctive "American Way" and sought to define it in ways that furthered their own political and social agendas. All of these groups had a strong interest in cementing national cohesion, and all promoted the notion of "consensus," even as they differed on the specific values and attributes that their fellow citizens shared. The compromises they made—and the alliances they forged—did much to produce the consensus culture that marked the public arena during the postwar years.

The roots of this consensus culture can be found not in the cold war era, as previous historians have suggested, but in the turbulent decade that preceded U.S. entry into World War II. Americans of diverse backgrounds and divergent agendas were alarmed by the chaos of the Depression years, as well as by the rise of fascism and communism abroad. To conservative industrialists and left-liberal intellectuals alike, these "alien" ideologies seemed to threaten the U.S. not only externally, but internally as well. To counter such threats—to shore up their vision of American democracy or the nation's economic system—diverse groups articulated their version of a unifying national ideology and sought to convince their fellow citizens of its merits. The resulting "cultural conversation" lasted nearly three decades and spawned Broadway plays, film shorts, comic strips, movies, radio shows, advertising blitzes, and cold war letter-writing campaigns.[13] It shaped cultural productions ranging from the Freedom Train to the radio serial *The Adventures of Superman*. Its legacies include terms that remain central to American political life—terms such as "free enterprise" and the "American Way," both of which were popularized in the late 1930s.

Two key struggles lie at the heart of this story, overlapped by a third. The first revolved around the shape and place of capitalism in American life. The economic collapse of the 1930s undermined the political and cultural authority of the nation's business community and called into question rarely challenged assumptions about the stability and course of U.S. society. In this context, President Roosevelt and his New Dealers promoted an "American Way" built around the twin pillars of majoritarian democracy and economic security for all Americans. Freedom from want, FDR argued, was a vital underpinning of democracy and something that could only be ensured by an activist government. Industrial unionists and those on the left wing of the New Deal coalition pushed FDR's vision even further, calling for an extension of majoritarian democracy from the political into the economic realm. In practice, such "industrial democracy" could take many forms, ranging from the spread of consumer and industrial cooperatives to a greater role for labor in corporate decision-making.

Corporate leaders and their allies responded to this challenge by launching an all-out campaign beginning in the late 1930s to reassert their authority and to shore up what they often referred to as the "American economic system." Regrouping after the initial shock of the Depression—and increasingly convinced that their problems lay not with New Deal "radicals" but with the American people as a whole—business groups launched a series of advertising and public relations campaigns designed to reeducate the public. They promoted a version of the American Way that celebrated individual freedom rather than majoritarian democracy and that posited a harmony of interests among classes. Replacing the beleaguered term "private enterprise" with the more resonant "free enterprise," they responded to New Deal and labor efforts to link Americans' economic and political rights with a linkage of their own: without economic freedom, they argued, Americans' political, civil, and religious liberties would disappear. Although business groups made only marginal headway in the late 1930s, they introduced themes and terms that would resonate through discussions of American political culture into the 1950s and beyond.

If debates over political economy formed one axis of the conversation on the American Way in the late 1930s, debates over the cultural definition of America formed another: How would a nation that elites had long defined as white and Protestant incorporate a diverse citizenry into its national identity and social fabric? The Depression took hold just as millions of "new immigrants" and their American-born children—and black Americans who had joined the Great Migration out of the South after World War I—were making a bid for greater political and social inclusion. The New Deal coalition welcomed many of these newly enfranchised Americans, but the Depression and escalating tensions abroad also produced a surge in anti-Semitism and other forms of ethnic and racial intolerance. Meanwhile, the successes of Fascist and Communist regimes abroad underscored both the possibilities and dangers inherent in cultural diversity. Many American opinion molders equated totalitarianism with enforced homogeneity and came to see diversity as a defining feature of democracy. The American Way, they argued, was the ability of diverse individuals to live together harmoniously. Yet such celebratory proclamations were often tinged with fear—fear that unbounded diversity could produce venomous hatreds that would ultimately tear a democracy apart. What was needed, many believed, was a broadly shared civic consensus capable of producing a stable and unified, yet tolerant and variegated, nation.

Responding to such concerns, diverse groups of Americans—liberal intellectuals, government officials, "new immigrant" and civic leaders, assimilated American Jews, and others—worked to blunt domestic intolerance and to broaden the bounds of national inclusion by promoting both cultural pluralism and a unifying American Way. They hailed America's demographic variety, even as they celebrated values that they argued were broadly shared by their fellow citizens. Those offering such prescriptive visions, however, defined the parameters of diversity and consensus in markedly different ways. Some cast America as a "nation of immigrants" or a "nation of nations," a collection of ethnically diverse individuals united by secular Enlightenment values. Others emphasized religious rather than ethnic diversity, suggesting that America was above all a "Protestant-Catholic-Jewish" nation. Advocates of this approach generally contended that religion was also a key unifying force. Americans, they proclaimed, were united by shared "Judeo-Christian" beliefs such as "the Fatherhood of God and the Brotherhood of Man" or the "sacredness of the individual."[14] Black Americans struggled with both paradigms since neither entirely acknowledged their unique history or the depth of the challenges they still faced. Still, some saw in this prewar impulse an opportunity to pursue "a politics of inclusion."[15]

A third axis of debate—the precise nature of America's foreign foe—overlapped with the other two. Beginning in the late 1930s, leftist intellectuals and artists, government officials, interfaith activists, conservative businessmen, and many others argued that an external enemy sought to turn Americans against one another—in short, to "divide and conquer" the nation. Liberals and leftists generally saw that enemy as fascism and tried to unite Americans in an antifascist consensus. Many defined fascism expansively, using it to condemn evils ranging from racial inequality and economic exploitation to red-baiting.[16] Other Americans, including ardent defenders of free enterprise, cast the nation's chief enemy as "totalitarianism," a term that encompassed communism as well. Many in this camp warned against *any* division that might sunder Americans. In their view, disgruntled workers or protesting blacks were as or more likely to provide an opening for the tactics of "divide and conquer" as were oppressive employers or purveyors of racial intolerance.

As these contrasting views of America's external enemy suggest, a central divide cut across all discussions of a unifying American Way. Many government officials and private elites—including influential voices in both the business and "intergroup" communities—used the language of consensus to promote *civility* across class, racial, ethnic, and religious lines. Denying or minimizing economic and power imbalances, they stressed the harmony of interests among various groups in American society and sought to shore up the status quo. Other Americans, however, put *equality* rather than comity at the center of their consensual vision. Civil rights activists, left-liberal intellectuals, and some advocates of the rights of labor tried to unite Americans around a set of values that they believed would ultimately lead to social change. Rather than ignoring power imbalances, they tried to use the language of consensus to correct them.[17]

These overlapping struggles over the precise nature of the American Way were ultimately reshaped by the politics of World War II and the cold war. The war against the Axis powers brought the federal government fully into the act of promoting national cohesion and produced an infrastructure of institutions devoted to publicly defining for Americans their common ground. It also forced groups on both ends of the political spectrum to curtail the vitriolic rhetoric they had sometimes used during the 1930s. In the postwar years, communism quickly replaced fascism as the nation's principal enemy. Many of those who had benefited most from the rhetoric of unity during World War II launched cultural programs designed to extend and reshape the wartime emphasis on common ground. The very energy that proponents of consensus devoted to their various campaigns, however, suggests that whatever consensus existed was fragile at best.

Inventing the "American Way" attempts to restore a sense of struggle and uncertainty to the emergence of a postwar consensus. At the same time, it sheds light on shifts at the center of U.S. political culture in the mid-twentieth century. Between the mid-1930s and the end of World War II, the focus of American liberalism—and of American politics more generally—moved from class-based concerns to a preoccupation with pluralism and individual rights.[18] This book suggests that the politics of consensus in the late 1930s and 1940s both spurred and reinforced that transformation. Many liberals who had previously worried about the dangers posed to the nation by economic inequality and an oppressive business elite became increasingly concerned that internal divisions of any sort might tear a democracy apart. Abandoning the language of progressive struggle, they promoted "tolerance" and "individual dignity" as core American values. At the same time, some in the business community sought to clothe their defense of American-style capitalism in the language of tolerance, pluralism, and national unity. In the postwar years, campaigns launched by intergroup activists on behalf of religious and sometimes racial tolerance garnered support from members of the business community who sought to burnish their image. Meanwhile, corporate leaders worked to discredit labor militancy by extending the message of social harmony and consensus at the core of such campaigns to cover class relations as well.

The relationship between religion and American public life also changed dramatically in the period covered by this book. Despite the nation's stated commitment to religious freedom contained in the Bill of Rights, virulent anti-Catholicism marked American politics into the 1920s and beyond. Anti-Semitism, too, surged after the turn of the twentieth century, assuming particularly venomous forms during the Great Depression. As late as 1931, a majority of the Supreme Court declared Americans to be a "Christian people."[19] Yet during and after World War II, the long-standing equation in public discourse of "Americanism" with Protestantism gave way rapidly, if incompletely, to the notion that the U.S. was a Judeo-Christian, "tri-faith," or broadly "God-fearing" nation.[20] This book links that transformation to the politics of consensus. To elites who were trying to define the nation through a contrast with Fascist or Communist enemies, the "interfaith idea" proved particularly useful. Both Fascists and Communists were said to embrace coercive homogeneity and to reject any religion other than that of the state. In this context, ecumenical religion could serve simultaneously as a symbol of American pluralism and American consensus.

In exploring such issues, this book seeks to illuminate the "myths, languages and arguments" that "serve[d] at least some Americans *as Americans*."[21] At the same time, it highlights the culture wars of mid-century—wars that have generally eluded our hindsight for two reasons. Many elite participants took pains to hide their differences in public and to suppress grassroots evidence of open dissent. At the same time, Americans have long shared a rich political language and a common set of motifs and historical references. "Vying for control of a common vocabulary, stealing each other's terms in hopes of investing them with radically altered meanings, political opponents have often left behind an illusion of consensus," Daniel T. Rodgers writes in his pioneering work *Contested Truths*.[22] Of no period of U.S. history is this truer than of the decades immediately following World War II: the meaning of terms such as "freedom" and "democracy" were bitterly contested during those years, even as the terms themselves were widely used. The ways in which Americans' common language and iconography both divided them and drew them together comprises one of the central themes of this book.

The conversation on consensus was carried on in many different registers and by many different voices. Because the dynamics of national identity in this period have only recently begun to attract attention from scholars, this book takes an inclusive approach—encompassing groups as diverse as left-liberal intellectuals, conservative manufacturers, interfaith activists, foreign policy strategists, and black Americans pressing for civil rights. This approach underscores the scale of the shift in American political culture at mid-century and suggests that the usual classifications applied to U.S. history in this period—political, racial, religious, labor and economic, cultural-intellectual, and diplomatic, among them—don't hold up when national identity is the subject under consideration. It also highlights connections between subjects and actors that are often considered in isolation. Finally, since the language of consensus concealed widely differing priorities, this approach helps reconcile invocations of consensus with the reality of conflict. Nevertheless, this book cannot hope to do justice to all of those involved in these debates. It focuses most heavily on individuals and institutions that were well positioned both to be heard and to contain dissenting voices.

More often than not, those with money and influence "won" the cultural battles of the 1940s and 1950s by shaping the terms of public debate. Not all Americans accepted their varied messages on the value of American-style free enterprise; the dangers of class, religious, and racial antagonism; and the need to combat first the Fascist and later the Communist threat. Nevertheless, they helped to forge a shared public vocabulary and to establish the framework in which many social and economic issues were ultimately addressed. That framework privileged individual freedom, national unity, and a shared faith in God above all else. In constructing and reinforcing this linguistic framework, they helped create a cultural reality.

While many established elites benefited from the nation's long-running conversation on consensus, they were not alone. Campaigns on behalf of religious, ethnic, and even racial "brotherhood" helped reshape American identity and reframe the boundaries of acceptable discourse, allowing many working-class ethnics and others to feel "at home" in America. Efforts to mobilize immigrants and their children into cold war propaganda campaigns often reinforced the nation's corporate order; but they also allowed first- and second-generation Americans to position themselves not as members of a threatening and alien minority, but as U.S. ambassadors and the staunchest of American patriots. Time and again, the issue of race proved a stumbling block for proponents of consensus. Still, the discourse on shared national values allowed black Americans to make limited gains. The language of individual freedom, faith, and national unity used pervasively by interfaith proponents, economic conservatives, and cold warriors was reclaimed and recast by southern blacks battling for de jure civil rights. In short, efforts to define a unifying national consensus gave religious, ethnic, and racial "outsiders" a powerful lever with which to pry open *some* doors of America's mainstream culture.

If the era's civic education campaigns helped open the door for certain kinds of social change, they slammed the door on others. Economic inequality didn't vanish with the end of World War II, but it was effectively taken off the table in the late 1940s and 1950s as a political issue. One reason for this was the widespread equation of the American Way—in sermons and civics lessons, movies and political speeches, public service advertising and press accounts—not with majoritarian democracy or egalitarian economic values but with *individual* freedoms, rights, and opportunities.[23] The focus on individual freedom proved a powerful tool in the fight against anti-Semitism, national origin quotas, and de jure racial segregation, but it made efforts to address institutionalized economic inequality politically difficult, if not untenable.[24]

The politics of consensus fractured in the upheavals of the late 1960s and early 1970s. In the era of Vietnam, youth protests, resurgent celebrations of ethnicity, and widely publicized urban riots and anti-busing violence, the varied elites who had worked for several decades to nurture and shape an illusory national consensus were no longer able to channel or contain dissenting voices. Many racial and ethnic outsiders who had once embraced the notion of shared American values and tried to shape the language of consensus to their own ends now rejected an idiom rooted ultimately in American patriotism. The economic productivity and affluence that had once seemed to succor national harmony and consensus now sparked sharp denunciations of American materialism and the maldistribution of wealth. The processes of fragmentation and polarization that first surfaced during the Johnson and Nixon administrations have only accelerated in recent decades, spawning debates over multiculturalism, the public role of religion, and, most recently, "red vs. blue" America.

The legacy of the consensus era survives, however, in institutions, political rhetoric, and assumptions about that past that continue to inform discussions of national unity and public values. Competing attempts to define core American values—to find common ground capable of uniting increasingly estranged groups of Americans—often take this period as their implicit backdrop. Proponents and critics of affirmative action, abortion restrictions, gay marriage, welfare and immigration reform, and a host of other issues invoke phrases and ideas popularized during this era. At a time when America seems more polarized than ever—yet when politicians and commentators continue to call for national unity and a return to the "vital center"—it is instructive to know how and why a fragile national consensus was shaped in the past, what it did for American political discourse and values, and what it inevitably could not do.[25]

PART I

Enemies at Home and Abroad (1935–1941)

CHAPTER 1

"Are We a Nation?"

In the spring of 1937, *Harper's* magazine announced a $1,000 essay contest to define a phrase that had suddenly begun to appear in newspaper headlines and on billboards across the nation: the "American Way." The term was not entirely new to America's political lexicon; but in the mid-1930s, it exploded into popular use. In the eighty years preceding Franklin Delano Roosevelt's election in 1932, the phrase appeared some 725 times in the pages of the *New York Times*, generally in either the negative ("not the American way") or the plural ("American ways and customs"). In the ten years following, it made some 2,230 appearances in the newspaper's pages and was frequently capitalized. Books began to appear entitled simply *The American Way* or *The American Way of Life*. Before 1933, only two volumes had used the phrase in their titles; one of these was *The American Way of Playing Ukulele Solos*.[1]

Those who wrote about the "American Way" were a diverse lot: a conservative economic columnist and an expert on adult education, representatives of what was then called the National Conference of Jews and Christians and the famous playwriting team of George Kaufman and Moss Hart. Henry Wallace, Roosevelt's progressive Secretary of Agriculture, weighed in on the topic with an article entitled "The Search for an American Way." So too did the liberal journalist and commentator Elmer Davis, librarians and bankers, the National Association of Manufacturers, and compilers of a reading list for Harvard College students.[2]

By early 1937, the phrase was being invoked so widely that the editors of *Harper's* felt it was time for clarification. The magazine invited its readers to help "restate" and "reinterpret" American traditions and ideals in light of the Depression at home and threatening ideologies abroad. "Words and phrases like 'democracy,' 'liberty,' 'the pioneer spirit,' 'equality of opportunity,' 'self-reliance,' 'local self-rule,' and 'constitutional government' mean different things to different people," the magazine's editors acknowledged. "We should like to see the essential American traditions and ideals separated from the un-essential and the outdated, so as to form a credo adapted to present and future needs." The need to articulate such a credo had never been greater, *Harper's* editors suggested. "The doctrines loosely known as communism and fascism have to-day virtually the emotional force of religions," they wrote. "It might be a good thing if those American ideas and ideals which many of us take for granted…could be formulated anew so that men and women of diverse politi-cal and economic views might join in accepting them with a will, feeling that they offer not only a link with the past but a guide to action." The magazine urged contestants to present the American creed in such a way as to "rally enthusiasm."[3]

The *Harper's* contest eventually attracted 1570 essays; but if the maga-zine's editors hoped it would reveal a widespread agreement on the nation's core values, they must surely have been disappointed. The contributions varied "from arguments for communism" to "arguments for old-fashioned aristocratic ideals," the editors later wrote, "from arguments for all manner of specific economic programs, such as systems of co-operatives or changes in the currency, to fervid defenses of the status quo; from up-to-the-minute discussions of the alleged glories or the alleged abominations of the New Deal to careful analyses of the backgrounds and principles of the early Colonists, the Constitution-makers, the Founding Fathers."[4] Ultimately, *Harper's* editors re-printed four essays. A construction engineer turned New Deal planner argued that "liberty has to be founded on security," while a Hollywood screenwriter equated the American Way with "economic democracy…a redistribution of income from the propertied to the propertyless." A German émigré also in-voked democracy but defined it as "political equality" and "social peace." An editorial writer for the *Baltimore Evening Sun* rejected all three formulations, arguing that neither democracy nor liberty was fundamental to Americanism. Rather, he declared, both were "logical outgrowths" of the "genuine" American principles: belief in "the dignity of the individual" and "a reasonable measure of respect for reality in politics." As *Harper's* columnist Bernard DeVoto noted dryly, "Anyone can shout 'American Way' in furtherance of his own interests and nearly everyone does."[5]

The *Harper's* essay contest—and the emergence of the term "American Way" more generally—testified to the urgency with which U.S. citizens turned to the question of America's national identity and shared values in the late 1930s.

American intellectuals and political leaders had wrestled with such issues since the earliest days of the Republic; but in the latter half of the Depression decade, domestic and international pressures converged to produce a particularly intense, self-conscious, and wide-ranging "cultural conversation" on the nation's collective identity.[6] "American Way" was not the only resonant phrase to appear at that historical moment. The historian James Truslow Adams introduced the expression "American dream" in his 1931 tome *The Epic of America*. By the end of the decade, playwrights, educators, journalists, ministers, and individuals ranging from Herbert Hoover to the immigrant writer Louis Adamic were employing the phrase to indicate an ideal or aspiration shared by all Americans.[7] Other writers discussed the "American creed" and the "American idea," both terms that also appeared far more frequently than they had in the past.

As the *Harper's* essay contest suggested, however, the widespread invocation of a common American way, dream, idea, or creed did not indicate the dawn of an era of harmony and consensus.[8] On the contrary, the proliferation of such terms in the late 1930s attested to a profound sense of anxiety—an anxiety shared by Americans across the political spectrum—about national identity and unity in an increasingly threatening world. The collapse of the national economy undermined long-standing power structures and called into question rarely challenged assumptions about the stability and progress of American capitalism. The maturation of "new immigrant" communities and the migration of thousands of blacks out of the South raised questions about the terms on which ethnic, religious, and racial "outsiders" would be incorporated into a society that had long been defined by elites as Anglo-Saxon and Protestant. Above all, the political triumphs of fascism and communism abroad—combined with fears that those ideologies were gaining ground in the U.S.—intensified concerns about America's core values, prompting those on the left as well as those on the right to try to define an alternative ideology cast in "American" terms. All this was reflected in the question posed by James Truslow Adams at the end of the decade: "Are we, as some have said, merely a hodgepodge of minorities? Or are we a nation with a common background and, despite our political battles, a continuing national ideal?"[9]

"Buried Under the Ruins"

The "crisis of Americanism" began in October 1929, when the "Great Bull Market" of the Twenties collapsed, wiping out in a matter of weeks almost 40 percent of the value of U.S. stocks.[10] Financial commentators initially dismissed the downturn as a speculative panic, but the crash was merely the portent of the Great Depression to come. Plunging stock prices helped upend the nation's overleveraged economy, causing thousands of banks and businesses to fail. Within five months, 3.2 million Americans were out of work; and two years later, unemployment had climbed to nearly 13 million, some 25 percent of the national workforce. By early 1932, the nation's industrial production was less than half what it had been just three years earlier.[11]

The economic catastrophe fundamentally challenged the way Americans conceptualized their nation. For the previous 150 years, most Americans had believed that, whatever one's individual fate, the nation as a whole was growing ever more prosperous. America's experience in the opening decades of the twentieth century had strongly reinforced this faith. Between 1900 and 1930, the nation's manufacturing output quadrupled, thanks in part to widespread factory electrification. The advent of mass production, consumer credit, and advertising produced in the U.S. the world's first mass consumer economy. Rural Americans for the most part did not share in this economic bonanza; but for those in the nation's urban centers, the prosperity was tangible. Middle-class families acquired washing machines, refrigerators, telephones, and automobiles, while urban workers bought canned foods, radios, and tickets to motion picture theatres.[12] "We thought American business was the Rock of Gibraltar," recalled E. Y. (Yip) Harburg several decades later. "We were the prosperous nation and nothing could stop us now."[13]

By the early 1930s, this national narrative of capitalist-driven growth and abundance seemed questionable at best, a monstrous delusion at worst. In Chicago, men fought over the contents of restaurants' garbage barrels and teachers fainted in their classrooms for want of food. In Stockton, California, people scavenged the city dump looking for half-rotten vegetables. In Appalachia, families subsisted on "such weeds as cows eat," and siblings sometimes alternated meals. Millions of Americans were evicted or lost heavily mortgaged houses and farms, and at least one million took to the road.[14] Millions more lost jobs or bank accounts, pared spending to the bone, or dropped out of school to help support their families. Yip Harburg lost his business, became a lyricist, and penned the song that would become the anthem of the decade: "Brother, Can You Spare a Dime?"

American society sometimes seemed on the verge of disintegration. In 1930 and 1931, food riots broke out in cities across the country, while rising frustration fueled mass marches of the unemployed. The following year, police and Ford Motor Co. security guards battled some three thousand hunger marchers outside the company's River Rouge plant in Dearborn, Michigan; four marchers died in the "Battle of River Rouge," and more than six thousand people joined the subsequent funeral procession, marching through downtown Detroit to the strains of the Communist Party's anthem, the "Internationale." By 1933, Midwestern farmers were dumping milk, blockading roads, and using vigilante justice to disrupt foreclosure proceedings. Meanwhile, cotton workers in California's San Joaquin valley joined in the largest agricultural strike in U.S. history. In 1934, general strikes paralyzed Toledo, Minneapolis, and San Francisco, and some four hundred thousand textile workers scattered from New England to the southern piedmont walked off the job.

To some, it seemed that capitalism itself was imperiled. "Not so many years ago in Russia all the sufferings of poverty...conceived a child...and its name was Bolshevism," a woman from Oil City, Pennsylvania, warned the director of President Hoover's Emergency Committee on Unemployment in 1930. "Right now our good old U.S.A. is sitting on a Seething Volcano," she continued. "In the Public Schools our little children stand at salute and recite a 'rig ma role' in which is mentioned 'Justice to all.' What a lie, what a naked lie."[15] Rexford Tugwell, a Columbia University economist and a member of Roosevelt's Brain Trust, agreed with at least part of the woman's assessment. "I do not think it is too much to say," he confided to his journal, "that on March 4 [1933, the day Roosevelt was inaugurated] we were confronted with a choice between an orderly revolution—a peaceful and rapid departure from the past concepts—and a violent and disorderly overthrow of the whole capitalist structure."[16]

Most Americans did not join in or put down strikes, engage in riots, or pursue vigilante justice. Nevertheless, the magnitude of the Depression, the scale of the social unrest, and the reaction of government and industrial leaders to both called into question the wisdom and authority of the nation's reigning elites. No episode did more to focus public attention on the failures of U.S. capitalism and its defenders in government than the fate of the "Bonus Army." In the spring and summer of 1932, thousands of unemployed army veterans converged on Washington D.C. to demand early payment of a bonus they were owed for their service in World War I. By June, as many as twenty-five thousand had arrived in the capital, some with their families. The Senate, however, refused to accede to their demands. In late July, when the "Bonus Marchers" failed to disperse, District of Columbia police tried to evict them from empty government buildings downtown (figure 1.1). A riot ensued and President Hoover ultimately sent in federal troops. Led by General Douglas MacArthur, the troops turned tanks and tear gas on the veterans and torched their encampment.[17] The fires burning in Anacostia spewed a smoky pall over

Figure 1.1. Bonus Marchers battle Washington, D.C. police in July 1932. Episodes like this reinforced a growing sense of unease in the United States and focused public attention on the failures of U.S. capitalism and its defenders in government (National Archives 111-SC-97560).

the nation's capital, as the dispirited veterans straggled back to a camp in nearby Johnstown, Pennsylvania. "I used to be a hundred-percenter," a man with a tear-streaked face said, referring to the arch-patriots of World War I. "Now I'm a Red radical. I had an American flag, but the damned tin soldiers burned it. Now I don't ever want to see a flag again. Give me a gun and I'll go back to Washington."[18]

The image of U.S. troops turning tanks and bayonets on unarmed veterans unsettled even many conservatives. In the country at large, it reinforced a growing sense of unease. "There is a feeling among the masses generally that something is radically wrong," Oscar Ameringer, an Oklahoma attorney, told a House subcommittee in 1932. "They say the only thing you do in Washington is to take money from the pockets of the poor and put it into the pockets of the rich. They say that this Government is a conspiracy against the common people."[19] The historian Gerald Johnson argued that few middle-class Americans—the midlevel bankers, insurance solicitors, and family practitioners who lived on his block—"cherish[ed] any serious doubts about capitalism." Even they, however, had developed a "new and decidedly critical attitude" toward certain aspects of the capitalist system "as it has been developed in this country." "It will be many a long day before Americans of the middle class will listen with anything approaching the reverence they felt in 1928 whenever a magnate of business speaks," Johnson explained. "The whole pantheon of their idols has been demolished. The Big Business Man, like Samson, has pulled down the pillars of the temple…and he is pretty well buried under the ruins."[20]

Thus, by the early 1930s, the authority of business and the equation of Americanism with laissez-faire capitalism were under siege on many fronts. These developments helped propel Franklin Delano Roosevelt and his New Dealers into office. The resulting ideological battle, however, was not fully joined until the second half of the decade. In 1933, industrialists and other economic conservatives were shell shocked and demoralized, and some believed they might be able to work with the new president. Within two years their views had changed. In early 1935, FDR introduced a sprawling package of legislation—dubbed by historians the "Second New Deal"—that effectively pulled the New Deal to the left. Developments in the second half of the decade also strengthened the hand of organized labor and spawned the Committee for Industrial Organization (later the Congress of Industrial Organizations). In the late 1930s, industrial unionists sought to extend FDR's vision, even as conservative industrialists regrouped and launched an all-out defense of laissez-faire capitalism in general.

The nation's traditional elites, white and heavily Protestant, took a leading role in these debates. Increasingly, however, they were joined by the ethnic, religious, and racial "outsiders" who made up the majority of the nation's working class and whose political aspirations were just beginning to be recognized by the New Deal. These new, or newly enfranchised, Americans helped fuel the debate over the nation's political economy, while raising questions about the scope and shape of American pluralism and the nature of the nation's binding values.

"The Foreign Element in This Country"

The Great Depression struck at a very unusual moment in American history—near the start of what one scholar has called "the great immigration interregnum."[21] For nearly 150 years, immigrants had poured into the United States from all parts of the world, with twenty-seven million arriving between 1880 and 1930 alone.[22] This era of mass immigration came to an end in 1924 when

Congress passed legislation banning all immigrants from Asia and slowing the influx of people from Southern and Eastern Europe to a trickle. In the late 1920s, migrants continued to arrive from impoverished regions of Mexico and Francophone Canada; but with the collapse of the U.S. economy, even those streams evaporated. Refugees, displaced persons, and individuals from the Western hemisphere filtered into the U.S. during and after World War II, but immigration did not again approach the levels reached during the early twentieth century until after the overhaul of the nation's immigration legislation in 1965.

The virtual cutoff of immigration to the U.S. inevitably shaped discussions of America's national identity and core values. Believing that a chapter in U.S. history had closed, some scholars in the late 1920s and 1930s turned their attention to America's immigrant past, finding there a source of national exceptionalism.[23] Meanwhile, the restrictive legislation of 1924 hastened the acculturation of immigrant communities and shifted political debate from immigration per se to the terms on which the U.S. should incorporate the new arrivals. Many first- and second-generation Americans sought full political and social enfranchisement—even as they sought to define an America broad enough to encompass them. Some "old stock" Americans chafed at this notion, clinging to visions of the nation rooted in "tribal" attributes such as whiteness, Anglo-Saxon or Nordic descent, or Protestantism. Others, recognizing that the new immigrants were destined to become a potent political and cultural force, tried to shape the values and political beliefs of these newest Americans.

The stakes in these debates were heightened by the nature of the immigrants themselves. The overwhelming majority of those who arrived in the U.S. between 1890 and 1924 came from Southern and Eastern Europe, although hundreds of thousands of Japanese, Armenians, Mexicans, Syrian Christians, and others also joined the immigrant stream. Diverse as these newcomers were, they shared several characteristics. To a far greater degree than earlier immigrants, they settled in the nation's manufacturing centers, where they were quickly absorbed into a newly industrialized working class. Moreover, unlike the elites who had long shaped public conceptions of "America," relatively few were Nordic or Protestant. The vast majority were Catholic, Eastern Orthodox, or Jewish, although some practiced Buddhism, Islam, Shintoism, and assorted other religions.

Although the "new immigrants" posed the most obvious challenge to America's national identity, they were not the only new arrivals in U.S. cities. Blacks had been trickling out of the rural South since the end of Reconstruction, but the outbreak of World War I launched what became known as the "Great Migration." During the war, half a million southern blacks journeyed north to take newly available jobs in the metalworking shops, automobile plants, and packing houses of cities such as New York, Chicago, and Detroit. Black Americans occupied the lowest rungs on the industrial ladder. Still, the urban centers of the Northeast and Midwest offered an escape from the economic peonage, disfranchisement, and lynch mobs that shaped black life in the rural South. By the end of the 1920s, another million blacks had moved north.[24]

Both the new immigrants and southern blacks were rapidly incorporated into America's industrial workforce, but they were not welcomed with open arms. Scores of prominent intellectuals such as the Progressive labor economist John R. Commons argued that Southern and Eastern European peasants belonged to "an inferior race that favors despotism and oligarchy rather than democracy."[25] Blacks were similarly scorned. Meanwhile, the American Federation of Labor invented the notion of an "American Standard of Living" and used it to link high wages to national identity. Union activists argued that Asian and some European immigrant groups should be barred from the country because of their willingness to work for "slave wages."[26]

With the U.S.'s entry into World War I, the focus of this cultural animosity shifted briefly to German Americans. When the war ended, however, many white Protestant Americans again targeted the new immigrant groups and racial minorities. Intellectuals and civic leaders pictured these groups as fomenters of labor unrest, threats to American jobs, catalyzers of "race suicide" among "old stock" Americans, and subverters of democracy itself. Race riots erupted in Chicago and other cities in 1919, while the Bolshevik Revolution helped spawn a domestic red scare with nativist overtones. In the early 1920s, a reincarnated Ku Klux Klan denounced Catholics and Jews as well as blacks. Meanwhile, a eugenics craze swept the nation, spawning scores of local and national societies, a eugenics "catechism" and sermon contest, and "Fitter Family" competitions at state fairs.[27] Such fears about "national division and the consequent destruction of American social cohesion" culminated in 1924 with Congress's passage of the Immigration Restriction Act.[28]

Ironically, the triumph of a culturally and racially restrictive definition of America in the 1920s set in motion demographic and cultural trends that would gradually erode that definition. By limiting the influx of foreigners to America's ethnic communities, the 1924 act accelerated the process of acculturation. The economic collapse of the early 1930s extended this process to those few immigrant communities unaffected by the legislation of the previous decade. The Mexican-American community in Los Angeles, for instance, was reshaped by harsh repatriation campaigns in the 1930s; over the course of half a decade, a community that had been comprised largely of immigrants was transformed into one dominated by their second-generation children.[29] Throughout the nation, this process of acculturation was further hastened by the intense attention that corporations, patriotic associations, settlement house workers, and others devoted to "Americanizing" immigrants during and after World War I.

One marker of the transformation occurring within immigrant communities was voter turnout. Large numbers of urban ethnics did not vote through the mid-1920s, either because they were not citizens or because they did not register or come to the polls. Rigid citizenship requirements deterred some, but many "simply did not find national party politics relevant to their lives." The combined impact of demographic shifts, prohibition, and the Great Depression changed that calculus. In some Chicago districts, the number of foreign-born *citizens* more than doubled between 1920 and 1930. During the same decade, many in the American-born second generation came of age. These new Americans increasingly concluded that they had a stake in the policies of the federal government. In 1928, they turned out in record numbers to vote for Democratic presidential candidate Al Smith. Four years later, they formed the backbone of the electoral majority that swept Franklin Delano Roosevelt into office.[30]

If new generations of Americans were increasingly taking their places in the voting booth, they were also starting to make their voices heard in the cultural arena. In 1930, most non-WASP Americans remained confined to comparatively low-paying jobs in the industrial working class. A growing number, however, had worked their way into positions of influence in the new culture industries that emerged in the opening decades of the twentieth century. Much has been written about the prominence of Jews in the movie industry during the 1930s and 1940s, but the Hollywood honor roll also included the Irish-American director John Ford, the Italian-American director Frank Capra, and Spyros P. Skouras, the son of an impoverished Greek shepherd who helped turn Twentieth Century-Fox into one of Hollywood's most powerful studios. Louis Adamic, a Slovenian-American who had immigrated to the U.S. at the age of fifteen, became a best-selling author in 1934 with the publication of his memoir, *The Native's Return*. Public relations and advertising, two comparatively new fields that produced much of the material heard on radio in the 1930s, also counted large numbers of Jews and Catholics among their staffers. So, too, eventually did the federal culture agencies established by the New Deal.[31]

Black Americans too made limited breakthroughs during the 1920s, although they faced even greater barriers to political and cultural incorporation than did the new immigrants. In the late nineteenth century, blacks had been effectively disfranchised throughout the South; but by 1930, roughly one in five lived in areas of the country where they could vote. Black Americans felt a deep-seated loyalty to the party of Lincoln, a loyalty that held through the presidential election of 1932. In 1934, however, black Americans threw their support behind the Democratic Party and Roosevelt's New Deal coalition, a permanent political shift that would shape U.S. politics for the rest of the century.[32]

If their exodus from the rural South gave blacks limited political clout, it also fueled rising expectations and a new spirit of cultural resistance. During the early 1920s, Marcus Garvey mobilized millions of black Americans into his Universal Negro Improvement Association by preaching a message of "race pride" and economic self-sufficiency. Garvey was profoundly cynical about the possibilities for black inclusion in white American society, but other black Americans harbored more hope. The National Association for the Advancement of Colored People (NAACP) had been founded in 1910, but it attracted broader public awareness in the 1920s with its campaigns against segregation, disenfranchisement, and lynching. Although relatively few blacks made inroads in Hollywood or Madison Avenue, the writers, artists, and musicians of the Harlem Renaissance attracted white patrons and an audience that transcended racial boundaries. Most Harlem Renaissance artists sought to define a distinctive black culture that could be a source of ethnic pride; many also stressed the contributions that blacks had made to American culture more broadly.[33]

Thus, by the mid-1930s, America's "new immigrants" and racial minorities were making a bid for greater political, social, and cultural inclusion. Their strong support for President Roosevelt was rewarded: the New Dealers went further than members of any past administration to incorporate Jews, Catholics, and blacks into the ranks of government and to administer federal programs evenhandedly.[34] The "new immigrants" and blacks also made up the backbone of the industrial labor movement that emerged in the late 1930s—a movement that, as Lizabeth Cohen has pointed out, was anchored in a multiethnic and multiracial "culture of unity."[35]

The generally inclusive ethos of the New Deal and the CIO has tended in historical accounts to overshadow a contrasting trend: the rise toward the end of the decade of virulent forms of intolerance.[36] Xenophobia waned after 1924, but it never disappeared; and the Depression fanned the banked embers of prejudice to life. As industries collapsed and unemployment soared, resentments between groups intensified. "In many places the foreign-born and those of their American-born children whose names had a so-called foreign sound were laid off first, before old-stock workers, sometimes even before the Negroes," the labor journalist Louis Adamic reported.[37] The decade's labor surplus allowed many employers to specify "WPX" (for "white, Christian, Protestant") in job advertisements and notices placed with employment agencies.[38] Finally, New Deal programs that put Americans of all racial and ethnic backgrounds on the same footing drew venom from some quarters. A "disgusted American" wrote Roosevelt aide Harry Hopkins in 1936 to complain about the individuals assigned to a Works Progress Administration sewing project in New York City. "Did you forget that there are still a few 'white Americans left,'" the anonymous letter writer asked. "Its the worst thing as far as placing is concerned. Nothing but colored, Spanish, West Indies, Italians + a hand ful of whites.... [I]f you don't see a race riot there it's a surprise." A Chicago man extended this sentiment to many other immigrant groups. "They should kick them all back to Europe as the majority of them are absolutely nogood," he wrote. "The foreign element in this country are allowed entirely to much leeway in practically every respect."[39]

Simmering economic resentments sometimes erupted into racial violence. On the West Coast, white men threatened those who hired Filipino laborers and threw dynamite bombs into the laborers' encampments.[40] Officials in Southern California and elsewhere repatriated thousands of Mexicans and Mexican Americans—in some cases forcibly.[41] In 1936, newspapers across the nation filled with stories about the secretive Black Legion, a Michigan-based vigilante group that, among other things, sought to help its members get and keep jobs. Members of the Legion flogged, kidnapped, and killed, and particularly targeted communists, Jews, Catholics, and blacks. While some argued that the Black Legion was an offshoot of the KKK, others saw it as "a modern forerunner of an American brand of fascism."[42]

If America's non-WASP minorities were frequent targets of ethnic, religious, or racial animosity, they could also be sources of such hostility. As the 1930s wore on, strains and warfare around the globe reverberated in the U.S. as well. Many Italian Americans hailed Mussolini's invasion of Ethiopia in 1935, seeing it as a sign of the resurgent glory of Rome. In response, black Americans in New York and Chicago boycotted stores owned by Italian-American merchants. American Catholics and Jews had long differed on a variety of social and political issues, but tensions between the two groups soared as a result of the Spanish Civil War.[43] Hitler's annexation of Austria and Czechoslovakia, the German and Soviet invasions of Poland, Stalin's conquest of Finland and the Baltic states, and the Nazi blitzkrieg across Europe in the spring of 1940 all rekindled dormant loyalties within immigrant communities.[44] Such developments threatened to turn Americans of diverse backgrounds against one another and fueled fears—even on the part of some liberals and leftists—that immigrants and their children could become conduits for various "alien" ideologies.

The Fascist and Communist Threats

The Depression and demographic change thus destabilized long dominant notions of "Americanism," opening the door to new voices and competing definitions of the nation. As the *Harper's* essay contest suggested, however, it was the successes of communism and fascism abroad—combined with fears that both doctrines were winning sympathizers in the U.S.—that gave efforts to define America's core values in the late 1930s new urgency. Taken together, communism and fascism provided Americans across the political spectrum with a fearsome ideological "other" against which the nation could and should be defined.[45] Those Americans who most feared communism and those who saw fascism as the greater danger rarely agreed on their concept of an ideal society; but in the late 1930s, both groups cast their visions in *American* terms. So too did many refugee intellectuals from other parts of the globe. By articulating and promoting an American idea, creed, or way of life, U.S. and foreign intellectuals, government officials, pundits, and business and civic leaders sought both to set the limits and possibilities of U.S. political culture and to provide a normative example to the world.

Communism had been on Americans' radar screen since the Bolshevik Revolution of 1917, but global developments in the 1930s added greatly to the sense of alarm in some quarters. Despite dire warnings, the Soviet Union had remained a political and economic pariah through most of the 1920s. Meanwhile, American corporations flourished virtually unchecked. That balance changed with the Great Depression. While capitalist economies everywhere ground to a halt, the Soviet Union engaged in forced and rapid industrialization, an achievement that impressed many foreign observers. Moreover, in August 1935, Stalin responded to the rise of Hitler by adopting the policy of the Popular Front; this allowed communists around the globe to ally themselves with socialists and "bourgeois" democrats in antifascist coalitions. The success of this policy was immediately evident in such countries as Spain and

France. In February 1936, Spaniards elected a Popular Front government, overthrowing a coalition of centrist and rightist parties and setting the stage for the Spanish Civil War. In France, too, the strategy transformed the communists into a mass party, and a Popular Front coalition triumphed in the 1936 elections. With a Socialist prime minister at the helm, the government limited work weeks and nationalized both the armaments industry and the Bank of France.

Fascism had gotten a later start than communism—both Benito Mussolini and Adolf Hitler built their movements in the 1920s—but it too benefited from the cataclysm of the Depression. As Germany's unemployment rate soared in 1930, so too did support for the Nazis among voters. The party, which had polled just 809,000 votes in 1928, garnered 6.4 million votes in 1930. Two years later, the Nazis won a plurality of seats in the German Reichstag; and in January 1933, Hitler was named chancellor. Liberals and leftists around the world watched in horror as the Nazis seized dictatorial power, abolished the German federal system, dissolved trade unions, burned books, and commenced the persecution of Jews. By early 1938, Italy had conquered Ethiopia, Japan was ravaging China, and Franco's forces seemed to be winning the civil war in Spain. Before the year was out, Hitler had annexed Austria and seized the Czechoslovakian Sudetenland.

These developments alarmed Americans on both the right and the left. Adding to their unease were signs that "communism" and "fascism" broadly defined might be gaining a toehold in the U.S. as well. Economic conservatives, who were keenly aware of what was happening in France, attacked the industrial union movement and decried the New Deal as "creeping state socialism." (A minority also likened the New Deal to fascism.) At the same time, they eyed with concern the emergence of a broad and multifaceted left-wing movement in the U.S. with strong ties to the CIO and Roosevelt's New Deal coalition and tangential connections to the Communist Party. At a political level, this movement encompassed such varied groups as New York's American Labor Party, Minnesota's Farmer-Labor Party, Wisconsin's Progressive Party, Washington's Commonwealth Federation, and the End-Poverty-in-California campaign of muckraker Upton Sinclair. Culturally, the movement counted numerous authors, critics, actors, screenwriters, musicians, and other intellectuals among its members. The U.S. Communist Party itself remained small, but it too capitalized on the Popular Front strategy, doubling its membership between 1936 and 1938 and billing communism as "twentieth-century Americanism."[46]

American industrialists and others in the business community worried in part about the appeal of "state socialism" to members of the middle class who had become disillusioned with the country's economic leadership. They were also deeply concerned about the views of first- and second-generation Americans. Because immigrants and their children clustered in the less skilled echelons of the working class, they were heavily represented in the industrial labor movement. As Michael Denning has shown, these groups also played an important role in the "cultural front."[47] Not surprising, when business groups launched their counterattack against the New Deal in the late 1930s, they aimed both to contain and to convert the nation's newest Americans.

If the specter of American socialism haunted economic conservatives, fears of domestic fascism had a similarly galvanizing effect on liberals and those on the left. Americans ranging from the activist lawyer Carey McWilliams to the prominent theologian Reinhold Niebuhr warned of a fascist menace within the U.S. with escalating urgency as the decade wore on. Articles reflecting such fears appeared not only in left-leaning magazines such as the *New Republic,* the *Nation,* and *American Mercury*, but also in publications such as the *Christian Century*, the *American Scholar*, and the *Saturday Evening Post*. In 1935, America's first Nobel laureate in literature, Sinclair Lewis, published *It Can't Happen Here*, a novel that envisioned the fascist takeover of the U.S.[48]

Leftists such as McWilliams saw evidence of fascism in phenomena as diverse as union busting, militarism, red-baiting, and vigilante justice.[49] Even those who defined the fascist threat more narrowly, however, were alarmed by the rise in ethnic and religious scapegoating during the decade, and particularly by the surge in anti-Semitism. Anti-Semitism was by no means a new phenomenon in America; but in the late 1930s, it appeared to take a far more virulent form. More than one hundred anti-Semitic organizations were created in the U.S. between 1933 and 1941; by one estimate, this was twenty times the number formed in the country up to that point.[50] In the past, domestic anti-Semitism had primarily taken the form of social or economic discrimination, but many of the new organizations—which boasted names such as the Silver Shirts, the American Nationalist Federation, Defenders of the Christian Faith, and the Knights of the White Camelia—resorted to violence. Some benefited from foreign support, even as they wrapped themselves in the mantle of Americanism.

One such organization was the German American Bund. Founded in 1936 by a Detroit autoworker, Fritz Kuhn, the Bund held mass rallies marked by uniforms and histrionics that eerily resembled those found in Munich and Nuremburg. The Bund had close ties to Hitler's Nazi party, yet Kuhn cast it as "a great American movement of Liberation" seeking to break the dictatorship of a "Jewish international minority." Bund meetings and marches featured

American flags, portraits of George Washington (whom Kuhn equated to Adolf Hitler), invocations of the Revolutionary War general Baron Von Steuben, and rousing renditions of "The Star-Spangled Banner" (figure 1.2). When the Bund held what it billed as a "mass-demonstration for true Americanism" in Madison Square Garden in February 1939 to celebrate George Washington's birthday, some twenty-two thousand Bundists and other sympathizers attended.[51]

Despite the Bund's direct ties to Nazi Germany, the individual who most alarmed many liberals was Father Charles Coughlin. In the early 1930s, the charismatic priest attracted an audience of millions to his weekly radio show, in which he attacked communism, railed against the gold standard, and called for the nationalization of the U.S. banking system. Coughlin also founded a political organization, the National Union for Social Justice, and launched a weekly newspaper. By 1934, he was receiving more mail than anyone else in the United States, including the president. Coughlin had long blamed the Depression on "money changers" and "international bankers"; but in 1938, he

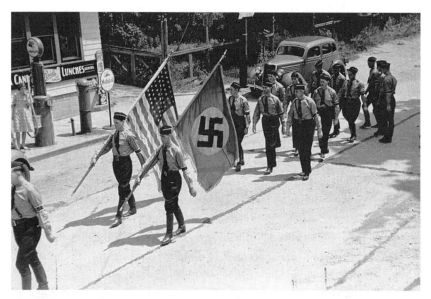

Figure 1.2. Members of the German American Bund march in Yaphank, New York in 1937. Although this gathering was small, a Bund rally at Madison Square Garden on Washington's Birthday in 1939 drew more than twenty thousand people. The surge in virulent anti-Semitism in the United States during the Depression fed fears on the part of many liberals and leftists that Americans too could succumb to fascism (Time & Life Pictures/Getty Images).

turned openly and stridently anti-Semitic. He repeatedly assailed "communistic Jews" and in one editorial lifted wording directly from a speech by Hitler's chief propagandist, Joseph Goebbels. By the end of the decade, Coughlin no longer attracted the huge and adoring audience he once had; still, a Gallup poll conducted in early 1938 showed that 10 percent of all American families with radios tuned him in regularly and that 83 percent of those who listened weekly approved of his message. Meanwhile, the Christian Front, a movement of Coughlin supporters formed at his urging, drilled its members in military tactics and stockpiled weapons. In cities such as Boston and New York, roving gangs of Christian Fronters smashed the windows of Jewish-owned stores and "engaged in open, Nazi-like brawls with Jews."[52]

The Black Legion limited its membership to native-born white Protestants, but the Christian Front flourished in Catholic immigrant neighborhoods in the urban Northeast. The founder of the German American Bund was a German immigrant, and the support of Italian Americans for Mussolini was well known. All this prompted some to view recent immigrants—those who had not yet been fully Americanized—as particularly susceptible to fascism. Staffers for the National Conference of Christians and Jews, for instance, argued that the organization should work more closely with organized labor as it tried to combat religious prejudice and particularly anti-Semitism. "This group," they explained, "includes a large percentage of foreign-born who have brought false beliefs into this nation."[53]

The Search for an "American Way"

Confronted with economic collapse and ideological threats both at home and abroad, a growing number of intellectuals, public officials, civic leaders, and others agreed with the literary scholar Howard Mumford Jones. "In a period of intense social strain," he declared in December 1935, "the country needs [the] steadying effect of a vital cultural tradition."[54] The poet and Librarian of Congress Archibald MacLeish chastised his compatriots for "morally disarming" America by elevating European over homegrown values. American intellectuals, he alleged, had "irresponsibly undermined the nation's historic principles and ideals," leaving it weakened in the face of the fascist threat.[55] Gilbert Seldes, the film critic and book reviewer who in 1932 produced the biting *The Years of the Locust*, charged four years later that writers were far more dangerous to the nation than industrialists or financiers. The former "merely ravaged the country's environment and resources," he wrote, while the latter imposed "an alien system of ideals upon America" that "prevented us from understanding ourselves."[56]

Such views only intensified as the decade drew to a close. The outbreak of war in Europe in September 1939, the German blitzkrieg in the spring of 1940, and particularly the fall of France that June gave the appeals of U.S. and émigré intellectuals a note of dire urgency. "One cannot counter the religious faith of fascism unless one possesses a faith equally strong, equally capable of fostering devotion and loyalty and commanding sacrifice," declared architectural critic Lewis Mumford in his 1940 call-to-arms *Faith for Living*. "If our democracy is to save itself," warned progressive educator George S. Counts in his presidential address to the American Federation of Teachers, "it must assert itself as a positive and aggressive social faith."[57]

Some commentators worried particularly about the threat to national unity and resolve posed by American ethnics. Such views were common on the right but extended in a rather different vein to many liberals and some on the left. In a 1938 article in the *Atlantic*, for instance, Howard Mumford Jones warned of the danger America would face if it allowed ethnic isolation and hostility between groups to undermine Americans' sense of common ground. Fascist and communist "dictator countries" posed a "serious...menace to political democracy" precisely because they had succeeded in making "patriotism glamorous," he argued. Americans needed a "patriotic renaissance," but one that would encompass *all* Americans, not just descendents of the *Mayflower* and "one-hundred-per-centers." "It is precisely the children and grandchildren of the millions who 'came over' some centuries after these earlier immigrations who need to have their imaginations kindled by American mythology," Jones wrote. "The gulf between the Boston Brahmins and the Boston Irish, old Detroiters and the swarming thousands of automobile workers...is not...going to be bridged by a bright recital of the French and Indian Wars." Jones concluded that "no race or religion or group or nationality can be permitted to assume that it has a monopoly of American history, and no race or religion or group or nationality can be permitted to feel it is excluded, if political democracy is to survive."[58]

Although some intellectuals and civic leaders focused on American ethnics, others concluded that even those with deep roots in the nation—and firm footing in the middle and upper classes—needed a tutorial on their own culture. For years Harvard University had largely ignored American topics in its curriculum; but in the late 1930s, it took a series of steps to rectify this imbalance.[59] Among other things, it published an extensive reading list on American history and culture, which it distributed to students, alumni, and interested members of the public. The preface lamented the fact that Americans' knowledge of their past often peaked in high school and faded thereafter. "One result of this ignorance and indifference is the lack of resistance of even well-educated persons to various forms of propaganda which would have them conceive 'Americanism' in terms of class, party, sectional, racial, or religious affiliation," the preface warned. It admonished readers against "a mere passive reading" of the books listed since that would "not make anybody a more intelligent citizen." Instead, readers should "be prepared to make [their] own syntheses, and answer [their] own questions. What is the American way of life? The American way of thought? How does it differ from European or Oriental ways of life and thought?"[60]

The compilers of the Harvard reading list urged readers to develop their own understanding of the "American Way"; but in the late 1930s, intellectuals, political leaders, and an array of civic organizations rushed to define this concept for all. Much hinged on the outcome of their efforts. At stake was the place and shape of capitalism in U.S. society. Would the power of labor unions and the federal government be strengthened? To what degree would business be regulated? Would the welfare state be expanded or forced to contract? At stake too was what might be called the cultural definition of America—the terms on which the nation's new immigrants and racial minorities would be incorporated into the U.S.'s national identity and social fabric. Would they be equals or second-class citizens? Would they be forced to shed their separate ethnic and racial identities, or would those identities be reconfigured? Would America continue to be seen as a predominantly white and Protestant nation? Behind these two groups of questions lurked a third: What role would the U.S., as actor or exemplar, play on the world stage? Among those eager to answer these questions were New Dealers, industrial unionists, and their foes in the boardrooms and press offices of corporate America.

CHAPTER 2

Industrial Democracy versus Free Enterprise

Many Americans first encountered the phrase "the American Way" on huge billboards that by 1938 had sprouted in hundreds of U.S. cities and towns. Shopping for groceries, heading to work, or entering an empty stretch of highway, they were suddenly confronted by a giant tableau of a cheerful American family picnicking, greeting Dad at the end of a workday, or taking a Sunday drive with the family dog. The foursome's bright smiles, comfortable car, and trellis-adorned home indicated that they had few material or psychological worries, an impression that bold lettering on the top of each sign underscored. "World's Shortest Working Hours," declared one. "World's Highest Wages," proclaimed another. "World's Highest Standard of Living," trumpeted a third. Script on the side of each billboard instructed viewers: "There's no way like the American Way."

The billboards, which were designed and distributed by the National Association of Manufacturers (NAM), must have seemed out of place to many Americans mired in the depths of capitalism's worst crisis. Nevertheless, they testified to the intensity of the debate over national values unleashed by the Depression. With other nations turning to communism and fascism for solutions to the global economic collapse, with America's capitalist idols knocked off their pedestals, Americans, too, began reexamining their political options. In this charged atmosphere, New Dealers, industrial unionists, conservative businessmen, and their various allies all seized on the language of Americanism and sought to define the nation in ways that furthered their own political and social agendas. Using new technologies and public relations techniques, they offered their own versions of America's history and core values and tried to set the limits and possibilities of U.S. political culture.

All addressed Americans' desire to be free of want, and all attempted to connect economic and political concerns. Beyond that, however, they framed the issue in profoundly different, even conflicting, ways. President Roosevelt, leaders of the Congress of Industrial Organizations (CIO), and others in the New Deal coalition stressed the majoritarian overtones of the word "democracy" and called for an activist government to help ensure Americans' economic security. Industrialists and their allies, by contrast, emphasized individual rights and the libertarian dimensions of American "freedom." They painted business, not government, as working peoples' true friend. The CIO, their allies to the liberal left on America's political spectrum, and even FDR for a time emphasized the struggle of "the people" against monopolistic capital and called for mutualistic responses to the economic crisis. Meanwhile, corporations and business groups promoted an "American Way" built on class harmony and a return to the pre-New Deal status quo. The ensuing battle—pitting "democracy" against "freedom," mutualism against individualism, and a progressive ethos against interclass unity—presaged contests that would continue into the postwar era.

FDR and the New Dealers

Shortly before ten o'clock on a cloudy night in late June 1936, President Franklin Delano Roosevelt arrived at the University of Pennsylvania's Franklin Field to accept the Democratic Party's unanimous renomination for president. Entering the stadium on the arm of his son James, FDR acknowledged the wild cheering of a crowd estimated at more than one hundred thousand people. He waited through the singing of "The Star-Spangled Banner," an invocation by an Episcopal bishop, and brief remarks by his vice president and several party officials.[1] Then FDR rose and addressed the assembly. "Philadelphia is a good city in which to write American history," he declared. "This is fitting ground on which to reaffirm the faith of our fathers; to pledge ourselves to restore to the people a wider freedom; to give to 1936 as the founders gave to 1776—an American way of life."[2] The president's ensuing address was not the "fighting speech" that most in the throng had expected or that many of FDR's advisors had urged him to give. Rather than assailing his Republican opponent, Roosevelt offered what the *New York Times* called "a statement of a philosophy."[3] He outlined the broad set of convictions that underlay the New Deal and that defined for FDR the American Way.

Roosevelt began his address in Philadelphia by invoking the image of a people united. Looking back over the previous four years, he declared that "rescue" from the depths of the depression had not been "a mere party task." "It was the concern of all of us," he asserted. "In our strength we rose together, rallied our energies together, applied the old rules of common sense and together survived."[4] In thus emphasizing Americans' shared problems, FDR reiterated a note he had struck many times as president. "I assume unhesitatingly the leadership of this great army of our people dedicated to a disciplined attack upon our common problems," Roosevelt had declared in his first inaugural address.[5] Two years later, the president had again used wartime metaphors—and invoked wartime unity—in a fireside chat defending the newly established Works Progress Administration: "This is a great national crusade to destroy enforced idleness which is an enemy of the human spirit generated by this depression," he had told his listeners. "Our attack upon these enemies must be without stint and without discrimination. No sectional, no political distinctions can be permitted."[6]

As this last quote suggests, FDR believed firmly that it was the responsibility of the federal government to serve Americans' *collective* interest—"to promote the general welfare," as he put it in 1935.[7] Roosevelt recognized the inherent tension between unchecked individualism and the needs of community; as president, he came down repeatedly on the side of the latter. "Only through the submerging of individual desires into unselfish and practical cooperation can civilization grow," he told an audience in Green Bay, Wisconsin, in August 1934.[8] Addressing a gathering of National Recovery Administration code authorities that same year, Roosevelt argued that the U.S. had gotten itself into the "difficult and dangerous situation" it faced in the bleak winter of 1932–1933, "due to the general attitude, 'Every man for himself; the devil take the hindmost.'"[9] In a speech in Los Angeles in 1935, the president recast liberalism by linking it to "human cooperation": "The faith of a liberal," he declared, "is profound belief not only in the capacities of individual men and women, but also in the effectiveness of people helping each other."[10]

This faith in cooperation—together with the assumption that Americans had harmonious interests—had shaped New Deal approaches to the economic crisis ever since Roosevelt's inauguration in March 1933. The president and his aides repeatedly worked to show farmers and industrial laborers that they needed one another's products and purchasing power.[11] New Dealers shunned solutions aimed at specific ethnic and racial groups even as they sought to administer federal programs evenhandedly. When Harold Ickes traveled to Atlanta in October 1934 to dedicate the first low-cost housing project for blacks, he did not single out Jim Crow for denunciation. Instead, he declared that "it is for the economic benefit of the whole country for all divisions of it to be prosperous."[12] FDR employed parallel logic when twice vetoing the "Bonus Bill" that had proved such a source of anguish to Herbert Hoover. "The Herculean task of the United States Government today is to take care that its citizens have the necessities of life," he explained in his first message vetoing the bill. "We are seeking honestly and honorably to do this, irrespective of class or group." Although all Americans honored the able-bodied veterans of the Great War, they should be treated no differently from their fellow citizens, he averred.[13]

On this summer night in Philadelphia, FDR reminded the gathered throng— as well as the millions of Americans listening to his speech on the radio—of their shared interests. He then warned them that all was not well in the world. "Clouds of suspicion, tides of ill-will and intolerance gather darkly in many places," he declared. Even in the U.S., "the rush of modern civilization itself has raised for us new difficulties, new problems which must be solved if we are to preserve to the United States the political and economic freedoms for which Washington and Jefferson planned and fought."[14]

In thus referring to "economic freedoms," FDR alluded to an additional theme at the core of his political philosophy: the "right," as he saw it, of all Americans to a measure of economic security. Roosevelt saw such economic security—particularly the right to "decent homes," "productive work," and "security against the hazards and vicissitudes of life"—as inextricably linked to freedom itself. "I am not for a return to that definition of liberty under which for many years a free people were being gradually regimented into the service of the privileged few," Roosevelt had declared in a fireside chat in September 1934. "I prefer and I am sure you prefer that broader definition of liberty under which we are moving forward to greater freedom, to greater security for the average man than he has ever known before in the history of America."[15] In early 1941, FDR would list economic security as one of the "four essential human freedoms." By then he would call it simply "freedom from want."[16]

Families and small communities, FDR believed, had once been able to provide such security, but "the complexities of great communities and of organized industry"—the "rush of modern civilization" to which he referred in Philadelphia—meant they could no longer do so. Economic security, Roosevelt had argued repeatedly, could now come from only one place: "the active interest of the Nation as a whole through government."[17] During his first term in office, FDR had pushed through Congress a wide range of programs designed to provide such "economic freedom." The New Dealers had set up work-relief programs such as the Civilian Conservation Corps and the Works Progress Administration. They had instituted agricultural price supports, federal guarantees for bank deposits and home mortgages, and—with the passage of the Social Security Act—pensions for the elderly. The Tennessee Valley Authority brought irrigation, electricity, jobs, and the promise of prosperity to a large swath of the rural and impoverished South. Finally, Section 7a of the National Industrial Recovery Act and the later, more powerful Wagner Act guaranteed workers' rights to organize and bargain collectively. Both measures strengthened the ability of organized labor to seek economic security for its members.

Such moves triggered a backlash. Economic conservatives charged that the administration was conspiring to subvert the Constitution and establish socialism, communism, or even fascism.[18] FDR admitted that the means he proposed for providing Americans with security were new, but he scoffed at what he called the "prophets of calamity."[19] Roosevelt had long argued that democracy was "not a static thing" but rather was "an everlasting march" that needed to evolve to meet changing social conditions.[20] The Constitution's framers, he believed, had allowed for such evolution by drafting a document that made possible "drastic changes in the methods and forms and functions of government without destroying the basic principles."[21] In a fireside chat delivered in June 1934, Roosevelt had compared the New Deal to the renovation of the old Executive Office Building then underway: just as the grand old building was being equipped with modern electrical wiring and plumbing, so, too, the New Deal was updating the federal government while keeping its basic purposes intact. "All that we do seeks to fulfill the historic traditions of the American people," FDR had said then. "Other Nations may sacrifice democracy for the transitory stimulation of old and discredited autocracies. We are restoring confidence and well-being under the rule of the people themselves."[22] Now, in Philadelphia, FDR returned to the same theme; he told his audience that he was pursuing the ideals of Washington and Jefferson by offering an updated version of the American way of life.

Having thus implicitly defended his policies, FDR went a step further. He suggested that economic security—"economic freedom," in his words—was an essential underpinning of Americans' political rights and indeed of democracy itself. Temporarily jettisoning his rhetoric of shared values, he suggested that those political freedoms were increasingly being threatened by a powerful economic minority.

In 1776 and the Revolution that followed, the president explained, Americans had sought and won their freedom from "the tyranny of a political autocracy." In the intervening years, however, "man's inventive genius released new forces in our land which reordered the lives of our people." Machinery, railroads, steam, electricity, the telegraph, the radio, mass production, and mass distribution had "combined to bring forward a new civilization" but also new problems for "those who sought to remain free." "Out of this modern civilization," FDR declared, "economic royalists carved new dynasties." This "new industrial dictatorship," he said, shifting metaphors, controlled the hours men and women worked, the wages they received, labor conditions, family savings, prices for farm products, and capital. No one except the royalists themselves were immune: workers, farmers, small businessmen and merchants, even "honest and progressive-minded men of wealth," had all found themselves under the heel of this new "despotism."[23]

This development endangered more than Americans' economic well-being. "For too many of us the political equality we once had won was meaningless in the face of economic inequality," the president declared. "For too many of us life was no longer free; liberty no longer real; men could no longer follow the pursuit of happiness." Against such "economic tyranny," American citizens "could appeal only to the organized power of Government." In electing Roosevelt and the New Dealers in 1932, the public had done just that.[24]

But this small clique of industrialists and their cronies had challenged the government's ability to take action. "The royalists of the economic order have conceded that political freedom was the business of Government, but they have maintained that economic slavery was nobody's business," FDR argued. "They granted that the Government could protect the citizen in his right to vote, but they denied that the Government could do anything to protect the citizen in his right to work and his right to live." Paraphrasing Lincoln, the president continued, "Today we stand committed to the proposition that freedom is no half-and-half affair. If the average citizen is guaranteed equal opportunity in the polling place, he must have equal opportunity in the market place." The American way of life, FDR suggested, encompassed not only political democracy but the measure of economic security required to make political democracy meaningful. It was up to the federal government to ensure both.[25]

In focusing on such "economic royalists," FDR was hearkening back to a rich strain in American political language and thought: progressivism. In the opening decades of the twentieth century, Progressive historians such as Vernon Parrington, Frederick Jackson Turner, and Charles Beard had cast American history as an ongoing struggle between "the people" and "the interests." "Behind the people stood virtue, democracy, and an ideal republic, while behind the interests stood alien monopolists associated with the evils of Europe, aristocracy, and capitalism," writes historiographer David Noble. "Inexorably, progress was pushed forward by the battle between good and evil unfolding in America."[26] A similar "progressive ethos"—positing "a dualistic struggle between a democratic insurgency and un-American monopolists"—animated numerous social and political movements in the late nineteenth and early twentieth centuries.[27]

In Philadelphia, FDR called the domestic struggle being waged by his administration "a war for the survival of democracy." In part, this reflected the proportions of the economic crisis: if men and women were not given a measure of security, if they could not feed and shelter their families, they might prove willing to surrender even their political rights. In the context of a diatribe against "economic royalists," however, the phrase took on added significance, highlighting the president's definition of democracy itself. That definition emphasized above all majoritarian rule—the rule, through government and elected leaders, of the common man. Men such as Thomas Jefferson, Andrew Jackson, Abraham Lincoln, and Theodore Roosevelt knew "that the majority often makes mistakes," Roosevelt would tell an audience in January 1938. "But they believed passionately that rule by a small minority unfailingly makes worse mistakes."[28] The Bill of Rights, FDR argued in another speech, was "put into the Constitution not only to protect against intolerance of majorities, but to protect majorities against enthronement of minorities."[29]

This view of American democracy served well a president who had won two sweeping electoral mandates, but it was not simply utilitarian. FDR's faith in the ability of "the people" to make sound decisions—like his belief that the federal government was obligated to ensure that all Americans were free from want—was deeply rooted. His tirades against economic royalists, by contrast, were more pragmatic. Temperamentally, FDR always preferred to stress the *harmony* of Americans' interests, to lead Americans in a united campaign against a common foe. The recession of 1937, Roosevelt's ill-fated court-packing scheme, and growing threats of war abroad changed the president's calculation in the closing years of the decade, necessitating a gradual rapprochement with the industrial elites he had for a time denounced. FDR's harsh antibusiness rhetoric peaked during the 1936 presidential campaign and faded thereafter. There were others, however, who extended this vision of America both in content and chronology.

Industrial Unionists and Their Allies

The presidency and the agencies of the New Deal gave FDR an unmatched podium for articulating his version of the American Way. But as the 1930s wore on, Roosevelt's vision was increasingly complemented and challenged by others. To the president's left, a more radical interpretation of the nation's history and core values emerged from industrial labor and socialist circles. Although this interpretation frequently converged with Roosevelt's—particularly on the need for an activist government to help ensure workers' economic security—it paid greater attention to workplace power and was more consistent in its portrayal of American history as a battle between "the people" and un-American capitalist "interests." This radical Americanism cast American workers and union organizers as the heroes of an ongoing struggle to save the endangered republic from "industrial Tories." The centerpiece of this progressive vision was "industrial democracy"—a recipe for extending majoritarian democracy from the political into the economic arena.

As Gary Gerstle has suggested, the roots of "insurgent Americanism" lay in the 1920s. The conservative Americanization campaigns of that decade severely weakened both labor and the left, but they also prompted many radicals and labor organizers to "redefine their politics in a way that fit[ted] American political discourse." During the 1920s, men such as Vito Marcantonio, Walter and Victor Reuther, John L. Lewis, Sidney Hillman, and A. J. Muste seized on American symbols and stated values and deployed them in the battle for workers' rights. Meanwhile, Socialists such as Harry Laidler and Norman Thomas attempted to regain legitimacy in the wake of the Bolshevik Revolution by redefining their aims in American terms. As United Mine Workers president John Lewis wrote in his 1925 book *The Miner's Fight for American Standards*, "The solution of most of the problems of American life can be found in a return to first principles—a reassertion in practice of the rules laid down by the Fathers of the Republic."[30]

Still, radical versions of "Americanism" remained on the margins of U.S. political discourse into the early 1930s. But as the Depression wore on, underscoring the gap between American dreams and American realities, leftists and labor organizers increasingly seized on it to motivate newly politicized—and in many cases, newly Americanized—workers. In 1932, organizers of the National Unemployed League chose July 4th weekend for their founding convention and called their central document "The Declaration of Workers' and Farmers' Rights." The following year, Socialists gathered four thousand unemployed or dissatisfied workers and Depression-pinched farmers in Washington at a Continental Congress for Economic Reconstruction. The delegates, drawn from "committees of correspondence," declared independence from a profit system that had "enthroned economic and financial kings…more powerful, more irresponsible, and more dangerous to human rights than the political kings whom the fathers overthrew."[31] In Wisconsin, Progressive Party founder

Philip La Follette declared that "liberalism is nothing but a sort of milk-and-water tolerance....I believe in a fundamental and basic change. I think a co-operative society based on American traditions is inevitable."[32] Even the U.S. Communist Party after 1935 declared itself to be the champion of "twentieth-century Americanism."[33]

Such individuals and organizations made up the left wing of the New Deal coalition. Indeed, some within the administration itself subscribed to similar views. In a 1936 article in *Scribner's* entitled "The Search for an American Way," Agriculture Secretary Henry A. Wallace argued that Americans needed to achieve "unity in diversity" by "evolving a concept of the general welfare grounded in both political and economic democracy." To do this, Americans needed to recognize that the nation had matured economically—that "certain types of economic liberty...cannot be tolerated any more than automobile drivers can be allowed to disobey a red light." While Wallace did not reject capitalism out of hand, he argued that Americans needed to place more emphasis on "cooperation, as distinguished from free competition." Thus far, he sounded much like the president he served. But Wallace continued:

> The only way in which democracy can survive the logical onslaught
> of the dictator-state aspect of Communism and Fascism is to
> develop the genuine cooperative idea to the limit. Producers'
> cooperatives are not enough. For the most part they merely take the
> place of middle men, and...they do not have any very profound
> effect on the people whom they serve. The cooperative way of
> life must pervade the community, and this means there must be
> consumers' cooperatives as well as producers' cooperatives, and
> ultimately industrial cooperatives. To live happily in a cooperative
> society takes an entirely different attitude of mind from that
> required in a society where free competition is the dominating rule.[34]

Wallace's version of the American Way was hardly communism. Still, in its implications for mutualism and worker control, it went far beyond the reforms instituted under the New Deal.

It was the CIO, however, that did more than any other group during the late 1930s and early 1940s to publicize, particularly to workers, a more radical understanding of the nation's history and core values.[35] The CIO's version of "Americanism" revolved around the notion of "industrial democracy," an idea that had first emerged in the U.S. during the 1890s and caught fire during the labor struggles that followed World War I. Embraced by Progressive reformers, labor leaders, socialists, and even some liberal business leaders, the term meant markedly different things to different people. To some, it signaled a social compact in which workers and managers would share power within the overarching framework of capitalism, perhaps through collective bargaining. To others, it "promised an end to hierarchy, centralized authority, and the degrading fragmentation of skills." To still others, "industrial democracy" meant the spread of producers' cooperatives or socialism in American clothes.[36]

The views of the CIO's founder and first president John Lewis, and thus of the early CIO, were deeply influenced by those of a one-time academic economist named W. Jett Lauck.[37] Lauck began working for Lewis and the United Mine Workers in the 1920s and quickly became one of the labor leader's closest advisors. During the 1930s, he drafted "almost all [of] Lewis's major addresses and publications." In the early years of the New Deal, Lauck also advised FDR on economic issues, and he has been credited with helping secure the inclusion of the union-protecting Section 7a in the National Industrial Recovery Act.[38]

As Lauck saw it, political democracy "in its modern sense" began in the American colonies in 1776. The establishment of the republic "upon democratic principles and rights of personal and civil liberty" was not accompanied by "class warfare" since "politically and socially, and in the holding of property, there were few distinctions in America at that time."[39] But subsequent economic and financial developments—particularly the Industrial Revolution and the excesses of decades like the 1920s—had produced a concentration of wealth and financial power that now fundamentally threatened the nation's political and social order. "A cabal of bankers and financiers 'working out its objectives silently, invisibly, and without official recognition' had come to dominate the American economy." In 1929, this plutocracy had plunged the U.S. into economic chaos. More than the economy was in danger, Lauck argued. "In the effort to shield themselves from public scrutiny and regulation, the 'Kings of Money and Lords of Finance' were perverting the Constitution and the Bill of Rights, corrupting the political processes, and regimenting the people. They would stop at nothing less than 'Tory Revolution.'" As if that weren't enough, the autocratic policies of America's financial and corporate leaders were nurturing "destructive radicalism," which threatened to undermine the political achievements of the Revolution.[40]

If Lauck and Lewis's retelling of American history sounded much like FDR's during the 1936 presidential campaign, their prescription for the nation's future pushed well beyond his. Roosevelt had great faith in the wisdom of "the people" as exercised through their elected representatives, and he called for "freedom" in both the political and economic arenas. His vision of democracy, however, was always more limited. Although FDR has often been portrayed as "the patron of labor's awakening," he was "a rather diffident champion" of unions. FDR believed that the best way to improve workers' lives, to ensure their freedom from want, was by relying on government regulation—by passing pension, unemployment, and wage-and-hour laws. He was at best a lukewarm supporter of collective bargaining rights, and he threw his support behind the pivotal Wagner Act only belatedly.[41]

Lewis, Lauck, and their compatriots in the CIO went further, contending that the only way to stop the forces of reaction and save the Republic was by extending democracy from the political to the economic arena. In his 1926 book, *Political and Industrial Democracy, 1776–1926*, Lauck had argued that employees should participate in corporate management through management-labor committees and employee ownership of common stock.[42] Within the industrial labor movement, the precise meaning of "industrial democracy" was a subject of intense contention during the late 1930s and 1940s, but all versions promised workers at least a measure of empowerment on the shop floor. For some, "industrial democracy" meant union representation and the system of collective bargaining over wages, hours, and working conditions set up by the Wagner Act. For others, it implied that workers should have a voice in "their employers' pricing and investment decisions."[43] As Lauck wrote to Lewis in a 1935 memo, industrial unionism was an "epoch-making crusade for humanity and democracy."[44]

In the late 1930s, these ideas filled the pages of CIO newspapers and echoed through the speeches of CIO officials, many of which were reprinted or broadcast by union-sponsored radio. Editorials and cartoons in the *CIO News* portrayed industrial unionists as champions of democracy, defending American values from "economic royalists" and "Tory employers" who were bent on imposing "autocratic rule over their workers."[45] A column by the CIO publicist Len De Caux, headlined "Wanted, More Paul Reveres!" argued that "home-grown American tories are trying to do to their country what King George III and all his British tories failed to do. The general idea of the American tories seems to be that democracy and freedom are bunk; and that the lower classes should be kept down by a judicious mixture of starvation and class legislation." De Caux warned that "the liberties and the very livelihood of millions of Americans are in serious danger today" and that "only the labor press conveys any real call of warning to patriotic Americans."[46]

As this column suggests, CIO organizers—and workers themselves—were quick to invoke the authority of America's patriotic pantheon. Strikers frequently carried American flags and likened their opponents to traitorous

"Tories." The *CIO News* highlighted the pro-labor credentials of Americans ranging from the radical pamphleteer Thomas Paine to the abolitionist and feminist Lucretia Mott.[47] But it was the old rail-splitter and champion of "free labor" Abe Lincoln whom CIO officials most frequently invoked. The CIO pamphlet *The Right to Strike—Keystone of Liberty* featured a quote from Lincoln on its cover: "Thank God we have a country where working men have the right to strike." A "Labor Facts" feature in the *CIO News* noted that when a general sent Union soldiers to replace striking printers in St. Louis in 1864, Lincoln quickly recalled the troops to duty and declared that he had no intention of interfering. And an article explaining industrial unionism noted that CIO president John L. Lewis shared Lincoln's birthday. CIO officials were also fond of paraphrasing Lincoln's Gettysburg Address. In 1938, Lewis told the first national convention of the CIO that "there has been born in America a new, modern labor movement dedicated to the proposition that all who labor are entitled to equality of opportunity, the right to organize, the right to participate in the bounties and the blessings of this country and our government." Two years later, Len De Caux wrote that "our idea of a 'new birth of freedom' is an expansion of collective bargaining and industrial democracy."[48]

If CIO officials made frequent reference to Lincoln and other national heroes, they also tried repeatedly to link the labor struggle to other rights and values that Americans, particularly their working-class constituents, held dear. The *CIO News* reprinted extensive excerpts of a speech by the chairman of the National Labor Relations Board in which, echoing FDR, he declared that the Wagner Act represented a "new liberty" comparable in its significance to the "ancient liberties" enshrined in the Bill of Rights. "Indeed, the constitutional liberties of freedom of speech, press and assembly, could not, in their aspects most important to working people, be enjoyed until this new liberty was created," he declared. A cartoon published in the newspaper in 1939 showed the hammer of "Big Business" using the chisel of "Wagner Act Amendments" to break the "Labor" link in the chain of democracy—a chain whose other links included "Free Speech," "Church," "School," and "Your Organization." "If you weaken or destroy the protection of one link in the chain of democracy, each of the others are successively and easily destroyed!" the caption warned (figure 2.1).[49]

CIO officials most often used the majoritarian language of "democracy" to capture their agenda, but they sometimes invoked "liberty" and "freedom" as well. The freedom they called for both reinforced and extended FDR's notion of "freedom from want." "The liberty we seek is different" from that sought by industrialists, declared John Lewis in his report to the 1938 CIO convention. "It is liberty for common people—freedom from economic bondage, freedom

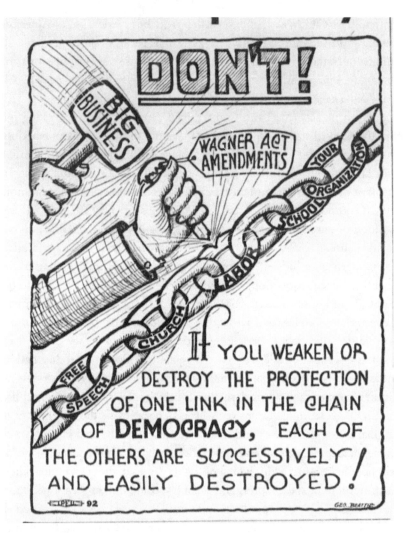

Figure 2.1. This cartoon appeared in the *CIO News* on 17 April 1939. Note its emphasis on the word "democracy," as well as its attempt to link organized labor to other institutions and values that Americans prized (courtesy of the AFL-CIO; reproduced by the Wisconsin Historical Society).

to regain again some human initiative, freedom that arises from economic security, and human self-respect." In a column in the *CIO News*, Len De Caux echoed these sentiments, painting "a very definite and concrete picture of what freedom means to millions of American working people today. It means in the first place a freedom which is often overlooked by high-falutin' liberals— freedom from low wages, intolerable speed-ups, layoffs and insecurity."[50]

In order to achieve such freedoms, however, workers had to be free to organize, and this in turn required the freedoms of speech, press, and assembly. Thus, CIO officials and organizers put particular emphasis on the freedoms guaranteed by the First Amendment, frequently portraying workers as the champions of the Bill of Rights. (They were aided in making this argument by the findings of a special Senate committee, chaired by Wisconsin Senator Robert M. La Follette Jr. The committee, formed in July 1936 to investigate corporate violations of workers' rights, uncovered numerous episodes of corporate espionage, intimidation, and violence.) On the 151st anniversary of the Bill of Rights, a cartoon in the *CIO News* showed the mighty arm of the CIO displaying the First Amendment to a gathering of plutocratic executives from "anti-union corporations" such as Ford Motor Company and Bethlehem Steel; tellingly, the executives were depicted in the tailcoats and top hats of Gilded Age robber barons rather than in the suits worn by twentieth-century executives. An accompanying column charged that Ford had denied its employees the right to speak and assemble "without the presence of spies and stool pigeons" and had violated freedom of the press by prohibiting the distribution of union literature.[51] John T. Jones, the CIO's legislative director, told a 1941 gathering of the Farmer-Labor Party in Duluth, Minnesota, that "the defense of the democratic way of life" required defense of such basic "democratic freedoms" as "freedom of thought, freedom of the press, freedom of assembly." These "democratic rights," he declared, "are attacked especially by those who are afraid that the full and vigorous operation of democracy will jeopardize their special positions of privilege and power."[52] As this suggests, the CIO, like FDR in the late 1930s, cast the Bill of Rights above all as a document securing the rights of the majority from an unscrupulous minority.

Despite this emphasis on majority rights, CIO officials were quick to remind listeners and readers that the organization stood for "equality of protection to any group, any minority, any religion." In part this reflected the realization of the CIO leadership that in order to build a class-based national movement, they would have to foster a "culture of unity" that crossed ethnic, religious, geographic, and racial lines.[53] At the same time, it evinced the efforts of the CIO leadership to link their agenda to events abroad. A cartoon in the *CIO News* in November 1938 showed a man representing the CIO standing shoulder-to-shoulder with FDR in a doorway labeled "American Democracy." Bearing rifles, the two men fended off a swastika-branded wolf that circled the carcasses of "labor unions" and "religious and racial minorities." In Germany, John Lewis declared in a speech the same month, the destruction of the labor movement preceded the persecution of Jews. "We cannot preserve democracy here in our country," he added, "if we encourage as a people the overwhelming tidal wave of criticism, slander and abuse for an American institution like the CIO that stands for the protection of the privileges of all Americans, whether they be gentiles or Jews or of any creed or religion, or any school of thought that maintains its respect for our institutions."[54]

Such arguments grew more pronounced in CIO rhetoric and writings as the fascist threat loomed ever larger on the horizon. The term "Tory" never disappeared from the CIO's vocabulary, but increasingly CIO officials likened their opponents—ruthless employers, congressional enemies of the Wagner Act, and the AFL's president William Green, among others—to fascists, European dictators, or fifth columnists. CIO vice president Reid Robinson addressed a convention of the Amalgamated Clothing Workers just as France was collapsing in June 1940. Many Americans believed that only traitors within could have catalyzed France's downfall, and Robinson told his listeners that America had had its own fifth column for a decade: this column, "opposed to our democratic institutions," was "made up of the group that believes that they can keep American people in the rolls of the unemployed," Reid declared. Later that year, a picket outside a Ford plant carried a sign reading "Hitlerism and Fordism versus Americanism and the Wagner Act." And when an office manager at the *Birmingham Post* threatened to don his Alabama state guard uniform and fire on those striking the paper, a *CIO News* editorial compared his language to that used by "Fascist bullies" and "Nazi storm troopers."[55]

The CIO was hardly alone in the late 1930s in warning about a domestic fascist threat. Still, its voice did not go unchallenged. Indeed, even as the CIO was emerging as an independent organization, U.S. corporations were gearing up for battle to define the nation's legitimate values. They too would invoke an "alien" ideology that now threatened America—totalitarianism—and they would use it to help popularize a new term in America's political lexicon: "free enterprise."

The National Association of Manufacturers and Corporate America

The rapidity with which the word "free enterprise" entered general usage in the late 1930s is stunning even by the standards of political speech. As late as 1935, the *Reader's Guide to Periodical Literature* did not have an entry for "free enterprise"; and in 1937, it was still referring readers to "laissez-faire." The words "free" and "enterprise" appeared side by side in the *New York Times* just thirty times between 1857 and 1934, and many of those references bore little resemblance to what is now meant by the term.[56] By contrast, "free enterprise," used as a synonym for the less evocative "private enterprise," appeared in America's paper-of-record 25 times in 1935, 114 times in 1937, and 220 times in 1940. By then, it had become a staple of Americans' political vocabulary.

The emergence of the term "free enterprise" during these years owed much to the changing political strategies of America's corporate leaders. Some businessmen, particularly those associated with the American Liberty League, had aimed their rhetorical guns at the New Deal as early as 1934. By 1937, however, the scale of this effort had shifted dramatically. Abandoning their historic focus on promoting individual products, legislative policies, or corporate images, U.S. corporations for the first time joined forces in a broad-based defense of laissez-faire capitalism in general. In advertisements, syndicated columns, cartoons, books, radio shows, and documentary films, the National Association of Manufacturers (NAM), the U.S. Chamber of Commerce, and a host of industrial giants tried to convince the American public that their interests and those of the nation's largest corporations were virtually indistinguishable. Painting a picture of class harmony and consumer prosperity—guaranteed by business, not by government—they dubbed this image "the American Way." Invoking the term "free enterprise," they countered mutualistic New Deal and CIO visions of the nation by emphasizing individual rights and the libertarian dimensions of "freedom."

American industry's willingness to close ranks and undertake such a campaign reflected its changing diagnosis of the problem business confronted. In 1934, the president of the U.S. Chamber of Commerce had complained angrily that the government was in the hands of an "organized mob."[57] At that point, however, FDR was still trying to use the National Recovery Administration to co-opt corporate leaders, and many of those leaders hoped to defeat him at the polls. By late 1936, the situation looked very different. The New Deal had veered sharply to the left; and despite a campaign of lobbying and frontal assaults, industrialists and their allies had failed miserably in their efforts to derail the Wagner Act, the Social Security Act, the Banking Act, the Public Utility Holding Company Act, and the president's tax program. Consumer and labor groups, including the CIO, were attacking cherished business prerogatives. Meanwhile, the Senate Committee chaired by Robert La Follette Jr., was making headlines with its charges of widespread corporate abuse. In November 1936, FDR won reelection in a landslide, aided in part by his denunciation of "economic royalists."

To many in the business world, all this suggested that a new strategy was needed—that the problem business confronted was not so much the New Deal specifically as the American public in general. "The public does not understand industry, largely because industry itself has made no real effort to tell its story," NAM president Robert Lund had warned as early as 1933.[58] Now others echoed that assessment. A contributor to *Public Opinion Quarterly* argued in 1937 that the "old easy reliance on the professionals of politics to temper the tides of popular unrest" had become "untrustworthy." Public relations expert Carl Byoir went further, predicting that unless business acted, "the whole capitalist system" could soon be destroyed by the "volcano" of public opinion. The dean of Columbia's school of journalism followed FDR's example in linking the struggle at home to world events. "Every citizen in the United States today," he declared in 1938, "is participating in a world war of ideas. This war may be as destructive of property rights, individual freedom, institutions and family life as a war involving material resources."[59]

But if business was to defend itself, it had to do more than simply proclaim its righteousness, commentators agreed: it had to explain to the public that their interests and those of the business community were aligned. "Research, mass production, and low prices are the offspring of business bigness" and its "justification," advertising guru Bruce Barton told a group of manufacturers in 1935. "This story should be told...just as continuously as the people are told that Ivory Soap floats or that children cry for Castoria."[60] Bank president Thomas Boushall told a group of southern businessmen in a widely reprinted speech that "the American people and American business have the same general concept of what we mean by the phrase 'The American Way.'" The problem, he argued, was that "the people" did not realize this. Business needed "to give a very clear definition when we refer to 'The American Way'" and to make clear to American citizens that business too "has the same concept and gives the same definition."[61]

Increasingly, corporate executives started to act on such advice. In the late 1930s, enterprises ranging from Goodyear and General Electric to the Aluminum Company of America and International Business Machines began running advertisements in magazines and newspapers defending the "American economic system." Large private utilities backed an Oregon-based news service that distributed lithographed editorials to some twelve thousand daily and weekly newspapers in small towns across the country. Chase National Bank, together with forty-five affiliates, sponsored a "business forum spiced with orchestral selections" that was broadcast Friday evenings over first the CBS and then the NBC radio network. General Motors launched one of the largest public relations campaigns—placing four-color ads in mass magazines such as the *Saturday Evening Post*, producing documentaries, and sponsoring the annual "Soap Box Derby" races under the slogan "It's the Soap Box Derby against the soap-box orators." During the weekly "General Motors Symphony Hour," the "Voice of General Motors" offered sound bites on employment, wage levels, and "the American system of free opportunity, free initiative, free competition." GM's "Parade of Progress," a traveling salute to that American system, logged twenty thousand miles touring the U.S. in 1936.[62]

All of these efforts reflected the rise over the previous two decades of the new field of public relations. As Stuart Ewen has shown, the idea of molding public opinion—of "engineering consent"—emerged in the U.S. in the 1910s and 1920s. During the Progressive era, corporate spokesmen and government officials had reacted to journalistic muckrakers by offering facts and rational arguments. During World War I, however, the Wilson administration tried to counter widespread isolationist sentiment by forming the Committee on Public Information (CPI). The creation of the CPI, or Creel Committee as it was often called, reflected a growing awareness of "public opinion" among political and business elites: the committee sought to "mobilize and channel popular enthusiasm" for the war by marshaling speakers and producing propagandistic ads, posters, and films. After the war, the growing influence of Sigmund Freud further undermined the faith of many elites in a rational public. In the 1920s, Edward Bernays, who was Freud's nephew as well as a foot soldier in the CPI, helped found the field of public relations by suggesting that corporate leaders and other elites could discreetly manipulate public emotions using slogans, symbols, and images.[63] In the 1920s, many corporations latched onto the new techniques in an effort to burnish their corporate images. In the late 1930s, they turned their public relations dollars to the task of salvaging "free enterprise" itself.

In their efforts to sell their views to the American public, corporations made extensive use of radio—a vehicle that reached even those who couldn't read. In fact, during the 1930s, business leaders pioneered the use of dramatization subtly to instruct Americans on political values without sounding shrill. (Developing this tactic in the realms of radio and sponsored motion pictures, they eventually carried it to television as well.) [64] No program better exemplifies industry's creation of a "usable" past through drama than *Cavalcade of America*, a weekly radio anthology launched by E. I. DuPont de Nemours & Co. in October 1935. DuPont, a major munitions manufacturer, had been investigated by the Senate's Nye Committee the previous year, and DuPont executives, together with their colleagues at General Motors, were some of the most active and influential members of the Liberty League. *Cavalcade of America* consisted of half-hour dramatizations of what a company press release called "little-known but authentic incidents in American history." "Inspirational in type," the press release continued, "the treatment offers a new and absorbing approach to history, the incidents being reenacted so as to emphasize the qualities of American character which have been responsible for the building of this country."[65] By the early 1940s, DuPont estimated that six million people listened to the show each week, and it ensured the program's continuing impact by offering recordings to schools and colleges for classroom use.[66]

Each show began with a short "announcement" stressing "the application of chemistry to human needs [and] showing how the chemist's art has contributed to the comfort and happiness of people in all walks of life."[67] But the show's instruction went far beyond chemistry. This can clearly be seen in an episode on Jane Addams that was broadcast in May 1940, five years after Addams's death and fifty years after the founding of Hull House. The brief episode, which starred Helen Hayes in the title role, followed Jane from her childhood to her acceptance of the Nobel Peace Prize; however, the dramatic tension—and most of the plot—revolved around a "little-known" and almost certainly fictional event during Jane's life at Hull House. As the *Cavalcade* scriptwriters told the story, Jane's activism on behalf of female workers and tenement dwellers antagonized a local sweatshop owner and an Irish ward boss, who both worried that she was giving immigrants "ideas...ideas [that] ain't doing us no good." The two men planted an article in the local paper, charging Jane with "meddling" in the affairs of working people and getting workers fired as a result. A mob, enraged by the article, attacked and ransacked Hull House. Desperate and financially strapped, Jane turned to the Manufacturers Association for help. Although she was initially rebuffed—a few members ran the kind of sweatshop Jane deplored—a manufacturer who grew up in the Hull House neighborhood sought her out after the meeting and presented her with a handful of large checks. "By the time I get through," he told her "every *decent* business man in Chicago—and there are a lot of them—is going to be rooting for you....Then we'll start on the politicians."[68]

The messages of this episode were clear. Although business, like any field, had a few bad apples, most manufacturers were honorable, even generous, men. In fact, some had grown up in immigrant neighborhoods themselves and, by embracing the "American Way," had made enough money to hand out large checks. The same could not be said of politicians, particularly Democrats such as the Irish ward boss in the drama or (by implication) the many who supported the New Deal. In the end, manufacturers, not politicians, were the working people's true friends. This version of history may have been only loosely rooted in reality, but it was designed to appeal both to middle-class Americans and to striving ethnic workers who might tune in *Cavalcade* on their radio dials.

Corporations such as DuPont and General Motors reached millions of Americans with their advertisements, sponsored events, and radio programs. But by the mid-1930s, some industrialists and business pundits had concluded that a more coordinated effort to reshape public attitudes was called for. When the editors of McGraw-Hill, publishers of *Business Week* and other trade publications, surveyed various industries in the wake of FDR's 1936 landslide, they found that companies' lack of agreement on the definition and goal of public relations left employees and communities "bewildered and confused by the efforts industry was making to tell its story and to defend itself." Casting itself as industry's savior, McGraw-Hill began conducting "Public Relations Forums" in major cities around the country to help "give industry a common approach to the problem."[69]

Although McGraw-Hill, the U.S. Chamber of Commerce, and other organizations entered the fray, the National Association of Manufacturers (NAM) quickly emerged as the central vehicle behind business's coordinated effort in the late 1930s to redefine America's political culture. Founded in 1895, the NAM had long used publicity to combat unionism and to "control national questions of importance to manufacturers." But the campaign the association launched in the mid-1930s was unique both for its scope and for its efforts to court, rather than chastise, the public. In 1934, following the takeover of the NAM by a group of conservative industrialists, the organization's new president tapped Walter Weisenburger, a combative ex-journalist and former executive of the St. Louis Chamber of Commerce, to head the public relations effort. Weisenburger and his staff worked closely with two newly formed committees of industry executives: one charged with overseeing the campaign, and a second formed to raise money for the crusade.[70]

The NAM's campaign did not get off the ground immediately; but by 1937, it was well underway. That year, the NAM spent nearly $800,000 on its information program, and it received another $3.25 million in in-kind donations of newspaper and outdoor advertising space and free radio time.[71] (The association's budgets continued to escalate throughout the decade.) Using that money, the NAM's public relations staff translated industry's message into what Walter Weisenburger boasted was "every media of public information": newspaper articles, op-ed pieces and cartoons; film strips, newsreels, and movie shorts; direct mail campaigns; magazine, newspaper, and billboard advertising; posters and displays for schools, factories, and store windows;

"payroll stuffers" and clipsheets for plant publications; radio programs; a speaker's bureau; bumper stickers; and pamphlets for use in schools and local libraries. Some of this material was translated into German, Hungarian, Swedish, Polish, Italian, and Yiddish, clearly indicating that the organization was trying to reach immigrant workers as well as the English-speaking middle class. The NAM's Industrial Press Service distributed news stories, editorials, and prematted comic strips to one-quarter of the newspapers in the nation, including many small weekly, daily, and foreign-language papers that used the material to fill space without mentioning its source. Likewise, hundreds of radio stations across the country broadcast the fifteen-minute drama *American Family Robinson* each week, without indicating that they had received it *gratis* from the NAM.[72]

While the NAM's public relations staff focused on producing this array of material, they relied on a vast network of local committees to distribute it. Adopting a tactic pioneered by George Creel and the federal CPI during World War I, the NAM urged its members to set up Special Committees on Public Information in their communities. Ideally, these committees would be composed of men who were "known to be interested in this subject," had "the contacts to raise money," were willing to "give some time to sitting down with editors, ministers, foreign language groups, heads of women's clubs, etc.," and were "influential enough to make their weight felt with newspapers, radio stations and other business people within the town." These committees would organize "civic progress" meetings and speaking engagements, distribute the NAM's propaganda locally, and raise funds for the association's advertising campaign.[73]

In preparing its "information" materials, the NAM staff strove to avoid defensiveness. Instead, it presented American industry as a "courageous, progressive force" and emphasized the self-interest of those to whom it directed its message.[74] Although NAM propaganda covered a range of themes—the "miracles" of industrial research, the "shared" burden of high taxes, the "myth" that machines eliminated jobs—its bottom line was always the same: the "American system" had resulted in a standard of living for all Americans that, even in the worst of times, was the envy of the world. In posters, pamphlets, speeches, and billboards, the NAM repeatedly drove home the message that Americans had higher wages, shorter working hours, and more cars, radios, refrigerators, and homes per capita than any other nation around the globe. By 1937, the NAM had settled on a phrase that captured the family-centered lifestyle this abundance supposedly made possible: the "American Way of Life."[75]

The NAM's publicity blitz thus co-opted and redeployed the notion of economic security—freedom from want—that was central to the politics of both the New Deal and the CIO. FDR had argued that only the federal government could provide such security and that, as the embodiment of the will of a majority of the people, it had a clear obligation to do so. The CIO went even further, denouncing businessmen as traitorous Tories and demanding more power for labor in the workplace. The NAM vehemently rejected both notions, in the process offering its own definitions of such core American values as "freedom" and "democracy."

Whereas left liberals in the New Deal and the CIO assumed that workers and their employers often had competing interests, the NAM built its social and political vision around the notion of social harmony. According to NAM materials, the interests of industrialists were virtually indistinguishable from those of other Americans. "One need not think very deeply to understand that the interest of labor and business—that is to say, the employer—are identical," read one item that the NAM supplied to factory publications in early 1938. "In the long run their interests do coincide because they are both parts of the same system."[76] Over and over, the NAM emphasized that "wage and salary workers" owned property (homes, cars, stocks, savings accounts, and insurance policies), that conditions for U.S. labor had improved markedly over the decades, and that towns and employees benefited when business did well. And like both FDR and the CIO, they turned frequently to Abraham Lincoln for support: "There is no permanent class of hired laborers amongst us," another NAM-authored article quoted Lincoln as saying. "Twenty-five years ago I was a hired laborer. The hired laborer of yesterday labors on his own account today, and will hire others to labor for him tomorrow."[77] Like the *Cavalcade* episode on Jane Addams, this article played to workers' dreams of social mobility.

Perhaps the most extended explication of this view came in a series of ads carrying the slogan "Prosperity Dwells Where Harmony Reigns," which the NAM placed in newspapers around the country in 1937. Some of the ads, undoubtly aimed at members of the middle class, stressed the dependence of home prices, small businesses, and city services on industry's payroll. Others reminded workers of the benefits and opportunities they gleaned from the American system. One hailed the "loyal partnership" between workers, capital, and management that had made the "average workman's lot" far better than that of his counterparts around the world. Another showed a worker on steel scaffolding waving to an executive in a chauffeured limousine: "I knew *him* when he pushed a wheelbarrow," the worker said. The final ad, aimed in part at first- and second-generation Americans, barely referred to business at all. Beside a picture of the Statue of Liberty, bold lettering demanded "*Are You* an American Citizen?" "A TRUE American…must be an American citizen not alone by accident of birth or privilege of naturalization," the copy continued:

> He must be an American citizen at heart, proud of his heritage of liberty and opportunity—willing to accept the duty of citizenship to protect American ideals.…
>
> Today many influences are at work to destroy the real value of your citizenship. They preach violence as opposed to reason. They strive to pit class against class—to gain advantage for the few without regard for the welfare of the many.…They undermine the spirit of co-operation and teamwork among all groups on which this nation has been built. Their success would spell the eventual breakdown of all that has made America mean "opportunity" for millions.

"These influences," the ad concluded, "CAN NOT succeed where Americans are awake to their duty as citizens. ARE YOU AN AMERICAN CITIZEN?"[78] The ad clearly suggested that anyone who did not foster "teamwork among all groups"—anyone who worked to foment class unrest—was not a true American.

The insidious "influences" to which this ad pointed were clearly not "economic royalists" or "industrial Tories." Businessmen, in the NAM's schema, were custodians of the people's interests. The great danger came from an overweening government that trampled on the rights and privileges of its citizens, in the process undermining the prosperity that only business could produce. "*When we give any Government increasing power to regulate our daily lives we are giving away one of the most sacred liberties any American citizen can possess,*" one NAM leaflet warned. "Governments *love* power! Don't give *any* Government the right to dictate *where* you shall work, *when* you shall work and *what* your wages shall be!"[79] An NAM booklet entitled *The American Way* reinforced this message, distinguishing between two kinds of government: "one in which the citizen is supreme and the government obeys his will; the other in which the state is supreme and controls the citizen." Implicitly contrasting the U.S. approach to that of totalitarian states, the booklet left little doubt which was, and should remain, the American Way.[80]

As such ads and pamphlets suggest, NAM staffers, like New Dealers and industrial unionists, cast American citizenship as, above all, a matter of shared values. The values they highlighted, however, differed sharply from those championed by FDR and the CIO. While FDR stressed majoritarian rule, embodied in the federal government, the NAM hailed individual liberties and the limits on government guaranteed by the Bill of Rights. While the CIO called for industrial *democracy*, which implied an extension of majority rule into the economic arena, the NAM stressed *freedom* of opportunity. The various definitions converged only on freedom from want.

Not surprisingly, the NAM fought an uphill battle. Its portrayal of business as the guarantor of prosperity worked only if it overlooked the ravages of the continuing Depression; this explains the NAM's tendency in the late 1930s to backdate statistics to 1929. Senator Robert M. La Follette's Committee on Civil Liberties investigated the propaganda onslaught as part of a larger probe into the union-busting activities of corporate America, and the *CIO News* reprinted some of the committee's findings. Many other Americans were reminded of the strained note in the campaign by pictures taken by some of the decade's most able documentary photographers: Margaret Bourke-White's famous shot of black flood victims lined up in front of an NAM billboard in Louisville, Kentucky, first appeared in *Fortune* magazine in 1937.

Nevertheless, by early 1939, the NAM believed it was making progress. In 1937, the CIO had introduced a new tactic—the sit-down strike—in its campaign against General Motors. Although the tactic brought the automaker to its knees, spreading sit-down strikes began to undermine middle-class support for the labor movement. Around the same time, FDR tried to counter Supreme Court antagonism to the New Deal with a disastrous plan to "pack" the court. Roosevelt's transparently political proposal backfired badly, eroding his stature even among many Democrats and New Deal supporters.[81] The full impact of these developments was not felt immediately; but by March 1939, Walter Weisenburger could report that public opinion had shifted to the right. Meanwhile, the economic downturn of 1937 and 1938, dubbed by some the "Roosevelt Recession," helped the NAM campaign in ironic ways. Schools and colleges, strapped for funds, used the association's *You and Industry* pamphlets as textbooks. Newspapers eager for economic news snapped up columns and other materials provided *gratis* by the NAM. And a drop-off in corporate billboard advertising opened more donated space for the NAM's American Way campaign. "We feel that the condition has changed from a situation in which we are a seller, trying to force our product, into what you might call a buyer's market," Weisenburger reported with obvious satisfaction. "This offers one of the greatest opportunities this association has."[82]

Weisenburger's optimism was not based on domestic events alone. By early 1939, rising tensions in Europe gave new resonance to several of the NAM's long-standing themes. With more attention focused abroad, the NAM's effort to contrast the American Way to foreign living standards seemed less labored than it had in the past. News reports on government initiatives in Germany, Italy, and Japan provided a powerful backdrop for NAM attacks on the growth of federal power in the U.S. Above all, international tensions and news reports from Germany made discord at home seem increasingly worrisome to many in the U.S. In January, one NAM speaker linked the association's advocacy of cooperation and harmony directly to events abroad. "I am proud to say that industry has made its start towards establishing this country's first line of defense—harmony between all groups in our economy," Fuller Barnes, an executive of the Associated Spring Company, told students and faculty at Hartford Theological Seminary. "If industry's good faith and good reasoning in this respect can be matched by other groups, we need not fear the tides of hate and madness that have swept other lands."[83] That same month, the NAM launched a new billboard campaign with the slogan "Let's All Work Together—It's an Old American Custom." "Dictatorships breed on misunderstandings between groups and classes," an item sent to plant publications explained. "They can never prevail here as long as we have a united America."[84]

Two events in the late summer and early fall of 1939 gave new energy to the NAM campaign. News of the Nazi-Soviet pact in late August gave credence to the argument that fascism and communism were really one and the same—that both were in fact "totalitarianism." A few weeks later, the outbreak of war in Europe raised the stakes for all Americans. "Now events abroad offer a dramatic back-drop against which the true value of the American Way can be measured," a staff memo exulted in the fall of 1939. "Americanism, the American system and all that they stand for have been set off in bold relief. As they survey war-torn Europe, as they see the spread of dictatorships and the ruthless suppression of rights and freedoms as commonplace here as the air we breathe and as they see Communism, Nazism and Fascism revealed as one and the same ideology, the American people are in a mood to recognize and count their blessings."[85]

If the war in Europe opened opportunities for the NAM campaign, it also called for a shift in emphasis. In the late 1930s, NAM officials and other corporate leaders had begun tentatively using the term "free enterprise"—in place of the less resonant "laissez-faire" or "private enterprise"—in an effort to link their economic agenda to the one value that virtually all Americans held dear. Now NAM staffers urged them to take a further step. "Free enterprise [will not] be saved as the result of appeals in the name of free enterprise alone," the staff memo argued. "Democracy and its preservation are the interest of every patriotic American today," it continued: "The public must be convinced that free enterprise is as much an indivisible part of democracy and the source of as many blessings and benefits as are our other freedoms of speech, press and religion." If the NAM's program "can emphasize effectively the inseparability of 'democracy' and 'free enterprise,' it may well be that the wave of enthusiasm and support for the former will carry the latter to unprecedented heights in public esteem."[86]

This notion of hitching industry's economic agenda to America's political values was not entirely new in late 1939. Both FDR and the CIO had linked their economic visions to political rights; and in early 1938, Raymond Moley had recommended that business do likewise. Moley, who had resigned from FDR's Brain Trust and become an advocate for American business, called on corporate leaders to "again and again make it clear that our economic system and our political system are essentially opposite sides of the same coin."[87] In his January 1939 Hartford speech, the NAM speaker Fuller Barnes had invoked "the threefold basis of our American way of life—religious freedom, private enterprise and representative democracy." The NAM's radio drama *American Family Robinson* had experimented with the same themes that summer.[88]

Nevertheless, the emphasis on democracy in late 1939 and 1940 posed a challenge to NAM stalwarts. The association's president, H. W. Prentis Jr., and many other NAM members were wary of the term, in large part because its majoritarian overtones had been used by President Roosevelt and others to justify the New Deal.[89] In ads, pattern speeches, and other materials, the NAM was always careful to refer to "representative democracy" or simply to "political freedom."

The NAM adopted this approach again in the winter of 1939–1940, when it launched a major new effort that became known as the "Tripod of Freedom" campaign. The NAM's president, H. W. Prentis Jr., explained the premise behind the campaign in a speech to manufacturers in April 1940. The "tripod of human freedom," Prentis told his audience, had three legs: "representative democracy," "civil and religious liberties," and "economic freedom, the institution of private enterprise." "Throughout the ages, these institutions have gone hand in hand," he continued. "They are inseparable. When one goes, all go." Then, borrowing an argument from the interfaith movement, he explained, "The same basic concept underlies them all—a religious concept common to Protestantism, Roman Catholicism and Judaism alike, the sacredness of the individual."[90]

If freedom's three foundations were inseparable, "free private enterprise" was the most vulnerable element in the trio, Prentis argued. "Even the Communist and Fascist and Socialist groups among us prate about their devotion to representative democracy and insist upon the preservation of civil and re-ligious liberties, at least so long as they themselves are not in power," he de-clared. "The attack always is against that other leg of the tripod, economic freedom." Prentis argued that "national economic planning" inevitably led to the erosion of both political democracy and civil liberties, since planners were required to control all "opinion-forming" agencies that might throw "monkey-wrenches into their carefully laid plans": "In other words, under na-tional economic planning, you would have here eventually just what you see in the dictator-controlled countries of Europe today: the suppression of all teaching except that which is in line with the general ideas of the government censorship of the press; the end of freedom of expression; and the destruction of religious liberty."[91]

This quote suggests one of the reasons that the NAM deemed the "tri-pod of freedom" imagery so useful. An NAM poll, probably conducted in 1940, showed that 96 percent of Americans believed that the abolition of religious freedom would violate their personal liberties, and 90 percent felt

Figure 2.2. This National Association of Manufacturers billboard in Dubuque, Iowa, testifies to the business community's growing use of the term "free enter-prise" in the late 1930s. The ad was part of the "Tripod of Freedom" campaign launched by the NAM in the winter of 1939–40 in an effort to connect what had once been called "private enterprise" to other treasured American freedoms (Library of Congress LC-DIG-fsa-8a05396).

the same about freedom of speech. By contrast, only 71 percent believed that the operation of private business was a basic American right, and 40 percent thought the right to strike was a fundamental liberty.[92] The NAM believed that the tripod of freedoms had "removed our objectives from the selfish category" and linked unfettered "free enterprise" to other values that Americans clearly held in greater esteem.[93]

Throughout 1940 and 1941, the NAM trumpeted the tripod of freedoms in every available forum. NAM billboards highlighted America's fundamental freedoms (figure 2.2) as did pamphlets, brochures, and the *American Family Robinson* radio show. *Primer for Americans*, a seventy-seven-page pamphlet designed for citizenship study by women's groups, broke down the "American Way" into three constituent parts: "privilege of self-expression," "right of self-government," and "opportunity of free enterprise." The hero of an NAM movie short dreamed that he was an attorney called upon to defend the American way of life. He summoned witnesses who testified to the nation's diverse freedoms and material abundance, then dramatized his concluding argument with the use of a small tripod.[94]

These intertwined freedoms, according to the NAM, constituted the rights and privileges Americans enjoyed; at the same time, their enjoyment defined the American. "To be an American—does it mean anything?" an article written by the NAM's staff for use in plant publications began. "Americans," the article continued, "include people of many races and religions—many ways of thinking, working, and living." What made these diverse individuals Americans? Not simply their residency "within...certain boundaries you find on a map." No, the article concluded, they were Americans because they could worship, associate, speak, read, and travel as they wished; because they could join political parties and vote freely for a government "whose authority is limited"; because they could choose their own occupation, spend and save earnings as they wished, and own and use property with a minimum of outside interference. "To be an American," the article declared, was to be "a free member of one of the freest societies on earth," a "civilization" built on "the fundamental principle...that the individual matters."[95]

The NAM's emphasis on individual freedom—like its emphasis on the dangers of an overweening government and the need for "teamwork among all groups" in American society—contrasted sharply with the vision of Americanism offered by both the CIO and New Dealers. Although neither the CIO nor FDR neglected individual freedom, both put their faith in majoritarian democracy and saw the greatest danger to America coming from a selfish and powerful minority. Industrial unionists also highlighted the fundamental inequality between labor and capital, an inequality that would need to be redressed before true "teamwork" would be possible. Some of the NAM's arguments, however, resonated with a different group—the motley collection of "intergroup" activists who in the years immediately preceding World War II sought to deploy an American Way to defuse rising tensions among America's ethnic, religious, and racial subgroups.

CHAPTER 3

In Search of Common Ground

On January 21, 1939, George Kaufman and Moss Hart's play, *The American Way*, commenced an eight-month run at New York's Rockefeller Center. The two men were best known for their lighthearted comedies, but this was a melodramatic epic. *The American Way* told the life story of Martin Gunther, a fictional German cabinetmaker who immigrated to Mapleton, Ohio, because he was determined to see his children grow up in a free country. Martin learned English and began a breathtaking rise up the town's economic and social ladder, transforming his small shop into a flourishing factory. His faith in his adopted country, however, transcended economic success: even the loss of his factory during the Depression did not shake Martin's faith in the American Way (figure 3.1).

Martin's grandson, Karl, was less convinced of his country's merits. Embittered by his family's financial losses and his own inability to find a job, Karl was recruited by an unnamed organization clearly modeled on the German American Bund. When Martin tried to dissuade his grandson from joining the group, Bundists beat the elderly immigrant to death. This violent act finally converted his mourning grandson, and in the play's final moments, Martin was given a hero's funeral. Eulogized as a true American, he was hailed as a man who "lived in tolerance and in peace among his neighbors" and who died fighting for the freedom "which he felt gave meaning to life."[1]

Kaufman and Hart's play might have given some solace to the businessmen clustered around the NAM; after all, its hero was a factory owner who was beloved by his neighbors and whose life story offered personal proof of the ability of Americans to transcend class boundaries. The play's principal contribution to the decade's discussion of America's identity and core values,

Figure 3.1. This scene of Ellis Island appeared in George Kaufman and Moss Hart's 1939 melodrama *The American Way*. The play suggested that the "American way" was the way of immigrants who had flourished under freedom and learned to live together by respecting their fellow man (Billy Rose Theatre Division, The New York Public Library for the Performing Arts, Astor, Lenox and Tilden Foundations).

however, lay elsewhere. Although the play never mentioned Hitler or the Bundists by name, its message was clear: the "American Way" was the way of immigrants who had flourished under freedom and learned to live together by respecting their fellow man. If a German-American Christian could be murdered by Bundists for his belief in tolerance and individual freedom, then Nazism and the bigotry it embodied were a threat, not only to Jews, but to all who subscribed to the American Way.

As Kaufman and Hart's play suggested, efforts to define a unifying American Way in the years immediately preceding U.S. entry into World War II were not limited to discussions of the nation's political economy. In the late 1930s and early 1940s, a growing number of opinion molders argued that a distinctive—indeed defining—feature of American life was the ability of diverse individuals to live together harmoniously. Casting America as the archetype of "unity within diversity," intellectuals, federal officials, and an array of civic groups emphasized the nation's diverse demographic strands, portrayed "intergroup" hostility as an alien import, and suggested that a deeply rooted ideological consensus made other forms of pluralism possible.

Efforts to highlight America's demographic diversity, as well as to reconcile that diversity with the need for national unity, stretched back at least to 1782 when J. Hector St. John de Crèvecoeur penned his famous *Letters from an American Farmer*. Indeed, America's "variety" had often been seen as "an inviolable sign of national exceptionalism."[2] Still, the scope and scale of efforts to champion cultural pluralism—and to curb cultural prejudice—in the late 1930s were startling, particularly in light of America's recent past. Well into the 1920s, prominent intellectuals and other powerful elites had warned against the "mongrelization" of the nation, voicing a fear that fueled the eugenics movement, immigration restrictions, and a resurgent Ku Klux Klan. By the late 1930s, the tenor of this national discussion had shifted dramatically. Intellectuals and civic leaders now hailed America's diverse ethnic, religious, and sometimes racial strains and argued that the U.S. had developed "the highest, most mature concept of human relations yet devised."[3] Existing organizations such as the Common Council for American Unity (CCAU) and the National Conference of Christians and Jews (NCCJ) redoubled their efforts to promote intergroup harmony as key aspects of the American Way. New organizations—the Council Against Intolerance, the Committee for National Morale, the Council for Democracy, the Institute for American Democracy, and many others—sprang up during these years to promote similar agendas.[4]

A complex array of developments abroad and at home spurred these efforts to both spotlight and tame American diversity. During the late 1930s, U.S. political observers frequently juxtaposed the American Way with "totalitarianism," a newly coined term used to capture the shared evils of fascism and communism. Since a coerced and homogeneous unity was one of these evils, the totalitarian threat made acceptance of diversity almost a definition of democracy.[5] Casting American variety in ethnocultural terms proved politically easier than it had been in the past, in part because of the clampdown on immigration to the U.S. in the 1920s. The restrictive legislation of that decade effectively took immigration off the table as a subject of national debate and hastened the acculturation of ethnic communities. In so doing, it made declarations of cultural diversity less threatening.

If global developments thus prompted many Americans to equate democracy with variety, they also underscored the dangers of unchecked difference. Intellectuals and civic leaders believed that warring factions had undermined national morale in Germany and France, paving the way for the political and military triumph of fascists. At the same time, U.S. newspapers, magazines, and newsreels were filled with stories about murderous clashes both between and within ethnic and national groups. In 1937, for instance, the *New York Times* opened the year with reports of virulent anti-Semitism in Germany and Eastern Europe that was threatening to turn "the recurrent Jewish tragedy" in that part of the world into "a final disaster of truly historic magnitude." In April, the paper reported the terror bombing of the ancient Basque city of Guernica by German bombers allied with Spanish nationalists; and in September, it told readers that Soviet purges had made the previous twelve months "the bloodiest since the early years of the Bolshevist [sic] revolution." December brought news of the Japanese "rape" of the Nationalist Chinese capital at Nanking—a three-week orgy of rape, torture, beheading, bayoneting, and machine-gunning that left as many as three hundred thousand Chinese dead.[6] And that was only 1937.

In this context, the U.S. looked to many American and foreign observers like a cosmopolitan haven; the generally inclusive ethos of the New Deal only strengthened this perception.[7] At the same time, many of those who hailed American pluralism and tolerance were driven in part by fear—fear that the U.S., too, might succumb to the hatreds ravaging other lands. America had a long history of nativism, racism, and religious intolerance, and the Depression only fueled such sentiments in some quarters. Moreover, rising tensions between nations in Europe and Asia had triggered what the immigrant writer Louis Adamic called a "powerful backwash of group feelings or national emotions" within America's ethnic communities. "The cleavages among the various groups [in America] are deepening," Adamic warned ominously in a speech he delivered widely in 1939 and 1940. "Groups are pulling apart into various corners, away from one another."[8]

Such fears meant that nearly all of those who emphasized America's pluralist makeup in the years immediately preceding World War II yoked diversity tightly to consensus.[9] By emphasizing the nation's demographic variety, they sought to distinguish the U.S. from totalitarian "others" and to make ethnic, religious, and racial minorities feel at home in the nation. By convincing Americans of diverse backgrounds that they shared fundamental beliefs, opinion molders sought to avert chaos and intolerance and to strengthen national morale. By declaring that America was a nation of diverse individuals bound by consensus, they sought to call such a nation into being and to provide an example for the world.

The fact that varied individuals and groups cast America as a diverse nation unified by certain core beliefs should not obscure key differences in the way they reckoned both pluralism and consensus. Some cast America as a "nation of immigrants"—or more broadly a "nation of nations"—united by the secular Enlightenment values enshrined in the Declaration of Independence and the U.S. Constitution. Members of the burgeoning interfaith movement, however, emphasized religious rather than ethnic diversity and saw in shared spiritual beliefs the source of the nation's common ground. Some antiracist social scientists, notably including Margaret Mead, emphasized Americans' immigrant *past* but focused on the assimilating power of American culture. Resurrecting the notion of "national character," they sought to reconcile the tension between unity and diversity by showing that Americans of diverse origins internalized certain key values.

Such differences mattered. An America pictured as a "nation of immigrants" implicitly left out both American Indians and blacks. Even those who advocated the broader "nation of nations" formulation often failed to recognize the unique history and challenges confronted by black Americans. Portrayals of the nation as "Protestant-Catholic-Jewish" sidestepped issues of ethnic and racial diversity and excluded atheists, secular humanists, and others who did not subscribe to one of these three major faiths. Margaret Mead saw prolonged intolerance as impeding the development of a shared "national character." Thus, her vision of the nation excluded both perpetrators and victims of racism.

Beyond all this loomed larger questions of comity and justice. If a fundamental agreement on values—an ideological consensus—was a necessary precondition for harmonizing diverse groups, then what was the content of that consensus and who controlled its boundaries? Should "tolerance" (or even "acceptance") extend to conservative businessmen? To communists and others on the left? To bigots? To those who condemned racial bigotry but made no move to dismantle segregation? In short, did the American Way mean greater *equality* for people of all backgrounds or simply greater *civility* within the context of the economic and social status quo? As Americans debated these issues in the late 1930s and early 1940s, the parameters of diversity and consensus—the limits of unity and inclusion—became contested terrain.

Louis Adamic and the "Nation of Nations" Approach

In the fall of 1939 and the spring of 1940, the Slovenian-American journalist Louis Adamic toured the U.S., lecturing to some one hundred audiences about his new project, a massive attempt to rewrite American history in a way that would integrate "Plymouth Rock and Ellis Island." Even a hundred years earlier, he argued, "the people of this country were largely derived from Britain" and were for the most part Anglo-Saxon and Protestant. (Adamic acknowledged the presence of "great numbers" of Negroes and Indians but argued that for various reasons both groups were seen as "outside the processes of American culture.") A century of immigration had changed that picture. "In the last hundred years, 38,000,000 immigrants came over; 24,000,000 in the last fifty years," Adamic wrote. "And the majority of them were non-Anglo-Saxons and non-Protestants, and were not very closely attached to the attitude to life called Puritanism." This shift had not been reflected in the nation's historical narrative or its sense of national identity. Adamic proposed to change that. He would write "an intellectual-emotional synthesis of old and new America; of the Mayflower and the steerage; of the New England wilderness and the social-economic jungle of the city slums and the factory system; of the Liberty Bell and the Statue of Liberty." "The old American Dream needs to be interlaced with the immigrants' emotions as they saw the Statue of Liberty," he declared. "The two must be made into one story."[10]

Adamic was a logical individual to undertake such a project. He had emigrated from the Austro-Hungarian Empire at the age of fifteen, learned English in New York City night schools, and become an American citizen while serving in the army during World War I. During the 1920s and early 1930s, he had worked as a West Coast journalist, befriending such activist writers as Carey McWilliams and Upton Sinclair and establishing his reputation as a radical democrat whose allegiance lay with the left wing of the New Deal coalition. Adamic's early work focused on class and labor issues, but his third book, a best-selling account of his return to Slovenia after a twenty-year absence, signaled a shift in emphasis. In the mid-1930s, Adamic began publicizing his "Plymouth Rock and Ellis Island" project through lecture tours and a lengthy questionnaire dubbed the "Broadside." He solicited letters from immigrants, their children, and "Old Stock" Americans about their experiences in and views of the U.S. Drawing on the thousands of responses he received, Adamic published four widely acclaimed books between 1940 and 1945 that became known collectively as the "Nation of Nations" series.[11]

Adamic was perhaps the most visible spokesperson for a vision of America that began to gain wide acceptance in the late 1930s—a vision that cast the U.S. as a "nation of immigrants" or, in the words that Adamic borrowed from Walt Whitman, as a "nation of nations." During these years, pioneers of intercultural education distributed materials on diverse ethnic and racial groups to teachers across the country in an attempt to promote cross-cultural understanding.[12] The Statue of Liberty, which for decades had been seen as an emblem of U.S. independence and "Franco-American friendship," was recast as a beacon "to the huddled masses of the Old World."[13] The Justice Department launched "I Am an American Day" to honor newly naturalized citizens, reinforcing its message of unity and diversity with both a radio program and a book of the same name.[14] Meanwhile, "Ballad for Americans," a rousing cantata composed for a Federal Theatre Project revue, celebrated "an Irish, Negro, Jewish, Italian, French and English, Spanish, Russian, Chinese, Polish, Scotch, Hungarian, Litvak, Swedish, Finnish, Canadian, Greek and Turk, and Czech and double Czech American." Written by John La Touche and Earl Robinson, both members of what Michael Denning has called the "Cultural Front," the song was popularized in late 1939 by the great black bass Paul Robeson. By 1940, MGM had snapped it up for a movie, school choruses were performing it across the country, and both the Republican and Communist parties used it in their national conventions.[15]

"Ballad for Americans" also became a theme song of the "American Common" at the 1940 New York World's Fair.[16] When the Soviet Union withdrew from the fair in the wake of the Nazi-Soviet pact, exposition designers decided to use the newly opened space to "demonstrate an idea diametrically opposed to the propaganda of the totalitarian states, . . . [namely] that America's greatness springs from the free and democratic institutions that allow her individual citizens and cultural groups to pursue happiness in their own differing ways." Fair organizers allowed different ethnic groups to take over the American Common for an evening, a day or a week, and to use the band shell, auditorium, and marketplace to "give its own distinctive 'country fair' with its own old-world bazaars and fiestas." As its name suggested, however, the American Common ultimately hailed diversity in the context of national unity. The Stars and Stripes towered over the Common on a "Liberty Pole," and each day ended with what organizers called a "brilliant patriotic gathering." "Here," one publicity release intoned, "will be America in its richest mingled traditions. Here will be the most direct and powerful answer to the dictators who would mold all peoples into the same rigid pattern."[17]

As this quote suggests, the celebration of America's diverse ethnic strains in the late 1930s and early 1940s in part reflected simply a new twist on an old tradition: invoking American diversity to argue for national exceptionalism. Many liberal intellectuals, government officials, and civic leaders also believed that a more inclusive vision of the nation was essential to cementing national unity and protecting political democracy during a time of international peril. Adamic and others worried about the physical and psychic effect of intergroup hostility on the individuals who were its targets. "Not a few old stock Americans go on believing they are on the inside track of a pattern of civilization and culture which was fixed long ago, once and for all," Adamic declared. This Old Stock prejudice, aggravated by the economic pressures of the Depression, kept America's newest arrivals from identifying with America, he believed: "When they say 'Americans,' they don't mean themselves." Such prejudice only reinforced Old World loyalties, exacerbating tensions among ethnic groups that had emerged as a result of hostilities abroad. Both old and new Americans, Adamic warned, were "becoming unhooked from the country's expansive and creative impulses, from the American Dream."[18]

As Adamic set about addressing these problems, his project quickly found institutional support. The Foreign Language Information Service (FLIS) had emerged from the federal Committee on Public Information during World War I and had worked for more than two decades to solve the "immigrant problem" by "educating away the misunderstanding and ignorance" that plagued both the foreign and native born; it did this largely by dispensing translated bulletins to the foreign-language press. In the late 1920s, the FLIS had fallen on hard times, but the rise of Hitler and growing tensions in Europe during the following decade resuscitated the organization. The FLIS's director, Read Lewis, was intrigued with Adamic's notion that a more expansive understanding of America's past and shared values could improve the morale of second-generation Americans and defuse religious and ethnic tensions like those he saw emanating from Europe. In the mid-1930s he recruited the young writer to help reorganize the agency and broaden its mandate. The FLIS and Adamic's "Nation of Nations" project also garnered significant financial support from the Carnegie Corporation. Energized by a new sense of purpose, Adamic and Lewis renamed the organization the Common Council for American Unity (CCAU) and launched a "little magazine" they entitled *Common Ground*. On the eve of World War II, they steered the CCAU into the forefront of a host of liberal groups that preached national ideological unity as an antidote to deepening religious, racial, and ethnic divides.[19]

Adamic, the CCAU, and their allies on the liberal left criticized the notion of a homogenous and static American culture and instead encouraged appreciation for the contributions of ethnic and racial groups to America's "culture in the making." At the same time, they rejected the ethnocultural essentialism embraced by the first advocate of cultural pluralism, Horace Kallen. Writing in an era of mass immigration and repressive Americanization campaigns, Kallen saw ethnic group consciousness as a bulwark against discrimination. Thus, he envisioned the U.S. as a loosely linked federation of relatively stable ethnic nationalities.[20] Two decades later, in the midst of the great immigration interregnum, the edges of America's ethnic enclaves had begun to blur. More important, Adamic, the CCAU, and many other liberals and leftists had come to see ethnocultural identity as a double-edged sword: it could enrich American culture and provide a temporary source of support for individuals as they merged "organically" into the nation, but rigid group loyalties could also fan the flames of prejudice that were ravaging Europe and threatening the U.S. as well.[21]

In fact, Adamic argued that the U.S. should "invite diversity" precisely because this was the best way to free *individuals* from the vice-like grip of ethnic pasts and "to produce unity in a democratic country." Suppression of diversity, Adamic argued, would tend to make cultural groups ashamed and defensive, driving them into "the concentration-camp-like foreign sections and ghettos and restricted residential districts." Inviting diversity, by contrast, "will encourage movement and dispersal, at the same time that it will work for harmony and fusion," Adamic wrote. "Inviting diversity brings out the basic sameness of people, just as the opposite results only in more and sharper differences."[22]

As this final line suggests, the "unity in diversity" that Adamic hoped to create rested ultimately on his proposition that individual Americans, whatever their background, shared a common set of values and aspirations. Adamic argued in his oft-delivered "Plymouth Rock and Ellis Island" lecture that both "old stock" Americans and those whose ancestors had arrived more recently had been propelled by a "surge toward freedom" and that both subscribed to the "American Dream." This dream was "a matter mostly of faith in the human individual and the concepts of liberty, fraternity and equality, of general welfare and democracy which were stated or embodied in the Declaration of Independence and the Constitution."[23] This emphasis on shared beliefs and values also permeated *Common Ground*. "Never has it been more important that we become intelligently aware of the ground Americans of various strains have in common," the editors declared in the opening issue, "that we sink our tap roots deep into its rich and varied cultural past and attain rational stability in place of emotional hysteria; that we reawaken the old American Dream, the dream which, in its powerful emphasis on the fundamental worth and dignity of every human being, can be a bond of unity no totalitarian attack can break."[24]

Thus, for all their celebration of ethnocultural diversity, Adamic and the CCAU put their greatest hopes for a just and harmonious society in the values shared by free individuals within the context of the American nation. The American Dream, Adamic argued, had many sources, and its appeal was potentially universal. "At its best, Americanism is nobody's monopoly, but a happy concentrate of some of the highest aspirations and tendencies of humanity at its best nearly everywhere at one time or another," Adamic wrote. "It is, among other things, a movement away from primitive racism, fear and nationalism, and herd instincts and mentality; a movement toward freedom, creativeness, a universal or pan-human culture."[25] Since Adamic believed that the U.S. best exemplified these "universal" Enlightenment-derived values, his writing often took on a celebratory tone. "America…embodies the highest, most mature concept of human relations yet devised," he argued in a 1943 article. "The unprecedented scope of this experiment in living together with relatively little friction has given the United States a unique status. To millions of the oppressed throughout the world 'America' is a magic name; it is paradise come true on earth."[26]

Such adulation might not seem surprising coming from some of the more conservative voices who embraced the "nation of immigrants" paradigm. Adamic, however, openly advocated racial equality and economic justice and was a stalwart of the Popular Front. His writings in the late 1930s and early 1940s put less emphasis on class issues than did his earlier work; still he argued in 1938 that America's philosophy of government "basically and generally…has no quarrel with the ideal of Communism, which is essentially the ideal of equality."[27] In the same article in which he extolled America as an earthly paradise, Adamic acknowledged that "we are still hampered by prejudice, by xenophobia, racism, isolationism, and 'class' distinctions."[28] In a private letter written in early 1939, Adamic noted that he was an American, "but displeased with much in present day America and passionate only in my feeling or idea that we have a chance here to create an amazing culture and civilization."[29]

As this final quote suggests, Adamic reconciled his conflicting views by adopting an approach often attributed to Gunnar Myrdal's famous 1944 study of race relations, *An American Dilemma*. Like Myrdal and many other liberals and leftists in the late 1930s and early 1940s, Adamic distinguished—always privately and sometimes in his public speeches and writings—between the America he saw and the America that was becoming.[30] "The United States is not anything finished and perfect, but a process in numerous ways and respects," Adamic argued in the speech he gave to audiences around the country. "The road ahead is long, and…we have to be patient." Adamic was optimistic that Americans were moving in the right direction. In stressing their core beliefs and common values, however, he was not simply celebrating the path his fellow citizens had taken; he was trying instead to nudge them down the long road ahead.

Black Americans generally applauded some aspects of Adamic's approach—particularly his equation of Americanism with individual freedom and equality and his judgment that America's ability to solve "the Negro question" would be the "ultimate test" of its civilization.[31] Some, however, challenged his optimistic tone. "The Negro teacher is expected to teach American democracy just as the white teacher does. But this idealism does not exist," a black teacher from North Carolina wrote in April 1940 in response to Adamic's questionnaire. "The student soon discovers the fallacy of this lesson. Doors of opportunity are closed in his face. He is crushed in more ways than one." Could the people of the United States afford to criticize Germany "for crushing the Jews," the teacher asked, "when people in America will hang Negroes up trees and cut off parts of their bodies for souvenirs?"[32]

What this and other black Americans were questioning was Adamic's judgment that the "Negro Problem" was simply "a section of the American Problem which involves all of us, white and black, old-stock white folk and people of recent-immigrant stocks."[33] Adamic believed this so fervently that when the white philanthropist Anson Phelps Stokes approached him in 1935 about plans being hatched by W. E. B. DuBois and others for an *Encyclopedia of the Negro*, Adamic brusquely suggested that they abandon the idea. "The Negro millions are part of the United States, not separate from it," he wrote Stokes, "and I feel that they belong, along with the Indians, Yankees, the Dutch, and the more recent immigrant strains, in a complete racial encyclopedia, which will tell us—the people of the United States: all of us—who we are, what we have in us, etc." Adamic was not alone in this view. In his dispute with Stokes and DuBois, Adamic successfully sought the support of the "young Turks" at Howard University, including economist Abram Harris, political scientist Ralph Bunche, and sociologist E. Franklin Frazier.[34] This group of young radical scholars fervently opposed what they saw as the "race chauvinism" of DuBois and his allies and instead placed their hopes for black advance and diminished race prejudice in interracial unionism.[35]

Adamic's refusal to distinguish sharply between the experience of blacks and other Americans was shared by most whites who celebrated the nation's cultural diversity on the eve of World War II. Those who orchestrated the era's public displays of cultural pluralism—government officials, intercultural educators, radio scriptwriters, and the heads of organizations like the CCAU, the International Institutes, and the World Fair's "American Common"—did not always share Adamic's radical politics, but they generally celebrated the history of the nation's diverse peoples and often emphasized the "gifts" that each had contributed to the national culture.[36] Black Americans were inserted into this panoply of progress, often without full recognition of their very different history and the unique challenges within American society that they continued to face.

The dilemmas this posed for black Americans were clearly apparent in Adamic's portrayal of the "Festival of Nations" staged by the St. Paul International Institute in April 1939. In preparation for the annual event, the city auditorium "was transformed into a market square in a composite Old World city of about the year 1850, when modern immigration to America began in earnest." With the help of a local architect, the edges of the vast space were transformed to suggest "the architecture of two dozen European and Asiatic countries." Participants—including blacks, who had been invited for the first time to take part—were supposed to don the costumes that their ancestors might have worn around 1850.[37]

This delighted most members of the city's ethnic communities, but it posed a problem for blacks. In the late 1930s, many black Americans were reluctant to call attention to their African heritage. Southern racists such as Mississippi senator Theodore Bilbo were actively promoting plans to ship American blacks to Africa, by force if necessary.[38] Moreover, the continent's residents were regarded as inept, corrupt, and savage by nearly all whites and even many progressive blacks. The attitudes of many black Americans started to change in 1935, with the Italian invasion of Ethiopia. Still, the evolution was gradual.[39] When the Council Against Intolerance in 1942 distributed thousands of classroom wall maps charting America's population by country of origin (e.g. "Ireland," "Sweden," etc.), blacks were the only group not identified geographically. On the advice of Walter White, executive secretary of the National Association for the Advancement of Colored People (NAACP), the Council used "Negro" instead of "Africa."[40]

For black Americans, such concerns clearly complicated the request that they don historically appropriate attire. In any case, in 1850—the date chosen by the organizers of the St. Paul festival—the ancestors of most black Americans were not in Africa but in chains. "The Negro group did not want to remind anyone of their ancestral slavery," Adamic noted. "They preferred contemporary clothes—black choir robes or starched white jackets and aprons."[41] This clearly disturbed Adamic, who believed that feelings of inferiority were as great a barrier to democratic unity as feelings of superiority. "Whatever one's background, one should not be ashamed of it, regardless of any prejudice against it," he wrote. "Shame of that sort is damaging to character and inner make-up, and it tends to turn one into a negative person outwardly."[42] Happily, in Adamic's account, "after seeing other groups in peasant and ghetto costumes, the leader of the Negro group appeared in the 'Americans All' procession in what she called her 'mammy clothes.' She had shed her defensive inferiority and for the first time really accepted her own background." Adamic hailed the festival as an example of "unity within diversity" that the entire nation might emulate.[43]

The leader of the "Negro group" at the St. Paul festival may have been willing to don "mammy clothes," but many other black Americans were understandably reluctant to celebrate their heritage as chattel. This was apparent when the Federal Radio Project of the U.S. Office of Education developed a twenty-six-part radio series entitled *Americans All—Immigrants All* to be broadcast over more than one hundred CBS-affiliated radio stations in late 1938 and 1939. The agency hired Gilbert Seldes, a critic, novelist, and playwright associated with the Popular Front, to write the script for the production. (Although Adamic did not initiate *Americans All,* he served as one of its advisors.) The series was designed to shore up democratic national unity by making nativism and other forms of intolerance seem unpatriotic. General episodes told the story of the mingling and integration of peoples in America and the disappearance of social and cultural divisions. Subsequent programs focused on a single outstanding attribute—for instance, the Scandinavian "gift for cooperation"—that each group had contributed to American culture. The show on "The Negro" followed this general pattern, emphasizing among other things the history of black workers in both the South and North. Seldes had incorporated some suggestions made by W. E. B. DuBois and Alain Locke. Nevertheless, when two officials in the NAACP's New York office read the script, they complained that it stressed "unduly the slave period and the Negro as a worker." "This script reads like a history of the progress of white people using the labor and talents of Negroes," they wrote. "It does not read like the history and progress of the Negro himself." The show was written to conclude with an African song and the Negro National Anthem, "Lift Every Voice and Sing," both sung by the renowned black baritone Jules Bledsoe. Just before airtime, however, the musical director scratched the scheduled lineup and substituted a song entitled "Black Boy." The substitution horrified black listeners including Locke, who called the song a "mammy interpolation." Locke and others persuaded CBS officials to rerecord the final fifteen minutes of the program so that wax recordings sent to schools and libraries wouldn't carry the song.[44]

These two episodes—the St. Paul "Festival of Nations" and the *Americans All—Immigrants All* radio series—suggest the tensions that existed over portrayals of unity and pluralism both within the black community and between many blacks and sympathetic whites, even those in the Popular Front. For instance, organizers of the World Fair's American Common wanted to use "Ballad for Americans"—the song popularized by Paul Robeson—during Negro Week. Members of the Negro Actors' Guild did not want the song used, because "it was not written by a Negro." They argued that black composers had difficulty getting audiences or artists to interpret their works, while most black interpreters used music written by people who weren't black. They were ultimately overruled, and "Ballad for Americans" closed the Negro Week program.[45]

Many black Americans thus resisted the specific vision of "unity within diversity" put forward by liberal and leftist whites such as Adamic. Nevertheless, some saw in this prewar discourse an opportunity to pursue what Barbara Savage has called "a politics of inclusion." [46] (They also recognized that it could contain an implicit loyalty test: The organizers of the New York World's Fair, for instance, declared that the purpose of the American Common was to "make loyalty to our country the only test of Christian or Jew, white or black, native or foreign born."[47]) Rather than celebrating their years in slavery, many blacks adopted an approach used by the former slave and abolitionist Frederick Douglass in the late nineteenth century: they presented themselves as the quintessential test of American democracy and urged Americans to live up to their ideals. As Lawrence Reddick, the curator of the New York Public Library's Schomburg Collection, wrote in a souvenir program distributed during the American Common's Negro Week, "The greatest gift of the Negro to America" was that "in one way or the other he has stood in every historic period, as a test of the sincerity, the real reality of the preachments of democracy." "And so today," Reddick continued,

> the drive for liberty, security and for equality of opportunity is
> a broad struggle by and for the common man. Since the Negro,
> historically, has borne the brunt of these social denials, he, perhaps,
> more than any other, appreciates the value and meaning of them all.
> The American Dream is the dream of the Negro. The dream of the
> Negro is the dream of an America which guarantees, in the words of
> Douglass, "all rights for all."[48]

As Reddick's words suggest, the vision of pluralistic unity and individual freedom promoted by Adamic and many others in the late 1930s and 1940s offered an opening to blacks, which some tried to appropriate. Ultimately, however, this consensual vision of the nation largely overlooked the entrenched problems of racial inequality.

Interfaith Unity as the "American Way"

In late May 1939, as Louis Adamic was preparing for his "Plymouth Rock and Ellis Island" lecture tour, a group of prominent New Yorkers—including such Broadway legends as Helen Hayes and Irving Berlin—gathered at the Center Theatre before the matinee performance of Kaufman and Hart's play *The American Way*. They assembled to confer on the two stars of the show, Frederic March and his wife, Florence Eldridge, the "badge of tolerance" awarded by the New York Round Table of the National Conference of Christians and Jews (NCCJ). In presenting the award, Helen Hayes warned against "attempts to import into this country discriminations and hostilities that have prevailed in other lands." "There is no room in this country for race hatred or religious intolerance," she declared. "Here we believe that a man has a right to be judged on his own merit and should not have to be subjected to any disabilities whatsoever on the ground of his racial origin or religious faith."[49]

Both Kaufman and Hart's play and Hayes's speech emphasized a point made repeatedly by Louis Adamic and many other advocates of the "nation of nations" approach in the late 1930s: bigotry and intolerance of various types were fundamentally incompatible with the American Way. Adamic and the CCAU acknowledged the existence of racism and nativism in the U.S., but they discounted the centrality of such ugly "-isms" to American culture by emphasizing Americans' lofty—and presumably shared—ideals. Meanwhile, the NCCJ and its allies cast "race hatred" and "religious intolerance" as alien imports, interlopers on American shores. Americans were united, both Adamic and members of the interfaith movement argued, by certain shared beliefs, chief among them their support for the freedom and dignity of the individual. The similarities between the CCAU and NCCJ approaches may be glimpsed in the fact that Adamic likely borrowed the name for his new magazine, *Common Ground*, from a book by the same name published in 1938 by a leading member of the interfaith movement.[50]

If members of the interfaith movement and those like Adamic who pictured the U.S. primarily as a "nation of nations" both placed pluralism within the context of a civic consensus, they differed in other key ways. While Adamic and his allies highlighted the nation's ethnic and racial diversity, the interfaith movement portrayed American pluralism as above all religious. The "badge of tolerance" presented to March and Eldridge by the NCCJ showed three hands clasped before the Statue of Liberty and was described by the *New York Times* as "symbolic of the Unity of American Protestants, Catholics and Jews for democracy, freedom and brotherhood."[51] Rabbi Morris Lazaron, the interfaith leader whose book likely inspired Adamic, called for recognition of the "common ground" shared by American Protestants, Catholics, and Jews.[52] Lazaron himself helped pioneer a vision of American "unity within diversity" that would become commonplace in America over the next two decades: the "tolerance trio." In late 1933, he joined a Presbyterian minister and a Catholic priest on a three-month, twenty-six-state "pilgrimage of understanding" sponsored by the NCCJ.[53] By the late 1930s, the NCCJ was dispatching "tolerance trios"—comprised of clergymen or prominent laymen from each religion—to schools, colleges, and civic forums around the country. They preached a vision of religious pluralism within a civic consensus, which the NCCJ dubbed "the American Way."[54]

If religion, in the NCCJ's view, was the chief repository of American pluralism, it was also the source of the nation's civic consensus. The NCCJ was perhaps the most visible arm of a growing movement among intellectuals and civic leaders in the late 1930s that argued that religious values, rather than the secular values of the Enlightenment, provided the crucial underpinning for American democracy.[55] Religion—specifically the belief in "the Fatherhood of God and the Brotherhood of Man"—"is the foundation of true democracy," declared the NCCJ's Jewish cochairman in a speech delivered in 1936 or 1937. He added that "the feeling that as we are brothers and have the same father [means] we must strive for the greatest good for all."[56] An NCCJ press release from February 1940 reiterated this argument, reinforcing and extending the analogy of family: "The democratic institutions by which we live are founded on a great religious insight, that under the Fatherhood of God we are all brothers and sisters...and all of us needing all the rest of us to make the family complete."[57]

The NCCJ frequently hailed America's heritage of religious freedom, calling it the nation's "most significant contribution...to the theory and practice of government."[58] This was not, however, an endorsement of atheism or even secular humanism. Rather, the NCCJ championed the notion, just emerging in the late 1930s, of a "Judeo-Christian tradition."[59] Protestants, Catholics, and Jews, the organization argued, shared one spiritual value essential to any democracy—the belief that every individual has "an inviolable personal dignity as a child of our one Father." This belief, in turn, led to the "religious values of liberty, justice and fraternity handed down to us by earlier generations of Americans." Now, however, these values were "being undermined," the NCCJ warned. "Emotional appeals to Protestants, Catholics and Jews to hate each other are being made by those who would be tyrants over us all."[60]

This view of America's heritage and values clearly minimized the nation's history of religious intolerance and downplayed real theological differences between groups. As early as 1931, the editor of the *Menorah Journal* warned that the NCCJ's approach suggested that "the differences are genuinely *NOT* differences, but misunderstandings. There are enough real, irreconcilable differences between Catholic and Protestant, Jew and Gentile, to make harmonious solutions gravely doubtful."[61] The Catholic hierarchy was particularly resistant to the NCCJ's approach, worrying that such cooperation would "imply that all religions were equally valid."[62] Still others, including Louis Adamic, found the interfaith movement's single-minded focus on religion troubling. In a 1939 letter to Rabbi Lazaron, Adamic warned against "simplify[ing] the problem [of intergroup tension] down to something that involves only the Jews as such and the Christians as such....You see so many of us are not especially Jewish or Christian."[63]

Adamic did approve of another aspect of the interfaith approach: its emphasis on *America*. But while Adamic and many of his allies on the liberal left used "Americanism" almost interchangeably with "universalism"—emphasizing what they saw as the fundamental *human* values shared by all Americans—the NCCJ put more explicit emphasis on the binding power of the nation-state. "The task of responsible leadership in America today is to lay before our citizens the larger loyalty to America which embraces the lesser loyalties of group and class and creed, the larger loyalty without which the lesser loyalties cannot be saved, or even the greatest loyalty of all—the loyalty of man to his Maker," Rabbi Lazaron wrote in his book, *Common Ground*.[64] Everett Clinchy, the Presbyterian minister who headed the NCCJ, put the matter more succinctly in a 1940 interview with the *New York Times*. The organization, he explained, was trying to bring about "a love for America so great that no one will be able to hate any group in the American neighborhood."[65]

The different approaches to achieving "unity within diversity" taken by the CCAU and the NCCJ can be attributed in part to the different histories of the movements they represented. The notion that the U.S. was a "nation of immigrants" or "nation of nations" emerged in the 1930s, propelled initially by intercultural educators, settlement house workers, labor organizers, and spokesmen for the "new immigrants" such as Louis Adamic; as Michael Denning has shown, this vision of "pan-ethnic Americanism" drew powerful early support from the cultural left.[66] The interfaith movement had a different genesis and different backers. In the wake of World War I, a broad-based Protestant revival coincided with a massive drive to "Americanize" immigrants. Many Protestant churches, urban missions, and other groups sought to "Americanize" the new immigrants in part by Christianizing them. Jewish groups responded angrily to such evangelizing efforts, leading in the mid-1920s to the establishment of a handful of groups designed to promote "goodwill" between Christians and Jews. Support for the nascent interfaith movement also benefited from the anti-Catholicism and anti-Semitism of the reborn KKK, which appalled many liberal Protestants.[67]

The efforts of liberal Christians and Jews to promote religious goodwill was thus tied from the beginning to debates over Americanism and national identity. The connection is made explicitly in a remarkable *New York Times* editorial, which appeared on Saturday, April 16, 1927. That date marked both the start of the Passover holiday and, in a rare calendric coincidence, the Vigil of Easter. The simultaneous celebration of Easter and Passover inspired the paper's editors to suggest quixotically that the two holidays be permanently fixed on the same date. Doing so, they argued, "would tend to give wider recognition to the part of religion in the life of the nation, to call special attention to what all of monotheistic faith have in common, and to teach...understanding and tolerance."[68] Four days later, a small group met to found the organization that would eventually become known as the National Conference of Christians and Jews.[69] For the next half century, the NCCJ would be the flagship of the interfaith movement.

Although the men and women who threw their weight behind the NCCJ in its early decades were religious liberals, many would hardly have been considered liberal in other contexts. The NCCJ's constitution declared that its purpose was to "promote justice, amity, understanding and cooperation among Jews, Catholics and Protestants in the United States, and to analyze, moderate and finally eliminate intergroup prejudices which disfigure and distort religious, business, social and political relations."[70] Despite the constitution's reference to justice, many of those who provided energy and financial support to the NCCJ in its early years were motivated primarily by "a conservative desire to hold American society together so that politics, education and business would function normally."[71] One such individual was Newton Baker, the NCCJ's first Protestant cochairman. Born in West Virginia, the son of a Confederate cavalryman-turned-country doctor, Baker went on to become a corporate lawyer and mayor of Cleveland before serving as Woodrow Wilson's Secretary of War. In 1932, many centrist and conservative Democrats hoped he would be their party's presidential nominee. After FDR's election, Baker was sharply critical of many New Deal initiatives; and in 1936, he led an unsuccessful effort to swing the Democratic Party platform to the right. Baker denounced racial prejudice and discrimination, but he was not a racial egalitarian: he referred to Negroes as an "infant race" and believed that few were capable of more than a basic education.[72]

Baker was hardly the only NCCJ stalwart whose sympathies lay with corporate America. Roger W. Straus, the organization's Jewish cochairman for nearly thirty years, was the son of the first Jew to serve in a presidential cabinet. Straus himself married into the Guggenheim family and, by the late 1930s, had risen to the position of chief executive of a mining conglomerate. Other early NCCJ backers included Edward Bernays, the founder of the public relations industry; Henry Breckenridge, a prominent New York attorney who joined Baker in the Democratic opposition to FDR; Supreme Court Justice Charles Evans Hughes Jr., who authored a number of decisions opposing the New Deal; investment banker Felix M. Warburg; and numerous members of the Ochs-Sulzberger family that owned the *New York Times*.[73] In 1940, the National Association of Manufacturers deployed a key NCCJ idea as part of its "Tripod of Freedom" campaign, and the following year a representative of the NAM addressed an Institute on Human Relations sponsored by the NCCJ.[74] NCCJ backers included many liberals as well, but from the start industrialists and their allies found a congenial home in the organization.

The NCCJ's early supporters also included a large number of prominent Jews. Liberal Protestants such as Newton Baker and Everett Clinchy helped found the organization; and, despite steadfast opposition from Rome, it enrolled some Catholics as well.[75] From the beginning, however, assimilated, anti-Zionist Jews played a particularly important role in the conference. Roger Straus contributed the $5,000 needed to launch the NCCJ, and nine of the ten initial affiliating organizations were Jewish. (The tenth was the Federal Council of Churches, a coalition of liberal Protestant denominations.) B'nai B'rith was the NCCJ's largest financial sponsor in its first few years. This heavy Jewish involvement was reflected in the Conference's original name: the National Conference of Jews and Christians. The name was changed in late 1938, coinciding with an effort by American Jews to downplay their role in the anti-Nazi effort.[76]

The NCCJ's name change signaled an important shift in the American Jewish community that would reverberate through the broader discussion of Americanism then underway. Anti-Semitism was hardly a new phenomenon in the U.S., but American Jews had long considered themselves safe from the most vicious forms of bigotry. This changed in the mid-1930s when Hitler sympathizers started distributing Nazi propaganda in the U.S. and the Depression triggered a surge in indigenous anti-Semitism; the popularity of Father Coughlin particularly alarmed many American Jews. Relatively assimilated Jews such as Kaufman and Hart felt a heightened awareness of their Jewish identities, and major Jewish organizations boosted their defense efforts in the domestic arena. One of these was the American Jewish Committee (AJC). Founded in 1906 by prominent German-American Jews, the organization differed from the American Jewish Congress in part because of its staunch opposition to Zionism. For most of its first three decades, the AJC had focused on aiding Jews abroad; in the mid-1930s, however, it turned its attention and fund-raising efforts almost exclusively to domestic defense.[77]

In 1936, with an initial war chest of $600,000, the AJC launched what it called the Survey Committee. This group, which never had more than thirty members, guided the AJC's defense effort until shortly before the U.S. entry into World War II. The Survey Committee included a smattering of prominent lawyers, investment bankers, advertising executives and politicians, as well as the editor of the *New York Post*, the brother of the publisher of the *New York Times*, the head of Viking Press, and the famed Hollywood producer David Selznick. Many of these men had never been active in a Jewish organization before. These men were by no means representative of all American Jews; in fact, one committee member remarked that they were "looked upon by the masses [of Jews] as representing the economic royalists, social snobs, and religious renegades in American Jewry." Nevertheless, they had the economic and social clout to make themselves heard.[78]

Members of the Survey Committee and AJC staffers believed that the fate of Jews was tied to the fate of liberalism and democracy. "To the extent that we can help promote attachment to the democratic ideal, we must do so," wrote Morris Waldman, the AJC's executive secretary. "We must make plain our opposition to extremism of both right and left varieties." The Survey Committee's program for 1937 reiterated the link between Jews and democracy and added that "the specific actions relative to educating the public on the truth about Jews must be integrated with the major task of maintaining peaceful relations between the various groups composing our population."[79]

When members of the Survey Committee spoke of "democracy," they were not necessarily hailing majority rule. After all, democracies could also produce majority tyrannies. Rather, like the conservative industrialists in the National Association of Manufacturers, they were invoking the minority-protecting freedoms though for different reasons, in the Bill of Rights, particularly religious freedom. Survey Committee members believed that a liberal, Bill of Rights-based democracy represented the best hope for minorities in a world increasingly divided between right and left. As board member Cyrus Adler put it, "If the liberals in the world fail and everybody becomes a Fascist or a Communist, then, of course, the Jews will fail also."[80]

Working through the Survey Committee, the AJC tried to discredit Nazism and shore up Americans' belief in religious freedom and the "human characteristics" common to all groups. In doing so, it relied heavily on what it referred to as "nerve center work"—influencing those individuals and groups who in turn molded public opinion. Throughout the 1930s, the AJC funded the work of anthropologist Franz Boas and called media attention to his antiracialist findings. It also produced and distributed pamphlets and books; maintained an active speakers' bureau; secured time for, wrote, or contributed to hundreds of radio programs; and arranged for dozens of newspapers and national magazines, ranging from *Reader's Digest* to the *New York Times*, to "carry and/or reprint material of interest to us." To work the "pro-democracy" message into films, and to screen out potentially inflammatory material, the AJC established a committee of sympathetic Hollywood writers and directors headed by the famous producer and Survey Committee member David Selznick. Finally, through direct subsidies or by tapping the pockets and expertise of its members, the AJC quietly channeled advice and financial support to dozens of organizations with similar goals.[81]

One of the groups that benefited most from the AJC's interest was the NCCJ. American Jews were split in the late 1930s between those who saw Judaism as an ethnocultural affiliation and those who viewed it solely as a religion.[82] The former group included many comparatively recent immigrants from Eastern Europe; they tended to belong to the AJC's principle rival, the American Jewish Congress, and to support Zionism. The AJC, by contrast, was led by third- and fourth-generation American Jews, often of German origin, who were horrified by anything that smacked of ethnic separatism. This group viewed Judaism entirely in religious terms and thus found the NCCJ's vision of American pluralism particularly appealing.[83] The AJC also saw the National Conference as an important ally in the effort to mobilize American Christians against both Nazism and domestic anti-Semitism. In 1933, the AJC reported that it was "making an effort to have the National Conference assume the position of importance in the U.S. that it merits." AJC staffers arranged newsreel coverage of the NCCJ's first "trio tour" and invented "Brotherhood Day," the nationwide celebration used for decades by the NCCJ to spread its themes. The AJC also quietly funded a study of Protestant textbook references to Jews, which was formally sponsored by the NCCJ. Finally, the AJC provided start-up funds for the NCCJ's Religious News Service, then used the wire service to feed its messages to the nation's Christian and daily press.[84]

Both the American Jewish Committee and the National Conference of Christians and Jews steered clear of defending Jews directly, fearing that this would only precipitate a "Jewish debate" in the United States. NCCJ director Clinchy warned in 1939 that an "open approach" to combating anti-Semitism and anti-Catholicism might actually fuel religious intolerance. Members of the AJC's Survey Committee clearly agreed: "Arguments that the Jews are *not* communists, that they are *not* war mongers, that they are *not* dishonest in business—these, though based on fact, only fan the flame of the anti-Semitic issue itself," they declared.[85] Instead, the Survey Committee called on the AJC and allied groups to shift the debate from "Jews vs. Nazis" to "Nazis vs. civilization/democracy [and] Americanism":

> It must be made perfectly clear that it is the *Nazis* who are the warmongers; the *Nazis* who are demoralizing foreign trade and thus creating unsettlement in the business world and unrest in the ranks of the unemployed; the *Nazis* who are fertilizing the soil for communism and who, in fact, have developed a "Brown Bolshevism" of their own; the *Nazis* who are attacking the bases of religion in all its forms; the *Nazis* who are undermining the home, abolishing liberal education, and destroying everything which modern men have come to respect.

"If the issue is stressed of 'Nazis vs. Civilization,'" the December 1939 memo continued, "the Jews will find themselves fighting shoulder to shoulder with all other right-thinking men."[86]

The reference in this memo to "right-thinking men" is suggestive because it underscores the degree to which religious tolerance, in the AJC's view, depended on ideological consensus. NCCJ representatives made a similar point when they defended religious pluralism by paraphrasing Booker T. Washington's defense of social segregation: "In all things religious, we Catholics, Jews and Protestants can be as separate as the fingers on a man's outstretched hand; in all things civic and American, we can be as united as a man's clenched fist."[87] Both quotes assumed a private arena of diversity and tolerance and a public arena of unity and consensus. How those arenas were defined, however, could lead to dramatically different political results. The CIO advocated religious and racial tolerance in an effort to unite workers of diverse backgrounds in a class-based coalition. When the NAM spoke up on behalf of intergroup harmony, by contrast, it was advocating cooperation between workers and owners as much as between ethnocultural groups. The fact that an analogy used to justify racial segregation could be marshaled on behalf of religious tolerance suggests some of the problems that would later develop with extending the NCCJ's vision of the "American Way" to blacks.

Similar tensions—over the nature of America's core values and the appropriate arenas for tolerance and consensus—emerged between the AJC and the NCCJ and some of the groups with which they were allied in the late 1930s. The AJC briefly funded the Council Against Intolerance in America, an organization founded in 1938 by James Waterman Wise. (Wise was a left-leaning writer and the son of Rabbi Stephen S. Wise, who headed the American Jewish Congress.) Like the AJC and the NCCJ, the Council Against Intolerance hailed religious freedom and called the Bill of Rights "the soul and spirit of the Constitution." The organizations differed, however, in other key respects. The Council, like Rabbi Wise and the American Jewish Congress, recognized Jews' ethnic identity, a position that made most AJC members quite nervous. The Council also emphasized *equality* as much as tolerance and was far more willing than the AJC or the NCCJ to highlight America's shortcomings and to denounce racial segregation. As this suggests, the organizations differed sharply on precisely what and whom should be tolerated. Reflecting the views of its founder, the Council Against Intolerance stressed the free speech guarantees of the Bill of Rights and tried to combat prejudice against radicals as well as against religious and racial groups. This approach worried many AJC members, who tended to be strongly anti-Communist and who wanted to sever any perceived links between Jews and the left. As one AJC staffer wrote in a memo evaluating the Council in October 1939, "No intelligent person desires to be tolerant of all things....Any attempt to combat intolerance toward the label 'radical' on the same basis as intolerance toward Jews, Negroes, and others, is founded upon a fallacy, since political prejudice arises from different sources and has different rationalizations than anti-Jewish and other prejudices."[88]

The NCCJ also steered clear of economic radicalism, a stance that was hardly surprising, given the social and economic profile of many of its supporters. In March of 1933, just days after FDR's inauguration, the National Conference of Jews and Christians circulated a manifesto calling on elected representatives to make emergency relief available through states and local agencies and to provide "adequate care of the aged" and tax reform. The manifesto, which was eventually signed by 160 prominent clergymen and laymen of various faiths, also called on legislators and leaders of industry and labor to work together to provide unemployment insurance, to check the breakdown in labor standards, and to create a national industrial planning board "to lay down farsighted lines of industrial control for human welfare." The document clearly evinced a deeply rooted concern about "the present cruel and unnecessary inequalities in men's opportunity to obtain and enjoy the earth's material blessings"; but its appeal to leaders of industry and labor, as well as politicians, assumed an underlying harmony of interests in the polity.[89] As the decade rolled on, FDR implemented the New Deal, and the CIO emerged at the forefront of the labor movement, the NCCJ fell silent on economic issues. Gradually, however, it began including economic classes in its list of those assailed by "group prejudice." A declaration circulated by the NCCJ and signed by more than 550 Protestant, Catholic, and Jewish lay and religious leaders in June 1939 warned of "the ultimate consequences of propaganda which advocates hatred against classes, races and religious groups." "The fires of prejudice burn quickly and disastrously," the document declared, invoking the example of Europe. "What may begin as polemics against a class or group may end with persecution, murder, pillage and dispossession of that group."[90] In February 1940, the NCCJ's invitation to observe Brotherhood Week denounced "voices" that "seek...to divide and weaken us" by setting "church against church, group against group, and class against class."[91]

In its list of hate-fomenting evils that Americans should resist, the 1939 NCCJ appeal began with "atheistic communism." (It then turned, in order, to fascism and Nazism, anti-Catholicism, anti-Protestantism, and anti-Semitism.) "Atheistic communism," it suggested, "seeks to destroy religion and to pit class against class in ruinous social and economic warfare." This was hardly the only link made between interfaith unity and anticommunism in the years immediately preceding World War II. In January 1938, the Chamber of Commerce in Jersey City, New Jersey, orchestrated a mass meeting to support Mayor Frank Hague in his efforts to stop what the mayor called the "Communist invasion" of the city by the CIO. In its front-page story on the event, the *New York Times* noted that representatives of business, civic, religious, and veterans organizations joined the speakers on the flag-flanked platform. "Catholic priests sat with Protestant ministers and Jewish rabbis were present," it reported.[92]

Taken together, these two episodes foreshadow the role the interfaith movement would play in coming years in constructing a national consensus defined against communism, as well as against fascism. To a nation trying to define itself against enemies deemed both totalitarian and atheist, the "interfaith idea" would prove particularly useful. By casting pluralism above all in religious terms, the interfaith movement would allow government officials and other elites to stress America's democratic diversity without reinforcing ethnic loyalties or divisions. At the same time, the notion that Protestantism, Catholicism, and Judaism were "the religions of democracy"[93]—that they were diverse representations of spiritual ideals and moral values that all Americans shared—reinforced the underlying cohesiveness of American society. In the face of irreligion or atheism, belief in *any* of America's "three great faiths"[94] could provide a basis for cultural unity. During World War II, the antifascist aspects of this argument would get the most exposure. In the postwar period, the emphasis would shift to anticommunism.

Margaret Mead and the Resurrection of National Character

In the spring of 1939, Margaret Mead and her husband, the British anthropologist Gregory Bateson, returned to the U.S. after several years of fieldwork in Bali and the islands of the Dutch East Indies archipelago. The two anthropologists had largely ignored politics during the interwar years. Because of prolonged absences from the country, Mead had not even voted since 1924. "I was living in a time perspective of a hundred years, and preparing the materials with which we would, hopefully, be better prepared for that long future," she later wrote. "Fascism, Communism, Nazism, Capitalism from such a long stand point, were perturbations, with which other people had to deal." The couple's return to the U.S. abruptly changed their perspective. Coming home to a world on the verge of war, they realized that Hitler "presented a terrible threat to everything we valued."[95] Mead and Bateson became convinced that it was time to turn their expertise "to the problems of our own society."[96] As they sought to do this over the next few years, they helped resurrect a concept that they and other cultural anthropologists had worked for two decades to undermine: the concept of national character.

Chief among the problems that Mead and Bateson identified on their return to the U.S. was the need to bolster national morale. They were hardly alone in this assessment. The rise of fascism—and particularly the announcement of the Nazi-Soviet pact and the outbreak of war in Europe—alarmed hundreds of American and refugee social scientists. The Nazi blitzkrieg and the stunning collapse of France in the spring and summer of 1940 compounded their concerns. Both American and foreign commentators blamed France's defeat not on military tactics but on a lack of national unity and morale. Some commentators, including the editors of the *Nation*, blamed France's spiritual paralysis on anti-Semitism, anti-Sovietism, and Anglophobia. Others, such as the French refugee writer André Maurois, looked to tensions between communists and right-wing groups in Depression-stricken France. The Reuters war correspondent Gordon Waterfield argued that "political and class divisions," particularly the "bitter feelings between big business on one side and the working classes on the other," had weakened the country "and prevented parliamentary government from functioning adequately." Waterfield's best-selling book, *What Happened to France*, paraphrased Abraham Lincoln in proclaiming the Third Republic "a nation divided against itself." "France has been beaten in a way that Republican Spain was not beaten, nor Finland, Poland, Norway or China," Waterfield declared. The French "appear to have lost heart."[97]

Such diagnoses prompted scores of social scientists, journalists, historians, and government officials—including many on the liberal left—to turn from analyses of economic and political inequalities in American society to the promotion of social harmony and national morale. The morale campaign that gained steam in 1940 and 1941 sought to combat isolationism and to bolster Americans' "sense of collective solidarity and responsibility" in the face of the fascist threat.[98] It attracted individuals as diverse as psychologists Gordon Allport and Kenneth Clark, anthropologists Margaret Mead and Ruth Benedict, public opinion specialists Elmo Roper and George Gallup, Interior Secretary Harold Ickes, journalist Louis Adamic, and playwright Robert Sherwood. Some of those involved paired a continuing—if muted—critique of U.S. capitalism with a renewed emphasis on the common ground shared by *all* Americans. Others followed the path taken by Harvard sociologist and Popular Front intellectual Talcott Parsons. Parsons had devoted his early career to "a critical study of the economic institutions of modern capitalism"; but in 1940, he joined the newly formed Council for Democracy and threw his energy into the morale campaign. In a memo drafted for the Council, Parsons warned that many of the "antagonisms" that had helped propel German fascists to power in the 1920s and early 1930s were present "in our own society now." Among these "antagonisms" he included anti-intellectualism, a tradition of racial nationalism, and hostility to big business on the part of America's "lower middle class." In subsequent writings and lectures, Parsons went further, suggesting that the emphasis on capitalism in studies of Western culture had distorted public discourse and sparked unnecessary social unrest. As Howard Brick has observed, Parsons increasingly came to "view society as a communal body and reform as the pursuit of harmony." While Parsons continued to advocate "the goal of mass welfare," he now "urged respect for established social elites in order to minimize mass upheaval," and he suggested that the role of government particularly in wartime should be to "reinforce" common values.[99] Parsons's transformation can be seen as part of a broader intellectual shift in the late 1930s and early 1940s sparked by the focus on national morale: increasingly, social scientists in various disciplines attributed conflict in American society to "misperceptions" rather than to a real collision of interests.[100]

Margaret Mead had never been explicitly concerned with economics or with conflicts between groups within the United States; in fact, her prewar work focused almost entirely on the South Seas. Nevertheless, as a cultural anthropologist and disciple of Franz Boas, she had been deeply involved for nearly two decades in an intellectual project that implicitly challenged the cultural homogeneity of the United States. In the late nineteenth and early twentieth centuries, the notion of national character often rested on arguments about the biological transmission of cultural values. Such racialist arguments fueled calls for immigration restrictions, as a means of imposing national unity. Meanwhile, Americanization campaigns were often premised on an evolutionary view of human culture: those at the forefront of such efforts generally saw themselves as helping "primitive" peoples progress toward greater civilization. Boas and his disciples rejected both arguments. They challenged biological determinism by calling attention to the overwhelming role played by culture in shaping human understanding and behavior. At the same time, they suggested that "culture" was not simply an attribute of "advanced" societies. Rather, cultures were organic wholes, structures of meaning that humans used to interpret all aspects of life. The relationship between cultures was relative, not evolutionary.[101] By showing those Americans who held power "that their own preferences were not absolute," Boasian anthropologists hoped to breed greater tolerance of cultural difference.[102]

Boasian anthropologists argued that culture was not biologically transmitted, but initially they had trouble explaining how cultures maintained themselves across generations. This began to change in the 1920s and 1930s when a loose group of anthropologists and psychologists centered around New York City and Yale began combining the insights of cultural anthropology with those of Freudian psychology.[103] For decades, students of child development, working within a Freudian framework, had explored the ways in which children learned social tradition; but these scholars primarily studied youngsters from the middle and upper classes of the U.S. and Europe, and they generally assumed that the personality traits shared by their subjects were human and universal.[104] Pioneers of "culture and personality" theory challenged this assumption. They argued that an individual's emotions and behavior were neither biologically determined nor universal; rather, they were strongly shaped by cultural patterns learned in childhood, often in infancy. As one social scientist explained, "The unique aspects of any society are determined and maintained by emotional habits learned in infancy by a majority of participating individuals." Such habits, developed through interactions with parents and others, were so "deeply organic" that they exhibited a "subtle primacy," shaping the individual's conduct throughout his or her life.[105]

In the 1920s and 1930s, most practitioners of "culture and personality" theory focused on American Indian tribes or on the inhabitants of remote villages or Pacific islands. Their studies often contrasted the "simple cultural harmony" of such places with the "fragmented neurotic civilization" of the capitalist West. Their work stressed both the holism of cultures and the resistance of cultures to change; thus, it could be invoked to support arguments for cultural pluralism in the U.S.[106] The implications of culture and personality research, however, depended heavily on the unit analyzed. As long as scholars assumed that ethnic, regional, religious, or racial subgroups were the prime carriers of culture, their studies tended to emphasize the internal diversity of modern nation-states such as the U.S. If they took the nation-state to be the principle carrier of culture, their analyses would inevitably underscore the *unity* of such societies.

This is the intellectual shift that Margaret Mead and many of her colleagues made soon after the outbreak of World War II. In the wake of the German blitzkrieg, Mead and Bateson joined more than one hundred other prominent anthropologists, psychologists, historians, journalists, and sociologists in a new organization called the Committee on National Morale (CNM). The brainchild of a philosophy professor-turned-Persian art expert, Arthur Upham Pope, the CNM sought to apply social science techniques to questions of unity at home and abroad. Mead headed the organization's Subcommittee on Comparative National Psychology and in this context began applying "culture and personality" theory to modern nation-states. Rather than focusing on the differences between ethnocultural groups in U.S. society, she and her colleagues now focused on what differentiated Americans from Germans and Russians from Japanese.

Mead and her colleagues took this step because they believed strongly in the righteousness and efficacy of social engineering.[107] Total war, Mead suggested, tested a nation's national character. Only by understanding "modal character structure" could the Allies put this powerful tool to use. "What is an American, a German, an Englishman, or an Australian?" Mead asked. "What is his peculiar pattern of strength and weakness, invincible under one set of conditions, infinitely vulnerable under another? In a last-ditch war," Mead concluded, "these will be the imponderables that count."[108] Mead and her colleagues hoped that by illuminating those factors they could help the U.S. and its allies avoid cross-cultural misunderstanding; develop more effective rationing, military training, and civil defense programs for the homefront; and craft propaganda tools for use abroad. Federal officials agreed: soon after the bombing of Pearl Harbor, many of the social scientists studying national character were brought into federal agencies, among them the Office of War Information and the Office of Strategic Services. On the day of the attack, Mead was invited to serve as executive secretary of the Committee on Food Habits, an offshoot of the National Research Council's Division of Anthropology and Psychology.[109]

While her husband and colleagues developed collective profiles of the Germans, Russians, and Japanese, Mead turned to her native land. In 1942, she published *And Keep Your Powder Dry*, the first book to apply the revived notion of national character to U.S. society. The book made an impassioned case for the unity of American culture and for an internalized consensus. American character, Mead argued, was an "expression of American institutions and of American attitudes which is embodied in every American, in everyone born in this country and sometimes even in those who have come later to these shores."[110] Now largely forgotten, the book was widely hailed at the time; well into the 1960s, it was required reading in classes on citizenship and American studies. Mead's volume also paved the way for a spate of national character studies written in subsequent years by academics and journalists such as D. W. Brogan, David Reisman, Henry Steele Commager, David Potter, and Max Lerner.[111]

Mead's book ostensibly placed the immigrant experience at the center of the national narrative: "We are all third generation," she declared in her pivotal third chapter. By taking the U.S. as her fundamental unit of analysis, however, she relegated cultural difference largely to the past and stressed a unity based ultimately on assimilation. If one Russian brother immigrated to the U.S. while another stayed behind, their children would be fundamentally different, she argued. The "American Peter" would become "a go-getting member of the Junior Chamber of Commerce" who disliked Stalin. The "Russian Ivan," by contrast, would find it nearly impossible "to understand what Americans mean by rugged individualism."[112] American national character was sufficiently distinctive, she suggested, that an observer would recognize Americans traveling abroad "whether they have come from Arkansas or Maine or Pennsylvania, whether they bear German or Swedish or Italian surnames."[113]

Mead's stress on assimilation reflected a shift in emphasis on the part of cultural anthropologists but not a complete revision in their thinking. Because Boasian anthropologists were renowned advocates of cultural relativism, scholars have often overlooked the role that assimilation played in their thinking. For more than three decades, Boas and his disciples had argued for the primacy of culture over biology—and attacked racialist thinking—by pointing to the convergence of immigrants to an "American" norm.[114] This emphasis is clearly apparent in the book that first brought the notion of cultural relativism force-fully to a popular audience, Ruth Benedict's 1934 classic *Patterns of Culture*. Benedict, a student and colleague of Boas and a close friend of Mead, made no secret of her moral agenda in writing the book. Decrying the "nationalism and racial snobbery" of the U.S. and other Western nations, she pleaded for tolerance for "aliens" and other outsiders.[115] The bulk of Benedict's book dealt with three non-Western societies—the Zuñi, Dobu, and Kwakiutl—which she used to explore the concept of culture, but her plea for tolerance rested on her contention that culture was not "biologically transmitted." To support this crucial piece of her argument, Benedict turned for evidence to the assimila-tive power of American society. "An Oriental child adopted by an Occidental family learns English, shows toward its foster parents the attitudes current among the children he plays with, and grows up to the same professions that they elect," she wrote. "The same process happens on a grand scale when entire peoples in a couple of generations shake off their traditional culture and put on the customs of an alien group." In fact, Benedict suggested that the culture of black Americans who lived in northern cities "has come to approximate in detail that of the whites in the same cities." "What really binds men to-gether is their culture—the ideas and standards they have in common," she concluded. The nation would substitute "realistic thinking" for "dangerous" and "misleading" "symbolism," if "instead of selecting a symbol like common blood heredity and making a slogan of it, [it] turned its attention rather to the culture that unites its people."[116]

Benedict, Mead, and other culture and personality theorists thus tried to combat prejudice—and to reconcile the tension between national unity and demographic inclusion—by focusing on a *national* culture that they be-lieved was embedded in the psyche of individual Americans. This focus on assimilation differentiated Mead and her colleagues from Louis Adamic. Adamic too believed that individuals of diverse ethnic backgrounds would gradually become Americanized, but he did not see this as the principle source of their common values. In Adamic's view, a belief in Enlightenment-derived values such as individual freedom and equality propelled immigrants to the New World; such values were not simply part of a culture acquired later. Adamic saw Americans' shared values as potentially universal. Mead, like the NCCJ, saw them as grounded in and bounded by the culture of the nation-state.

Racism and nativism entered Mead's account only briefly—as a barrier to full assimilation. In a short but telling passage on aggression, she sug-gested that an "American boy" might encounter black, Puerto Rican, Mexican, Irish, and Sicilian children who had very different ideas about fighting. In the

Sicilian case, Mead made clear that she was referring to first-generation children, who had not yet been fully assimilated. "Negroes," however, had a "view of what is fair" that had been "dangerously skewed by the circumstances that they themselves have been too long 'fair game' for white people."[117] If victims of racism could thus be excluded from Mead's vision of the American character, so, too, could those who enshrined racist belief. In fact, the one group Mead explicitly excluded from her analysis was southerners. "The generalizations in this book should be regarded as based primarily on the North, Middle West and West," Mead suggested in a footnote. The South's "bi-racial classification of humanity" so affected its culture that any attempt to generalize about both the North and the South would "be too abstract to be fruitful."[118]

Having defended the notion of American character, Mead turned to its content.[119] America, she emphasized, had a "moral culture," one which "bristle[ed] with words like *good* and *bad*." This was by no means a universal quality. The Samoans, for instance, emphasized grace and awkwardness rather than morality. The Balinese were more concerned with "whether a given act would make people feel *paling*, the Balinese word for the state of not knowing where you are." Mead noted that Americans' unusual focus on morality was reinforced by their child-rearing techniques. American parents took responsibility for punishing their children, whereas parents in most societies "call[ed] in gods, or scare dancers, or relatives" rather than risk facing their children's "hostility and hatred." Such practices produced in American children a conscience, an attribute that Mead deemed "very rare and special."[120]

Americans shared an internalized morality with most other Judeo-Christian cultures, but other aspects of the national character distinguished Americans from Europeans, Mead suggested. Americans, she observed, were eternally in motion, with no fixed sense of geographic or social place. Like third-generation immigrants, they purposefully forgot their European ancestors and looked instead to their American past—hometowns, popular culture, voluntary associations, and military service—to produce shallow common bonds. They expected to leave their fathers behind occupationally, geographically, and socially, just as their fathers had once left their grandfathers behind. This forward gaze and perpetual upward striving was embodied in Americans' relationship to the founding fathers. "Washington does not represent the past to which one belongs by birth," Mead wrote, "but the past to which one tries to belong by effort."[121]

If Mead believed that all Americans were "third generation," she saw their character structure as fundamentally Puritan. Not only were they moralistic, but also, like the Puritans, they linked success and goodness, believing that "wealth was the inevitable reward of virtue and industry." Mead considered this to be one of the nation's "most distinguishing characteristics." "On it is based our acceptance of men for what they have become rather than for what they were born," she wrote. "On it is based our faith that simple people...are worthy of a hearing in the halls of the great. On it is based our special brand of democracy."[122]

Critical as Mead believed this moral code to be, she also saw it as exceedingly fragile—something that required "very special circumstances" in order to flourish. The link between virtue and success had flowered in the U.S. while withering in England because America's "pioneer conditions" fueled "a great and expanding economy." During the Depression, Mead observed, this "moral keystone" of the American character had "taken a body blow." If Americans ever lost it entirely, she warned, the consequences would be devastating: If Americans became convinced that "it's all a matter of pull, of who you know, that working hard doesn't get you anywhere nowadays," they might sink into a "cynicism which could well form the basis of an American fascism."[123]

Despite the ominous note in these passages, Mead remained optimistic. The key to saving the American character was redefining America's playing field and the meaning of success. World events, horrific as they were, had opened just such an opportunity by making it clear to all that the world needed to be "built new, according to a new plan." Americans now had the chance to become "devoted entrepreneurs" of this noble cause. "Building the world new" did not mean simply remaking it in America's image, Mead cautioned. Rather, it meant creating "from a hundred cultures, one culture which does what no culture has ever done before—gives a place to every human gift." To accomplish this, Americans would have to study other cultures closely, but Mead believed that only Americans had the energy, practicality, and "moral framework of basic human rights" to make it happen. Devotion to this cause—the cause of restructuring world culture after the war—would, in turn, help Americans fight well, Mead declared. Her compatriots, she argued, would fight "only if they believe, with every fiber in their being, that their cause is just—and new."[124]

Thus, Mead ultimately ended on the same note struck by numerous other activists and commentators in the late 1930s and early 1940s. America, she suggested, was a nation of immigrants who had discovered the secret to transethnic harmony and who could carry that message to the globe. This secret was embodied in the shared beliefs and values that made a demographically diverse nation possible—in what Mead called the "American character," what Adamic called the "American Dream," what representatives of the NCCJ called the "American Way," and what a visiting Swedish economist would soon immortalize as the "American Creed."

The "War Work" of Gunnar and Alva Myrdal

In September 1938, Gunnar Myrdal arrived in the United States to take the reins of a study on the American Negro proposed and funded by the Carnegie Corporation, a study that would eventually become known as *An American Dilemma*. The study inquiry had first been suggested in late 1935 by Newton Baker, the Carnegie trustee who also served as the NCCJ's first Protestant co-chair. It was made possible in part because the foundation had decided not to fund another ambitious project: the "Encyclopedia of the Negro" promoted by W. E. B. DuBois, which Louis Adamic had so fiercely opposed. When Carnegie Corporation president Frederick Keppel finally selected a scholar to head the study, he relied on the recommendation of two former officials of the Rockefeller Foundation. One of those officials was Lawrence K. Frank.[125] A founder of the child development movement in the United States, Frank had introduced Margaret Mead to several of the psychiatrists and psychologists who proved so influential to her culture and personality work. In addition, Mead's and Frank's families shared a house in the early 1940s while Mead was drafting *And Keep Your Powder Dry*.[126]

As this web of incidental connections suggests, Myrdal's study was embedded from its inception in an intellectual milieu that focused on combating intolerance and disunity in the U.S., and fighting fascism abroad, by emphasizing the beliefs and values that diverse Americans allegedly shared. Baker, Adamic, Mead, and the various organizations to which they were attached disagreed on many specifics, but all cast America as the archetype of "unity within diversity"—a nation in which a civic consensus allowed a heterogeneous citizenry to live together in peace. Moreover, all believed that by broadcasting their visions—by using books, magazines, public pageants, school programs, and speaking tours to educate the American public—they could call such a nation into being. This U.S. discourse on Americans' common ground clearly had a profound impact on Gunnar Myrdal and his wife, Alva. As Myrdal's biographer has noted, the couple "arrived at an exaggerated notion of the importance of the American creed partly by listening to American intellectuals from the fall of 1938 to the spring of 1940."[127]

The Myrdals' own intellectual backgrounds also predisposed them to look for shared national values. Gunnar had begun his career as a neoclassical economist who believed that the free market was the most efficient way to spread national wealth. His views shifted in 1929–1930 when Rockefeller Foundation fellowships brought the couple to the U.S. and they witnessed firsthand the stunning collapse of the U.S. economy. The failure of neoclassical economics to cope with this disaster altered Gunnar's political and economic views; and upon his return to Sweden, he turned his intellectual energy to social engineering and the promotion of the welfare state. Mydral differed from most social engineers, however, because he believed that social scientists should state explicitly their assumptions about what was right and wrong, good and bad, just and unjust. Moreover, he argued that in a democracy, they "should attempt, in so far as possible, to draw their value premises from the general beliefs and values of the people."[128] Alva, meanwhile, had spent her fellowship year meeting with social and child psychologists—including some involved with the developing field of culture and personality theory—and visiting school civics classes in which "American" values were taught.[129] When the couple returned to Sweden, they joined the Social Democratic Party and worked to build broad national support for the party's policies. A book on Sweden's "population crisis," which they coauthored in 1934, reflected their newfound interest in identifying and cementing national values. "History has never seen a balanced and harmonious society that was not grounded in secure values within a collective psychology," they wrote.[130]

When the Myrdals returned to the United States in 1938, they were buffeted by the same combination of hopes and fears that affected many other liberal and leftist intellectuals. During their first visit, the couple had been appalled by the enormous inequities in American society, as well as by the nation's lack of social and economic planning; they believed the nation's laissez-faire liberalism derived directly from the American emphasis on individual freedom. A decade later, the U.S. seemed transformed. The prolonged Depression had forced Americans to accept more social responsibility, the Myrdals believed, and the "humanitarian pragmatist" FDR had wrought the greatest change in the American social system "since the revolution." The moralism of American culture, which seemed oppressive in 1929, looked like a virtue in the global context of the late 1930s. American individualism, which the Myrdals had previously viewed as an obstacle to reform, now seemed a sign of the nation's energy and spirit.[131]

During their Rockefeller year, the Myrdals had been particularly struck by the array of European immigrants who made the U.S. their home; they wondered what bonds held such a diverse country together. In his writings from that time, Gunnar Myrdal noted the "throng of races" that divided the working class. He also likened America's "political indoctrination" of its children and immigrants—through civics and Americanization classes—to that undertaken by the Soviet Union and Italy. The result, he argued, was that when individuals were asked about their political beliefs, they "use conventional and stereotyped stock phrases which may have little bearing on…behavior."[132] When the Myrdals returned to the U.S. at the end of the decade, the tenor of their observations had changed. They emphasized the rapidity with which diverse European immigrants were assimilating into American culture, forging a common identity, and learning to live side by side. By contrast, their European kin were slaughtering one another in pogroms and on the battlefield.[133]

Even as the Myrdals celebrated America's social harmony, however, they shared with many other American liberals and leftists a concern that fascism could "happen here." In a June 1939 interview with a reporter for the *St. Louis Post Dispatch*, Gunnar wondered aloud whether Americans were committed to preserving their democracy.[134] Alva examined the same question in articles written for Swedish magazines that fall. She compared Father Coughlin's views to the early ideology of the Nazis, noting that both were anti-Semitic and hostile to capitalism. Alva saw the South—with its "great class inequalities" and "racial persecution"—as the other possible source of American fascism, although she believed the South's "fascism" was more "old-fashioned" and "feudalis[tic]."[135] Still, Alva cast these unsettling tendencies as the exception in America. As Walter Jackson has noted, she "framed the conflict between fascism and democracy as an ideological and moral conflict" and "optimistically predicted that democratic values would win out over class and racial inequality in America."[136]

The Myrdals' own beliefs and experiences—as well as the intellectual environment in which they found themselves in the late 1930s—thus primed Gunnar to think about the problem of race in America in moral and ideological terms. Nevertheless, this focus did not emerge immediately. When Mydral submitted a memo to Carnegie president Keppel in January 1939 tentatively laying out his approach, he paid great attention to the economic "determinants" of black life and behavior and did not mention the "American creed." In a memo written the following summer, he introduced the idea of the "American state religion" but did not emphasize it over other factors.[137]

In the end, it was not in America, but in Sweden, that the central argument of *An American Dilemma* emerged. The German blitzkrieg in the spring of 1940, which so alarmed American intellectuals, had an even more powerful effect on the Myrdals. The German Wehrmacht had launched its offensive in early April by invading Denmark and Norway, and to many observers it seemed that Sweden could be next. Both Myrdals were determined to be in their homeland during its moment of crisis. In early May 1940, they sailed for Europe with their children on the only ship available: a Finnish freighter packed with dynamite. Arriving in Sweden, they were appalled by the politics of neutrality they found. To head off an invasion, the Swedish government had agreed to continue trading with Germany and to allow some Nazi troops to cross the country by rail to and from Norway. The government also restricted press coverage of Germany and the war, opened letters, and censored telegraph and telephone communications. "Sweden is in the pocket of Germany," Gunnar Myrdal complained to a colleague in the U.S.[138]

As the Myrdals' worked in the spring and summer of 1940 to strengthen their country's "ideological defenses," they increasingly found themselves turning to the example of the United States. Sweden was a democratic society, but they worried that the average Swede would not be as vigilant as his or her American counterpart about the erosion of rights and liberties. To alert Swedes to this danger and to strengthen the nation's ideological preparedness, the Myrdals coauthored a book entitled *Kontakt med Amerika* (Contact with America), which they published in 1941. The second chapter—"Den amerikanska trosbekännelsen"—developed their notion of the "American Creed." Americans, they argued, shared a fundamental consensus of values that transformed a continental and culturally varied democracy into a stable and unified land. The U.S. still had "glaring inequalities," they admitted, but "ahead of every other country in the whole Western world" it "has a living system of expressed ideals for human cooperation which is unified, stable, and clearly formulated." Sweden's political belief system consisted of "latent, unpracticed principles." By contrast, America's shared ideals "have been made conscious and articulate in all social levels."[139]

In 1929, Gunnar Myrdal had suggested that Americans simply parroted "stock phrases" when asked about their political beliefs. Now the couple argued that every American had the basic tenets of the American creed "stamped in his consciousness."[140] How was this possible, they asked? Part of the answer, they argued, could be found in shared celebrations of national heroes and historic events. Making a point similar to one made by Mead, they noted that only the U.S. celebrated the birthdays and deaths of famous people long deceased. The Myrdals also credited the U.S. political and legal system, especially the Supreme Court, as well as American churches and schools. Alva Myrdal, who shaped the book's discussion of education, drew heavily on her experience with public schools in the Midwest and experimental progressive schools launched in the U.S. during the previous decade. Generalizing from these—and largely ignoring both segregated schools and traditional private institutions—Alva argued that American schools brought together children from diverse ethnic and religious backgrounds and taught them democratic values and the tools needed to cooperate.[141]

What were those democratic values? To the Myrdals the "American creed" meant, "above all, civil rights, civil liberties, a free press, and democratic decision making." They saw these ideals as rooted in the Enlightenment and embedded in the U.S. Constitution. Although Americans did not always match their shared values, the Myrdals assured their audience that "there is scarcely any doubt that the national value system is continually increasing in influence." It was in this context—a lesson on ideological "resistance" preached to fellow Swedes—that Gunnar Myrdal developed the argument that would eventually frame *An American Dilemma*. Americans did not always act on the American creed, because it sometimes conflicted with their "local ideologies" or "interests," he argued. Nevertheless, even reactionary southerners defended the national ideology. "The Negro problem, just like all other difficult social problems, is therefore in the first place a problem in the Americans' own heart," Myrdal concluded. *This* was the American dilemma.[142]

Kontakt topped the Swedish best-seller list and became an important resistance book in occupied Norway. Gunnar Myrdal returned to the U.S. in March 1941 and that summer began drafting his seminal study of "the negro problem and modern democracy." In conceptualizing the project, Myrdal drew on the key concepts that he and Alva had developed in Sweden.[143] The resulting book, published in 1944, became one of the most influential books ever written in America and one of most important sociological studies ever. It influenced federal policy and Supreme Court decisions and "set the respectable parameters for the study of race in the United States for the next quarter century."[144] The notion that Americans shared a deeply rooted consensus on values—and that the U.S. "race problem" was fundamentally moral, psychological, and ideological—would shape American understandings of race through at least the mid-1960s.

Of *Kontakt* the Myrdal's daughter, Sissela Bok, has written, "the most astounding points of view, sometimes emanating entirely from their own hopes and fears, are presented as facts. All writers are prone to such overstating, but Alva and Gunnar…offer[ed] personal interpretations of abstruse matters as obvious to all who had their eyes open."[145] In later years, the Myrdals acknowledged that they might have been more critical of the U.S. in a different context; *Kontakt*, they noted, was written as a "preparedness" or "resistance" book rather than as a scholarly volume.[146] *An American Dilemma* drew on extensive research by a huge staff and eventually ran to nearly fifteen hundred pages. It was clearly a scholarly effort, yet it too had an ideological goal. While he was writing the book, Gunnar believed that it would help Americans see clearly the difference between their values and those of Nazi Germany; in so doing, it would help shore up home front morale. Interviewed nearly four decades later, he referred to the book as his "war work," adding "I think this meant much for what the book came to be."[147]

In the late 1930s and early 1940s, Alva and Gunnar Myrdal—like Adamic, Mead, representatives of the NCCJ, and dozens of other individuals and organizations—invoked an American consensus for political ends. Individuals and groups arrayed across the political spectrum stressed Americans' shared values in an effort to combat intolerance and promote social harmony at home and to steel their fellow citizens to withstand "alien" hatreds and ideologies. They differed, however, not only in the way they defined Americans' shared values, but also in the way they cast the relationship between this prescribed consensus and the nation's legal and social status quo. Groups such as the NAM and often the NCCJ emphasized *civility* across class, religious, and other lines and promoted an image of the nation that denied or minimized economic and power imbalances. Meanwhile, civil rights activists and left-liberal intellectuals such as Louis Adamic, James Waterman Wise, and the Myrdals put *equality* at the center of their unifying visions. Rather than trying to convince their fellow citizens that U.S. society was already virtually flawless, they tried to unite Americans around a set of values that would ultimately lead to social change; rather than ignoring power imbalances, they tried to use the language of consensus to correct them. The balance between these two visions of America's core values would soon be strongly influenced by America's entry into World War II.

PART II

The Politics of Unity during World War II (1942–1945)

CHAPTER 4

The Spectre of "Divide and Conquer"

On December 7, 1941, Japanese warplanes attacked the U.S. Pacific fleet at Pearl Harbor, bringing the U.S. into World War II. The following day, the *CIO News* ran a cartoon contrasting "The American Way" with "The Hitler Way" (figure 4.1). One panel depicted Uncle Sam presiding over the table of "Voluntary Agreement," flanked by pleasant-looking men representing "Labor" and "Management." The other panel pictured "Shackled Labor" being whipped by a storm trooper wielding "Anti-Labor Bills." The second image contained resonances of the sharp antibusiness rhetoric that had characterized the industrial labor movement since its coalescence in the mid-1930s: the picture indicted not only Nazi Germany but also implicitly those in the U.S. who sought to hogtie organized labor. The first image, however, suggested an alternative that had been largely missing in previous *CIO News* cartoons: an "American Way" of collective bargaining and harmonious business-labor relations, with Uncle Sam playing a powerful mediating role.[1]

The appearance of this cartoon in part reflected leadership changes within the CIO, but it also foreshadowed developments in the United States during World War II. The bombing of Pearl Harbor and the entry of the U.S. into the war brought the federal government fully into the act of promoting national cohesion. It also provided an opening to a variety of private groups who sought to use the calls for social and ideological unity to their own ends. During the mid- to late 1930s, industrial unionists, their allies in the left wing of the New Deal coalition, and at times even the president himself,

Figure 4.1. This cartoon appeared in the *CIO News* the day after the bombing of Pearl Harbor. While the cartoon continues to equate "antilabor bills" with Nazism, it also envisions an alternative "American way" marked by harmonious agreement between labor and management (courtesy of the AFL-CIO; reproduced by the Wisconsin Historical Society).

had argued that selfish and undemocratic business elites posed the greatest threat to America's civic institutions and values. At the same time, a variety of right-wing populist movements combined hostility to corporate America with racist and anti-Semitic appeals.[2] With the U.S. now fully engaged in the war, this populist rhetoric largely disappeared. Instead, groups and individuals across the political spectrum warned of the Nazi tactic of "divide and conquer" and promoted harmony and cooperation between various subgroups in U.S. society. Consensus—a consensus defined by a common enemy—came to be seen as the *sine qua non* of the "American Way."[3]

Beneath this broad canopy of consensus, however, sharp ideological differences remained. Many liberal and leftist intellectuals, labor organizers, and others who had joined the Popular Front coalition during the late 1930s saw the war above all as a worldwide battle against "fascism," a term they employed expansively to cover evils ranging from anti-Semitism to economic exploitation. These Americans hoped to use the struggle to promote an "anti-fascist" consensus at home and abroad and to bring about a more democratic and egalitarian social, political, and economic order. Casting the war as an all-out contest between "freedom" and "slavery," they argued that Hitler and his minions were using racism and red-baiting to divide Americans. From their positions in federal propaganda agencies and a variety of private groups, they sought to extend the economic agenda of the New Deal and to promote ethnic, religious, and racial equality.

These promoters of a broad antifascist consensus were countered from the beginning by others who used calls for national harmony to shore up the corporate order and to reinforce existing power relations in U.S. society. Some of these Americans viewed the war as a fight among nations or peoples rather than a battle of ideas; they sought to unite all Americans in a pro-American coalition against the Germans, Italians, and Japanese. Others, particularly conservatives, portrayed the nation's enemy as totalitarianisms of both right and left. The latter view had wide appeal during the twenty-two months of the Nazi-Soviet pact, but it was complicated by the Nazi invasion of the Soviet Union in June 1941. Rather than openly condemning America's wartime ally, many who favored this approach focused on promoting civility and "selling America to Americans."[4]

As this suggests, the emphasis on national unity and consensus during the war was a double-edged sword: Red-baiters, union busters, and purveyors of ethnic, religious, and racial hatred could be cast as Nazi agents, but so too could those who forcibly advocated social change. In the end, groups on both ends of the political spectrum were forced to curtail the vitriolic rhetoric they had deployed during the late 1930s. This was particularly apparent in the economic arena. The CIO largely abandoned its "militant idiom" during the war, opting to ally itself with the federal government in a bid to expand its membership.[5] Business groups also moderated their tone. The U.S. Chamber of Commerce and even the National Association of Manufacturers backed away from frontal assaults on unions and the New Deal. Instead, they and their allies worked to recapture cultural authority by convincing Americans that all would benefit from a harmonious, highly productive, and consumer-oriented postwar society, one in which business rather than government took the lead.

The Infrastructure of Consensus

The U.S.'s involvement in World War II produced an infrastructure of institutions devoted to publicly defining for Americans their common ground. While some of these organizations predated the Japanese attack on Pearl Harbor, most were spawned or greatly strengthened by the nation's war effort. Some would continue to operate into the postwar years, becoming crucial vehicles for promoting or shaping a cold war consensus on American public values. During the war, however, the range of competing voices meant that battles to shape America's wartime consensus proceeded on many fronts.

The federal agency officially charged with defining the meaning of the war to Americans on the home front was the Office of War Information. Eager to avoid the "calculated hysteria" that had marked federal propaganda efforts during World War I, FDR initially opposed the formation of any such agency. Pressured by key advisors, he eventually established an Office of Facts and Figures (OFF) in October 1941 and charged it with disseminating "factual information on the defense effort." Archibald MacLeish, the Librarian of Congress who was brought in to head the new agency, mapped out a "strategy of truth" that called for providing hard facts to the media, often with little accompanying interpretation. This approach, however, left the business of interpretation entirely to the private press, radio networks, and Hollywood. Public opinion specialists argued that "the separation of data from inspiration was both artificial and crippling"; and by May 1942, MacLeish himself agreed. The "key to unity in fighting this war," he wrote Roosevelt, is "[a] full knowledge of what we are fighting for, coupled with assurance that we can win our goals." The following month FDR took MacLeish's suggestion and folded the OFF into a new agency with broader powers, the Office of War Information (OWI).[6]

The OWI was hardly the only federal agency working to build a wartime consensus among Americans. In fact, the Treasury Department undoubtedly reached at least as many civilians through its war bond campaigns as did the writers and artists of the OWI. Treasury Secretary Henry Morgenthau Jr., the only Jew in Roosevelt's cabinet, was an early opponent of the Nazi regime. Even before the U.S. entered the war, he had decided "to use *bonds* to sell the *war*, rather than *vice versa*."[7] The administration continued to emphasize defense bonds' ideological—as opposed to simply economic—role, even after the Japanese attack on Pearl Harbor. By offering all Americans a stake in the war effort, by linking personal financial security to national defense, federal officials hoped to buttress national morale and create a "channel for unity" behind the war effort. Such considerations shaped all aspects of the wartime bond campaigns. In an effort to ensure that all Americans could buy bonds, the Treasury Department created "Series E" bonds, which were sold only to individuals, and saving stamps, which even children and the poor could afford. The department mobilized the national media as well as Hollywood celebrities into its selling campaign, but it also worked with groups representing virtually every segment of the American population: farmers, workers, women, schoolchildren, black Americans, and a variety of religious and ethnic groups.[8]

While the consensus-building messages of the OWI and the Treasury Department reached virtually all American civilians, the sixteen million men and women who served in uniform during the war received their instruction on the nation's unifying values and wartime aims primarily from the armed forces. In 1940, the army instituted an orientation course for new recruits, which consisted primarily of pamphlets prepared by scholarly experts and lectures delivered during basic training. By mid-1941, Army Chief of Staff General George C. Marshall had decided that something further was called for. Filmmakers and artists ranging from Frank Capra to Theodore S. Geisel (aka Dr. Seuss) were recruited to make morale-boosting documentary films under the auspices of the United States Army's Information and Education Division. In 1943, both civilian and military leaders began to worry that the lack of a common enemy after the war might lead to widespread social unrest. Working with the American Historical Association, the army produced a series of *G.I. Roundtable* pamphlets designed to educate troops on the nature of the enemy, the reasons they were fighting, and the shape of the postwar world.[9]

Working alongside these branches of the federal government was a multitude of private groups. One of the most central to the politics of consensus both during and after the war was the War Advertising Council. The very existence of the Council testified to the resurging power of business during the war. In the fall of 1941, many Madison Avenue executives had been "running scared." The advertising industry's profits had been hard hit by the Depression, and, with companies increasingly switching production from consumer durables to armaments, the future looked bleak. Moreover, rising popular suspicions of

Madison Avenue had led in 1938 to the first federal regulations on advertising; many in the industry feared further consumer-driven attacks. They worried particularly that the federal government might not consider advertising "a legitimate business expense for the purpose of corporate taxes and war contracts." In November 1941, more than six hundred advertising, industry, and media executives gathered in Florida to brainstorm ways to head off government controls. Taking their cue from James W. Young of the J. Walter Thompson agency, the conferees settled on a plan to burnish the industry's image by embracing "public service" advertising; this step would have the additional benefit of allowing advertisers to defend free enterprise in the name of the public interest.[10]

The bombing of Pearl Harbor less than a month later derailed those initial plans but opened new opportunities to the ad men. The Roosevelt administration now sought to use advertising to sell its domestic programs to the public. Both before and immediately after Pearl Harbor, however, administration officials met resistance when they approached media organizations directly about donating advertising space for critical wartime campaigns.[11] When Madison Avenue executives organized the War Advertising Council in early 1942 and offered their services to the federal government, their offer was quickly accepted. The federal government increasingly relied on the quasi-private Council: between 1942 and 1945, it orchestrated scores of "information campaigns" on behalf of a wide variety of federal agencies. It promoted war bond sales, military and womanpower recruitment, good nutrition, and blood donations; fought inflation, absenteeism, employee turnover, and "loose talk" about the military; and urged the conservation of everything from rubber and fuel to tin cans and kitchen fats.[12] In the process, the Council helped boost public support for business and impressed federal officials with advertising's power. It forged a link between the White House and Madison Avenue that would prove vital to the politics of consensus long after the war had ended.

If the War Advertising Council was one important quasi-private conduit of information, Hollywood was another. The director of the OWI, Elmer Davis, recognized that films were the "easiest way to inject propaganda ideas into most people's minds" because moviegoers were so absorbed in the on-screen action they did not realize their views were being shaped.[13] In early 1942, Davis established a liaison office in Hollywood to help shape and vet studio films. Hollywood did not always follow the OWI's script. Nevertheless, it generally proved a staunch ally in the federal government's overarching campaign to unify Americans behind the war effort.

While the War Advertising Council and the Hollywood studios were two of the most important private channels of wartime meaning, they were hardly alone. Virtually every institution and organization that had entered the contest to define America's core national values in the late 1930s maintained their efforts during the war. Many stepped up their activities, couching their appeals in terms of consensus and unity. In late 1942, for example, the Council Against Intolerance began publishing a monthly guide for educators entitled *American Unity*; it continued issuing the publication throughout the war. With federal approval, the National Conference of Christians and Jews carried its message of interfaith harmony into hundreds of U.S. army camps; its message was further reinforced by the newly instituted United Service Organizations. Meanwhile, dozens of colleges and universities across the country instituted programs in American studies or American civilization. These groups and many others realized that, in defining the meaning of the war for Americans—in defining the grounds on which Americans should unite—they were in fact helping shape the postwar world.

"Divide and Conquer"

The message that Americans got from every quarter during World War II was encapsulated in the phrase "divide and conquer." This was the strategy, they were told, that Hitler had used to gain power in Germany and later to topple France. Now, the Nazi regime would attempt to foment social division in the U.S. as well. Thus, defeating the Axis depended above all on national unity.

During the war, this message became a staple of the federal government's domestic propaganda campaign. In his State of the Union message, delivered one month after the Japanese attack on Pearl Harbor, President Roosevelt warned Americans to "guard against divisions among ourselves" and to be "particularly vigilant against racial discrimination in any of its ugly forms." A few months later, the Office of Facts and Figures issued a pamphlet entitled *Divide and Conquer*, which charged that Hitler and his agents were "sow[ing] seeds of hate and disunity" among Americans. The theme also showed up in speeches by Justice Department officials; in pamphlets, "fact sheets," and movie shorts produced by the OFF and the OWI; in war bond advertisements and other public service messages produced by the War Advertising Council; and in Frank Capra's famous morale-boosting films that became known collectively as the *Why We Fight* series.[14] When the OWI launched a "Stop That Rumor!" campaign in 1943, it noted that "hate rumors" were the most common and dangerous type. The OWI identified Jews, Catholics, and Negroes as common targets of such rumors, but it also listed blood banks, draft boards, business, unions, the Russians, and the British. Hate rumors, the OWI clarified, are "the ones that express prejudice, animosity or hostility for religious, racial, social or economic groups other than the enemy."[15]

A similar theme emanated from a range of Hollywood films. The low-budget picture *Hitler's Children*, which became a "sleeper" sensation in 1943, showed how the Nazi tactic of divide and conquer could destroy the family. So too did the Broadway hit-turned-screenplay *Tomorrow the World* (1944).[16] The 1944 thriller *Lifeboat*, directed by Alfred Hitchcock and based on a story by John Steinbeck, transferred the drama to the North Atlantic. As the film opens, a German U-boat torpedoes a luxury ocean liner and is in turn sunk by the stricken ship. A small group of survivors—including a socialite reporter-photographer, a radical Czech American merchant seaman, a business tycoon, a Cockney radio operator, a nurse from Kansas, a badly wounded German-American stoker, and a black steward—find themselves adrift in a lifeboat. When they rescue the lone survivor of the submarine, the Nazi captain, he ruthlessly tries to divide and conquer the fractured group. He almost succeeds, taking the helm of the lifeboat after the others are unable to agree on a leader and steering them toward a mid-ocean rendezvous with a German supply ship. The Nazi quietly eliminates one of the Americans, pushing the wounded and delirious stoker overboard while the others sleep. Only in the final moments of the film are the remaining occupants of the lifeboat able to overcome their differences and kill the German in what the *New York Times* described as "a rush of horrified rage." The fragile unity of the Allied survivors is symbolized and cemented by two blossoming romances—one between the Kansas nurse and Cockney radio operator, another between the wealthy socialite and the radical seaman.[17]

In underscoring the need for Americans to surmount their divisions of class, politics, ethnicity, and race, *Lifeboat* dramatized what Lary May has called the "conversion narrative" of World War II films. In the 1930s, studios turned out pictures that promoted what one screenwriter called the "spirit of the New Deal broadly defined." "To overcome social and economic corruption," May writes, "heroes commonly shed their loyalty to the rich" and allied with the lower classes, thus realigning cultural and political authority. This story line was particularly apparent in movies starring Will Rogers and in Frank Capra films such as *Mr. Deeds Goes to Town* (1936) and *Mr. Smith Goes to Washington* (1939). World War II produced a very different conversion narrative. Increasingly, heroes and heroines reached across class and cultural lines, not to challenge official institutions and expose greedy businessmen and corrupt politicians, but to save the nation from a foreign enemy. In movies ranging from *December 7* (1942) and *Casablanca* (1942) to *Lifeboat*, consensus became "the nation's core value, whereas distinct ethnic as well as class interests [were] now seen as alien to public life."[18]

May and other historians have suggested that the emphasis on overcoming divisions during the war—on uniting in a consensus defined by a common enemy—was inherently conservative. Certainly, the NAM and other business groups sought both before and during the war to counter the demands of labor and the continuing threat of the New Deal by arguing that "dictatorships breed on misunderstandings between groups and classes."[19] But the language of "divide and conquer" was used by those on the left as well as those on the right: a variety of liberal and left-leaning organizations used it to discredit everything from ethnic, religious, and racial prejudice to union busting and red-baiting.

The slippery political nature of "divide and conquer" rhetoric is clearly revealed in a wartime episode involving Frank Capra's famous *Why We Fight* series. When the army recruited the famous filmmaker to produce the series in early 1942, Capra quickly assembled a team of Hollywood writers. He soon fired most of them, charging years later that their scripts were filled with "Communist propaganda." In fact, Capra's correspondence at the time suggests that he fired the men, not because of his own convictions, but because he was being pressured by the army and by members of the House Special Committee on Un-American Activities. The Special Committee, forerunner to HUAC, had been headed since its formation in 1938 by the Texas Democrat and virulent red-baiter Martin Dies. Dies repeatedly decried the "purveyors of class, racial and religious hatred" and argued that communism (like fascism) was an "alien force tearing at American unity." According to Capra, members of the Dies committee who were also on the House Appropriations Committee had threatened to cut off funding for the project because some of Capra's chosen writers were too "red."[20]

If anticommunists on the Dies committee charged leftists with turning Americans against one another, those they targeted simply reversed the allegation. When screenwriter John Sanford learned of his dismissal from the project, he sent Capra a letter of warning. The war "can be lost if we are divided against ourselves," he wrote:

> It can be lost if Gentile is played off against Jew, black against white, rich against poor, labor against capital, hammer-and-sickle against stars-and-stripes.... To spike one anti-fascist voice today (whether it be the voice of a communist, a reputed communist, or no communist at all) is to spike one gun at a time when all guns—good,

poor, and obsolete—should be shooting till their barrels get too hot to be held.[21]

Sanford was a member of the Communist Party, and in the 1950s, he was blacklisted for taking the Fifth Amendment before HUAC. In 1942, however, he too could deploy the language of "divide and conquer," drawing on rhetoric that had been used by antifascist leftists for several years.

Antifascism versus Pro-Americanism: Competing Visions of Consensus

During the war, leftists, liberals, moderates, and conservatives could all use the language of national unity and social division for one simple reason. "Divide and conquer" was a strategy used by the enemy. It said nothing about *who* or *what* that enemy actually was.[22] In fact during the early years of the war, the precise nature of America's enemy—and thus of the consensus defined by that enemy—was a matter of considerable debate.

Many on the liberal left saw the war as a global battle against fascism in all of its myriad manifestations. Although they virulently condemned the actions of Hitler, Mussolini, and Hirohito abroad, they did not limit their vision of fascism to Germany, Italy, and Japan. As Daniel Geary has observed, antifascism during the 1930s and early 1940s was "a political posture that called for radical reforms toward economic reconstruction and racial equality in a democratic constitutional order." Many antifascists applied the "metaphor of fascism" to a wide range of domestic evils, including lynching, nativism, anti-Semitism, union busting, capitalist exploitation, and red-baiting.[23] Viewing the war as a cataclysmic battle between ideologies and ways of life, they sought to shape an antifascist consensus both at home and abroad.

The most eloquent and prominent spokesman for this position during the war was Roosevelt's hand-picked vice president Henry A. Wallace. In a speech delivered six months after Pearl Harbor, Wallace cast the war in phrases borrowed from Lincoln's famous "House Divided" speech. The war was a "fight to the death between the free world and the slave world," Wallace declared, establishing an analogy that within a few years would assume a very different meaning. "Just as the United States in 1862 could not remain half slave and half free, so in 1942 the world must make its decision for a complete victory one way or the other." The previous 150 years, Wallace suggested, had been a "long-drawn-out people's revolution," designed to give "the common man" everywhere a better standard of living, the skills and time to read and write, and the ability to "think and work together." According to Wallace, this "people's revolution" had begun in America in 1775, but it had spread around the world—to France in 1792, to Latin America in the Bolivarian era, to Germany in 1848, and to Russia in 1917. The current war was a Nazi-led "counterrevolution" by which "Satan now is trying to lead the common man of the whole world back into slavery and darkness." The effort, Wallace predicted, would not succeed. Not only would the Allies win the war, but also "the common man will smoke the Hitler stooges out into the open in the United States, in Latin America, and in India. He will destroy their influence." The war would usher in a "century of the common man," in which the values embedded in the New Deal and invoked in FDR's Four Freedoms address to Congress would be extended both in the U.S. and around the globe.[24]

Wallace's "Century of the Common Man" speech was a direct response to another vision of America and the postwar world offered some fifteen months earlier by the publishing magnate Henry R. Luce. In a famous *Life* magazine editorial entitled "The American Century," Luce envisioned a postwar Pax Americana in which the U.S., like Britain before it, presided wisely over the world, remaking the globe in its own image. America, Luce argued, should become in the twentieth century "the dynamic center of ever-widening spheres of enterprise," "the training center of the skillful servants of mankind," the "Good Samaritan" feeding the world's hungry, and the "powerhouse of the ideals of Freedom and Justice." America had flirted with collectivism under the New Deal, but its devotion to self-reliance, independence, and equal opportunity remained strong. The "promise of adequate production for all mankind, the 'more abundant life,'" was a "characteristically American promise," Luce argued, despite the fact that it was often made by "demagogues and proponents of all manner of slick schemes and 'planned economies.'" "It is for America and for America alone," Luce concluded, "to determine whether a system of free economic enterprise—an economic order compatible with freedom and progress—shall or shall not prevail in this century."[25]

The visions offered by Wallace and Luce shared certain similarities. Both invoked the language of freedom, and both envisioned a postwar world in which the promise of abundance would be extended to all.[26] Both also saw the U.S. and its values as engines driving this postwar change around the globe. Here, however, the parallels ended. Wallace cast the war as a struggle to the death against fascism everywhere and portrayed the American and Bolshevik revolutions as advancing the same cause. Luce implied that communism was at least as alien to the American Way as fascism. Wallace displayed a deep commitment to economic democracy and suggested that government action might well be needed to achieve freedom from want. Luce, like the NAM and other economic conservatives, depicted free enterprise and political democracy as inherently intertwined. Wallace did not attack the wealthy per se, but he emphasized the march of the "common man" and warned against men of means who sought to secure their fortunes by "lur[ing] the people back into slavery of the most degraded kind."[27] Luce, by contrast, privileged stability, order, and established hierarchies of power. Above all, Wallace—like Louis Adamic, Gunnar Myrdal, and many others on the liberal left—believed that the U.S. had fallen short of its noble goals. Luce, by contrast, saw the pre-New Deal U.S. as a perfected model for the world.

Luce's editorial was written in February 1941, four months before Hitler invaded the Soviet Union and severed the alliance that had helped popularize the notion of a "totalitarian" bloc. Nevertheless, many commentators continued to counterpose the U.S. to a totalitarian—rather than a fascist—"other" during the war. A few on the left used the term "totalitarianism" to emphasize their disagreements with Stalin. Many more on the right applied the term more broadly to condemn not only Soviet-style communism but also the encroachment of the state into economic, religious, and interpersonal affairs. When Walt Disney produced an anti-Nazi cartoon short, *Chicken Little*, in 1943, animators originally used the word "fascism" to describe the beliefs held by the evil and conniving Foxey Loxey. Disney, a staunch anticommunist who had suppressed a strike within his own studio, insisted that the word be changed to "totalitarianism," despite the expense and time required to reanimate the sequence. Although the Soviet Union was never explicitly mentioned in the film, the point, one of the animators later explained, was to "make it sound like we're condemning Russia too."[28]

Within the government, the antifascist viewpoint was most strongly represented by the liberals and leftists associated with the OFF and the OWI. These included writers and artists such as Archibald MacLeish, Malcolm Cowley, Robert Sherwood, Arthur Schlesinger Jr., Henry Pringle, Ben Shahn, and Francis Brennan, as well as members of the Foreign Language Division like Alan Cranston. Like Henry Wallace, these men generally cast the war as a fight "for freedom and against slavery," a "people's war" that would lead to the extension of "freedom of speech, freedom of religion, freedom from want, [and] freedom from fear."[29] They worked to convince Americans that the nation's enemy was the ideology of fascism, even as they tried to sideline those Americans who appeared to subscribe to fascist beliefs. Extending their antifascist argument into the domestic arena, they argued that the best way to recruit diverse

Americans into the war effort was by actively combating "discrimination of any sort due to race, color, creed, or national origin."[30] At every turn, however, they encountered opposition from others both within and outside of the government who had a different view.

The OWI progressives, for instance, argued repeatedly during the war that America's enemies were fascist ideologies and their proponents—the Nazis, the Italian Fascists, and the Japanese warlords—rather than the German, Italian, or Japanese people. The vast majority of people living in the Axis countries, the OWI contended, were simply "dupes"—dupes who had to be "liberated" from their "despotic rulers" and eventually welcomed into the postwar "brotherhood of man."[31] This distinction, however, proved too subtle for many Americans, including some within the administration. Many sided with Robert Maxwell, the director of the children's radio show *The Adventures of Superman*. When an OWI official in 1943 encouraged Maxwell to tone down the program's virulent attacks on the Germans and Japanese, the director responded:

> I control the destinies of three juvenile radio programs with
> audiences running into the millions. I can, in some small way,
> formulate ideologies for these youngsters.... I am, at the moment,
> teaching this vast audience to hate.... And, unfortunately, there is
> no cleavage between the individual and the state whose ideology he
> defends. A German is a Nazi and a Jap is the little yellow man who
> "knifed us in the back at Pearl Harbor."

To argue otherwise, Mr. Maxwell concluded, was simply to "make for confusion."[32] In the case of the Japanese, many in the government and the media went further still: despite evidence to the contrary, they cast not only Japanese but all Americans of Japanese descent as potentially traitorous.[33] Although the OWI repeatedly protested such portrayals, it did not have the means to enforce its approach.

If OWI staffers could not convince other opinion molders of the innocence of enemy civilians or Japanese Americans, they also had trouble when they tried to marginalize potential fascists at home. Many Italian-American *prominenti*, members of the community's conservative leadership, had supported Mussolini up until the moment the U.S. entered World War II. Alan Cranston, the head of the OWI's Foreign Language Division, noted that his group had tried to "abolish the long-established leadership of the pro-fascists by ignoring them." Their efforts were thwarted, however, by the Treasury Department, which appointed many of the *prominenti* to Italian-American war bond committees. Cranston complained that the Treasury Department had appointed Generoso Pope, an Italian-language press baron who had been a staunch Mussolini supporter, to head a key war bond committee. When anti-fascists in the Italian-American community refused to serve with Pope, the Treasury Department appointed a dozen more Italian-American conservatives, to the dismay of Cranston and others on his staff. By early 1943, the OWI had largely abandoned its efforts to undermine the *prominenti* and settled instead for trying to unite all Italian Americans—and eventually Americans of all nationality groups—in a broad "Americans All" coalition that "stressed pro-American themes."[34]

Even as liberals and leftists in the OWI tried to convince Americans that fascism was the enemy, they worked to further the goals of the broader anti-fascist campaign—strengthening and extending the goals of the New Deal and combating discrimination at home. A leaflet entitled *How to Raise $16 Billion* advocated withholding taxes as a means of spreading the burden of paying for war. *Battle Stations All*, a pamphlet dealing with inflation, supported price and rent control, increased taxation, and other steps designed to "tak[e] the profit out of war." It also called for guaranteeing people at least their minimum essentials of food, clothing, shelter, transportation, and recreation. *Negroes and the War* not only lauded the contribution that black Americans were making to the war effort but also described the educational and economic advances they had made under the New Deal. The pamphlet praised the role of the Works Progress Administration and the National Youth Administration and described the New Deal as ringing "like a pleasant bell in the ears of the American Negro." The OWI manual *When Radio Writes for War* urged the authors of radio programs not to portray Negroes as "the Stepin Fechit type, the minstrel man, the stooge, the dumb domestic, the guy always being chased by ghosts."[35]

Outraged conservatives saw in such booklets—with their support for economic redistribution and greater racial equality—evidence of totalitarian tendencies on the part of the administration. Moreover, such materials did not represent the only voice of the OWI. Many of the liberal writers, artists, and researchers in the agency had joined the OFF when it was headed by Archibald MacLeish, the poet laureate of the Popular Front. When the OFF was merged into the OWI in June 1942, Gardner Cowles Jr., a Midwestern newspaper publisher, was appointed to head the domestic branch. A liberal Republican and staunch supporter of Wendell Wilkie, Cowles backed Roosevelt's foreign policy but opposed many aspects of the New Deal. He also believed that the OWI's principal role was to coordinate government campaigns on the home front.

He established the Bureau of Campaigns within the agency and strengthened the OWI's ties to the advertising industry. As a result, the antifascists increasingly found themselves competing for influence and resources with staffers drawn from Madison Avenue. These men and women showed little interest in portraying the grimmer aspects of the war or in promoting domestic reform. Instead, they sought to rally support for specific government programs by "selling America to Americans."[36] They oversaw sentimental, patriotic, and upbeat campaigns that generally reinforced the nation's corporate order. The liberal chief of the OWI's graphics bureau complained that such Madison Avenue techniques had "done more toward dimming perception, suspending critical values, and spreading the sticky syrup of complacency over the people than almost any other factor."[37]

The growing tensions within the OWI came to a head in the spring of 1943. Cowles reorganized the domestic branch, bringing its writers, artists, and researchers under the direct control of several men who favored the "advertising technique."[38] Price Gilbert, a former Coca-Cola executive who had been appointed to head the Bureau of Graphics and Printing, shelved vivid posters of Nazi brutality created by Popular Front artist Ben Shahn, replacing them with folksy American scenes by magazine illustrator Norman Rockwell. (Shahn and a colleague responded by producing a poster of the Statue of Liberty carrying four bottles of Coke in her upraised hand. The motto on the poster declared "The War That Refreshes: The Four Delicious Freedoms!") Meanwhile, William Lewis, a former vice president of the Columbia Broadcasting System, curbed the work of the writers, telling them they could write "only to specification" and killing a proposed pamphlet on the nation's food supply.[39] In April, some fifteen men and women resigned from the OWI en masse. In a letter to the *New York Times*, they charged that the agency was becoming an "office of war ballyhoo."[40] One of the resigning writers, Arthur Schlesinger Jr., went further in a private letter to literary critic Bernard DeVoto. "The advertising men have been striking out for more and more power over the whole domestic information policy," he wrote. "It has meant an increasing conviction that any government information campaign likely to affect a vested business interest should first be approved by that interest. It has meant a steady replacement of independent writers, newspapermen, publishers, mostly of liberal inclination, by men beholden to the business community for their livelihood and thinking always as the business community thinks."[41]

The mass resignation was the beginning of the end for the OWI's domestic branch. By early 1943, the agency was under intense fire from conservatives in Congress, who controlled both houses after the fall elections of

1942. Republicans and southern Democrats both saw the agency as promoting the agenda of FDR and the New Deal. The public release of Frank Capra's *Prelude to War*—despite the dismissal of much of the original screenwriting team—only fueled such attacks. Army Chief of Staff General George C. Marshall intervened personally to direct congressional anger away from the Capra films. The OWI, however, was not so lucky. Conservatives attacked the pamphlets on taxation and inflation and argued that *Negroes and the War* was both partisan pleading and an attempt to force an "alien" philosophy—racial equality—on the South. The ranking Republican on the House Appropriations Committee declared that OWI films, radio scripts, and publications were "partly drivel, partly insidious propaganda against Congress and for a fourth term," and occasionally "along communistic lines." In June 1943, a coalition of Republicans and southern Democrats slashed funding for the domestic branch of the OWI.[42]

The resignations and funding cutbacks at the OWI in mid-1943 silenced the staunchest and best-positioned advocates of a progressive, anti-fascist consensus within the federal government. In so doing, they effectively amplified the voice of the business community. Many corporate, advertising, and public relations executives hoped to use the war to reestablish their cultural and political authority. America's new role as the "arsenal of democracy"—together with surging wartime production—gave them the opening. The war revived corporate profits, restored national prosperity, and allowed those who had once been dubbed "industrial Tories" to wrap themselves in the mantle of patriotism. Still, many businessmen realized that such developments would pay few political dividends in the postwar period unless they were brought to the attention of the American public. Many corporations also worried about keeping their names in the public eye at a time when they had few or no consumer goods to offer. They solved both problems by taking the advice of the Young & Rubicam advertising agency, which instructed potential clients to "serve the company" by "serv[ing] the nation."[43]

The War Advertising Council orchestrated such efforts. Federal agencies, often working through the OWI's Bureau of Campaigns, funneled requests for support to the Council. The Council ranked requested campaigns by relative importance, then assigned them to volunteer ad agencies, which developed campaign themes and compiled supporting facts. The resulting "campaign guides" were distributed to companies and industry associations for use in privately sponsored advertisements. (Companies were free to select the campaigns and themes they wished to use.) In some cases, the Council itself provided free advertising mats and other materials, for which the print media and outdoor advertisers donated space. The Council also supervised the presentation of public service announcements on the radio by creating and supervising a radio allocation plan. Finally, it forwarded "fact sheets" on important topics to various media outlets. Both the print and broadcast media drew on these fact sheets when drafting editorials or assigning and reporting stories.[44]

The War Advertising Council took its cues from the federal government; nevertheless, this system transferred a great deal of control over wartime propaganda from the public to the private sector. Although the federal government selected the issues addressed in public service advertising campaigns, Madison Avenue increasingly framed the messages Americans received. Not surprising, messages conceived by the War Advertising Council and disseminated by the Council or corporate advertisers had more in common with the vision of Henry Luce than with that of Henry Wallace. In aggregate, these campaigns equated the American Way not with greater equality or security but with the freedom of individuals to consume. They suggested that U.S. industry, not the federal government, was best able to guarantee Americans' "freedom from want."

During the war, Americans had only to open their newspapers or magazines, turn on the radio, or walk through the streets of their city or town to see or hear messages that linked brand names or corporate logos to the war effort: the consumption of Pabst Blue Ribbon beer or Pepsi-Cola to stepped-up wartime production, a gift of Charles-of-the-Ritz cosmetics to the purchase of war bonds, or Cannon percale sheets to the donation of blood.[45] OWI writers had condemned such efforts to tie "commercial plugs in with war messages," warning that such linkages represented a tasteless effort to "capitalize on the gravity of the war."[46] By contrast, it was precisely this strategy—intertwining "sacrifice and self-interest"—that the War Advertising Council and private advertising agencies recommended when persuading corporate clients to run public service ads. A 1943 ad for Chesterfield cigarettes featured a smiling female solderer, Chesterfield dangling from her lips, and urged female readers to contact the U.S. Employment Service Office.[47] Bendix Home Appliances emphasized its patriotic contribution in an ad showing a woman singing as she hung out the wash: "My Bendix lies over the ocean, my Bendix lies over the sea, my Bendix does wash for the navy, instead of the laundry for me."[48] Many ads touted awards that companies had received from either the military or the Treasury Department for achieving wartime production or bond sales goals.

Such ads suggested that individual companies were going all out for the war effort. Many also reminded Americans of how good they had it—not only compared to the nation's fighting men, but also compared to civilians in other countries. "Sure you've got the money...So have lots of us," declared an anti-inflation ad prepared by the War Advertising Council. (The ad went on to urge Americans to save, rather than spend, the money they had.) An anti-inflation ad sponsored by the Bowery Savings Bank of New York noted that "old-fashioned thrift" was "one of the reasons why we have more to eat and more to wear—and pay less for necessities—than men and women in many other countries."[49] "We were Spoiled...and Thank God for it!" Chrysler exclaimed in a *Saturday Evening Post* ad promoting war bonds. "We bought things that only the very rich could afford in other countries. Shop girls dressed as well as the smartest women in Paris." Chrysler added that this "American way of living" was not only "the envy of the world," but "probably saved the world": "To meet your demand for more and still more cars at the prices you wanted to pay, you made us at Chrysler, for example, build the production system that was later to pour out weapons to our fighting men."[50]

Such ads conveniently overlooked the ravages of the Depression and the war-wrought devastation of other lands, while crediting corporate America for Allied successes. Government defense spending was fueling the nation's economic boom, but ads generally ignored this fact. Instead, they attributed the nation's prosperity—both past and present—to "old-fashioned" American values, harmonious business-labor relations, and the prowess and ingenuity of American business. "Hardships taught our forefathers the virtue of self-reliance and the need for cooperation," Budweiser proclaimed, under a picture of New England Puritans. Those same values would win the war, and "in peace-time that same unity of effort will keep America strong and prosperous."[51] In a remarkable ad entitled "Strange Fruit," Wyandotte Chemicals Corporation recast the title of the antilynching ballad that Billie Holiday had popularized a few years earlier. The tree in the ad was adorned not with African-American bodies but with the products of an abundant consumer society: a magazine, a rayon dress, photographic film, an airplane, and a bottle of perfume. All these, the ad copy suggested, were derived from wood using a chemical manufactured by the company. "Money may not grow on trees," the ad declared, "but miracles do."[52]

Both the War Advertising Council and corporate advertisers acknowledged that many products were not immediately available to home-front consumers. At the same time, most linked appeals for wartime sacrifice to the promise of postwar consumption.[53] This was particularly true of the many ads that urged Americans to purchase war bonds or to save money in order to head off inflation. "Buy an Extra War Bond for You—and Me," a soldier instructed his wife in a 1944 ad placed by the Eureka Vacuum Cleaner Company in *McCall's*:

> I want you to buy an extra War Bond and put both our names on it. And when you've bought that extra Bond…I want you to buy yourself a dress…something soft and something blue. Because *out here* that's how I think of you—and thinking of you I think of all the fun we'll have together when I come home…buying things for the most wonderful house in all the world….our house, the house I'm going to build for you.

Such ads suggested that Americans were fighting not for freedom of speech or religion but for a right to buy toasters, refrigerators, and Cadillacs. These goods and many others "had marched away to war," but they would return after Victory Day when American would "meet its destiny of peace and plenty."[54] In fact, many ads suggested that the right to purchase such goods—and the system of free enterprise that produced them—were core American values. "How *American* it is…to want something better!" proclaimed ale-maker P. Ballantine & Sons in an ad showing two female war workers pocketing war bonds.[55] The makers of Sparton radios envisioned a father talking to his young son. "We have so many things, here in America, that belong only to free people," he said.

> The right to free speech and action.
> Warm, comfortable homes.
> Automobiles and radios by the million.
> Electrical machines to keep and cook our food; to wash and clean
> for us.[56]

The Stewart-Warner Corporation struck a similar note in an ad urging Americans to observe reduced speed limits and to buy war bonds. "Will you *ever* own another car? Another radio? Another gleaming new refrigerator?" the manufacturer of auto parts and appliances asked. "Those who live under dictators merely dream of such possessions." Although a picture of a dark swastika topped the ad, the reference to "dictators" suggested a broader interpretation of the enemy.[57]

In the meantime, all Americans needed to do their part. Materials produced by the antifascist writers and artists in the OWI had praised New Deal programs and often advocated government solutions for pressing wartime problems—for instance, price and rent controls as an antidote to inflation.

By contrast, campaigns orchestrated by the War Advertising Council generally emphasized the responsibility of individual citizens. In one Council ad, "the PATRIOTIC Mrs. Jones" fought inflation by continuing to use a chipped teacup and by "wearing her clothes for another year—and another." In a second, "us little guys—us workers, us farmers, us business men" fought inflation in part by foregoing purchases and price hikes and by not "ask[ing] higher wages for our work." A third ad showed a fish labeled "John Q. Public" enticed by the baited hook of "depression." "Don't get hooked again!" the ad declared. "To avoid the kind of depression we had after the last war—WE MUST HEAD OFF INFLATION NOW! And the best way to do that is to save your money." "If you don't [keep prices down], who will?" a fourth ad asked rhetorically. "Uncle Sam can't do it alone."[58]

Some ads were explicitly political, sounding the same themes used by the NAM and other business groups in the late 1930s. An ad sponsored by Liberty Motors & Engineering Corporation played off FDR's "Four Freedoms," declaring the "U.S. System of Free Enterprise" to be "The Fifth Freedom."[59] A series of ads run by the Nash-Kelvinator Corp. in 1943 and 1944 showed American servicemen dreaming about the country to which they would eventually return. "The future *I'm* after is so big nobody's ever going to hand it to me on a silver platter!" declared one sailor stranded in a lifeboat. Another, being carried out of a Pacific jungle on a stretcher, thought of the men who had come before him. "And all I ask is the chance *they* had, the chance of an individual fighting man when the chips are down…and the opportunity to go ahead in a land where nothing and nobody cuts great men down…where no false power builds little men up…where every man and woman and child is a free *individual*."[60]

The Politics of Moderation

In 1943, the celebrated muckraker George Seldes self-published a book entitled *Facts and Fascism* that explicitly linked fascism abroad and at home. "There are many powerful elements working against a greater democracy," Seldes argued, "against an America without discrimination based on race, color and creed, an America where never again will one third of the people be without sufficient food, clothing and shelter, where never again will there be 12,000,000 unemployed and many more millions working for semi-starvation wages while the DuPont, Ford, Hearst, Mellon and Rockefeller Empires move into the billions of dollars." Seldes argued that the National Association of Manufacturers and the business empires it represented were "the center of American Fascism," the U.S. equivalent of the industrialists who had funded Mussolini and Hitler. His attack, however, did not stop there. "When it comes to relating foreign Fascism with native American Fascism there is a conspiracy of silence in which the OWI, the American press, and all the forces of reaction in America are united," Seldes wrote. "Victory over foreign Fascism is certain," he predicted, but the job at home remained "unfinished." Partly because of the unwillingness of American liberals and leftists to take on corporate conservatives, American civilians would "have to continue to fight native Fascism for many years." Otherwise, Seldes warned, "we will stupidly have dropped the victory won in Africa, in Italy, in Germany and in Japan."[61]

Facts and Fascism was a highly unusual wartime tract. What made the book so exceptional was not Seldes's antifascist vision but his unstinting attack on other Americans. Although many liberals and leftists shared Seldes's hopes for a more egalitarian future, most believed that the first step toward securing that future was defeating the Axis powers, a step they believed required national unity. Moreover, the stress on social cohesion during the war—as the essential countermeasure to the Nazi tactic of "divide and conquer"—opened both purveyors of prejudice and promoters of protest to charges that they were aiding the enemy. Both factors contributed to what Seldes dubbed a "conspiracy of silence." Most Americans who saw fascism as a global concern moderated their tone on the home front during the war. Although some in the OWI and elsewhere sought to sideline profascist groups, they generally shunned all-out attacks on domestic enemies. Instead, they focused on unifying Americans behind the war effort and using the war to promote egalitarian values.

This strategy can clearly be seen in the wartime activities of the labor movement, particularly the CIO. Although the CIO represented only one-third of all organized workers during the war, it dominated key industries such as steel and automobiles that were at the heart of the defense buildup. Moreover, its energy and vision had driven labor's mobilization during the late 1930s. In those years, CIO officials and the *CIO News* regularly joined Seldes and other leftists in launching blistering attacks on the NAM and its political and business allies; they dubbed their domestic enemies "economic royalists," "industrial Tories," and increasingly "American fascists." These rhetorical salvos were matched by militant on-the-ground tactics. As Robert Zieger has observed, "To be for labor meant marching on picket lines, facing police truncheons, and fighting for workers' rights."[62]

The CIO's retreat from this approach began in late 1940, when the soft-spoken Philip Murray replaced the fiery John L. Lewis as president of the organization. Lewis was an isolationist who viewed developments abroad through the lens of 1917: he believed that British imperialists were trying to drag the U.S. into a European "bloodbath" that would ultimately endanger the labor movement, and he saw FDR's defense policies as misguided, if not dishonest. Murray and his supporters, by contrast, believed that Hitler had to be stopped. They remained committed to bolstering labor's power and to improving the living standards of workers, but they argued that the best way to do this was by standing by the president who already had helped labor achieve unprecedented gains. Moderating their antibusiness tone, they threw their weight behind the accelerating defense buildup, arguing at the same time for increased labor participation in managerial decision-making and national planning. In essence, the CIO leadership moved away "from raw, class-conscious politics" to "a view of workers as participants in a broad civic coalition."[63]

The U.S.'s entry into World War II accelerated this strategic shift, a move that was reflected in *CIO News* articles and cartoons like the one contrasting the "Hitler Way" with the "American Way." It was also evident in an influential book published in early 1942 by two of Murray's longtime associates on the Steel Workers Organizing Committee. In *The Dynamics of Industrial Democracy*, Clinton Golden and Harold Ruttenberg argued for collective bargaining, a union shop, and "the participation of organized workers in management." These steps, they argued, were critical to both "the establishment and maintenance of industrial peace" and the "attainment of full production." Moreover, collective bargaining represented "the extension of the basic practices and principles of democracy into industry." Although Golden and Ruttenberg continued to call for radical reforms and to liken industrial citizenship to political citizenship, their tone was hardly confrontational. This was underscored by the fact that Russell W. Davenport, chairman of *Fortune*'s Board of Editors and a former speechwriter for Wendell Wilkie, agreed to write the book's foreword. "When you read this book you move from a crazy world into a rational one," Davenport wrote. "You leave behind the world of the last ten years, in which strikes, lock-outs, and riots marked the inability of men to recognize a common interest or a common goal." Golden and Ruttenberg, he suggested, had mapped out "a new world in which a common interest binds men together and a common goal is in some measure achieved."[64]

If U.S. involvement in the war delegitimized organized labor's "militant idiom," it also undermined unions' most potent weapon—the strike.[65] Within weeks of the declaration of war, the CIO and other labor organizations had agreed to a "no-strike pledge" promulgated by FDR. Many workers did engage in work stoppages during the war, but most were short and triggered by the "day-to-day indignities" suffered in "hectic wartime workplaces"; many involved only a single department or shift. Meanwhile, polls conducted by the Gallup organization between 1942 and 1944 showed that four out of every five Americans favored some form of antistrike legislation. Such views extended to union members, who were for the most part strongly patriotic. CIO vice president Sidney Hillman noted in 1943 that workers would defend their own strikes, while condemning those of others in the labor movement.[66] Indeed, when John L. Lewis led a half million coal miners on an extended strike that year, polls showed that he was the most unpopular man in America—with an "unfavorable" rating that put him on the same plane as Hitler and Hirohito.[67]

The approach of the CIO's leadership during the war involved a calculated bet—a bet that if organized labor abandoned its militancy at least temporarily, it could solidify its alliance with the federal government and emerge from the war in a better position to make its voice heard. In some respects, this bet paid off. Despite strong opposition from the NAM and other business groups, FDR established the National War Labor Board (NWLB) vested with a broad range of powers.[68] The NWLB quickly instituted a "maintenance of membership" clause that swelled union ranks at a time when millions of new workers— teenagers, housewives, migrant farm workers, and others with little historic commitment to the labor movement—were flooding into defense plants. Instead of collapsing, the CIO's membership more than doubled between 1939 and 1944, despite the departure from the organization of six hundred thousand members of Lewis's United Miner Workers union.[69] Longer hours, overtime provisions, incentive pay plans, and vacation benefits (often taken in the form of double-time pay) led to a 27 percent rise in real earnings during the war for workers in the manufacturing sector.[70]

If the war bolstered organized labor's numbers and swelled the pocket-books of individual workers, it nevertheless reduced unions' cumulative power. Over the course of the war, the NWLB increasingly shifted from a "prestigious forum for the presentation of [labor's] interests" to an "inflation-fighting agent" interested primarily in limiting wages."[71] Although workers' average weekly earnings soared 65 percent during the war, this reflected overtime hours more than wage gains. At the same time, the profits recorded by corporations almost doubled.[72] Meanwhile, the implied linkage between labor's "no-strike pledge" and the government's "maintenance of membership" guarantee effectively transferred union power to the federal government. "The wartime 'contract' that emerged" between organized labor and the national government was markedly different from the "bold visions of shared decision-making" laid out by Murray and others at the start of the war, Alan Brinkley has written: "Instead of an active participant in the councils of industry, the labor movement had become, in effect, a ward of the state."[73]

If the wartime emphasis on national unity prompted labor leaders to abandon their militant tone, it had a similar effect on America's business community. This was not because corporate America had decided it was out of the woods. The war restored the prestige and profitability of U.S. industry, but it also greatly expanded the federal government's role in the economy. Federal defense contracts kept war plants humming, while federal regulatory agencies oversaw everything from pricing to wage rates. Many corporate, advertising, and public relations executives believed that their efforts to "sell" the public on the abstract concepts of free enterprise and individual liberty had been generally successful. But what did "free enterprise" mean in practice? The real issue facing industry was no longer "private enterprise versus collectivism," a top NAM staffer told the War Congress of American Industry in December 1942, but "private enterprise versus 'modified enterprise'"—"*to preserve individual initiative in the management of property; not merely the right of the individual to own property.*"[74] Such concerns were widely shared and remained strong throughout the war. As Thomas D'Arcy Brophy, president of the Kenyon & Eckhardt advertising agency, wrote investment banker Prescott Bush in August 1944, "Regardless of the outcome of the [upcoming presidential] election, free enterprise is in for a fight."[75]

Nearly all members of the business community feared expanded federal control of the economy after the war, as well as a resurgence in the political power of organized labor. They were not, however, of one mind about the scope of the danger. "Traditional or practical conservatives" viewed unions as "illegitimate," distrusted the federal government, and called for the "dismantling" of most New Deal programs. By contrast, moderates and "more sophisticated" conservatives believed that business should work to curb rather than to destroy the New Deal. They sought to preserve corporate and managerial prerogatives but saw a role for the government in promoting economic growth and preventing "wild economic fluctuations." They also believed that unions—properly contained—could make workers allies, rather than enemies, in the drive for greater production and "industrial stability."[76] The emphasis on national unity and consensus during the war gave moderates the upper hand and forced even traditional conservatives to modulate their tone. Instead of launching all-out attacks on unions and the federal government, many in the business community emphasized what they argued was the natural harmony of interests produced by modern American capitalism.

One example of this shift was the wartime transformation of the nation's largest business group, the U.S. Chamber of Commerce. Throughout the 1930s and into the 1940s, the Chamber of Commerce's leadership had been almost as fanatical as the NAM in its opposition to the New Deal. In the spring of 1942, however, a group of young, mostly Western, members revolted against this old guard and installed as president a youthful and energetic Spokane entrepreneur, Eric Johnston. Johnston quickly reoriented the organization, making peace with FDR, urging businesses to learn to live with unions, and praising America's wartime economy—with its emphasis on teamwork and massive production—as a model for the future. In hundreds of interviews, speeches, op-ed pieces, and other forums, Johnston urged Americans to embrace the politics of cooperation, consumption, and economic growth.[77] He quickly became the most prominent spokesman for business's new consensus-oriented approach.

Johnston most fully explicated his vision in a 1944 manifesto entitled *America Unlimited*. America, Johnston declared, was "a civilization of abundance." All Americans were capitalists "in their psychology" because they did not accept "the status into which birth and fate have cast them." During the economic catastrophe of the Depression, however, Americans had lost sight of this common ground. Although Johnston was critical of certain aspects of the New Deal—its attempt "to legislate by administrative decrees," its tendency to centralization, and its emphasis on "defeatist ideas" such as make-work programs and "plowing under"—he argued that the greatest evil of the period was its "spirit of vendetta and class warfare." That spirit had been fueled by both New Dealers and those who opposed the administration. The war, Johnston believed, had rescued the nation from this spiritual morass by reminding Americans of "a fact which has been true all along, but concealed from sight—that the areas of agreement transcend by far the areas of conflict." Business, labor, and the government were now working together to put the economy into overdrive, in the process benefiting all. Johnston argued that this spirit of consensus and teamwork should be extended into the postwar period. Business should recognize labor's right to bargain collectively (although not the union shop), while labor and government should work to remove "physical, political, and psychological obstacles to the free flow of enterprise capital." If more was produced, there would be more to divide. The result, Johnston enthused, would be "an economy of the people, by the people, for the people"—a "people's capitalism" of high productivity and high consumption that would contrast sharply with both the "capitalism of private monopoly and special privilege" and with the "bureaucratic capitalism" of Moscow and Berlin.[78]

Johnston's approach was widely embraced by more moderate or pragmatic members of the business community, including those associated with groups such as the Business Advisory Council, the Committee for Economic Development, and the Advertising Council. But even businessmen who did not share Johnston's desire to reconcile with organized labor and the New Deal were forced during the war to reckon with his vision. The NAM, for instance, underwent a turbulent internal battle, as hard-line members tussled with pragmatists in the organization and particularly on the professional staff over the association's public relations approach.

For most of the previous decade, the NAM had tried to convince the public that, in the words of one staff memo, "the continuance of [all government] regulation will lead the country into collectivism." The pragmatists argued that this approach wasn't working: "Even if true, that contention cannot be sold to the public." Most Americans, they continued, believed firmly in "the symbol of free enterprise," but they also attributed the debacle of 1929 to "shortsighted selfishness and a lack of vision on the part of businessmen." The public "felt that the nation's economic leadership had failed, and it transferred this leadership to government because government was the only agency that offered to help us out of the mess." Given this history, the pragmatists argued, it would be nearly impossible to convince the public that government controls were illegitimate. Instead, the business community should argue that such controls were unnecessary. Rather than taking a negative approach—"oppos[ing] *unsound* proposals to promote security, higher living standards and enlarged opportunities"—the NAM and its allies should emphasize a positive message: They should "convince the public that businessmen have such sound motives and so much economic vision that there is no need" for government intervention.[79] The business community, in other words, should present itself as best able to provide those things Americans most wanted: jobs, consumer goods, economic security, and opportunity.[80]

This approach meant convincing the public that the business community had "come of age" since the 1920s, when it "occasionally used its economic freedom sincerely, but mistakenly, against the general welfare."[81] The NAM pragmatists contended that the best way to do that—to convince the public "that business men are both *eager* and *competent* to achieve the nation's goals"—was "to associate the postwar problems facing America with a successful *accomplishment* in which industry *already* has demonstrated its eagerness and capacity to solve the nation's problems." That accomplishment was "obviously" wartime production. The public needed to be convinced that high productivity—achieved through the harmonious cooperation of consumers, investors, workers, and managers in a free enterprise system—was the best way to achieve "full employment, reasonable economic security, higher living standards, opportunity for progress, economic justice, personal liberty, and other legitimate postwar desires of the American people."[82] High productivity could also be achieved through "regimentation and compulsion," as Hitler had shown, but the price of productivity thus achieved was "religious, civil, political and economic freedom."[83] (Here NAM pragmatists hearkened back to a theme pioneered during the "Tripod of Freedoms" campaign in 1939 and 1940.)

Many conservatives in the NAM were leery of the approach the pragmatists proposed. Nevertheless, NAM staffers took steps during the war to refocus the organization's efforts. At the association's urging, companies ranging from the Aluminum Company of America to Boeing Aircraft held "Soldiers of Production" rallies during which NAM speakers linked high productivity to high standards of living and urged "partnership" between workers and managers; hundreds of thousands of employees attended such rallies, and radio carried them to millions more. The NAM also stepped up its efforts to reach "opinion moulders" in agriculture, women's organizations, education, and churches. At NAM urging, for instance, business groups in dozens of cities held local and regional conferences with religious leaders, designed to reduce or eliminate "the misconceptions of motive and interest known to exist toward organized management in this influential group." Business attendees at such meetings stressed that industry had seen the light—that it had acquired "an enlarged social vision developed out of ten years of economic tribulation and depression." They also noted that the two groups had a common interest in "seek[ing] a state of society in which the worth, dignity, and potential of the individual are primary considerations." Such a society, the business representatives emphasized, required that all forms of freedom—"political, religious, and economic"—be preserved. Finally, they argued that the best way to achieve higher living standards, economic justice, and the "maintenance and extension of our American freedoms" was "through one basic method—*greater production*."[84]

These themes were also at the heart of an advertising campaign commissioned by NAM staffers and developed in late 1944 and early 1945 by the Kenyon & Eckhardt advertising agency. The campaign was designed to promote a "progressive free-enterprise, free-market" model for the economy and to portray business as "forward-looking" and "dynamic" rather than as "Bourbonistic."[85] Although "ostensibly" addressed to "Mr. and Mrs. America," the campaign was actually intended to "sound a keynote for some thousands of other business men to repeat" in luncheon speeches and interviews.

Organizers also hoped "to reach the wholesalers of public opinion—editors, educators, and the like."[86] Ads in the campaign emphasized the sense of common ground that Americans had rediscovered during the war and portrayed high production as the key to postwar prosperity. "Government handouts" would "result only in more and more debt," but high productivity would allow Americans to "earn more, buy more, have more." Such a high-production, high-consumption economy required the cooperation of both business and the public. Business needed to make "full use of the technological 'know how'" it had acquired during the war and to pledge itself to "a just and enlightened wage policy." The public's role was political. It needed, among other things, to work for lower taxes and "labor policies that establish the responsibilities of both labor *and* management." Ads encouraged readers to write for a free booklet that provided more information.[87]

Fearing that the campaign would appear partisan and thus be discredited, the NAM held it until after the 1944 presidential election.[88] The Kenyon & Eckhardt ads began appearing in mid-December, and dozens of other large corporations prepared to tie their own advertising to the effort.[89] By late January, however, the NAM's campaign was under fire. Conservatives on the NAM's board, led by Chrysler finance chairman and former Liberty League member B. E. Hutchinson, attacked the free booklet, challenging its assumption that "everyone should have a job." They also argued that it offered unrealistic examples of what employees could expect to earn and that it "tacitly accept[ed] a growing labor movement."[90] Although many board members supported the campaign, it was ultimately scuttled.[91] Many of its key themes, however, would reemerge after the war in campaigns organized by Kenyon & Eckhardt's president Thomas D'Arcy Brophy on behalf of a reconstituted Advertising Council.

The deadlock between pragmatists and conservatives within the NAM was finally broken in the late spring of 1945, when Eric Johnston and the U.S. Chamber of Commerce joined the CIO and AFL in promulgating a "Labor-Management Charter." The charter committed organized labor "to respect managerial rights" and "eschew the nationalization of industry," but it also recognized the "fundamental rights of labor to organize and engage in collective bargaining." Praised by FDR as well as prominent Republicans, the charter was ultimately endorsed by the *Wall Street Journal* and such industry leaders as Charles E. Wilson of General Electric and Winthrop Aldrich of Chase National Bank. Although the stunned NAM refused to climb on board, key members of the leadership now joined most of the association's staff in calling for a more pragmatic public relations approach. The NAM's positions remained very conservative—it continued, for instance, to lobby against the Wagner Act and for antistrike legislation—but it increasingly portrayed these positions as promoting the public interest and thus placed "the onus of industrial discord on unions for refusing to accept reasonable reforms." In late 1945, the NAM hired a top public relations firm to insert its message—"management serves the public interest"—into a wide range of radio entertainment and news programs. The NAM's refocused "moderate" strategy helped it torpedo a national labor-management conference convened by Truman just after the end of the war. More broadly, it helped transformed the NAM into "a potent political force" in the postwar years.[92]

Business groups were by no means alone in learning to deploy the language of shared values during the war. The language was also used by those arguing for greater religious, ethnic, and racial inclusion. Ultimately, no group would benefit more from the combined emphasis on unity and pluralism during the war than those who argued that America was a tri-faith nation.

CHAPTER 5

"The House I Live In"

On April 22, 1944, a group of Howard University students converged on Thompson's, a moderately priced chain restaurant in downtown Washington, D.C. Like most restaurants in the nation's capital, Thompson's was segregated. Sixty-five students entered the restaurant and, after being refused service, sat down quietly and began to read. Others picketed outside. "Are you for Hitler's Way or the American Way?" their signs read. "We Die Together. Let's Eat Together."

Six black GIs soon noticed the picketers and joined the students inside. White servicemen were also eating in the restaurant and white military police asked the black soldiers to leave. When they refused, an MP lieutenant asked them to leave as a personal favor: the army did not want to be embarrassed "in case of an incident." The black GIs kept their seats. Ultimately, the military police were forced to order all servicemen, white and black, out of Thompson's. Four hours later, the management of the restaurant chain directed that the students be served.[1]

As their placards suggested, these Howard University students were attempting to bend the language of wartime unity and consensus to their own ends. Invoking an "American Way" that they clearly contrasted to the racist practices of Hitler, they suggested that any American who did not support integrated dining facilities sympathized with Nazis. In this instance, their strategy worked, perhaps in part because the army was eager to avoid a racial incident. In many other cases, however, those pushing for more egalitarian treatment were dismissed as troublemakers, traitors to an "American Way" that often put civility and social harmony above all else.

If calls for national unity—and appeals to a consensus defined by a common enemy—shaped debates over the nation's political economy during the war years, they also had a profound effect on discussions of ethnicity, religion, and race. Federal agencies, political commentators, Hollywood, the news media, and an array of civic organizations celebrated America's "democratic diversity" in speeches, movies, radio shows, educational pamphlets, and a variety of other venues. Such paeans to cultural pluralism were designed both to bolster the morale of the nation's heterogeneous population and to distinguish the U.S. from its fascist (or totalitarian) enemies. At the same time, federal officials and many civic leaders worried about the potential for social unrest—or even violence—as Americans of widely differing backgrounds were flung together in military training camps and overcrowded war production centers. Thus, even as they hailed America's diverse demographic strands, they appealed for "tolerance" in the name of national defense.

This formulation made pluralism a corollary of consensus. It promoted a more inclusive vision of U.S. society by recognizing the contributions that ethnic, religious, and racial "outsiders" had made to American life. It also provided a powerful rhetorical tool with which to condemn bigots and bullies of all stripes. At the same time, this vision of unity and difference emphasized teamwork and assumed that all groups in American society were working toward the same ends. Distinct ethnic, religious, racial, regional, or class interests were legitimate only to the degree that they could be aligned with or subsumed within the values and interests of the nation as a whole. The implications of this linkage of pluralism to consensus had markedly different implications in the arenas of ethnicity, religion, and race.

"Our Enemies Within"

Even before the Japanese attack on Pearl Harbor, some groups promoting cultural pluralism and intergroup harmony in the U.S. hoped to link their cause to the issue of national security. In early 1941, for instance, staffers at the American Jewish Committee (AJC) argued that the Nazi blitzkrieg of the previous year gave the organization "a unique opportunity to discredit anti-Semitism not merely in terms of Americanism, decency and fair play, as in the past, but also in terms of American defense and national survival."[2] Many Americans believed that only a fifth column could explain Germany's string of military successes, and particularly France's speedy collapse in June of 1940.

Playing off of Nazi racialism, both the AJC and its ally, the National Conference of Christians and Jews (NCCJ), argued that bigots formed just such a fifth column. Anti-Semitism, the NCCJ's Everett Clinchy argued, was a "Nazi trick" that Hitler had used to divide and undermine Western democracies.[3]

In the months leading up to Pearl Harbor—and particularly after the U.S. entry into the war—a host of liberal organizations joined the AJC and the NCCJ in preaching tolerance in the name of national unity and defense. Schools and civic groups across the country showed the NCCJ filmstrip *The World We Want to Live In* and listened to conference speakers decry religious conflict as "a trick to weaken and destroy us." The Council Against Intolerance spread the theme through annual Independence Day celebrations in several cities, which were broadcast over national network radio. It also distributed to schools materials urging tolerance, including the aptly named magazine *American Unity*. A group called Citizens for Educational Service Inc. issued a pamphlet entitled *Footprints of the Trojan Horse,* which depicted anti-Semitism as a device being used to destroy democracy one minority at a time. These examples could be multiplied many times over.[4]

Some of this material used rhetoric every bit as hysterical as that used by nativists during World War I or by red-baiters in the postwar years. For instance, the Chicago chapter of the NCCJ issued a brochure entitled *No Ocean Separates Us from Our Enemies Within*. The document opened to a collage of Nazi storm troopers, bombed-out buildings, and stricken women and children refugees. "Enemies Within Hastened the Fall of Democratic, Liberty Loving Nations Abroad—National Defense Demands National Unity," the brochure intoned. Only then did the brochure make clear that these internal enemies were those who "propagat[ed] lies, suspicion, misunderstanding and intolerance among American citizens of every creed and race."[5]

With the U.S. entry into World War II, this plea for tolerance in the name of national unity became a staple of the federal government's domestic propaganda campaign. The war triggered the greatest internal migration of Americans since pioneers poured over the Appalachians more than a century earlier; by the end of the war, one in every five Americans had left their homes, many for military service or for urban centers of defense production in the North and East.[6] As Americans with different accents, eating habits, religions, political beliefs, and skin colors encountered one another for the first time, both the opportunities and the dangers loomed large. The federal government stepped in to help shape the outcome. Less than a month after the Japanese attack on Pearl Harbor, President Roosevelt warned employers against discharging or refusing to hire workers "simply because they were born abroad or because they have 'foreign-sounding' names." "Remember the Nazi technique," the president continued. "Pit race against race, religion against religion, prejudice against prejudice. Divide and conquer!"[7] An OWI manual distributed to the producers of radio shows declared simply, "Men and women who foster racial prejudices are fighting for the enemy."[8]

In 1944, the American Jewish Committee privately took credit for "making the phrase 'divide and conquer' a household phrase in American life."[9] This is an overstatement, but it contains a germ of truth. The AJC and groups such as the NCCJ with which it worked closely were among the first to cast arguments for tolerance explicitly in terms of national unity and defense; in fact, the AJC helped fund many of the private groups that decried the divisive results of prejudice both before and during the war. Moreover, the Office of Facts and Figures contacted both the AJC and the NCCJ shortly after the bombing of Pearl Harbor for help in crafting an anti-Nazi message.[10]

In any case, the AJC, the NCCJ, and the various organizations with which they were allied greatly amplified the government's message. For instance, they may well have been responsible for a series of advertisements decrying various forms of domestic intolerance that appeared in labor newspapers toward the end of the war. In the fall of 1944, four such ads appeared in the *ITU News*, a bimonthly magazine published in Woonsocket, Rhode Island, by organizers of the Independent Textile Union. Although the ads included a line at the bottom urging Americans to buy war bonds, the bulk of each ad was devoted to a warning about America's "enemies within." "America has its snipers, too!" screamed one ad, under a picture of a darkened street haunted by a sniper and his victim. "They don't stalk through the streets with guns in hand. They don't shoot down children who are out after curfew. But they talk carelessly, unwisely and intolerantly." These American snipers, the ad continued, were "playing Hitler's game by sniping at 'those Catholics,' 'those Jews' or 'those Protestants.'" According to the ad, Hitler also sought to turn "Negro and White, each against the other" and to set "native-born against naturalized citizen[s]." It concluded with an admonition to "Be big…be liberal…be tolerant…Be American!"[11]

The other ads in the series carried similar messages. "Is Hitler Winning a 'Secret' Victory?" asked one. "The Hitler plan of setting class against class, of stirring up racial and religious hatred, is making insidious headway right here in this country—even though our fighting men are giving up their lives to wipe out these prejudices forever." A third ad offered Americans an "Invitation to Committee Suicide" under a picture of a revolver and an engraved card reading, "Hate the Protestants…Hate the Catholics…Hate the Jews." [Figure 5.1] The fourth ad pictured the mother of two American servicemen. The woman knitted sweaters for her soldier sons, sent them chocolate cakes, and urged her husband to purchase more war bonds. But despite such

Figure 5.1. This image graced the 14 August 1944 cover of *The Union*, a publication put out by the CIO-affiliated International Union of Mine, Mill and Smelter Workers. A similar image appeared in the *ITU News*, published in Woonsocket, Rhode Island, by organizers of the Independent Textile Union. The ITU version, however, dropped the line about Negroes and added text at the bottom that equated tensions between classes to racial and religious hatred (courtesy of the United Steelworkers; reproduced by the Wisconsin Historical Society).

patriotic acts, the ad charged, this woman was an enemy agent. Through her "thoughtless remarks" about neighbors of different religions, skin colors, and ethnicities, she spread "hatred and distrust" among groups of Americans. "As surely as though you landed on these shores in the dark of night from a submarine, bent on blowing up factories and burning bridges," the ad warned the woman, "in spite of your charming manner and your all-out war record, lady, you are a *saboteur*."[12]

As Gary Gerstle has noted, the message of cultural pluralism and tolerance contained in these ads appealed to the French Canadian workers who made up the bulk of the Independent Textile Union. French Canadians had faced fierce anti-Catholic prejudice in America, and "the nation's decision to attach so much importance to the fight against religious discrimination appeared to them an unprecedented opportunity to integrate themselves into American life." Moreover, the language of loyalty and betrayal that suffused the ads undoubtedly resonated with workers who were being pressured by the government to give their full support to the war effort. In the later years of the war, ITU leaders themselves increasingly adopted the language and sentiments contained in the ads. In doing so, they embraced a version of cultural pluralism that emphasized the rights of ethnic individuals rather than of ethnic communities. (As the "Sniper" ad declared, "We're *all* Americans if we believe in the American ideal of 'inalienable rights,' of 'equality of opportunity'...of 'freedom of the individual!'") This, writes Gerstle, "threatened to undermine...the ethnic enclave's communalist orientation," an orientation that provided one of the sources of its labor radicalism.[13]

Moreover, these ads—like other private and governmental appeals for tolerance during the war—often equated tensions between classes to racial and religious hatred. Some versions of the "Suicide" ad, for instance, suggested that "Capital is profiteering" was as much an example of treasonous bigotry as "The Negro is rebelling" or "Attack the Jews." (This cast in a more colorful vein the OWI statement that economic groups—like religious, racial, or social ones—were illegitimate targets for "prejudice, animosity or hostility.") Such propaganda for tolerance challenged "the notion that the relations between capital and labor formed the central political and moral question of modern American life," Gerstle observes. At the same time, it obscured "the fundamental inequality in capital-labor relations."[14] Both these ideas had been central to the vision of Americanism offered by the industrial labor movement and its left-liberal allies before the war. During the war, however, these assumptions were undermined, not only by the conscious campaigns of America's business community, but also by the federal government and many of the private organizations that sought to instill the values of cultural pluralism and intergroup harmony in the American people.

"Steam from the Melting Pot"

The notion that bigots were "enemies within" was not the only method used to promote tolerance and cultural pluralism during the war. One of the most common formulas for portraying—and thus furthering—America's pluralistic unity was that used in more than a dozen World War II combat films. During and after the war, Hollywood turned out numerous combat films featuring platoons, bomber crews, or other small combat units comprised of men of widely varying backgrounds: a WASP from New England, a Kansas farm boy with a German surname, an Irish Catholic, a Jew or Italian from Brooklyn, a southerner, a Polish American from the Midwest, and so on. These films showed diverse Americans—Americans divided by region, ethnicity, religion, class, rank, service, and sometimes race—uniting to battle the Nazi or Japanese enemy, sacrificing when necessary for the common cause. The same formula was widely employed in radio shows, books, cartoons, and other formats.

Scholarly discussions of these films and similar cultural artifacts have focused particular attention on their "roster[s] of exotic ethnic surnames."[15] One historian has argued that "ethnicity and region of origin" were the "key differences" reflected in these movies, precisely because many liberals assumed that such attributes among whites were "of no real consequence."[16] Other scholars have invoked the "sprinkling of Italians, Poles, Irish, and Scandinavians" in such films as evidence of the wartime "celebration of the ethnic diversity of the American people."[17] To still others, they offer evidence of the ultimate triumph of the "nation of nations" approach espoused by Louis Adamic.[18]

There is no question that the "Americans All" approach to national unity during World War II diverged sharply from the "100 percent Americanism" that dominated public discourse during World War I. Nevertheless, the scholarly emphasis on wartime celebrations of ethnicity has tended to mask lingering concerns on the part of both private groups and many federal officials about the loyalties and predilections of America's foreign nationality groups. In the late 1930s and early 1940s, left liberals such as Louis Adamic and his colleagues at the Common Council for American Unity worried nearly as much about tensions *among* America's ethnic groups as about prejudices aimed at them by the native born. Both the AJC and the NCCJ cast intolerance as an alien rather than a homegrown philosophy and defined bigotry, particularly anti-Semitism, as an Old World disease. Thus, they saw recent immigrants— those who had not yet been fully Americanized—as particularly susceptible to prejudice.[19] Such fears were not limited to cosmopolitan leftists and inter-group liberals, and they did not abate when the U.S. entered World War II. In a September 1942 article entitled "Steam from the Melting Pot," *Fortune* warned that ethnic Americans might form a fifth column. The nation's foreign-language groups, the magazine declared, comprised "a replica of explosive Europe on U.S. ground."[20]

Federal officials too worried about loyalties and prejudices imported from the Old World. While some in the government saw ethnic groups as an asset—a powerful weapon able "to influence opinion and events in their native countries abroad"—others feared that the loyalties of foreign-nationality groups to overseas homelands could pose an internal security risk, disrupt domestic unity, and ultimately undermine the war effort. Such concerns prompted the Roosevelt administration to create several wartime agencies devoted specifically to monitoring and influencing the political actions of America's ethnic communities. These included the Foreign Nationalities Branch of the Office of Strategic Services and the Foreign Language Division of the Office of War Information. Older agencies—the State Department, the FBI, and the Department of Justice—also played a role in these efforts.[21]

Government officials focused some of their concerns on American citizens and residents with ties to the Axis powers, but their anxieties were not limited to these ethnic groups. They also worried that simmering tensions within and among immigrant groups—the strains between various Slavic nationalities, for instance—might erupt, hindering the war effort.[22] Similarly, they feared that Old World hatreds—such as the Polish hatred of the Russians—would hurt America's ability to cooperate with her allies. Such concerns were exacerbated by evidence that overseas interests and governments were trying to manipulate America's foreign-language groups.

Philleo Nash served as special assistant for Domestic Operations in the OWI from 1942 to 1945 and as a special consultant to the Secretary of War in 1943. In both positions, he was responsible for observing, reporting on, and helping craft policy toward America's foreign-language and racial minority groups.[23] In a memo dated June 3, 1943, he warned that American Slovaks, Italians, Magyars (Hungarians), Croatians, and Germans "have been subjected, during the past decade or longer, to foreign propaganda influences hostile to the American way of life, anti-democratic in spirit, working to utilize this country's foreign language populations for political and economic purposes connected with the European, not the American, scene." The Slovaks, for example, "have been subjected to tremendous pressure by both Germany and Hungary seeking to weaken the Czechoslovak Republic by turning Slovaks against it." The Germans sought to destroy the Republic, while the Hungarians merely wanted additional territory, "but the result of their combined activities has been to create such widespread confusion in the minds of Slovak-Americans as to blind them to the real issues of the war." "It is no exaggeration to state," Nash continued, "that an alarming proportion of Slovak-Americans to this day are fearful of the effect an Allied victory in the war will have on the so-called 'Slovak state' and Slovak 'independence.'"[24]

The catalyst for Nash's 1943 memo was the wildcat strike by members of John Lewis's United Mine Workers' union. "Of the 500,000-odd coal miners now out on strike, thus jeopardizing the entire American war effort, approximately 400,000 are men of foreign birth or the sons of immigrants," Nash wrote. Most of the striking miners belonged to one of the foreign-language groups that he had cited as subject to foreign pressure, with the Slovaks being the largest group. "It is a striking fact that the overwhelming majority of the strikers belong to those foreign-language groups which have been least able to assimilate and which have been subject to the heaviest pressure of foreign interests," Nash declared. "The great majority of the coal miners now on strike are ignorant of the broad issues at stake and see no reason why they should place the interest of the United States as a whole before their own interests."[25]

Nash was a liberal Democrat and New Dealer whose family had long been involved in the struggle for racial equality. He himself was a staunch advocate for civil rights within both the Roosevelt and Truman administrations.[26] Yet during the war, Nash clearly put the need for unity behind the war effort above all else. He saw strikes as illegitimate and believed that the willingness of immigrants and their children to walk off the job provided evidence that they had not yet been fully Americanized. This example suggests the moderating impact that the drive for national unity during the war had on many in the liberal community.

One possible solution to the perceived problem of "dangerous" ethnic loyalties was to convert those loyalties into assets by transforming ethnic Americans into U.S. ambassadors. This approach was advocated by voices as divergent as Louis Adamic's and those of the editors of *Fortune*. In his 1941 book *Two-Way Passage*—and in subsequent meetings with the president, Eleanor Roosevelt, and other administration officials—Adamic urged

U.S. policymakers to use American ethnics to "ignite" an "American revolution in Europe." He proposed that U.S. immigrants and their children, organized into national advisory groups, be allowed to develop postwar plans for their ancestral homes, then return temporarily to administer liberated countries after the war. These ethnic Americans would bring peace to Europe, not by "policing" the Continent or imposing democracy from without, but by "cut[ting] loose the vicious tentacles of hate, narrow nationalism, oppression and frustration" that kept the *inherent democracy* in the hearts of Europeans from flowering. Only the U.S. could accomplish this task: Europeans would know that the Americans came not as "strangers; not [as] conquerors or invaders, or intruders—but [as] visitors. We are their nephews and second cousins."[27] This "Passage Back" idea, Adamic suggested, would also help ease America's ethnic tensions, "straighten[ing] out the kinks and quirks in our American innards which come from the 'old country,' from the fact that we're ex-Europeans, escaped Poles and Croatians and Czechs and Scandinavians and Englishmen." Rather than being torn apart by European conflicts, American ethnics would unite around the notion of bringing freedom and democracy to their respective homelands, Adamic predicted. Helping establish a "United States of Europe" would allow ethnics like himself to be "just plain Americans while we're citizens of the world."[28]

Fortune, too, called for mobilizing immigrants in a foreign crusade. Given that millions of first- and second-generation Americans "cannot yet get Europe out of their system," the magazine declared in its September 1942 article, the "only sensible attitude...is to transform our foreign stock into the world's greatest task force of political warfare." Such a move would overcome Old World allegiances and animosities by rallying immigrants to America's cause. "There is dynamite on our shores," *Fortune* warned, "and we should explode it in the right direction."[29]

During the war, the OWI made limited use of this approach. It used antifascist émigrés and high-profile ethnic Americans in its *Voice of America* broadcasts, but such radio programs were designed to shape views abroad, not at home. The federal agency that did the most to mobilize entire immigrant communities—and to channel ethnic loyalties into national allegiance—was the Treasury Department. During war bond drives, Treasury officials and their liaisons in the War Advertising Council worked closely with foreign-language radio stations and with ethnic organizations. They urged ethnic Americans to hold bond drives in traditional costumes and to sell ethnic food at bond rallies. Many immigrant groups clearly understood the message they were being given: buying war bonds was a way to retain their ethnic identity, while demonstrating their loyalty to the nation.[30]

Such campaigns called on first-and second-generation Americans to subsume their ethnic loyalties within their loyalty to the nation. But how was that national loyalty to be defined? Alan Cranston, the liberal New Dealer who headed the OWI's Foreign Language Division, complained in a 1942 speech that many German-language newspapers in the U.S. ran articles on war bonds, rationing, and civilian defense but refused to publish "a single word" condemning Nazism. "If they fail to separate themselves and their people from the Nazis," he asked rhetorically, "how can they possibly expect the rest of the world to make any distinction between the Germans who worship Hitlerism and the Germans who hate Hitlerism? How can they expect Americans in the midst of a death struggle with the Nazis to continue to treat German immigrants as loyal, full-fledged Americans?"[31] This comment suggests that Cranston—like many other left liberals in the OWI—equated American loyalty with staunch antifascism. Many Treasury Department officials clearly disagreed. They equated American loyalty with a willingness to participate wholeheartedly in the war effort, and they worked closely with groups and individuals in immigrant communities whom some in the OWI believed to be profascist.

Similar disagreements divided former allies outside of the federal government. In 1944, Louis Adamic broke abruptly with the Common Council for American Unity (CCAU) and his one-time friend and backer Read Lewis. During the course of the war, the Slovenian Adamic had become deeply involved with the politics of his Yugoslavian homeland and had emerged as a strong supporter of the communist resistance leader Josef Broz Tito. The CCAU, meanwhile, worked with *Amerikanski Srbobran*, a Pittsburgh-based newspaper published by the Serb National Federation, which both Cranston and Adamic believed to be profascist and antidemocratic. In a lengthy memo accompanying his resignation, Adamic suggested that the CCAU's unquestioning embrace of pluralism led it to defend "divisive and dangerous foreign language papers under the slogan of American Unity." He further accused the CCAU of changing an OWI press release on the Nazi persecution of Jews into a statement about the "unconquered men and women of Europe," before translating the press release for use by foreign-language papers. The CCAU, Adamic charged, had "a policy of 'avoiding controversial issues' in such a way as to obstruct, rather than promote, the cause of democracy in the United States."[32] This general criticism seems misplaced, since the CCAU's magazine *Common Ground* attacked both racial segregation and the internment of Japanese

Americans during the war.[33] Still, it points to a critical issue about which even liberals during the war disagreed: what common values united the nation, and how far should tolerance and pluralism extend?

"Believing Americans"

If one solution to the "foreign nationalities problem" was to transform ethnicity into a weapon of war, another solution was to recast American pluralism in religious terms. Tolerance of diversity was widely seen as a primary marker of democracy—a key feature that distinguished the unity of the U.S. from the uniformity of fascist or totalitarian states—but that diversity could take many forms. By speaking of Protestants, Catholics, and Jews rather than of Scandinavians, Slovaks, and Jews, federal officials and other opinion molders could emphasize America's cultural diversity without reinforcing potentially problematic loyalties to foreign homelands.

In the context of World War II, this approach had an additional advantage: it transformed difference into sameness, allowing a single parameter to serve as a symbol of both pluralism and consensus. America had a long and bitter history of anti-Catholicism. Anti-Semitism, too, had surged since the turn of the century and had taken a particularly virulent turn during the 1930s. Still, the idea of religious freedom had long been central to America's national identity. FDR reinforced this connection in January 1941 when he listed religious freedom as one of the "four essential human freedoms" that his policies were designed to secure. During the war, the president and other federal officials repeatedly argued that freedom of religion was "one of the principles for which we are fighting this war."[34]

This vision of the U.S. contrasted sharply with American portrayals of the Axis powers. Today, most Americans think of the Nazis as primarily anti-Semitic, but that is not the way they were portrayed before and during World War II. In a speech in late October 1941, for instance, Roosevelt argued that Hitler's plan was "to abolish all existing religions—Protestant, Catholic, Mohammedan, Hindu, Buddhist and Jewish alike." "The property of all churches will be seized by the Reich and its puppets," the president declared.

> The cross and all other symbols of religion are to be forbidden. The clergy are to be forever silenced under penalty of the concentration camps, where even now so many fearless men are being tortured because they have placed God above Hitler.

> In the place of the churches of our civilization, there is to be set
> up an International Nazi Church—a church which will be served by
> orators sent out by the Nazi Government.[35]

These sentiments were extended to the other Axis powers as well. An OWI publication, *Enemy Japan*, declared that "the official propagandists have taken the simple religious practices of the [Japanese] home and by channeling them through the official machinery of the State have developed the separate national cult, State Shinto." Through the practice of State Shinto, the document continued, "Japanese children are taught the supremacy of the State over the individual, just as in Nazi and Fascist countries."[36]

The notion that the U.S. was fighting an irreligious enemy—an enemy hostile to *all* faiths other than that of the state—allowed religion to play two different, but complementary, ideological roles. "Freedom of religion" could mean both the freedom to adhere to one's own particular faith *and* the freedom to be religious. This approach, which cast religion as a source of unity as well as diversity, had been promulgated by the NCCJ and allied groups since the early 1930s. FDR himself presaged many of the themes the government and others would strike during the war when he delivered a radio address on behalf of the NCCJ's "Brotherhood Day" in February 1936. The day had been set aside, Roosevelt noted, so that "we can meet, not primarily as Protestants or Catholics or Jews but as believing Americans."

> We who have faith cannot afford to fall out among ourselves. The
> very state of the world is a summons to us to stand together. For as I
> see it, the chief religious issue is not between our various beliefs. It is
> between belief and unbelief. It is not your specific faith or mine that
> is being called into question—but all faith.

It was because of that threat, the president concluded, "that you and I must reach across the lines between our creeds, clasp hands, and make common cause."[37]

During the war, this vision of America as religiously diverse, yet spiritually united, appeared in numerous venues: presidential speeches, OWI pamphlets, Hollywood films, the *Why We Fight* series, and numerous cartoons, textbooks, brochures, radio shows, and other materials produced by an array of private groups. Not surprising, the groups that did the most to promote this vision of the U.S. included the NCCJ, the AJC, the B'nai B'rith Anti-Defamation League, and the religious social welfare agencies that came together to form the United Service Organizations (USO). During the war, these groups worked closely with military officials and federal agencies—as well as with Hollywood producers and others—to promote a vision of intergroup tolerance and national unity pictured above all in religious terms. The role of such private organizations only increased after Congress cut off funding to the domestic branch of the OWI in June 1943.[38]

With federal approval, the NCCJ carried its version of the "American Way" into hundreds of U.S. army camps. The army incorporated NCCJ materials into GI orientation courses, and "tolerance trios" visited military installations from Norfolk to Nome. These traveling emissaries conducted "trialogues" before assembled troops, in which they argued that religion was a foundation of democracy, and religious intolerance was thus a danger to America's very foundation. The NCCJ estimated that, in just the first year of the program, more than two million soldiers and sailors attended interfaith meetings or saw the NCCJ film *The World We Want to Live In*. The NCCJ also distributed millions of tri-faith prayer cards, as well as pamphlets with such titles as *United in Service* and *American Brotherhood*. In 1943, the NCCJ's Clinchy lectured on interfaith tolerance to every graduating class of both the Army and Navy Chaplains' Schools.[39]

The NCCJ's message of interfaith tolerance and national consensus was reinforced by the "practical ecumenicity" of the military: nondenominational chapels, an ecumenical Army and Navy Service Book, and a distinctive "Chaplains' Scarf."[40] It was also buttressed by the activities of the USO, which provided recreational opportunities to service personnel and defense workers. Under the organization's umbrella, six national religious agencies—the Young Men's Christian Association (YMCA), the Young Women's Christian Association (YWCA), the Jewish Welfare Board, the Salvation Army, the National Catholic Community Services, and the National Traveler's Aid Association—operated canteens, dance halls, clubs, and recreation centers at more than eighteen hundred locations across the country.[41] A board of directors, which included many prominent businessmen, raised funds for the organization, but it also received federal funding.[42] Through brochures, books, and other materials made available at its centers, the USO promoted a vision of the nation that emphasized both religious tolerance and an ecumenical national consensus. The USO, commented one USO-YMCA leader, was "a demonstration not only of national unity but even more of our basic unity through faith in religion."[43]

NCCJ officials clearly saw their military camp program as an opportunity, not only to shape life in the armed forces, but to head off postwar tensions of the sort that followed WWI. When former Texas governor James Allred addressed sailors assembled at Camp Wallace near Galveston on behalf of the NCCJ, he noted that many veterans would be "leaders in their home communities" after the war. Allred described his own encounter with the Ku Klux Klan after World War I and suggested that it was his friendship with a Catholic and a Jewish shipmate that had kept him from joining the cloaked raiders. He warned his audience that "when this war is over there will be another set of organizers of hate movements" who "will want veterans to join to make their hateful plans seem patriotic." "We congratulate you on your new-found unity," Allred told the sailors, and "we ask that you see to it that hate movements do not get going in the places you live." The NCCJ reprinted Allred's remarks and distributed them widely toward the end of the war.[44]

Although the NCCJ focused significant attention on the military, it did not neglect civilian society. NCCJ staffers, for instance, argued in 1942 that the NCCJ should work more closely with organized labor because "this group includes a large percentage of foreign-born who have brought false beliefs into this nation."[45] (Similar reasoning prompted the American Jewish Committee to launch a National Labor Service in 1945 to "sluice" comic strips, posters, and editorial copy to the nation's unions and labor press.[46]) Cities across the country celebrated the NCCJ's Brotherhood Week during the war, while schools and newspapers used pamphlets, comic books, press items, and other materials distributed by the conference. One such comic book told the story of "three pals"—George Foster, Blaine Kehoe, and Gershon Ross—who had played together on their high school football team. Little distinguished the three friends except for their religions, which were glimpsed through their names and their culinary habits: Gershon's mother cooked gefülte fish, while Blaine could not eat meat on Fridays. After Pearl Harbor, all three enlisted in the war against the "Japs," each with a different service. Each man was killed in action while urging his buddies to "carry on." The final scene in the book depicted the three buddies, arm-in-arm, walking above the clouds. "The three pals will never meet on earth again, but they have done their job gallantly and well; and their spirits mingle as in days of old," the caption read. "Catholic, Protestant, Jew....They died, as they lived...in true brotherhood....Americans All!"[47]

The "three pals"—like the characters in Hollywood's combat films—were fictitious, but a real-life episode in early 1943 followed a similar script and gave the interfaith movement an enduring symbol. On February 3, the U.S. troopship *Dorchester* was torpedoed off Greenland and quickly sank, killing hundreds of servicemen and four army chaplains—two Protestants, a Catholic, and a Jew. As the story was pieced together by the Jewish Welfare Bureau and others, the four chaplains gave up their life vests so that others could survive. The story was widely retold in newspapers and other forums, and posters showing the four chaplains holding hands and praying together on the deck of the sinking ship were distributed nationally. Reproduced on postage stamps, in stained glass windows at West Point and the Pentagon, and in many other artifacts and locations around the country, this image of interfaith and American consensus and unity became one of the most familiar to emerge from the war[48] (figure 5.2).

Groups such as the NCCJ and the USO were at the forefront of efforts to recast American pluralism and consensus in religious terms, but the tri-faith vision of the nation also found support in the business community. The NCCJ had long attracted support from prominent industrialists, in part because it promoted social harmony and emphasized the "dignity of the individual" as a central feature of the American Way. When NAM staffers encouraged businessmen to hold local and regional meetings with clergy during the war, they noted that participants "should include a church group selected and invited by the leaders of the three principal denominational groups (Protestant, Catholic,

Figure 5.2. This postage stamp depicts the four chaplains who gave their lives during the sinking of the troopship *U.S.S. Dorchester* in 1943 and became wartime symbols of American diversity and consensus. The original stamp design included the words "Catholic, Protestant, and Jewish" in addition to the reference to interfaith unity; those words were omitted from the stamp issued in 1948. This may reflect the increasing emphasis in the public arena during the cold war on Americans' shared faith rather than their diverse religious affiliations.

and Jewish)." Conference organizers followed these recommendations; and in cities such as Brooklyn, Chicago, and Los Angeles, the number of Catholic and Jewish religious leaders attending NAM-inspired meetings between 1941 and 1943 actually exceeded the number of Protestant ministers attending.[49]

The combined efforts of the federal government, the NCCJ, the USO, and many other private groups propelled the interfaith movement to new heights during the war. Religious prejudice by no means disappeared—anti-Semitism actually peaked in 1945—but the "interfaith idea" emerged as a powerful symbol of both American pluralism and American consensus.[50] During the war, the notion that the U.S. was a nation of diverse but "believing" Americans—a nation, in particular, of Protestants, Catholics, and Jews—rivaled portrayals of the U.S. as a "nation of nations." In the postwar period, as American enmity shifted from fascism to "atheist communism," religion would increasingly supplant national origin in discussions of both prejudice and diversity in American life.

"More 'American' Than the White Majority"

In the fall of 1945, the NCCJ sponsored a nationwide essay contest for high school students with the theme "The Best Example of Teamwork I Know." Essays were supposed to illustrate "how Americans of diverse backgrounds work together for the good of their school or community, or the nation." The winning composition, dramatized by Hollywood film stars, was to be featured on a national radio program during American Brotherhood Week in February 1946.[51]

Nobukazu ("Noble") Oyanagi, a Japanese American student living in St. Paul, won the contest. Noble wrote about the day that his family was taken from their home in Tacoma, Washington, to the Pinedale Assembly Center near Fresno, California.[52] "As we worked in our home until the train time preparing to leave, in popped one of our dearest friends—Callahan by name, an Irishman if there ever was one," wrote Noble. Callahan took time off from work to drive the Oyanagi family to the train station, where Noble found all of his "buddies" waiting. Joe Mineth, an Italian, and Gus Martigopolus, a Greek, carried the Oyanagis's luggage to the train concourse. Another friend gave Noble a comic book. As the train started to pull away, Noble saw "chums of every nationality" who had come to see him off—"Eric Liljas, a blond Swede; Bobby Feldman, a Jewish pal; the entire Wing family, who, although their homeland was ravished by the Japanese, had no harsh feelings toward us."[53]

Here was a picture of pluralistic America helping to "ease the burden of evacuation" for the Oyanagi family.[54] But there was much that the story left out. Shortly after Pearl Harbor, three FBI agents had come to the family's home, searched the residence, and—without explanation—taken Noble's stepfather with them. Told they would soon have to evacuate, the rest of the Oyanagi family quickly sold off the inventory of the family grocery store and stored their household furnishings in a church building. Taking only what they could carry, Noble, his mother, and his two older brothers boarded a train and "traveled with shades down and accompanied by military carrying side arms and rifles."[55] Three months after arriving at Pinedale, the family was transferred to the Tule Lake internment camp in northern California. Noble himself spent a year and half at Tule Lake, before joining an older brother who had been allowed to leave the camp to attend college in St. Paul. When Noble's high school English teacher handed him the essay assignment, his parents were still in the camp.[56]

Perhaps because of the uncertainty of his family's situation, Noble mentioned none of this in his winning essay. Instead, the teenager wrote, "It was truly teamwork in action that I witnessed that day." But teamwork for what? Neither Noble nor his friends challenged the legitimacy of the evacuation, although the youth did note that for him it was a "gloomy, dismal day." Rather, the essay—and certainly the accompanying press materials—implied that internment was simply the sacrifice Japanese Americans had to make for their country, just as other Americans had to invest in war bonds, donate blood, or forego strikes. By celebrating the pluralistic unity of the friends who accompanied the Oyanagis to the train station, the essay and attendant publicity deflected attention from the justice of the internment policy itself.

Noble's essay, although written some weeks after V-J day, provides a striking example of the potentially conservative implications of linking tolerance to national unity during the war. Wartime celebrations of American pluralism highlighted the contributions of diverse cultural groups to U.S. society but rarely addressed the terms of their inclusion in the nation. Meanwhile, appeals for tolerance in the name of national unity stressed comity and social harmony above all else. Such appeals could be used to condemn bigots and bullies, but they could also be used to critique those who protested too vigorously. Thus, they provided at best a weak tool with which to critique national policy, contest existing power structures, or protest the economic and legal status quo.

As this suggests, the promise of the wartime discourse on pluralism and consensus was limited when it came to the nation's racial minorities—particularly

Japanese Americans and blacks. U.S. propaganda of all sorts stressed the racism of the Nazis, just as it stressed their hostility to all forms of legitimate faith. This gave activists an opening. Some linked appeals for American "brotherhood" to demands for civil rights and civil liberties or portrayed segregation and institutionalized discrimination as a Nazi tactic to "divide and conquer." Racial prejudice, however, was embedded far more deeply in American law and social custom than were ethnic and religious prejudices. Thus, challenges to racial prejudice—and particularly efforts to secure *equality* rather than mere civility—were far more likely to trigger social unrest. Federal policymakers and many in the intergroup movement hoped to dampen racial hostility and to bolster the morale of black Americans; at the same time, they worried about antagonizing whites. When it came to issues of race, the federal government and many private groups trod cautiously—preaching tolerance and working to defuse racial violence, while balking at the concrete steps needed to end discrimination and dismantle Jim Crow.

Federal officials had plenty of reason to be concerned about the challenge to national unity posed by issues of race. Even after the attack on Pearl Harbor, some black Americans felt a measure of sympathy for Japan, which claimed to be fighting white European colonialism in Asia. This argument seemed all the more convincing to some in the black community since America's staunchest ally, Great Britain, oversaw a large empire comprised primarily of brown and black people. Black Americans did not support Hitler, but many likened British imperialism and American racism to the Nazi's treatment of Jews, Gypsies, and other "undesirables." Their anger at the U.S. was not limited to the American South. Major defense employers regularly discriminated against blacks, in many cases encouraged by unions. During the war, the army and navy assigned black recruits to segregated units and trained them almost exclusively for noncombatant roles as cooks, dishwashers, stewards, stevedores, and hard laborers. The Marine Corps and Army Air Corps accepted no blacks in the early months of the war. Adding insult to injury, the military segregated blood plasma, although the plasma of blacks and whites was identical.

Wartime conditions only heightened the opportunities for festering racial hatreds or resentments to explode into violent clashes. During the war, some seven hundred thousand black civilians—as well as hundreds of thousands of whites—left the South mostly for overcrowded war production centers in the West and North.[57] The influx of black workers triggered scores of "hate strikes" by whites, who resented the sight of "former janitors or cafeteria workers running a drill press or lathe."[58] Competition for scarce housing triggered bloody confrontations—usually instigated by whites—in Detroit; Chicago;

Beaumont, Texas; and other cities. Meanwhile, northern blacks who joined the military often found themselves shipped to training camps in the South, where they were subjected to the humility of segregation for the first time. Many of the worst racial clashes broke out in such training centers, as well as in army and navy encampments in such far-flung locations as Lancashire, England, and Guam.[59]

Most black leaders went to great lengths during the war to stress the loyalty of their people to the American cause. In a 1942 article in the *American Mercury*, the author J. Saunders Redding recounted the mental process through which he came to realize that "I believe in this war." Although there was much about the war he did not like, ultimately "this is a war to keep men free," Redding wrote. "We Negroes here in America know a lot about freedom and love it more than a great many people who have long had it." Black Americans needed to continue to struggle "to enlarge freedom here in America," but "our first duty is to keep the road of freedom open," Redding concluded.[60] Asked to address the question "Should the Negro Care Who Wins the War?" the influential black educator Horace Mann Bond argued that the "Negro in the U.S." was in fact the "quintessential American." He elaborated, playing on lingering concerns about the loyalty of immigrants and their children: "By ancestry, by birth, and by the tradition of his history, the Negro is, indeed, more 'American' than the white majority," Bond wrote. "The very fact of [the Negro's] separation from any past or present national existence—German, English, Welsh, Scotch, Irish, Swedish, Italian, Polish, Finnish, Hungarian, or what have you— guarantees the purity of his national allegiance to the American ideal, and his relative freedom from the bastardizing influences of the 'mother-country consciousness' which has so corrupted America in recent years."[61]

Despite such assurances, concerns about black loyalty and morale both immediately before and during the war gave civil rights activists a limited political lever. The first to grasp this possibility was A. Philip Randolph, the powerful head of the all-black Brotherhood of Sleeping Car Porters. In the summer of 1941, Randolph threatened to lead one hundred thousand blacks on a march on Washington to protest segregation in the armed forces and racial discrimination in defense industry hiring. As Carey McWilliams later observed, the march was called "during the period of national emergency proclaimed after the fall of France," a period when American leaders were particularly alert to the dangers of internal disunity. FDR tried to convince Randolph to call off the march, but the union leader would not budge. The president found he could only prevent the march by issuing an executive order banning racial discrimination in the defense industry. The Fair Employment Practices

Commission, set up as a result of the president's order, had limited enforcement powers. Still, as McWilliams noted, it marked a historic reversal of the federal government's "laissez-faire policy based on the assumption that there was nothing the federal government could do to protect the civil rights of citizens of the United States."[62] That policy had been in place since the end of Reconstruction. The establishment of the FEPC thus marked a key turning point on the road to the postwar civil rights movement.[63]

Randolph's success in the summer of 1941 emboldened other civil rights advocates. The nation's largest-circulation black newspaper, *The Pittsburgh Courier*, had earlier dismissed Randolph's strategy as "a crackpot proposal." Now it called for a "Double V" campaign—"victory over our enemies at home and victory over our enemies on the battlefields abroad." The CIO, at its November 1941 convention, condemned discrimination in hiring as a "direct attack against our nation's policy to build democracy in our fight against Hitlerism"; a year later it founded a permanent Committee to Abolish Racial Discrimination (CARD).[64] In 1942, the Council Against Intolerance made national headlines when it called for an integrated army division.[65] That same year, students at the University of Chicago, inspired in part by Randolph's example, organized the Congress on Racial Equality (CORE). CORE cells quickly sprouted in other cities and began holding interracial demonstrations to integrate theatres, restaurants, bus lines, skating rinks, and other facilities.[66] The Howard University students who sat in at Thompson's in April 1944 drew their inspiration from both Randolph and CORE.

Such efforts often met resistance, and many organizations that advocated racial "tolerance" as an essential feature of the American Way stopped short of promoting equality. In March 1942, for instance, NCCJ staffers recommended that the organization take on race more directly and shift from "publicizing the ideal of tolerance" to attacking actual instances of intolerance through direct action. The organization's president and board of trustees rejected the proposal. When the Conference's "tolerance trios" visited army camps, they spoke to troops rigidly segregated by race.[67] A comic book entitled *They Got the Blame: The Story of Scapegoats in History* was distributed by the YMCA and other groups promoting religious, ethnic, and racial harmony. The comic denounced the "torture" and "terrorizing" perpetrated by the Ku Klux Klan in the past but suggested that "the Negro race is today approaching the political, economic and social position which the American Way of Life guarantees to all."[68] (The comic also discussed Irish immigrants, Catholics, and Jews, but no other group required a similarly reassuring statement.) Even the CIO's Committee to Abolish Racial Discrimination (CARD) adopted a relatively cautious approach. During the war, CARD sponsored conferences designed to further racial understanding, mobilized support for the FEPC, pushed for nondiscriminatory public housing, and encouraged unions to push for contract clauses that prohibited discrimination in hiring. Nevertheless, as Robert Zieger has argued, "Its statements stressed good citizenship, reasoned appeals, and moderation." CARD "discouraged racial militancy," and its publications largely avoided the issues that most often caused racial tensions in the workplace, including disputes over job assignments and the promotion of black workers.[69]

Operating within this constraining environment, black Americans made what progress they could. In the fall of 1942, Frank Capra hired the black scriptwriter Carlton Moss to work on an army orientation film entitled *The Negro Soldier*. The army hoped the film would help bolster the morale of black GIs and defuse racial tensions in the military by teaching "comradely regard across racial lines." Moss decided to "ignore what's wrong with the army and tell what's right with my people." He hoped that by doing so he would prompt whites to ask, "What right have we to hold back a people of that caliber?" The resulting film contrasted Nazi racism to the "American Way," hailed the contributions of black Americans to past wars and iconic moments in American history, and followed a light-skinned black soldier through Officer Candidate School. The film managed to avoid any reference to slavery, Jim Crow, or racial segregation in the army, but it was filled with images of well-dressed, responsible, church-going, and patriotic black Americans.[70]

The army originally intended to show the film only to black recruits; but when it was finished in early 1944, black activists and social scientists in the army urged that it be shown to white soldiers as well. Army brass and top officials in the War Department personally screened the film and required a series of specific changes designed to avoid antagonizing whites. For instance, they demanded that a sequence showing a white nurse massaging the back of a black solider be cut, even though the army used white medical staff to treat black GIs. After a series of test screenings before both black and white audiences, the army made *The Negro Soldier* mandatory viewing for soldiers of all races at U.S. replacement centers. It also released the film to civilians.

Despite the film's failure to confront racial inequalities directly, the NAACP and other civil rights groups worked overtime in the final years of the war to promote the film both to commercial theatres and to schools and civic organizations. In an era when most Hollywood films used blacks as comic relief, *The Negro Soldier* marked the beginning of a turning point. Alfred Hitchcock's film *Lifeboat*, released the same month as *The Negro Soldier,* also included a black American in its diverse and "democratic" crew, and it was this man who ultimately disarmed the Nazi submarine captain. The black, however, was a steward, and, when given the chance, he refused to vote on who should captain the lifeboat.[71] Moreover, he was the only member of the crew who did not join the frenzied mob that beat the Nazi to death toward the end of the film. The image of a black man killing a white—even an avowed enemy—was still far too controversial in wartime America.

Both *Lifeboat* and *The Negro Soldier* appeared just months after race riots erupted in cities across the country, threatening to turn American unity into a shambles. The trouble began in Mobile, Alabama, in late May when white ship-yard workers rioted over the promotion of black welders. In early June, gangs of white soldiers and sailors—destined for the bloody war in the Pacific—prowled the Mexican American districts of Los Angeles, beating up youths wearing zoot suits and anyone else who got in their way. In mid-June, a race riot shook Beaumont, Texas, and in late June, Detroit exploded. By the time federal troops were called in to quell the violence, twenty-five blacks and nine whites lay dead, while nearly a thousand were injured. In August, a race riot in Harlem claimed six black lives and sent hundreds more to the hospital.

The race riots of 1943 shocked Americans, focusing a spotlight on ra-cial tensions across the country and launching what quickly became known as the "Civic Unity Movement." In the months that followed, hundreds of cities, states, religious groups, and community organizations set up commit-tees designed to investigate and defuse tensions among ethnic, religious, and particularly racial groups. Racial liberals and civil rights advocates generally applauded this move. Robert Weaver, the New Dealer who would eventually become America's first black cabinet secretary, wrote in *Phylon* in 1944, "The most outstanding feature of this development has been the official recogni-tion of the race problem in the North."[72] In 1951, Carey McWilliams argued that the civic unity movement had brought the struggle for racial justice to the attention of community leaders across the nation and helped to "organiz[e], for the first time, a public opinion on the subject."[73] Some historians have suggested that this network of organizations "shaped the incipient civil rights movement in the years before protests against racial discrimination gained widespread national attention."[74]

If these committees focused attention on the "race problem," however, they also shaped the way it was understood in many quarters. Thus, their actions underscore the ambivalent legacy of America's wartime discussion of plural-ism and consensus for issues of race. Some groups did take steps to promote civic unity by addressing underlying issues of racial inequality. In 1945, for instance, the mayor's Civic Unity Committee in Seattle worked with the local transit company, the bus drivers' union, and the Urban League to reverse a long-standing ban on hiring black drivers.[75] In 1949, the Toledo Board of Community Relations took credit for convincing local hospitals to hire black nurses and for persuading Toledo hotels to open their doors to all customers.[76] Such achievements generally resulted from behind-the-scenes blandishment. Most civic unity committees shunned litigation and direct action—tactics that, after all, would increase racial tensions by antagonizing discriminators.

Ultimately, as its name suggests, the civic unity movement was most concerned with promoting social harmony. The Seattle Mayor's Committee persuaded local newspapers not to print stories about confrontations between whites and blacks on the city transit system and to play down the return of Japanese Americans to the West Coast. It worried that coverage of both issues would inflame racial tensions and perhaps even incite further violence.[77] In Chicago, tensions over housing, particularly black efforts to move into neighborhoods claimed by whites, led to "chronic urban guerilla warfare" between 1944 and the end of the decade. Yet hundreds of racial "incidents"—ranging from vandalism to arson bombings to full-scale riots involving thousands— were barely covered by the city's major metropolitan dailies. The Mayor's Committee on Race Relations and its successor, the Chicago Commission on Human Relations, convinced the city's white-owned papers that covering such episodes would only fan the flames of racial unrest.[78] Such steps helped sustain an image of racial harmony and consensus well into the postwar period that was often at odds with events on the ground.

"The House I Live In"

In the waning months of World War II, the black folk singer Josh White performed a patriotic ballad entitled "The House I Live In" in venues around New York City. At roughly the same time, Frank Sinatra made a ten-minute film short built around, and titled after, the same song (figure 5.3). Both Josh White's and Frank Sinatra's version of the song opened with the same stanza, a stanza that began and ended with a simple question: "What is America to me?" The two versions of the song, however, answered that question in strikingly different ways. A comparison of these two cultural productions suggests both the ways in which a progressive, antifascist vision of America was tamed during the war and the way that issues of pluralism and tolerance were increasingly cast in religious terms.

Figure 5.3. In the Oscar-winning film short *The House I Live In* (1945), from which this publicity shot is taken, Frank Sinatra chastises a gang of bullies for beating up on a Jewish schoolmate. Although the film has been hailed for promoting racial tolerance, its appeal to brotherhood and American unity is cast largely in religious terms (Photofest).

"The House I Live In" had been penned in the fall of 1942 by the Popular Front songwriting duo of Earl Robinson and Lewis Allan. That October, the New York-based Youth Theatre included it in a "left-patriot revue" entitled *Let Freedom Sing*, and the following spring it received a rousing reception at a May Day rally in Union Square.[79] White's rendition of the song was in keeping with this Popular Front tradition. He answered the opening question with phrases that boldly captured the left-liberal, antifascist vision of the nation. America was not comprised solely of the white, native born, and middle class. Rather, it included "the folks beyond the railroad," "my neighbors white and black," and "the people who just came here, or from generations back." Both versions equated America with democracy, but only White's explicitly cast that vision in economic terms: "A land of wealth and beauty, with enough for all to share." Finally, while White's rendition clearly celebrated America's political freedoms—invoking the town hall and the soapbox, as well as Lincoln,

Jefferson, and Paine—it also emphasized "the tasks that still remain." In fact, White ended the song on this note of hope as yet unfulfilled: "With its promise for tomorrow / That's America to me."[80]

The film version of the song contains few of these politically charged references. Instead, Sinatra answers the opening question with a string of sentimental—and largely innocuous—images of America and its people. America is a plot of earth, a street, the local grocer, "the howdy and the handshake," the corner newsstand, and the churchyard. Sinatra sings of "the worker at my side," but more pointed references to class division are excised. America's cultural diversity is alluded to in only one abstract line: "All races and religions, that's America to me." In fact, when Lewis Allan, the song's lyricist, realized that his line about "my neighbors white and black" had been cut, he became so angry that he had to be removed from the theater.[81] Allan, who had earlier penned the powerful antilynching ballad "Strange Fruit," considered this explicit reference to racial harmony central to the song's meaning. He also used the phrase "The House I Live In" as the title of a brief poem that began with the line "bigot-tree" and ended with the word "lynched."[82]

Journalists at the time and scholars after have praised the film short for promoting racial tolerance.[83] Yet the film's overall appeal for tolerance, brotherhood, and American unity is cast largely in religious terms. The film opens with Sinatra, playing himself, crooning a melody during a recording session. Leaving the studio for a cigarette break, he encounters a gang of boys beating up on a schoolmate. When Sinatra asks what the problem is, the leader of the bullies cries, "We don't like his religion!" The boy, apparently, is Jewish. After several more exchanges—during which Sinatra suggests the gang members are Nazis rather than Americans—the singer gives the youth his lecture: "Religion makes no difference—except maybe to a Nazi or someone who's stupid," Sinatra declares. "Why people all over the world worship God in many ways. God created everyone. He didn't create one people better than another."[84]

National origin as a parameter of diversity is mentioned, but de-emphasized in the film. Sinatra notes that his father came from Italy, although he himself is an American. "But should I hate your Dad because he came from Ireland or France or Russia?" he asks the boys. Sinatra then returns to religion, retelling a true story that was widely invoked by the interfaith movement. A few days after Pearl Harbor, he tells the boys, as footage of ships and bombers fill the screen, a U.S. bomber located and successfully attacked a "Jap" battleship. "The pilot of that aircraft was named Colin Kelly, an American and a Presbyterian," Sinatra declares. "Do you know who dropped the bombs? Meyer Levin, an

American and a Jew. Do you think maybe they should have called that off because they had different religions?" he asks rhetorically.

If national origin gets limited attention in the film short, class divisions and the color line are entirely ignored. None of the boys pictured are black; and in the film, as in the song, Sinatra makes no explicit references to color. Even an issue of central concern to black Americans during the war—the military's segregation of black and white blood plasma—is played out in the film in religious terms. Sinatra learns that the chief bully's father was an army sergeant who received several blood plasma transfusions after being wounded. The Jewish boy's parents both donated blood. "I betcha maybe your pop's blood helped save his Dad's life," Sinatra tells the Jewish boy. Then turning to the bully, he asks, "Do you think, if he'd known about it in time, your father would rather have died than to take blood from a man of a different religion?" Of course, during the war, this was hardly an issue: Jewish and Christian blood plasma, unlike black and white, was mixed.

Such omissions and adaptations are particularly surprising given the collection of men who came together to make the film. Screenwriter Albert Maltz was a member of the Communist Party and was ultimately jailed as one of the Hollywood Ten. Mervyn LeRoy directed and coproduced the short; thirteen years earlier he had directed the gritty and explosive film *I Am a Fugitive on a Chain Gang.* Sinatra, who had been called a "dirty guinea" while growing up in Hoboken, New Jersey, had been giving impromptu talks on racial, religious, and ethnic tolerance at high schools around the country; a few weeks before the release of the film, he spoke to an audience of five thousand in Gary, Indiana, after a high school's acceptance of black students prompted a walkout by whites.[85] All of these men, together with producer Frank Ross and the RKO studio, donated their time and resources, while Allan and Robinson waived their song royalties.[86] Proceeds from the film short were donated to ten charities. Among those who benefited were such leaders in the battles for organized labor and civil rights as the Abyssinian Baptist Church in Harlem, the Highlander Folk School in Tennessee, the Fellowship House in Philadelphia, and the California Labor School in Los Angeles.[87]

It is unclear why these men made the film they did. Perhaps they feared that a film that explicitly confronted racial and economic injustice would be kept out of theaters or would not attract an audience. Certainly, in the context of wartime discourse, couching arguments for tolerance in religious terms was a far safer bet. *The House I Live In* was distributed to theaters free of charge by RKO in the fall of 1945. Hailed by critics and applauded by intergroup activists and the media, it won a special Academy Award in 1946 for its promotion of "tolerance and brotherhood."[88] In its central concerns and formulations, the film looked backward, but it also foreshadowed the direction that discussions of American unity and consensus would take in the postwar years. There would be one central difference: Soviets and their Communist allies would soon replace Nazis and "Japs" as the enemies threatening to divide and conquer Americans.

PART III

Shaping a Cold War Consensus (1946–1955)

CHAPTER 6

United America

On April 16, 1946, millions of children across America sat down before dinner to listen to their favorite nightly radio drama, *The Adventures of Superman.* For more than six years, the "Man of Steel" had appeared regularly on stations affiliated with the Mutual Broadcasting System and battled mad Nazi scientists, sinister and disloyal Japanese Americans, and radioactive monsters. The story line that began that night, however, was different. Entitled "The Hate Mongers Association," it pitted Clark Kent/Superman and his sidekick Jimmy Olsen against a secretive group called the Guardians of America. The Guardians were trying to prevent an interfaith council in Metropolis from constructing a community clubhouse and gymnasium "for the use of all boys and girls in the neighborhood, regardless of race, creed or color." They first set fire to the store of a druggist named David Hoffman, then badly beat a boy named Danny O'Neill who had seen them set the fire. "It isn't just the Catholics, or the Jews, or the Protestants they're after," Kent told Jimmy. "Their game is to stir up hatred among all of us—to get the Catholic to hate the Jew and the Jew to hate the Protestant, and the Protestant to hate the Catholic. It's a dirty, vicious circle, and like Hitler and his Nazi killers, they plan to step in and pick up the marbles while we're busy hating one another and cutting each other's throats. It's an old trick but for some reason a lot of us still fall for it." For the next five weeks, Superman battled not the Scarlet Widow, der Teufel ("the Devil") or the Atom Man—but bigoted Americans.[1]

"The Hate Mongers Association" marked a turning point for Superman. As a journalist for the *New York Herald Tribune* noted, after "years of pure blood, thunder and atomic energy," the caped avenger had begun crusading for "tolerance." In June 1946, Superman fought "The Clan of the Fiery Cross," which was trying to run a Chinese family out of town.[2] (Tipped off by a Ku Klux Klan infiltrator, the show's writers worked real KKK rituals and passwords into the show.[3]) In September, the Man of Steel helped pin a murder on a crooked political boss, who had been accused by veterans "representing the three faiths" of discriminating in job appointments.[4] In early 1947, when the Knights of the White Carnation schemed to keep boys with foreign-sounding names off the West Side High School basketball team, Superman restored the team and exposed the Knights. He also revealed that they had slain a prominent businessmen who had tried to expose their discriminatory actions.[5] Clark Kent/Superman was drawn into many of these crusades by his friend Jimmy Olsen, who was involved with a nonsectarian boys club appropriately named "Unity House."[6] By 1948, Kellogg Co., which sponsored the program, was including short talks on tolerance "before and after each episode by either the 'Superman' actor himself or by the announcer of the program."[7] When Superman made the leap to television in 1951, the show's producers highlighted his newfound mission in their introduction: Superman, the announcer intoned, was fighting "a never-ending battle for Truth, Justice, and the American Way."

Superman's recruitment into the fight for the "American Way"—an American Way built around notions of tolerance and teamwork—reflected a shift in strategy on the part of some in America's business community. Parents, teachers, intergroup activists, and child welfare organizations had long lobbied the producers of comic strips and children's radio shows to make their fare more socially conscious, generally with little success.[8] In late 1945, however, William B. Lewis, radio director at the Kenyon & Eckhardt advertising agency, latched onto the idea as a way of showing that "the interests of the community and those of a commercial advertiser" were not incompatible.[9] Kenyon & Eckhardt had the Kellogg Co. account, and Lewis set *Superman* director Robert Maxwell to work on the idea. (Maxwell was the same individual who in 1943 had told OWI officials that he was "teaching this vast audience [of youngsters] to hate.") In crafting the story line for "The Hate Mongers Association," Maxwell consulted with experts ranging from Margaret Mead to officials at the National Conference of Christians and Jews (NCCJ).[10] Meanwhile, Lewis sold the idea to Kellogg Co. executives.

Their bet paid off. Listener ratings soared, reaching 4.5 million per week by March 1947 and making *The Adventures of Superman* the most popular children's radio program.[11] Two years later, it moved from a fifteen-minute daily slot on the Mutual Network to a full half-hour three times a week on ABC.[12] Enthusiastic letters poured in from parents and educators, and news organizations ranging from *PM* to *Newsweek* lauded the show. The American

Newspaper Guild, the NCCJ, and the American Veterans' Committee honored the series, as did the Calvin Newspaper Service, which provided news and syndicated columns to more than a hundred black newspapers across the country.[13] (Meanwhile, the anti-Semitic evangelist Gerald L. K. Smith denounced Superman as "a disgrace to America" and, in Georgia, the Grand Dragon of the KKK tried unsuccessfully to launch a boycott of Kellogg's Pep cereal.) As a Kenyon & Eckhardt executive told the *New Republic* in early 1947, "This tolerance theme is good business."[14]

At one level, the revamping of *The Adventures of Superman* provides an early example of what is today called socially conscious advertising: Kellogg Co. sought to boost its image and sales by presenting itself as responsible and community minded. At a deeper level, however, the program's makeover can be seen as part of a wide-ranging and multifaceted effort by an array of influential elites in the immediate postwar years to recapture the sense of national unity and teamwork that had pervaded public discourse in the U.S. during World War II. Those engaged in this endeavor included social scientists who worried about threats to social cohesion posed by the "group mind"; intergroup activists who hoped to extend their wartime antiprejudice campaigns; business, advertising, and public relations executives determined to derail the rising power of labor and to halt or roll back the policies of the New Deal; and officials of the Truman administration who sought to unify Americans behind their emerging cold war policies.[15] The motives of these diverse elites differed sharply, as did their precise definition of the values around which Americans should unite. What they shared was a fear of social unrest or upheaval that prompted them to promote a consensual and harmonious vision of the nation.

The breadth and depth of such concerns can be glimpsed in a lecture series held at Columbia University in the waning months of World War II and published in 1947 under the title *Unity and Difference in American Life*. Participants in the symposium ranged from Columbia historian Alan Nevins to Howard University sociologist E. Franklin Frazier, from foundation official Lawrence K. Frank to public relations pioneer Edward Bernays. Many of the dozen individuals who contributed to the published volume stressed Americans' need to recapture common ground after the war. Frank noted that "the democratic faith" required Americans to "encourage individual differences and diversities of all kind." "But," he added, "if we hope to maintain social order, we must find or create some unity, at least in the form of some basic assumptions, some common values." Robert M. MacIver, the Columbia sociologist who edited the volume, linked the need for social harmony to both American identity and the nation's place in the world: "Of all nations, of all countries, ours depends more than any other on the cultivation of co-operativeness and good will between groups," he wrote. "Without that there is no such thing as an American way of life; without that it is very difficult to know that America stands for anything."[16]

But what would produce such cooperativeness and goodwill? What actions or beliefs were required to reinforce this harmonious vision of the American Way? Frazier, addressing "The Racial Issue," argued that the only way for Americans to achieve true national unity was to repudiate the racial "caste system" and fully to integrate "the Negro into our economic, political, and social organization."[17] Other contributors, however, prescribed a mental "reorientation." Rabbi Louis Finkelstein, president of the Jewish Theological Seminary and director of the institute that sponsored the lecture series, argued that Americans needed to be encouraged to think about "the common interests of people as against their diverse interests." "A trade union may regard its interests as opposed to those of the employer; the southern Negro has his quarrels with the southern white," the rabbi noted.

> But the more thoughtful in each group will realize that beyond these divisive interests, there are centripetal ones, shared by opposing groups. The prosperity of an industry often has more effect on the lives of the employees and employers than the results of their struggle against one another. The prosperity and well-being of the South as a whole is more significant in the life of both whites and Negroes than is their relative position in the struggle for power.

Americans ignored such common ground at their peril, Finkelstein argued. Recent events around the globe had shown the threat "to all groups and institutions of democratic lands from emphasis on that which divides us rather than on that which unites us."[18]

Finkelstein's comments suggest one of the reasons that many liberals—even many who supported civil rights and a greater level of economic security for all Americans—abandoned the language of progressive struggle in the postwar years and instead both celebrated and invoked values that they argued were broadly shared by their fellow citizens.[19] Foreign powers and ideologies certainly posed a threat to democratic societies such as that of the U.S., but many believed that the greatest danger to such societies lay within—in the centrifugal forces that, if exacerbated or left untamed, might tear a democracy apart. Many American liberals and European émigrés believed such internal strife explained both the Nazi rise to power in Germany in the early 1930s and the stunning collapse of France in 1940.[20] The dangers of postwar division seemed particularly great in the U.S., where pronounced differences of race, region, ethnicity, and religion compounded those of class, occupation, and ideology. In a 1945 report prepared for the Twentieth Century Fund, consumer advocate Stuart Chase argued that if farm, labor, and business pressure groups weren't curbed and the general interest made paramount, American democracy could succumb like France's had in 1940 or be replaced by a dictatorship like those seen in Germany and the Soviet Union. "Even Germany was a democracy once," Chase warned.[21] Four years later, Arthur M. Schlesinger Jr. invoked similar fears when he used a portion of W. B. Yeats's famous poem "The Second Coming" as an epigraph to his 1949 manifesto, *The Vital Center*:

> Things fall apart; the centre cannot hold;
> Mere anarchy is loosed upon the world...

The poem, composed in 1919, expressed Yeats's cyclical view of history. To many American liberals in the wake of World War II, however, it seemed to capture the danger faced by modern democratic societies.[22]

In their search for shared American values, many liberals took the path advocated by Finkelstein, focusing less on the power imbalances in American society than on the possibilities that individual freedom and economic abundance might open to all. This emphasis enabled them to make common cause with moderates in the business community. Corporate moderates were more inclined than their conservative peers to embrace collective bargaining and a limited role for the state in buoying the national economy. Still, nearly all opposed efforts to curb corporate autonomy by giving workers or the state greater control, and the vast majority wanted to halt or roll back the more radical features of the New Deal.[23] In an effort to achieve these ends— to reestablish their authority by positioning themselves as socially conscious community leaders—moderate business leaders embraced the cause of intergroup tolerance and teamwork. Many had also concluded that hostility between workers of various ethnic, religious, and racial backgrounds could undermine postwar productivity, endangering the high-production– high-consumption society that was at the heart of their consensual vision of America. Finally, the language of tolerance and teamwork could be extended beyond cultural groups to relations between labor and management as well. Schlesinger recognized the alliance emerging in the postwar period in his foreword to *The Vital Center*. Liberals, he argued, "have values in common with most members of the business community—in particular, a belief in free society—which they do not have in common with totalitarians."[24]

Schlesinger's reference to "totalitarians" highlights a final emerging link among intergroup liberals, many businessmen, and the federal government. During World War II, those who argued for tolerance in the name of national unity most often invoked a common enemy who sought to "divide and conquer" Americans. During the war, the precise identity of this common enemy was vigorously contested: those on the liberal left portrayed fascism as the nation's principal other; many conservatives cast totalitarianism in this role; and others looked simply to the Axis powers. The language of antifascism allowed liberals and leftists to promote civil rights and economic egalitarianism and to decry red-baiting alongside other forms of prejudice. In the months immediately following V-J Day, many liberals—including those who wrote for *The Adventures of Superman*—continued to invoke fascism as the force threatening to divide and conquer Americans. With the Axis powers defeated, however, this argument proved less and less persuasive. Meanwhile, the Truman administration quickly shifted its attention from the fascist to the communist threat. By 1948, many other American liberals had done the same. The communist threat, like the fascist one, could be deployed against ethnic, religious, and racial prejudice, but it was less effective in arguing for economic egalitarianism. At the same time, it opened the door to a new form of ideological intolerance: red-baiting.

Wanted: "Indoctrination in Democracy"

Long before the Japanese surrender, federal officials, military leaders, and a range of civilian elites worried about the breakdown in social order that might follow the war. They had ample cause for concern. Military service and the lure of jobs in defense plants had uprooted millions of Americans, throwing people of diverse backgrounds, habits, and beliefs together in army camps, transient communities, and crowded production centers. Postwar demobilization would unleash some eleven million veterans onto the American economy, and many experts believed that postwar cutbacks in federal defense spending would trigger an economic downturn, if not a full-blown depression. Notwithstanding the passage of the GI Bill of Rights, intense postwar competition for housing and jobs seemed certain. Adding to the social cauldron, more than 110,000 Japanese Americans had been forcibly relocated from their homes on the West Coast and would have to be reintegrated into an American society that, in many areas, remained hostile. Meanwhile, organized labor and black Americans, who had largely put their aspirations on hold during the war, seemed sure to push for greater political power and more social and economic equality. The race riots and strikes that had exploded across the U.S. in the summer of 1943 seemed only to foreshadow larger problems once America no longer had shared enemies and a common wartime goal.[25]

Those who worried about social unrest were haunted by the "spectres of 1919."[26] In the wake of World War I, more than four million workers had walked off the job, creating the biggest work stoppage the U.S. had seen to that point. The year following the war was marked by some thirty-five hundred strikes, including a bitter police strike in Boston, a general strike in Seattle, and walkouts by coal miners, steelworkers, telephone operators, and textile workers. Lynch mobs rampaged through the South, and race riots broke out in some twenty-five cities and towns. Across the country, returning servicemen attacked socialists, immigrant workers, and blacks. Meanwhile, a spate of bomb threats and bombings triggered a virulently anti-immigrant "Red scare."[27] President Roosevelt was alluding to all this when he told Americans in January 1944, "We on the home front must see that history shall not repeat itself in postwar hatred and intolerance."[28]

In the months immediately following V-J Day, it seemed to many federal officials and business and civic leaders that history *was* repeating itself. Reconversion from a wartime to a peacetime economy strained American society, fueling inflation, igniting smoldering social tensions, and unleashing pent-up demands. The industry-labor alliance that had buoyed corporate America's profits and prestige during the war unraveled. In November 1945, 225,000 General Motors autoworkers went on strike, demanding a 30 percent wage increase without a comparable rise in prices and—in a bid for true partnership in corporate decision-making—public access to the automaker's books. Over the next year, more than five million American men and women walked off the job in the greatest strike wave in U.S. history.[29] Huge walkouts—occasionally accompanied by violent confrontations—swept through the automobile, steel, railroad, and electrical industries; and a strike by four hundred thousand soft-coal miners in May 1946 threatened to bring the shaky U.S. economy to its knees.

These strikes worried a wide range of American elites, but to many in the business community, they seemed a particularly ominous sign. General Motors fended off the demand of the United Auto Workers that it open its books, and other strikes focused on higher wages, better hours, and job security. Still, many corporate leaders shared the concerns of one advertising executive who warned in 1946 that "business (which rose in public esteem during the war) is again being pictured as the 'villain' in the American drama."[30] The coming months, many believed, would determine America's long-term economic and political fate, and the prognosis was far from clear. The Congress of Industrial Organization's Political Action Committee (CIO-PAC), formed in 1942 to work for a social welfare state, had been widely credited with securing Harry Truman's spot on the 1944 Democratic ticket. Now it was gearing up again. With many economists predicting the return of recession or even depression to the U.S., industry executives and their allies saw the labor unrest as a sign that the New Deal might soon be revived and extended.[31]

The spread of "state socialism" elsewhere around the globe fueled their fears. In France, Italy, and Czechoslovakia, Communist parties emerged from the war as the strongest political blocs. In China, the Soviet-backed Red Army advanced steadily, while in Latin America, leftist parties seemed to be gaining support. Most alarming to many American businessmen was Winston Churchill's defeat at the hands of the British Labor Party in democratic elections. If Britain's beloved wartime leader could be overthrown by an avowedly socialist opposition, it might be only a matter of time before "creeping state socialism" resurfaced in the U.S. as well.

Business groups were by no means alone in watching postwar developments with a growing sense of unease. Many who sought to promote religious, ethnic, and racial harmony were also alarmed by the tensions that the end of the war had unleashed. Throughout the South, black veterans returned home and headed to their county courthouses to register to vote; they also demanded better treatment in other arenas. Their actions frequently drew a violent response from intransigent whites. In Georgia, South Carolina, and Tennessee, black veterans and others who demanded their rights were gunned down or beaten for their "uppity" actions. In late February 1946, a confrontation between a white store clerk and a black navy veteran led to a standoff between whites and blacks in Columbia, Tennessee. Hundreds of highway patrolmen were ordered into the town; they cordoned off the black district and began stealing, searching homes without warrants, and firing indiscriminately at residents. Ten people were wounded, and more than one hundred blacks arrested; two of those jailed were later shot by Columbia police. (Although whites started the confrontation and were responsible for most of the violence, initial news reports stressed black responsibility for the "disorders.")[32] Eight months later in Athens, Alabama, a mob of up to two thousand whites rioted, injuring more than one hundred black residents.[33] Such episodes prompted one southern civil rights activist to warn of the rise of "fascism" in the American South.[34]

The South had no monopoly on postwar racial confrontations. On the West Coast, ruffians threw bricks through the windows of houses occupied by Japanese American veterans, and whites tried to prevent Chinese Americans from moving into some neighborhoods. In Philadelphia, blacks and whites fought in the streets with clubs, bricks, and milk bottles.[35] In December 1946, a white mob in Chicago battled police in an effort to prevent blacks from moving into a veteran's housing project near the airport and stockyards—the first of many such housing riots in Chicago. Although news of such confrontations was often suppressed by local "civic unity" committees, enough seeped out to alarm many intergroup activists. In a speech delivered to an NCCJ subcommittee as tensions at Chicago's Airport Homes escalated, community organizer Saul Alinsky warned that the city was on the verge of a major race riot. In terms of race relations, he declared, Chicago was in "the worst spot we've been in for years."[36]

Not all postwar unrest was triggered by either economic issues or race. Reports of a surge in juvenile delinquency alarmed many federal officials, civic leaders, and opinion molders, as did news that veterans were resorting to violence to achieve even admirable ends. In Athens, Tennessee, in August 1946, a group of veterans stunned the nation by laying siege to a jail, where local officials were counting ballots from the county primary election. The veterans, inspired in part by lectures and discussions on democracy they had received in the army, had put together a fusion slate to oppose the local political machine. When it appeared that the machine was stealing the election—roughing up poll watchers, shooting a black man who tried to vote, and dragging ballot boxes to the jail to be "counted"—supporters of the fusion party resorted to techniques they had learned at war: after waging a six-hour gun battle with equipment seized from a nearby armory, the ex-GIs used dynamite and demolition techniques to blow a hole in the building and rout those inside. Even many who supported the veterans' cause were alarmed by their methods. "Violence begets violence," editorialized the *New York Times*. "A precedent was set in Athens, Tenn., that could be a real danger to this country."[37]

Taken together, this wave of strikes, race riots, and other forms of unrest convinced diverse elites of the need to "re-sell Americanism to Americans."[38] When the NCCJ's entertainment division met in Manhattan in December 1945, the attendees—including Eric Johnston and famed producer David O. Selznick—called for a "militant brotherhood" to offset racial and religious prejudices that had emerged since the end of the war. Johnston had just left his post as head of the U.S. Chamber of Commerce to assume the presidency of the Motion Pictures Producers and Distributors of America. He warned of "the salesmen of dissension, the rabble-rousers and hatemongers" who were "seeking to exploit post-war dislocations and post-war nerves." The solution, Johnston suggested, was a "program of group relations" designed to rebuild national unity and "a more conscious appraisal and defense of American values."[39] Attorney General Tom Clark echoed these sentiments in a speech a year later. "The aftermath of the war has brought its characteristic cynicism, disillusionment and lawlessness," Clark warned in late 1946. "Indoctrination in democracy is the essential catalytic agent needed to blend our varying groups into one American family."[40]

In the months and years that followed, business organizations, federal officials, intergroup activists, foundations, universities, and many in the advertising, movie, and public relations industries heeded that advice. Independently and together, they launched a range of cultural projects—educational programs, advertising campaigns, comic strips, movies, radio shows, and public pageants—designed both to buttress national unity and to shape a consensus on America's unifying values. Some liberals and leftists put equality and free speech at the center of the American Way, arguing (as E. Franklin Frazier had) that the nation could only create abiding national unity by living up to its egalitarian values. Many others, however, privileged civility over equality. They tried to paper over differences and to contain dissent and unrest. They sought to "reorient" Americans, shaping a consensus on American public values by creating the illusion that such a consensus already existed.

"The Best Public Relations Plan for Business That Was Ever Devised"

Although many groups participated in this cultural project, no organization was more central in the decade following V-J Day than the Advertising Council. A peacetime reincarnation of the War Advertising Council, the Advertising Council provided a vital link between the White House, the nation's business community, and the news and entertainment industries. It also worked closely in the postwar period with a variety of organizations that were trying to promote an American Way rooted in ethnic, religious, and racial tolerance. The notion of "public service advertising" implies a national consensus—a broadly shared set of values and social norms—and the Advertising Council worked hard to present itself as all encompassing and nonpartisan. Thus, it provides a useful window into the shifting and sometimes uneasy alliances forged in the postwar period among a range of different groups.

The very existence of the Advertising Council testified to both the continuing strength of anti-New Deal sentiment in America's business community and the conviction on the part of Madison Avenue executives, federal officials, and others that such an institution could help shape public attitudes about issues of national importance. Born in part out of an effort to stave off consumer regulation of advertising, the War Advertising Council had helped "sell" federal programs to the public during the war. In the process, it burnished business's image, impressed federal officials with advertising's power, and established a powerful working alliance between moderates in the business community and the Roosevelt and Truman administrations. After the Japanese surrender, the War Advertising Council confronted the issue of demobilization. If the Council disbanded, many advertising executives feared, Madison Avenue—and business more generally—might lose much of the goodwill it had gleaned. Instead, the Council reorganized as a private nonprofit foundation dedicated to "public service" advertising. (The reorganized Council also dropped the word "War" from its name.)

The Advertising Council's justification for this decision—which contrasted "democracy" with centralized federal control—provides an early glimpse of the philosophy it would bring to many of its campaigns. "Advertising helped us to fight our greatest war, yet remain a democracy," the Council boasted in a 1945 report. "The reason why it did is simple." A warring nation had to acquire scrap, conserve gas, boost its food supply, and man merchant ships—or risk losing the war. "Government cannot do these things. Only the people can. And the people must either be compelled or persuaded—there is no other way," the Council argued. Advertising "enabled this country to fight through our first global war—with a minimum of compulsion. In a period when the trend towards centralized controls might well have become an irresistible force, this was a service of lasting significance to every business and every citizen."[41]

Tools of mass persuasion, so essential during the war, were needed even more in its wake, the Council argued. America "no longer has the supremely unifying cause of Victory. The trend will be to stop pulling together, to stop working for the common good. Group clashes promise to be renewed, old hatreds revived; new war-born discords seem almost inevitable." Moreover, at this critical moment, the federal government was "liquidating" its Office of War Information (OWI). "Should business likewise scrap its information leadership, there would then exist no coordinated method for informing and inspiring the people, or securing public action," the Council warned ominously.

Advertising Council executives truly feared the fracturing of the nation along class, religious, ethnic, and racial lines, and they believed in the power of advertising to counteract such trends. For all their talk of social responsibility, however, they also recognized that the Council was "the best public relations plan for business which has ever been devised."[42]

Luckily for Advertising Council stalwarts, the national media generally supported the plan. The Council's success depended on the willingness of radio networks, major newspapers, national newsmagazines, and outdoor advertisers to donate space and time for public service messages and to include themes from Council campaigns in editorials and news stories. (Advertising Council officials believed, with reason, that if the national media embraced their framing of key public issues, many local media outlets would follow suit.) When War Advertising Council representatives met with editors of *Time*, *Life*, and *Fortune* in the summer of 1945 to solicit their postwar support, some of the editors raised questions about whose interests the Council represented; they were mollified when told that the Council represented the "voice of business." In the end, the Council won financial backing from associations of broadcasters and publishers, as well as from newspaper and outdoor advertising groups. In the late 1940s and early 1950s, the roster of those who served as Advertising Council directors or committee members included top executives in newspaper empires like the *Washington Post* and the Scripps-Howard newspaper chain; general-interest magazines such as *Time, Look,* and *Sunset*; and the national broadcasting networks NBC, ABC, and CBS.[43]

The Truman administration was also eager to maintain a conduit to the American public, particularly as it tried to win support for continued U.S. internationalism in the late 1940s. During the war, liaisons to the War Advertising Council were housed in the Office of War Information. When the OWI was disbanded, Truman moved these functions into the White House itself, a practice Eisenhower continued. Despite their formal titles as White House aides, the individuals who filled these positions generally came from the advertising industry and often identified more closely with Madison Avenue than with administration officials and policies.[44] The arrangement gave the Advertising Council unusual access to the president and conferred on it "considerable prestige."[45] It also blurred the distinction between the War Advertising Council, which worked solely for the federal government, and its peacetime successor, which was an independent organization.

From the late 1940s on, the Advertising Council worked to influence both elite opinion and the broader American public in a variety of ways. Beginning in early 1946, it organized regular White House conferences on pressing national issues that brought together administration officials, Advertising Council directors, and influential individuals who served on the Council's various advisory committees. A conference in February 1950, for instance, drew more than one hundred prominent attendees, including Secretary of State Dean Acheson; Atomic Energy Commission chair David Lilienthal; Marshall Plan administrator Paul Hoffman; executives of General Motors, Proctor and Gamble, Standard Oil, and IBM; CBS's Frank Stanton; Motion Picture Association head Eric Johnston; and Philip Graham of the *Washington Post*.[46] Such meetings bolstered the reputation and influence of the Advertising Council, while giving the administration an opportunity to garner elite support for its programs. In October 1947, Truman administration officials used one such meeting to build industry and media support for the Marshall Plan in advance of submitting cost estimates for the European recovery effort to Congress.[47]

Beginning in 1950, the Advertising Council also brought together business and foundation executives, union representatives, prominent academics, and other opinion molders in a series of roundtable discussions designed to "create a *consensus* [on the nation's core values] that *could* become the possession of the average man."[48] The Council contended that the nation's founding documents—the Declaration of Independence, the Constitution, and the Bill of Rights, in particular—had been conceived in an agrarian age and needed to be updated to match changing conditions: "The impact of industrialization, the growth of great corporations and the development of a type of capitalism found no where else in the world have so altered our social, political and economic systems that the old documents do not now sufficiently define the American Way," one internal memo declared.[49] In an attempt to shape national debate, the Advertising Council sponsored discussions on topics ranging from "The Moral and Religious Basis of the American Society" to "People's Capitalism." Proceedings of these roundtables were collected in a book entitled *What Is America?* which was published by Simon & Schuster and distributed by the United States Information Service overseas. The Advertising Council also sent digests of the discussions to fifteen thousand "educators, college presidents, editors and leaders in business and professional life." These pamphlets were later used by educators in many of the nation's burgeoning citizenship and American studies programs.[50]

With its White House conferences and American Round Tables, the Advertising Council attempted both to mold and to publicize elite opinion on national values. Most of its energy, however, was focused on reaching the broader public through a series of "public service" campaigns. In the postwar years, the Council conducted campaigns on behalf of issues ranging from

Better Schools and highway safety to racial and religious tolerance, European recovery, and the American Economic System. Many daily and weekly newspapers reprinted Advertising Council messages, while nearly eleven hundred magazines and more than nine hundred outdoor advertising companies donated space. (The costs of running Advertising Council materials were generally subsidized in part by regular newspaper, magazine, or billboard advertisers.) Network radio still abided by the radio allocation plan devised during World War II, which slotted public service spots into network broadcasts and included Advertising Council messages in national commercial advertising and entertainment programs. Finally, local radio stations, Sunday newspaper supplements, trade and industry journals, and corporate in-house magazines made frequent use of Advertising Council copy.[51] It is difficult to measure the overall impact of Council campaigns on public attitudes. Still, one indication of their impact on national discourse is the popularity of the figure "Smokey Bear" (created to promote fire prevention) and the widespread use in the late 1950s of the term "people's capitalism," a term heavily promoted by the Advertising Council.

In conducting its postwar campaigns, the Advertising Council operated much as it had during World War II. There was, however, one crucial difference. Before V-J Day, federal agencies set the Council's agenda: the War Advertising Council conducted campaigns solely for the federal government, and it automatically accepted all administration requests for aid. After the war, the Council's board—a collection of advertising and marketing executives drawn from ad agencies, corporations, and media groups—exercised far greater control. "In the old days, the advertisers agreed to take any message which we prepared for them," explained Charles W. Jackson, the Truman administration's chief liaison to the Council. "Under this new arrangement, they reserve the right to accept or reject messages as they see fit." Significantly, the Council also offered assistance to some private organizations whose requests for campaigns were deemed worthy and noncontroversial.[52]

In deciding which campaigns met these dual criteria, the Advertising Council realized that it needed to appear nonpartisan. For this reason, the reorganized Council in 1946 appointed a Public Advisory Committee (later renamed the Public Policy Committee) consisting of "15 to 20 outstanding leaders of public opinion" drawn from "different segments of our population." Issues were deemed to have "passed from the stage of public controversy"—and thus be an acceptable field for Council action—if an act of Congress had charted a "national course of action" *or* if a particular request received the support of three-quarters of the advisory committee. Ostensibly, this setup insured that the Advertising Council accepted only projects "in the best interests of the public as a whole." Members of the Public Advisory Committee, however, were appointed and removed by the Advertising Council, and the group only considered campaigns that had already been approved by the Council's Board of Directors. In 1949, Charles G. Mortimer Jr., the General Foods marketing executive who chaired the Council's board, reassured William Randolph Hearst that the Public Advisory Committee "most definitely" did not "run the show." The committee's most important function—acknowledged in some Advertising Council materials—was "to remove any suspicion that the Council's intent was to propagandize for business."[53]

"United America"

In 1946, members of the Advertising Council, like businessmen across the country, watched uneasily as wave after wave of strikes swept the nation. State socialism had already leapt the English Channel, and to many in the business community it seemed that, if nothing were done, it would be only a matter of time before socialism jumped the Atlantic as well. Thus, even as they sought to reconstitute their organization for peacetime, members of the Advertising Council began searching for ways to rekindle the spirit of national unity that had buoyed production and profits during the war.

One of those at the forefront of this effort was Thomas D'Arcy Brophy, president of the Kenyon & Eckhardt advertising agency and a founding member of the Advertising Council's Board. A descendent of Irish Catholic immigrants to Butte, Montana, Brophy had attended a Jesuit college in Washington State, earned a B.S. from the Massachusetts Institute of Technology, and served in the army during World War I. Brophy had joined Kenyon & Eckhardt in 1931, but two years later, a serious car accident had left him badly burned on his face, hands, and legs. After nearly thirty plastic surgery operations, Brophy had returned to Kenyon & Eckhardt. He was soon elected president and started transforming the agency into one of the nation's advertising powerhouses. In 1944 and 1945, Brophy and his agency had worked closely with the pragmatists in the National Association of Manufacturers (NAM), developing the advertising campaign that eventually drew fire from NAM conservatives. Brophy had also helped organize the United Service Organization, the interfaith group that provided recreational opportunities to military personnel and defense workers during the war. Perhaps reflecting Brophy's leadership, it was Kenyon & Eckhardt's vice president for radio who transformed *The Adventures of Superman*.[54]

As Brophy cast about for ways to shore up free enterprise and to buttress American unity, his attention was captured by the mass turnout at rallies celebrating "I Am an American" day across the nation. The holiday honored those citizens who had been naturalized or reached majority during the previous year. Launched in 1938 by Chicago's Hearst newspaper as a promotional gimmick, it had been transformed into a national holiday by Congress in 1940. During the war, the Immigration and Naturalization Service became a major sponsor of the event. On May 19, 1946, half a million people gathered in New York's Central Park to hear speeches by New York mayor William O'Dwyer, a Catholic priest, a Protestant clergyman, and a Jewish rabbi, interspersed with musical entertainment. On the same day, tens of thousands packed a similar rally at Boston Common, and seventy-five thousand people braved a heavy rain storm to attend a celebration in Chicago. Huge crowds also gathered in Baltimore, Detroit, and Los Angeles. These numbers—together with the willingness of the New York crowd to join in a mass recitation of a patriotic credo—deeply impressed Brophy. "What was behind it?" he asked rhetorically in a memo prepared for colleagues at the Advertising Council. "A deep desire on the part of millions of our people, and especially the millions of foreign born, to reaffirm their faith in American freedom."[55]

Brophy proposed that the business community harness this patriotic energy by organizing a "super-radio program" to be broadcast nationally every Sunday evening. The show would feature acts by top radio entertainers interspersed with brief talks on "Americanism" by a Catholic prelate, a Protestant clergyman, a Jewish rabbi, and a prominent layman "who has come up the hard and American way." Rather than attacking communism or state socialism directly, these men would extol American traditions and opportunities. "Salesmanship can sell Americanism to Americans as well as it can sell soap and motor cars," Brophy exuded.[56] Brophy eventually dropped the idea for a radio show, throwing his energy instead into the American Heritage campaign that is the subject of chapter 7. His proposal, however, highlights several key themes that would emerge, and intertwine, in Advertising Council campaigns in the postwar years: promotion of ethnic, religious and sometimes racial tolerance and teamwork; support for American-style capitalism; and anticommunism.

The Advertising Council threw its weight behind the effort to promote religious and ethnic tolerance a few months after V-J Day, when it agreed to help the NCCJ promote Brotherhood Week in February 1946. The NCCJ had been remarkably successful during the war at spreading its message of interfaith tolerance and civic consensus, and it emerged from the conflict with a new sense of vigor and possibility. At the same time, NCCJ staffers and board members—like those associated with other intergroup organizations—spoke ominously about the dangers of resurgent intolerance. At an NCCJ board meeting in November 1945, one speaker noted that all Americans were minorities of one sort or another—whether by virtue of their religion, their race, or their profession. "We have learned through the dreadful years of hatred which led to the World War that by developing hate against whatever minority may be chosen to be a scapegoat, evil demagogues can become destructive dictators," James N. Rosenberg warned. Such hatred, he added, "can destroy our country."[57]

When the NCCJ first launched Brotherhood Day in the early 1930s, it focused on promoting Protestant-Catholic-Jewish amity and the day was observed primarily from the pulpit. During the war, both the time allotted to the celebration and its message had broadened considerably. The NCCJ continued to emphasize the nation's religious pluralism and to portray Americans as bound by a shared belief in "the Fatherhood of God and the Brotherhood of Man," but Brotherhood Week emerged as a national celebration of American unity and consensus. This trend continued in 1946. At the suggestion of Hollywood producer David Selznick, cochair of the event, organizers renamed the week-long commemoration "American Brotherhood Week," a name they believed had "wider universal appeal in approaching the whole country."[58] This broader focus was also apparent in the slogan chosen for the 1946 observance: "In Peace as in War—Teamwork." As the *New York Times* reported, the American Brotherhood program entailed "mobilization of a vast public opinion against all prejudices that divide one American against another, and establishment of a positive program of civic cooperation among all groups."[59]

This appeal for "teamwork"—which condemned class "prejudices" and tensions as well as ethnic, religious, and racial ones—heralded a shift in emphasis within the NCCJ in the postwar years. Industrialists and other businessmen had always felt more comfortable with the NCCJ than with other organizations that promoted religious and racial tolerance, many of which were further to the left. In the late 1940s, however, corporate support for the conference mushroomed. Airline president Thomas E. Braniff signed on as Catholic cochair in 1946; five years later, Ford Motor Company vice president Benson Ford was installed as Protestant cochair. (Both men succeeded academics.)[60] Roger W. Straus continued to serve as Jewish cochair; so by the early 1950s, all three of the conference's top officials were prominent industrialists. Businessmen, corporate lawyers, and advertising executives also served on many of the NCCJ's committees. Meanwhile, corporate contributions rolled in, including a $1 million grant from the Ford Motor Company Fund in

1951, which allowed the NCCJ to construct a new headquarters building near the United Nations.[61]

This burgeoning business support for the NCCJ in the late 1940s and 1950s reflected a constellation of factors. A growing number of prominent corporate leaders were Catholic or Jewish and thus had a personal interest in promoting a religiously inclusive and socially harmonious vision of American society. Some businessmen had also been alarmed by the eruption of "hate strikes"—primarily aimed at black war workers—during World War II. Although corporations discriminated against blacks in a variety of ways, wildcat walkouts and tensions between workers of different religions, ethnicities, and races threatened the high productivity that had been essential during wartime and that was a centerpiece of the business community's postwar vision.[62] Finally, as Brophy realized, appeals for tolerance and unity could be used to harness the patriotic sentiments of many working-class ethnics and could be expanded to cover relations between labor and management as well. In May 1946, one NCCJ staffer recommended the latter move in an internal memo: "There will be no peace in America so long as there is class warfare," he wrote. "It should therefore be one of the great tasks of the Conference to educate for cooperation between Labor and Management in contradistinction from strife."[63] The NCCJ followed this advice. In 1948, the board approved a resolution to "bring brotherhood into the industrial field." The following year it set up a Commission on Labor-Management Organizations, which launched "Teamwork in Industry" projects in industrial plants around the country.[64]

It was in this broader context that the Advertising Council decided to take on American Brotherhood Week, expanding the observance to a full nine days. With Advertising Council support, the NCCJ recruited former Minnesota governor Harold Stassen to serve as general chairman and President Truman to serve as honorary chair. Spyros Skouras, president of 20th Century-Fox, headed the movie committee; William S. Paley, president of CBS Inc., coordinated radio's contribution; and Advertising Council chairman James Webb Young guaranteed Madison Avenue's support.[65] This network of prominent sponsors paid off. More than a hundred regularly scheduled radio programs—including such popular shows as the *Jack Benny Program*, the *Edgar Bergen/Charlie McCarthy Show*, Walter Winchell's news broadcast, and *Truth and Consequences*—ran special announcements on American Brotherhood Week or incorporated the theme into their programs. Radio shows written specifically for the observation also appeared on all of the major networks.[66] Theatres across the nation screened a three-minute film short entitled the *American*

Creed, which was produced by David Selznick and featured Jimmy Stewart, Ingrid Bergman, Eddie Cantor, Katherine Hepburn, Edward G. Robinson, and Shirley Temple, among others. Moviegoers were also asked to join the "American Brotherhood" by contributing a dollar and signing a short pledge composed by Selznick:

> I pledge allegiance to this basic ideal of my country—fair play for all.
> I pledge myself to keep America free from the disease of hate that destroyed Europe.
> In good heart I pledge unto my fellow Americans all the rights and dignities I desire for myself.
> And to win support for these principles across the land, I join the American Brotherhood, sponsored by the National Conference of Christians and Jews.[67]

Despite the reference in this pledge to "fair play," American Brotherhood Week promoted teamwork and unity above all else. After all, the prizewinning essay written by Noble Oyanagi, celebrating his family's send-off to an internment camp, was also written for this 1946 celebration.

Building on the connection established during American Brotherhood Week, the NCCJ approached the Advertising Council in June 1946 about conducting an ongoing public service campaign designed to "build a united people" by combating "intergroup hatred and prejudice."[68] The Advertising Council's Public Advisory Committee quickly approved the proposal and gave it "top priority." The Council tapped Lee Bristol, vice president of advertising at Bristol-Myers Company, to coordinate the campaign and asked the New York advertising agency Cecil & Presbrey Inc. to oversee the creative work.[69] The American Jewish Committee and the Anti-Defamation League of B'nai B'rith soon joined the NCCJ as sponsors, contributing financially to the costs of producing ads and other materials.[70] The resulting "United America" campaign (which was sometimes also called the "Group Prejudice" campaign) ran from mid-1946 until the end of 1952.

The Advertising Council's involvement with the United America campaign reflected many of the same factors that had attracted corporate support to the NCCJ. In the early decades of the century, the advertising industry had been a bastion of white Protestants; as late as 1931, the editors of *Who's Who in Advertising* had casually remarked that "adherents to the theory of Nordic supremacy might relish the fact that blue-eyed advertising men are in the majority."[71] By the late 1940s, however, the industry's demographic profile was changing. Significant numbers of Jews and Catholics now worked on

Madison Avenue, and they increasingly occupied prominent positions in major agencies; Samuel Dalsimer, the Cecil & Presbrey vice president who helped orchestrate the United America campaign, was also a member of B'nai B'rith's Anti-Defamation League.[72] An Advertising Council staffer recognized the interest such individuals took in "intergroup tolerance and understanding" in a letter sent to officers at major advertising agencies in July 1946. "Ordinarily we ask one advertising agency to do the creative work in any campaign," he wrote, "but, in this instance, knowing how many advertising agency people are interested in the subject, we are asking a number of agencies to cooperate in the preparation of material." Eleven agencies ultimately contributed to the campaign.[73]

Such personal interest only partly explained the Advertising Council's embrace of the NCCJ proposal. In a press release announcing the United America campaign and in letters sent to media outlets and potential supporters, the Council repeatedly linked appeals for tolerance and social harmony to postwar productivity and the nation's stature abroad. Both were issues of particular concern to the business community and to the Truman administration. "Racial and religious antagonisms" in the U.S. "menace existing institutions," "interfere with production in offices, shops, mines [and] factories," and "constantly threaten to break out into open acts of destructive violence," the Advertising Council warned in one such letter. "Division in the U.S. creates an impression throughout the world that America is weak and our country's position and prestige is thoroughly lowered in world affairs."[74]

Similar messages echoed through the radio spots, radio and television "fact sheets," advertising mats, car cards, window displays, outdoor posters, and other materials the Advertising Council distributed to national advertisers and media outlets. "We have two great tasks before us: (1) to build a peaceful world; and (2) to press forward on the home front to high production and prosperity," the Council declared in radio and television fact sheets distributed in the late 1940s. "A divided America, with Protestant against Catholic, Christian against Jew, white against black, native-born against foreign-born, could only serve both to break our production drive and announce to the world that our democracy has failed." The Council urged broadcasters and advertisers to convey these dangers to the public, and it frequently compared bigotry to a dreaded disease. The "individual citizen" could "help keep America strong," it declared, by "isolating and quarantining group antagonism" and by "alertly guarding himself and his family against infection by racial prejudice."[75] The alternative, one radio spot suggested, was foreseen by Abraham Lincoln: "*A house divided against itself cannot stand!*"[76]

Campaign materials generally urged Americans to "accept—or reject—people *on their individual worth*," to shun rumors against a race or religion, and to "speak up ... *against* prejudice, *for* understanding." "Remember—*That's Being an American*," many United America ads declared. One print advertisement, released in March 1948, linked discrimination in the economic arena explicitly to "a lower living standard for *all*." The ad reprinted an illustration from the report released by President Truman's Committee on Civil Rights the previous fall. It then quoted Eric Johnston, when he was president of the U.S. Chamber of Commerce: "The withholding of jobs and business opportunities from some people does not make more jobs and business opportunities for others. Such a policy merely tends to drag down the whole economic level. You can't sell an electric refrigerator to a family that can't afford electricity."[77]

This ad, like most of the other materials produced as part of the "Group Prejudice" campaign, appealed primarily to the self-interest of its audience.[78] Its explicit condemnation of discrimination and inequality, however, was unusual. In framing the campaign, the Advertising Council followed the lead of many of the organizations that had argued for tolerance in the name of national unity during the war; as a result, it emphasized social harmony far more than equality. Campaign materials generally stressed the "antagonisms" and "divisions" that bigotry produced, not the inequities it fostered. This emphasis on a united America begged one important question: Would protest against such inequities similarly imperil the nation?

In their effort to promote national harmony, campaign organizers steered clear of issues that seemed particularly controversial. One ad distributed in early 1948 asked "Who's a Bigot?" and offered "A Self-Quiz for Everyone Who Wants to Be a Good American!" Readers were encouraged to take the quiz and to check their responses against the answer key. The quiz contained probing queries designed to expose "group-thinking," but several questions were eliminated from the final version of the ad. Among those cut were: "Should members of different races and religions marry?" and "Should members of all groups be admitted to any one social club?" In the eyes of campaign coordinators, such questions seemed more likely to open than to heal societal rifts.[79]

Not surprisingly, the issue of black-white relations required particularly delicate handling if the façade of unity was to be maintained. In December 1946, the Advertising Council discouraged the National Association for the Advancement of Colored People, the Council for Democracy, and the

American Jewish Committee from forming and staffing a parallel organization to work specifically with broadcasters. The Council argued that such an initiative would disrupt its radio allocation program and added that such projects should not be undertaken by people who didn't have a strong knowledge of the media industry.[80] The move highlights the Advertising Council's desire to retain credit for the campaign and to control the way national messages about tolerance were framed.

Efforts to contain the racial issue were also apparent in 1948 when the Advertising Council suspended broadcasts related to the United America campaign for at least four months prior to the presidential election. Truman had proposed a sweeping civil rights program early in the year; when the Democratic Party convened in July, a coalition of liberal and labor delegates insisted that it be explicitly endorsed in the party platform. This move prompted a walkout by southern Democrats who quickly formed the States' Rights or Dixiecrat party and nominated South Carolina governor Strom Thurmond for president. "United America has been kept off the air...because the problem of interracial equality has become a political issue," an Advertising Council committee reported. It recommended that the campaign be reinstated after the election because "the campaign is good for the Council public-relations-wise at normal times."[81]

Indeed by the late 1940s, the "United America" message was being disseminated widely through a range of media. Radio was the strongest supporter of the campaign, largely because of the radio allocation program that had been set up during the war. The Advertising Council reported that the campaign received more than 831 million radio listener-impressions in 1947, nearly 923 million listener-impressions in 1948, and more than 1.1 billion such impressions in 1949. Radio spots aired on such popular national programs as Drew Pearson's "Washington Merry-Go-Round," the Jack Benny Program, the George Burns and Gracie Allen Show, the Abbott & Costello Show, and the NBC Symphony Orchestra. The Council also reported that its proof sheets for newspaper ads generated more than nine thousand mat orders in 1948 and an even higher number in 1949. (By mid-1948, some one hundred white southern dailies had used United America materials, an indication of change in Dixie as well as a sign that many of these ads trod lightly when it came to race.) Popular and trade magazines, comic books, buses, subway cars, and commuter trains also carried Group Prejudice material, and a television spot produced in 1949 was distributed to over seventy television stations. In 1948, schools, churches, and individuals requested some twenty-five thousand reprints of ads.[82]

Increasingly, these materials appealed for religious and racial tolerance by warning in overheated language of the communist threat. During the war, those who sought to combat various forms of bigotry frequently invoked an enemy who was seeking to divide and conquer America. In the immediate postwar years, the Advertising Council and other groups tried to resurrect this ideological framework. With the Axis defeated, the precise nature of America's insidious enemy initially was far from clear.[83] By mid-1948, however, this ambiguity had been resolved: rising tension with the Soviet Union had produced a new villain for the drama.

The rapid shift from antifascism to anticommunism can be glimpsed by comparing two versions of a United America ad prepared by the Kenyon & Eckhardt agency and released to the media in February 1948. The advertisement pictured six American celebrities along with a brief description of each: Susan Hayward (Protestant), Spencer Tracy (Catholic), Eddie Cantor (Jew), Frank Sinatra (Immigrant's Son), Marian Anderson (Negro), and Sonny Tufts (Mayflower descendent). The bold-faced caption below these faces read: "But Who Cares?" In the original draft of the ad, which was selected for the campaign in the fall of 1946, Paul Robeson represented blacks, while Edward G. Robinson stood in for Jews. Both men remained active on the political left, and by 1948, the Advertising Council no longer considered them suitable models for Americans.

By the early 1950s, many of the ads distributed as part of the United America campaign powerfully reinforced an anticommunist consensus— often in language that was strikingly reminiscent of the ads lauding religious and ethnic tolerance that had appeared in labor newspapers during World War II. "HOW TO COMMIT SUICIDE" blared one ad released in 1950: "No, not you!—but possibly your country." Ads produced by the Advertising Council in conjunction with Brotherhood Week in 1952 were even more direct. "Are You One of Stalin's Puppets?" asked one (figure 6.1). "Did *you* help make him a *COMMUNIST?*" asked another. A third ad pictured a kindly older woman— clearly shocked—exclaiming "Me…A Red?" This ad, like its wartime counterpart, informed the lady that "those things you've been saying about other people are doing the Communists' work for them."[84]

The wartime ads had often equated tensions between classes to racial and religious hatred. Increasingly, ads produced for the United America campaign took a similar turn. Radio spots and ads distributed in the first two years of the campaign condemned "group strife" but made no explicit references to tensions between workers and managers. By the early 1950s, however, such references were routine. One 1951 ad—"…only silly humans do that!"—showed

Figure 6.1. This public service ad, distributed by the Advertising Council during Brotherhood Week 1952, fueled anticommunism even as it argued for tolerance between other groups in American society (courtesy of the Advertising Council and the University of Illinois Archives).

one bird lecturing another before a sign that read "NO Catholics, Jews, Protestants." The copy of the ad departed from this avian setup, proclaiming "There are those who would give their eyeteeth to see America divided into arguing factions—Labor against Management—Christian against Jew—White against Negro" (figure 6.2). Other ads reversed the direction of class animosity, condemning "Management against Labor."

The Advertising Council discontinued the United America campaign at the end of 1952, largely because of declining financial support from the campaign's original sponsors.[85] By then, however, other Council campaigns incorporated several of its key themes. "Religion in American Life," launched in 1949 at the behest of General Electric president Charles E. Wilson, promoted interfaith unity by emphasizing the shared faith in God that allegedly distinguished Americans from their communist foes. (The Advertising Council agreed to undertake the campaign only if it were conducted on an interfaith basis and advertising materials featured Protestants, Catholics, and Jews.)[86] That campaign, which continued into the 1960s, was only one of many in the postwar years that reinforced an anticommunist consensus. Meanwhile, a series of Council campaigns on economic issues reinforced the notion that individual freedom was a core American value and cast teamwork as essential to postwar prosperity.

Defending "American-Style" Capitalism

In the fall of 1945, officials in the Office of Price Administration (OPA) asked the Advertising Council to run a campaign on behalf of price controls. Severe inflation had plagued the U.S. after World War I; in the wake of V-J Day, it again emerged as one of the most serious and contentious issues facing America. OPA officials, as well as many labor and consumer advocates, favored extending wartime price controls well into the reconversion period. Corporate leaders and business groups such as the NAM and the Committee for Economic Development (CED), by contrast, wanted the controls eliminated. They argued that an unfettered market would spur production and eventually stabilize prices. Not surprising, Advertising Council executives sided with the business community. Somewhat reluctantly, they agreed to run a campaign but allotted it a mere two weeks of radio time.[87]

In the coming months—as strikes spread across the nation and the debate over price controls and the OPA intensified—the Truman administration continued to lobby the Advertising Council to take on the issue of inflation. The

Figure 6.2. The Advertising Council distributed this public service ad in 1951 as part of its "United America" campaign. The text of the ad equates labor protests against management to religious and racial hatred (courtesy of the Advertising Council and the University of Illinois Archives).

Council, however, dragged its feet. Finally, in the fall of 1946, it responded, circulating a confidential proposal for a "Production Urgency" campaign. The proposal suggested that stepped-up production, not price controls, was the best way to curb inflation and to head off "a serious and possibly disastrous downswing" in the economy. Such higher productivity could only be achieved "if all of us make it a common goal," the proposal declared. "We need national unity now as never before." The Council proposed a "national campaign of public information" designed to "rally all elements of our national life around a central goal of increased production."[88]

The Production Urgency campaign never got off the ground, but the proposal provided a blueprint of sorts for one of the Advertising Council's central postwar endeavors. In the late 1940s and 1950s, the Council ran a series of campaigns designed to buttress the "American Economic System" and to promote what the Council—adopting a phrase coined by Eric Johnston during the war—would eventually call "People's Capitalism." These campaigns advanced many of the same ideas and values promoted by the NAM in the late 1930s and, with more success, by businessmen during the war: the high standard of living made possible by American capitalism, the need for harmony and teamwork to reap the benefits of that economic system, the centrality of individual freedom to the American Way, and the inseparability of the nation's economic, religious, and political liberties. Increasingly, the Advertising Council also spotlighted a theme that some in the business community had experimented with during the war. American capitalism, they suggested, had been transformed over the last few decades: no longer the cutthroat version advocated by Adam Smith and decried by Karl Marx, it was now capitalism "of, by and for the people." Chastised by the Depression, corporate leaders had seen the light and were now among the most civic-minded and responsible of American citizens.

The Advertising Council was by no means alone in launching economic education campaigns in the postwar years. In the late 1930s, the business community had been reeling under the combined onslaught of the New Deal and a reinvigorated labor movement.[89] The war had restored the prestige and profitability of American industry—and temporarily tamed labor—but it had also expanded the federal government's role in the economy. Businessmen had hoped that this federal role would recede as soon as the war ended, but debates during reconversion over price controls and other issues reawakened their fears. Industrialists won some victories in 1946 and 1947—most dramatically, passing the labor-curbing Taft-Hartley Act over President Truman's veto. Still, Truman's stunning victory in 1948—in a presidential election marked by "one of the sharpest class votes in American history"—led many in the business community to fear that the New Deal would be revived and extended.[90] In addition to opposing Taft-Hartley, Truman had proposed a full employment bill and national health insurance and lobbied Congress to establish a permanent Fair Employment Practices Commission. Even his preferred strikebreaking tactics—seizing vital industries and drafting strikers—hardly reassured businessmen worried about advancing state control.

Propelled by fears of a renascent New Deal, the NAM, the U.S. Chamber of Commerce, the CED, and dozens of other business groups and corporations jumped into the cultural breach, attempting to shape a national consensus that was conducive to unfettered corporate expansion and economic growth. Over the next decade, they conducted sweeping public relations campaigns designed, in the words of NAM president Claude Putnam, to "sell—to resell, if you will—to free Americans the philosophy that has kept us and our economy free."[91] In 1952, *Fortune* editor William H. Whyte Jr. estimated that American industry was spending at least $100 million annually on such projects.[92] By that year, Robert Griffith has observed, "the detritus of these campaigns lay scattered about America's cultural landscape in books, articles and pamphlets, in motion pictures, on billboards and posters, on radio and television, on car cards in buses, trains, and trolleys, even in comic books and on matchbook covers."[93]

The Advertising Council thus had plenty of company, but its efforts differed from those of individual corporations and many business groups in several respects. Because of its close ties to both the White House and the national media—ties developed during the war—the Council was able to exercise an influence on public discussion that extended far beyond its own advertising campaigns. Moreover, the War Advertising Council had been a quasi-public entity during the war—privately run but working solely for the federal government—and many Americans were unaware of its postwar transformation. The voluntary continuation of the radio allocation program set up during the war and its extension into the new television market meant that many Advertising Council "spots" received ample air time and ran without corporate sponsors. Broadcasters also used Council "fact sheets" to work campaign messages into plots and dialogue. Finally, the Advertising Council presented its campaigns as representing a national consensus; all materials it produced explicitly stated that they had been endorsed by representatives of business, organized labor, and the general public.

The effort required to produce even the appearance of consensus can be glimpsed in the behind-the-scenes maneuvering that preceded the Advertising Council's launch of its long-running American Economic System campaign. In late 1946, a joint committee of the Association of National Advertisers (ANA) and the American Association of Advertising Agencies (AAAA) asked the Advertising Council to undertake a campaign designed to "improve public understanding of our economic system." According to the joint committee,

Gallup polls showed that the vast majority of Americans believed in the "five fundamental principles" of that system: private property, a free market, profit and wage incentives, competition, and "government regulation—but not government control." Yet the public often violated these principles in practice, supporting such issues as "confiscatory taxation" and "the peacetime continuance of OPA." This showed that Americans "lack the necessary knowledge to appraise those issues accurately," the joint committee declared. "The *actions* of broad masses of the American people prove they *do not* understand the economic system under which they live."[94]

The ANA and the AAAA were the two largest advertising organizations in the country, as well as constituent members of the Advertising Council. Together, they were fully capable of undertaking a campaign like the one they proposed.[95] They turned to the Advertising Council because it offered one singular advantage: the appearance of nonpartisanship. As Howard Chase, the General Foods executive who headed the joint committee, stressed when he announced the effort to the press, this campaign would be "completely unbiased and absolutely free from any material which will benefit business interests to the exclusion of other segments of the economy." This nonpartisanship would be guaranteed by the Advertising Council, which "by Government charter, may operate only in the public interest."[96]

On the last count, Chase was misleading: although the Advertising Council had liaisons in the White House, it had no government charter. It did, however, have its Public Advisory Committee (PAC). When the Council began to consider the campaign in early 1947, that nineteen-member committee included the presidents of Harvard University and Hunter College; the famed theologian Reinhold Niebuhr; pollster George Gallup; former New York governor Herbert Lehman; Helen Hall, director of New York's Henry Street Settlement; and Howard University economist E. Franklin Frazier. (Frazier left the PAC within months and was replaced by Charles Houston, legal advisor to the NAACP.) Although Advertising Council directors derided the committee's decision-making power in private, they never underestimated its legitimating force. Even a controversial campaign, if approved by this diverse group, could be presented as embodying a national consensus. Advertising Council vice chairman William Reydel noted in January 1947 that without the PAC, "the Council might have been unable to consider" an economic education campaign.[97]

Securing the blessing of the PAC, however, initially proved tricky. When the group first considered the joint committee's proposal in January 1947, members raised a host of objections:

The economic philosophy expressed in the presentation sounds too "laissez-faire" and "right-wing Republican." The campaign as proposed, stresses production to the exclusion of distribution and, more particularly, of the distribution of the benefits of increased productivity. The themes seem to claim and promise too much and to ignore weaknesses and dangers in our economic system, such as major depressions.[98]

Niebuhr questioned whether the undertaking could be termed "noncontroversial" at all. At a subsequent meeting three months later, Harvard President James Conant argued that the characteristics of America's economic system should be "listed as 'goals' rather than actualities."[99]

In the end, two members of the advisory committee proved particularly central to the approval and subsequent course of the campaign. Evans Clark, executive director of the Twentieth Century Fund, was the man tapped by Advertising Council executives to chair the PAC. Clark ultimately helped bring both AFL president William Green and CIO president Philip Murray on board. He countered arguments made by some union officials that the campaign would undermine labor's postwar position. He also urged labor leaders "to court public opinion," reminding Murray in particular of public hostility to unions.[100] When the PAC considered the American Economic System campaign in early 1947, Clark emerged as one of its most vocal defenders. He argued that it would "concentrate the attention of the American people on the extraordinary productivity of the country," adding that it "should emphasize what productivity has accomplished in terms both of wealth and of freedom."[101]

Clark belonged to a group of liberal thinkers whom historian Meg Jacobs has dubbed "purchasing-power progressives." In the wake of World War I, these liberals "saw mass consumption as a great liberating force that would preserve democracy, enhance the quality of life, and forestall destabilizing economic cycles." This view led them to see workers as consumers as well as producers and to push for both higher wages and industrial unionism. Clark himself married *Nation* editor Freda Kirchwey, worked for New York City's Socialist aldermen, and spent two years with a Soviet trading bureau. In 1920, he cofounded the Labor Bureau, which helped hundreds of unions negotiate with employers. Eight years later, department store magnate Edward Filene recruited Clark to head the Twentieth Century Fund, a foundation that Filene had created to promote the politics of purchasing power. In 1934, Clark and the Twentieth Century Fund did research for the drafters of the Wagner Act; the following year, they provided "expert evidence" that helped secure congressional passage of the bill.[102]

Given this history, why did Evans support a campaign that has been interpreted by one historian as "overtly political and illiberal"—part of a broad-based effort by America's business community to undermine the Wagner Act and other key provisions of the New Deal?[103] A key to this apparent shift can be found in a report drafted near the end of World War II by another "purchasing-power progressive," Stuart Chase. *Democracy Under Pressure: Special Interests vs. the Public Welfare* was commissioned by the Twentieth Century Fund and introduced by Clark. In the interwar period, men like Clark and Chase supported industrial unionism as a way of securing higher wages—and thus greater purchasing power—for millions of unskilled and unorganized immigrant workers. Chase's 1945 account, however, suggested that whatever power imbalance had once existed between labor and business had been largely redressed. In the wake of the Wagner Act, Big Labor had joined Big Business and Big Agriculture as an economic monopoly that threatened to trample on the interests of consumers—particularly "the 75 per cent of American workers who are not in the labor movement." Chase argued that the efforts by some unions to "crack open the Little Steel formula" during the war made them—as well as business and farm groups—"chief offenders on the price control issue." His chapters on labor exuded particular fury over wartime strikes. "In a community engaged in total war, a strike of war workers, or those who supply war workers, is in effect a strike against the community, not against the bosses," Chase wrote. "The fact that the miners are now well enough organized to freeze city dwellers, or shut down war industry, or bring the railroads to a standstill is no great satisfaction to the rest of us."[104]

Such reasoning helps explain why Clark found the proposal for a public service campaign stressing unity, teamwork, and the shared interest of all Americans in rising productivity appealing. In 1935, Clark, Chase, and other proponents of the Wagner Act "saw the right to organize as the middle way between an outdated laissez-faire system and an intrusive, even totalitarian, state."[105] *Democracy Under Pressure*, however, warned that a "spirited free-for-all" between the "Big Three" could rip American democracy apart, paving the way for just such authoritarianism.[106] A proponent of mass consumption, Clark cared deeply about both expanding productivity and ensuring that the benefits of productivity were widely shared. He was less concerned with empowering labor politically or giving unions a say in corporate decision-making. Ultimately, his vision of American society—like that of Eric Johnston and many business moderates in the postwar years—rested more on social harmony than on progressive struggle.

The second member of the PAC who proved pivotal to the campaign was Boris Shishkin, the AFL's chief economist. A Russian émigré whose Catholic mother had sheltered Jews during pogroms in Odessa, Shishkin was a strong supporter of both intergroup tolerance and civil rights. (He served on the Fair Employment Practices Committee during the war and later on President Truman's Committee on Civil Rights.) On labor and economic issues, however, Shishkin was more conservative than some union officials. The son of a Tsarist military attaché, he was a staunch anticommunist. He had a Ph.D. in economics, but no shop-floor or organizing experience, and his prescription for reconversion emphasized high production and mass purchasing power. In 1948, the year the Advertising Council formally launched the American Economic System campaign, Shishkin left for Paris to serve as a labor representative on the Marshall Plan.[107]

Shishkin helped Clark convince top labor leaders to endorse the "American Economic System" campaign. More important, he helped steer the campaign out of the bog of controversy on the PAC. Shishkin suggested that Clark appoint a subcommittee to further review the proposal and then served on the subcommittee alongside CED chairman Paul Hoffman and Hunter College president George Shuster. (Shuster resigned before the campaign got off the ground, and Clark took his place.) These three men worked closely with the joint committee and Advertising Council staffers to modify the campaign, securing, for instance, an explicit endorsement of collective bargaining. They then convinced the full PAC to sign off on the proposal. Only Shishkin, Hoffman, and Clark, however, reviewed specific campaign materials. Shishkin's name appeared on every ad produced for the campaign, representing labor's endorsement.[108]

The Advertising Council finally launched the American Economic System campaign in November 1948, the week after Truman's surprise victory in the presidential election. The final campaign drew on the work of four advertising agencies, as well as the Twentieth Century Fund, which produced a widely distributed campaign guide entitled *The Miracle of America*. A newly established Industries Advisory Committee raised large sums to support the campaign from corporations such as General Foods, General Electric, Eastman Kodak, and Standard Oil of Indiana. By the spring of 1950, the Advertising Council reported that campaign ads had appeared in hundreds of popular magazines, Sunday supplements, daily and weekly newspapers, and trade publications, as well as on nearly four thousand billboards and ninety thousand posters in commuter trains, subways, street cars, and buses. The Council also claimed credit for 1.7 billion radio listener-impressions. It had distributed nearly eight hundred thousand copies of *The Miracle of America,* largely to schools and companies. Independently, *Scholastic Magazine* and the U.S. Army reprinted the pamphlet for distribution to students and troops.[109]

As finally approved, the campaign revolved around what the Advertising Council called "the most distinctive economic fact about America—our prodigious ability to mass produce."[110] This enormous productivity, on display during the war, had given Americans "the highest standard of living ever known by any people in any country at any time." It had produced shorter working hours, lower prices, higher wages, greater profits, and more jobs. Thus, "expanding productivity" was "a national necessity," both the product and safeguard of American freedoms.[111] "Productivity...stimulated by political, religious and economic freedom plus an unrivalled teamwork," one ad prepared for retailers in 1949 declared, "that's the American way!"[112] The emphasis on productivity as a *safeguard* of American freedoms increased dramatically at the end of the decade as a result of rising international tensions and the outbreak of the Korean War. Increasingly, the Advertising Council cast productivity as essential not only to better living standards, but to defeating the Communist threat. One ad produced for the 1951 campaign showed a Catholic priest standing in the rubble of his bombed-out church. "Is World War 3 *inevitable?*" it asked. No, it answered. If Americans could "pull together" and produce all out, they could "swing the balance for freedom and peace."[113]

As this ad suggests, calls for labor-management unity were central to the American Economic System campaign. While the campaign endorsed collective bargaining, most ads, radio spots, and other materials emphasized "teamwork": "management that pays reasonable wages and takes fair profits," "labor that produces as efficiently and as much as it can." The ad that launched the American Economic System campaign began with the banner statement: "Sure, America's going ahead...*if we all pull together!*" (figure 6.3). Thanks to support from the Magazine Publishers of America, the full-page ad ran in 134 national publications, most of which sponsored it as a "public service."[114] Another ad told a parable about a "Happiness Machine": the machine wasn't perfect, but it was "better than anything else that's ever been tried." Unfortunately, managers, laborers, farmers, and consumers fought "over who should get the most happiness," in the process destroying the machine. The ad proposed a "better ending." The miracle machine could be further improved—"without even working harder"—if the people just "work[ed] *together.*"[115]

Both the celebration of American capitalism and the emphasis on harmony and teamwork in these ads could also be found in the NAM campaign of

Sure, America's going ahead...

if we __all__ pull together!

Let's compare *yesterday* with *today* ...that will give us an idea of what tomorrow can be!

Machine Power: Since 1910 we have increased our supply of machine power 4½ times.

Production: Since 1910 we have more than doubled the output each of us produces for every hour we work.

Income: Since 1910 we have increased our annual income from less than $2400 per household to about $4000 (in dollars of the same purchasing power).

Work Hours: Yet, since 1910 we have cut 18 hours from our average workweek—equivalent to two present average workdays.

HOW have we achieved all this? Through the American kind of teamwork! And what is *teamwork?*

American teamwork is management that pays reasonable wages and takes fair profits—that provides the best machines, tools, materials and working conditions it possibly can—that seeks new methods, new markets, new ideas; that bargains freely and fairly with its employees.

Our teamwork is labor that produces as efficiently and as much as it can—that realizes its standard of living ultimately depends upon how much America produces—that expects better wages as it helps increase that production.

Teamwork is simply working together to turn out more goods in fewer man-hours—making things at lower costs and paying higher wages to the people who make them and selling them at lower prices to the people who use them.

What we've already accomplished is just a foretaste of what we *can* do. It's just a start toward a goal we are all striving to reach: better housing, clothing, food, health, education, with ever greater opportunities for individual development. Sure, our American System has its faults. We all know that. We still have sharp ups and downs in prices and jobs. We'll have to change that—*and we will!*

It will continue to take *teamwork*, but if we work together, there's no limit on what we can all *share together* of even greater things.

Approved for the

PUBLIC POLICY COMMITTEE

of The Advertising Council

by:

EVANS CLARK, Executive Director, Twentieth Century Fund
BORIS SHISHKIN, Economist, American Federation of Labor
PAUL G. HOFFMAN, Formerly President, Studebaker Corp.

Published in the Public Interest by:

SPONSOR'S NAME

What we have already accomplished is just a foretaste of what we can do—if we continue to work together!

WANT TO HELP? MAIL THIS!

PUBLIC POLICY COMMITTEE
THE ADVERTISING COUNCIL, INC.
11 West 42nd Street, New York 18, N. Y.

I want to help.

I know that higher wages, lower prices, shorter hours and larger earnings can all result from producing more goods for every hour all of us work.

Therefore, I will ask myself how I can work more effectively every hour I am on the job, whether I am an employee, an employer, a professional man or a farmer.

I will encourage those things which help us to produce more and add to everyone's prosperity—things like greater use of mechanical power, better machines, better distribution and better collective bargaining.

I will boost the good things in our set-up, and help to get rid of the bad.

I will try to learn all I can about why it is that Americans have more of the good things in life.

Please send me your free booklet, "The Miracle of America," which explains clearly and simply, how a still better living can be had for all, if we all work together.

Name

Address

Occupation

Figure 6.3. The Advertising Council's long-running American Economic System campaign lauded "teamwork" and high production as the keys to prosperity for all. This full-page ad ran in more than 130 national publications, including newsmagazines such as *Time* and newspapers such as the *New York Times* (courtesy of the Advertising Council and the University of Illinois Archives).

the late 1930s. Another element of the American Economic System campaign, however, suggested that segments of the business community had embraced the lesson preached by pragmatic NAM staffers during the war. The Advertising Council repeatedly acknowledged that American capitalism was not yet perfect, that the system still had its faults. This dose of humility allowed the Council to suggest that businessmen had learned from their mistakes. It also allowed them to frame the terms in which those "imperfections" were discussed. One widely reproduced ad—entitled "How to tune a piano!"—showed three men with axes chopping the instrument to bits. "Sure, these men are crazy," the ad declared. "But they're using the same kind of thinking a lot of people have been using on the American economic system lately."[116] The message of the ad was clear: What American capitalism needed was a tune-up, not an overhaul.

By the early 1950s, the Advertising Council and others in the business community were beginning to take the next step—to argue that American capitalism had been fundamentally transformed and democratized over the past few decades. In February 1951, the editors of *Fortune* devoted an entire issue of the magazine to "USA: The Permanent Revolution"; within months they had repackaged it as a book. "Fifty years ago American capitalism seemed to be what Marx predicted it would be and what all the muckrakers said it was—the inhumane offspring of greed and irresponsibility," the magazine's editors wrote in a book based on the issue: "But American capitalism today is actually nothing of the kind. There has occurred a great transformation, of which the world as a whole is as yet unaware.... There has been a vast dispersion of ownership and initiative, so that the capitalist system has become intimately bound in with the political system and takes nourishment from its democratic roots."[117] The struggle in America was no longer between the proletariat and the bourgeoisie, the editors concluded, but between Big Labor, Big Agriculture, Big Little Business, and Big Business. "And where, in this regrouping of U.S. economic power, do we find the sense of responsibility that ought to go with the power if the nation is to increase its productivity?" they asked. "The only place it can be found in any force is in the individual business enterprise."[118]

Two other books published within a year of the *Fortune* volume—Peter Drucker's *The New Society* and Frederick Lewis Allen's *The Big Change*—made similar arguments. So did dozens of magazine and newspaper articles. In April 1951, when the Advertising Council held its first roundtable to define the American Way, it invited as participants both Drucker and Russell Davenport, who had helped edit *U.S.A.: The Permanent Revolution*.[119] The notion that America had evolved a new form of capitalism—a form marked by "a greater diffusion of power than any other system"—was introduced into the 1952 presidential campaign by Republican hopeful Harold Stassen. Borrowing the phrase coined by Eric Johnston during the war, Stassen called this new variety "people's capitalism."[120]

Although the Advertising Council did not coin the term "people's capitalism," it did much in the late 1950s to publicize both the phrase and the concept. Council president T. S. Repplier spent six months in Europe, the Middle East, and Asia in early 1955 studying U.S. and Communist propaganda methods. Upon his return, Repplier and the Council proposed that the U.S. refute directly communist charges that America's economic system was "exploitative" and "obsolete": the U.S. should emphasize its new form of capitalism—"capitalism of, by, and for the people"—"thus liberating from the Russians a word made famous by the Constitution of the United States and by Abraham Lincoln."[121] The proposal was greeted warmly by the White House; and within months, the Advertising Council was working with the United States Information Agency (USIA) on a People's Capitalism exhibit to be taken abroad. The Council also promoted the concept strenuously at home, encouraging business leaders, politicians, and journalists to highlight the term in speeches, articles, and ads. Finally, it invited prominent academics, businessmen, and journalists to participate in a series of roundtable discussions on "people's capitalism," then distributed digests of the proceedings to educators, editors, and other opinion molders.[122]

The text of the People's Capitalism exhibit laid out many of the central concepts promoted by the Council. American society was founded on "a belief in God," a conviction that "all men are created equal," and a philosophy: "The State exists only to serve the individual, not the reverse." These ideas had helped produce "a dynamic new kind of capitalism which benefits *all* the people." American workers shared in the "rewards" of industrial productivity, benefiting from shorter hours and greater purchasing power. As a result, America was "becoming classless" and "almost everybody [was] a capitalist." In 1900, the exhibit explained, most capital for business expansion came from a few banking houses; in 1956, by contrast, "nearly every American owns life insurance, has a savings account, or belongs to a pension plan—and much of these funds are invested in industry." The resulting lifestyle benefits were enormous: virtually all Americans enjoyed access to free education, "more leisure for cultural development," and comfortable single-family homes.[123] The exhibit illustrated its argument by showing pictures of the family of Ed Barnes, a Pennsylvania steelworker and union member, at home, at play, and in church.

Two buildings anchored the exhibit, underscoring its narrative arc: a log cabin stood at the entrance and visitors left via a prefabricated five-room steel home, complete with a dishwasher, garbage disposal, and television.[124]

In February 1956, the People's Capitalism exhibit opened at Washington D.C.'s Union Station for a brief "test preview." The USIA hoped to use comments on the exhibit—particularly from the city's foreign residents—to fine-tune its message. Some twenty-five thousand people passed through the exhibit over the next ten days. The voluminous response from American citizens—journalists, government officials, and area residents—reveals both a widespread embrace of the basic assumptions behind "people's capitalism" and cracks in the consensus.

Some of those who wrote simply applauded the exhibit. Many others accepted its central story line but critiqued aspects of the presentation. President Eisenhower suggested that the exhibit emphasize Americans' religious tolerance by showing pictures of "Catholic, Protestant and Jewish places of worship side by side." He and others also urged the USIA and Advertising Council to amplify their discussion of American cultural life "since foreign peoples accuse Americans of having no cultures and no souls." Many critics wrote that the houses looked too perfect—that even the log cabin would inspire envy in parts of the world and that the modern house did not have a "lived-in" look. Exhibit organizers incorporated many of these suggestions—securing the pictures requested by Eisenhower, doubling the space devoted to culture and religion, replacing the original log cabin with a reproduction of "the kind in which Abraham Lincoln lived in his youth," and procuring some used furniture and kitchen equipment for the modern home.[125]

Exhibit organizers appear to have ignored two other concerns raised by some viewers: the lack of colored faces in the exhibit and the argument that Ed Barnes's annual salary of $6,000 placed him far above the "average American."[126] One of the most penetrating letters came from Alma Scurlock, a resident of Washington D.C., who had worked in the field of community relations with the American Friends Service Committee. "I view with considerable concern, and even some alarm," she began, the selection of a family from Fairless Hills, Pennsylvania, to represent "our way of life." Fairless Hills and the adjoining community of Levittown were new developments that had been built for workers at U.S. Steel. Although the company employed some blacks, they were unable to buy homes in either subdivision. "No Negro has ever lived in either of these communities, although they total over 1,000 homes," Mrs. Scurlock wrote. "This is the largest all-white community which has persistently refused all appeals to change its segregation policy." She suggested that exhibit organizers shift their focus to Concord Park Homes, a planned community less than ten miles away. Concord Park, she suggested, was not "typical," but rather "ideal"—a place where "families of all backgrounds live together in harmony and peace in the truly American way."[127]

Alma Scurlock's letter points to a tension between two visions of the American Way. Both saw intergroup harmony as central to America's national identity and to the nation's message to the world; they differed, however, on how to achieve that end. The more conservative vision, promoted by the Advertising Council and many others, prescribed civility: Americans were to work together, without fundamentally challenging the status quo. The other vision, which Scurlock clearly shared, emphasized social change. As E. Franklin Frazier had argued more than a decade earlier, Americans could only achieve true national unity—real intergroup harmony—by overturning their racial "caste system." The American Way, viewed through this lens, was not so much a description of the present as an ideal to be attained. The tension between these two visions of the American Way was starkly apparent during the Freedom Train campaign of the late 1940s.

CHAPTER 7

The Freedom Train

Of all the postwar efforts to promote a consensual vision of the "American Way," none was more ambitious than the Freedom Train and the accompanying "American Heritage" campaign. Between September 1947 and January 1949, a red, white, and blue locomotive dubbed the "Spirit of 1776" carried a glittering array of American documents and artifacts through hundreds of cities in all forty-eight states. The train's contents included Thomas Jefferson's "rough draft" of the Declaration of Independence, George Washington's annotated copy of the Constitution, the original Bill of Rights and Emancipation Proclamation, and the flag that was planted at Iwo Jima. The train's journey was coordinated with one of the largest peacetime ideological campaigns ever undertaken in this country. Conceived in the Attorney General's office, organized by movie and advertising executives, and financed by America's largest corporations, the Freedom Train and American Heritage campaign portrayed a nation that was unified, consensual, and inclusive.

This veneer of unity, however, concealed an ongoing contest over America's core values. Although a handful of corporate and advertising executives exercised powerful control over the project, they did not operate in a vacuum. A close examination of the Freedom Train and American Heritage campaign reveals a series of conflicts and compromises, power struggles, and unexpected alliances involving a diverse array of groups: an administration worried about domestic unrest and a deepening cold war, National Archives staffers with New Deal inclinations, interfaith groups who hoped to use the campaign to promote religious tolerance, Communists who denounced it as a reactionary cover-up, and black Americans fighting for integration and civil rights. With so many groups vying to define the American Way, even a word as seemingly central to national identity as "democracy" eventually was cast aside. Under the banner of "freedom," Americans with widely divergent interests used the Freedom Train both to underscore conservative consensus and to promote social change.

"Indoctrination in Democracy": The Idea of a "Bill of Rights" Train

The idea for the Freedom Train emerged from the Attorney General's office in the spring of 1946. One early April day, William Coblenz, the Justice Department's assistant director of public information, took a lunchtime stroll to the National Archives. Inside the cavernous stone building he found a "trickle of tourists" viewing a display of German surrender documents together with Hitler's last will and testament. Coblenz, who had been assigned by the Justice Department to keep tabs on "lunatic fringe literature," worried about the "distortion and confusion" he saw in the U.S. on "basic public issues." Struck by the erosion of liberties revealed in the German documents, Coblenz wished that more Americans could see them. But few Americans would ever make it to Washington to view the display. Reflecting on this, Coblenz conceived of a traveling exhibit that would take the papers to the people. As he saw it, one side of a train car would display copies of historic U.S. documents such as the Bill of Rights, while the other side would carry a chronicle in pictures and papers of Hitler's Third Reich. That way, Americans could compare their own heritage of civil liberty with the destruction of such freedoms under the Nazi regime.[1]

Coblenz quickly brought his idea to the attention of Attorney General Tom C. Clark. Clark, a genial Texan and one of the moderate Democrats Truman had appointed to his cabinet the previous year, was a former corporate lawyer who had nevertheless earned a reputation during the Roosevelt administration as a Justice Department trust buster. During the war, Clark had helped coordinate the internment of Japanese Americans on the West Coast, and he would go on to lead the Truman administration's Communist purge. At the same time, Clark shocked his southern colleagues by demanding that black Americans be admitted to the Federal Bar Association and resigned as president when the association resisted. In 1947, he became the first U.S. attorney general to file an amicus curiae brief in a civil rights case.

Clark seized on Coblenz's idea of a traveling "Bill of Rights exhibit" as a way of halting the postwar "disintegration of...our American unity."[2] In mid-1946, both domestic and international events made this seem particularly crucial. Reconversion from a wartime to a peacetime economy was straining American society, igniting smoldering social tensions. In the months since Germany's surrender, the Soviet Union had tightened its control of Eastern Europe, and the international communist movement had abandoned its wartime "popular front." In a rare speech on February 9, Stalin stressed the incompatibility of communism and capitalism. Two weeks later, as U.S. officials groped for an explanation of this hardening line, George F. Kennan fired off his famous "Long Telegram," arguing for the deep historical and psychological roots of Soviet aggression. On March 5, Winston Churchill introduced the phrase "iron curtain" to the world. A contrast with Nazism had triggered Coblenz's brainstorm; but by the late spring of 1946, Americans were girding for ideological battle against a very different foe.

Armed with strong endorsements from Clark and President Truman, Coblenz and staffers at the National Archives began organizing an exhibit. To hold costs down, they kept the project simple. A single refurbished train car would carry documents, prints, and photographs telling "the story of the establishment, growth and defense of the rights and freedoms that belong to each one of us as an American citizen." The exhibit car would be hitched to the back of freights and would move from city to city for three to four months. Most of the documents would be facsimiles (thus cutting the cost of insurance), and publicity would be left to local U.S. Attorneys. The entire project was expected to cost between $15,000 and $25,000.[3]

By early fall, however, it was becoming clear that even this modest sum was too high. With the war over, neither the Justice Department nor any other federal agency had an extra $20,000 in its budget to preach good citizenship. What's more, a Republican congressman had gotten wind of the project and was denouncing it as an administration election-time ploy. In September, Clark finally decided to delay the "Bill of Rights exhibit" until after the midterm elections. And in a move that would fundamentally alter both the scope and message of the train, the Attorney General decided to seek private funds.[4]

Clark's first call was to Edwin Weisl, a prominent New York attorney and an old friend of the Attorney General's.[5] Weisl was traveling on the West Coast with a client, Barney Balaban, the president of Paramount Pictures. When Clark called, Weisl put Balaban on the phone. Within minutes, Clark had a pledge for the $20,000 he needed.

Balaban, the oldest son of Russian Jewish immigrants, combined a history of fighting religious and racial intolerance with an Horatio Alger's belief in the American Way. Balaban's father had owned a small grocery store on Chicago's

West Side; the son made a fortune by establishing a chain of "deluxe" movie theatres, the first in the country with indoor cooling systems. In 1926, Paramount bought a controlling interest in the chain, and a decade later—when Depression overcommitments pushed the studio toward bankruptcy—it brought in Balaban to reorganize its operations. At 59, Balaban was a living embodiment of the American dream.

Unlike many other Jewish studio executives of the era, Balaban acknowledged his roots. He had stayed in New York after joining Paramount and remained active in Jewish community affairs. (In 1946, he was serving as a national cochairman of the United Jewish Appeal.) A collector of Americana, Balaban had the previous year presented the original manuscript of the Bill of Rights to the Library of Congress in "appreciation for the freedom which drew...(his) parents to this country from Europe." He had also joined other movie magnates on an industry committee of the National Conference of Christians and Jews (NCCJ). In the Freedom Train Balaban saw "a wonderful vehicle for creating good will among various racial and religious groups."[6]

But Balaban also believed that such a project should remain in the hands of the private sector. In a speech in early 1946, he called on Hollywood to make more films about American democracy and to send abroad "only those pictures that accurately reflect our national life." At the same time, he decried the efforts of many European governments to regulate the movie industry and attacked plans for a State Department-sponsored informational film program. Informational movies would be more credible if shown by the private sector, he argued, and studios should be allowed to reap the profits.[7]

Balaban applied the same logic to the Attorney General's proposal. In offering to bankroll the exhibit, he suggested that Clark send Coblenz to New York to discuss alternative ways of running the project. When Coblenz arrived at Balaban's Manhattan office in mid-October, he found that the magnate had assembled a roomful of Paramount executives to discuss the establishment of a "nonpartisan" foundation to run the exhibit. Balaban and his associates also proposed that a special train be devoted to the project, that it tour for a full year rather than merely a few months, and that it carry original documents instead of facsimiles. Finally, they urged the Justice Department to widen the impact of the train by enlisting the national media in a massive educational campaign tied to the exhibit.

Clark and Coblenz quickly agreed to the plan and invited representatives of the national media to a follow-up luncheon at the Attorney General's office that December. Meanwhile, Balaban delegated his assistant, Louis A. Novins, to work full time on the project. Novins, 37, had been an assistant attorney general of Massachusetts before joining Paramount and, like his boss, was active in Jewish community affairs. Energetic and organized, he was destined to play a pivotal role in what would eventually become the American Heritage Foundation.

While government officials and studio executives discussed plans for a "Bill of Rights Train," Thomas D'Arcy Brophy, the New York advertising executive, was quietly circulating his proposal for a "super-radio program" modeled on "I Am an American" Day. Brophy had seen the proposal for a "Production Urgency" campaign designed to unite the nation around "the good old-fashioned American will to work." He argued that a campaign focused narrowly on economics would likely misfire. "The causes of our national unrest are deep and complex," he contended. "They cannot be cured simply by an adjuration to get off our seats and go to work—even with a promissory slogan about the good that full production would bring for all." Instead, Brophy argued that the key to rebuilding national unity lay in a broader if "homelier" appeal.[8]

Brophy's proposal won quick applause from the handful of prominent businessmen and foundation heads to whom he showed it. But several reminded him that "if such a program should be sponsored by business, it would greatly dilute its effectiveness." Brophy approached NBC about running the program as a public service but was still discussing the plan with the network when the Advertising Council received an invitation to the Attorney General's "Bill of Rights Train" lunch.[9] At that moment, Brophy knew his problem had been solved:

> We have available through the Advertising Council radio time and newspaper and magazine space conservatively valued at $10,000,000 which can be used now, this year—not for a frontal attack on Communism by "big business" which would be bad, but in support of a campaign sponsored by the Attorney General of the United States to re-sell the America we and our forebears have built, to the millions of Americans who thoughtlessly take it all for granted, and are generally unaware of any threat to our way of life.
>
> These millions are the balance of power in this country. We all have great faith in their collective judgment, but that faith should not lull us into a sense of false security in the face of what we know is being done by those who do their zealous best to stir up class and other antagonisms.
>
> The Attorney General's campaign...would present many opportunities to present powerful economic facts which should be

brought out. Its broad theme can be expressed in the copybook maxim, "Don't kill the goose that lays the golden eggs."

Here is a great opportunity to tell the truth to the people of this country by the means we know best how to use—Motion Pictures, Radio, Newspapers, Magazines, all methods of mass persuasion developed to a high state of perfection in America by American Business.[10]

When Attorney General Tom Clark convened his luncheon on December 10, 1946, no attendee was more enthusiastic than Thomas D'Arcy Brophy.

The Private Sector Climbs on Board

Both Novins and Brophy thought the luncheon a smashing success. The forty-three attendees represented every sector of the national media and in-cluded the publisher of the *Washington Post,* the heads of both major radio networks, the president of 20th Century-Fox Film Corp., and the songwriter Irving Berlin. Attorney General Clark delivered a rousing speech (carefully scripted by Novins), in which he attacked both "statism" and various forms of intolerance. "All over the world there appears to be a struggle between one form of 'state-ism' and another," Clark warned. "Whether it's fascism, com-munism or the various degrees of socialism - it's not the American brand of democracy as we know it." Even at home, America's "democratic structure" was being tested. Among the culprits: "alien ideologies," Old World rivalries and hatreds, and "professional bigots" who "pervert the sacred right of free speech to place one American against another, one creed against another, one race against another." The solution to this problem, Clark suggested, was the "dramatic projection of a single idea"—"the development of American democracy as the fullest expression of individual freedom, human rights and the dignity of man."[11]

By the meeting's end, the attendees had enthusiastically endorsed the plan for a Liberty Train. But, as Brophy had hoped, they adopted one significant change: the contrast with Nazi Germany was dropped since "that government was not unique" in its suppression of civil liberties. Instead, the exhibit would simply celebrate "the American way of life."[12]

From this point on, control over the project shifted rapidly from the Attorney General's office to the train's private-sector backers. (This crucial shift—never total—was lost to most Americans, who assumed that the train was run by the federal government.) Novins and Brophy increasingly took charge, courting the U.S. Chamber of Commerce, the American Bankers Association, and the National Association of Manufacturers at a meeting in early January. Meanwhile, Brophy approached Winthrop Aldrich, the conservative chairman of Chase National Bank, about heading the emerging foundation.[13]

Brophy knew Aldrich from their work on a wartime campaign to raise funds for the United Service Organizations. Aldrich, a Harvard-educated lawyer from a prominent Rhode Island family, had gradually been drawn into banking by his brother-in-law, John D. Rockefeller Jr. Although he had enraged his fellow bankers in 1933 by calling for a complete separation of commercial and investment banking, Aldrich later earned a reputation as an outspoken critic of the New Deal. By all accounts a stiff and formal man, Aldrich nevertheless had the kind of contacts in the business community that the incipient foundation badly needed. When the American Heritage Foundation was finally incorporated in mid-February 1947, Aldrich was named chairman; Brophy, president; and Novins, executive vice president.[14]

Brophy and Aldrich quickly turned to the problem of raising money. Balaban had offered to pick up the tab for the original exhibit, but the project's new organizers envisioned a train and accompanying media campaign many times as costly as Coblenz's modest proposal. In early 1947, Brophy persuaded the Advertising Council to take on the American Heritage campaign as a public service, thus ensuring millions of dollars in donated time and advertising space. Meanwhile, Aldrich hosted a luncheon at the Union Club in New York City to garner pledges from major American corporations. He also appointed a score of business leaders to raise funds from their respective industries.[15]

The American Heritage Foundation would later stress that financing for the Freedom Train project came from labor groups, communities, and private citizens, in addition to businesses. In fact, *all* of the money raised while the exhibit was being organized—and more than 90 percent of the dollars collected in the project's first nine months—came from wealthy individuals and America's largest corporations. E. I. du Pont de Nemours and Co., General Electric Co., Standard Oil of New, Jersey and U.S. Steel Corp. each pledged $20,000 or more. Eastman Kodak Co., R. J. Reynolds Tobacco Co., the major film studios, and a host of other companies gave $10,000 to $20,000 each. And "private citizen" John D. Rockefeller Jr. donated an additional $25,000.[16]

These businesses received no special rights to advertising or product tie-ins. (Airline executives lobbied for a "Freedom Plane" to complement the train but were turned down.) Rather, in wooing businessmen, Brophy and Aldrich repeatedly stressed the "enlightened self-interest" that should open corporate coffers. By underscoring the common heritage of all Americans—and the stake every citizen had in "freedom"—the campaign would help derail the antibusiness antagonism that had surfaced during the Depression and that threatened to resurge if the U.S. economy faltered. "We have a very limited time in this country to condition ourselves to withstand a major assault of forces which if successful, would seriously weaken, if not destroy, our democratic institutions," Brophy warned Aldrich in a memo about fund-raising strategy. "Only last week I saw a CIO sponsored motion picture, admirably produced, in which the American economic system was damned at every turn....We should act while the average American is relatively prosperous, for discontent grows with bad times!"[17]

American Heritage Foundation officials saved such sentiments for private memos and conversations. Publicly, they stressed the inclusive grassroots character of the organization. The foundation, Brophy declared in a speech delivered in New York's Federal Hall, "is purely a citizens' group. It is non-partisan, non-controversial and entirely supported by voluntary contributions from public spirited organizations and individuals." Aldrich echoed these sentiments in a letter to Philadelphia's mayor: "I should like to make it unmistakably clear that this program will be conducted entirely on a non-partisan basis. The themes to be used through the various media at our disposal will be confined to the *common* heritage of *all* Americans."[18]

Brophy, Novins, and Aldrich did take some steps to legitimate this claim. They invited William Green and Philip Murray, the presidents of the AFL and CIO respectively, and Robert Sproul, president of the University of California at Berkeley, to serve as vice chairmen of the foundation. (Having labor leaders and major business figures on the same board "would be very much in the spirit of this undertaking," Brophy noted in a memo to Aldrich.) In order to give the foundation "catholic strength," they also took pains to secure trustees from both political parties, all three major religions, all regions of the country, and both sexes. Recognizing the "imperative public relations need" of having a "leading American negro" on the board, they named Walter White, executive secretary of the National Association for the Advancement of Colored People (NAACP).[19]

Ultimately, however, control of the Freedom Train and the American Heritage campaign remained in the hands of the ruling triumvirate and their handpicked staff. Brophy and Aldrich rejected some of Attorney General Clark's nominees for the foundation's board of directors, and internal memos suggest that Green, Murray, and Sproul learned of major decisions no sooner than other board members. Walter White's membership on the board of directors appears to have had little impact on the foundation's policy on racial matters.[20]

Contested Truths

The stated goal of the American Heritage Program was to inspire Americans to a more active citizenship by "emphasizing and dramatizing" their common heritage. But determining precisely what that common heritage was proved troublesome. Even the most basic of terms—"democracy"—could spark heated debate. This became clear at a White House conference called in late May 1947 to rally public support for the Freedom Train project.

The 175 hand-selected guests at the conference composed a Who's Who of America's social, economic, civic, and media worlds. (In order to keep the project "nonpartisan," politicans weren't invited.) Guests ranging from Henry Ford II and director David O. Selznick to the Urban League's Lester Granger listened to speeches by the Attorney General and officers of the American Heritage Foundation. Toward the end of his speech, foundation president Thomas Brophy unveiled the proposed slogan for the nationwide media campaign: "Work at democracy to make democracy work."[21]

This emphasis on "democracy" alarmed some attendees. As Aldrich later reminded Brophy, "A number of people raised the question as to whether the program of the Foundation did not have political implications because of the emphasis on the word 'democracy.' You and I came to the conclusion that in the future we would use the word 'freedom' instead of 'democracy' in connection with our publicity." Brophy quickly appropriated a slogan that had been used by the National Association of Manufacturers in the late 1930s—"Freedom Is Everybody's Job"—and promised to downplay the word "democracy" in all subsequent printed material.[22]

Why such controversy over a word that had been used to rally Americans to war for at least two generations? In the early Republic, many political elites feared "democracy," which they equated with mob rule. But Andrew Jackson helped popularize the term, and by the early twentieth century, politicians regularly wrapped themselves in its mantle. American doughboys marched into World War I to save the world for democracy; in the early years of World War II, a powerful "democratic revival" essentially equated "democracy" with "the American way of life."[23]

Some conservative attendees may have feared the linguistic link between "democracy" and the Democratic Party. But the debate likely ran deeper, for by mid-1947, "democracy" had become a contested term. "Among the most controversial words of our era is 'democracy'," philosopher Sidney Hook declared in the March issue of *The New York Times Magazine*. "There never was a period when it had an absolutely clear meaning, but the passage of time has obscured rather than clarified its connotations." When the American delegation meeting in Moscow to discuss the future of Germany was asked to give its definition of democracy, delegates had trouble defining the term.[24]

Much of this confusion resulted from the growing tendency to define "Americanism" against communism rather than fascism. Although Americans of both left and right generally agreed that Nazi Germany was not in any sense a democracy, the same was not true of the Soviet Union. Some liberal and leftist intellectuals distinguished between the "economic" democracy of the Soviet Union and the "political" democracy of the United States. (Indeed, in 1942, Vice President Henry Wallace had told a Madison Square Garden audience, "Some in the United States believe that we have overemphasized what might be called political or Bill of Rights democracy.") Meanwhile, the CIO called for an "industrial democracy" with economic implications reaching far beyond the political democracy most conservatives were willing to embrace. If conservatives had any doubts that liberals and leftists were co-opting the term, they could look to the most recent edition of Alexis de Tocqueville's *Democracy in America*, with its glowing foreword by British political scientist and Labor Party leader Harold J. Laski.[25]

Meanwhile, American conservatives were beginning to argue that democracy and totalitarianism were not incompatible—an idea that would have been heretical a mere five years earlier. Friedrich A. von Hayek, an Austrian-born economist, popularized this view in 1945 with his best-selling manifesto *The Road to Serfdom*. Hayek argued that fascists, socialists, communists, and liberal democrats had all come to rely on ideas of national economic planning that led inevitably to totalitarian serfdom. By ignoring the rights of the individual, Hayek suggested, democratic majorities could create states every bit as totalitarian as those led by malevolent dictators. One magazine reader, extending this theme, argued that Puritan Massachusetts had been just such a "totalitarian democracy." Still other conservatives argued that the United States was not a "democracy" at all but a "republic."[26]

"Freedom" had none of these troublesome overtones. It was, as Daniel T. Rodgers has written, "the obverse of the twentieth century's new totalitarianisms; it was, in a word, everything that fascism and communism were not." Moreover, for those concerned about a revival of the New Deal, "freedom" had convenient economic resonances. An expansive term, "freedom" could encompass everything from freedom of religion to "free enterprise," the phrase economic conservatives had invented in the late 1930s to replace "private enterprise." Thomas Brophy clearly recognized these linguistic and philosophical links: the American Heritage program "sets the stage" for the Advertising Council's "American Economic System" campaign, he wrote a colleague who was coordinating the latter project. "Political freedom permits free enterprise to operate, free enterprise gives political freedom its economic strength for survival."[27]

Ultimately, the organizers of the American Heritage campaign settled on the nation's "heritage of individual freedom" as the point on which Americans most widely agreed.[28] But if they came to this term partly because of its economic overtones, they were also forced to recognize its social implications. To be truly free, an individual had to have freedom of choice, unhindered by the restrictions and prejudices of others. Thus, "individual freedom" could also be invoked by those arguing for religious and racial tolerance and inclusion. As Sheldon Waldo, an attorney who welcomed the Freedom Train to Jacksonville, Florida, said: "If in our hearts we secretly possess a feeling of superiority because of our association with a particular faith, whether it be Protestant, Catholic or Jew, we have to that extent denied freedom to a fellow man." Although Waldo did not say as much in his speech, the same argument could be applied to black Americans.[29]

Defining the American "Consensus"

Even before the American Heritage Foundation had been incorporated—let alone settled on a slogan for the Freedom Train campaign—Louis Novins had turned his attention to ensuring that the documents on the train matched the sentiments of its sponsors. In January 1947, he and others spearheading the effort appointed a Committee on the Selection of Documents to choose suitable items for the train. Officially, the committee consisted of National Archivist Solon J. Buck; Librarian of Congress Luther H. Evans; and A. S. W. Rosenbach, a private collector of Americana from Pennsylvania. Unofficially, Novins's voice carried the most weight, for he represented the train's financial backers.[30]

National Archives staffers under the supervision of Elizabeth S. Hamer had already been working for months on what had been known as the "Attorney General's Bill of Rights project." By late 1946, they had compiled a list of suggested documents for the train. As they saw it, the first half of the exhibit would trace the rise of democracy and civil liberties in the New World from the English Magna Carta through Virginia's ratification of the Bill of Rights in 1791. The second half would carry the story into the present, with displays on civil rights for blacks and women; the extension of civil liberties to the U.S. territories of Alaska, the Philippines, and Guam; and the establishment of the United Nations to project the "Four Freedoms" around the globe.[31]

This original proposal presented an upbeat and progressive vision of American democracy. It also reflected the New Deal sympathies of Hamer and others selecting the documents. A display entitled "Bonds of Friendship" was to include the program of a mass meeting held in New York in March 1917 to celebrate "the triumph of Russian Democracy." A series of photographs and foreign-language posters would highlight the array of immigrant groups that had contributed to America's pluralistic culture. A section on the need for eternal vigilance was to contain President Roosevelt's 1941 executive order establishing the Fair Employment Practices Commission (FEPC) and President Truman's 1946 executive order setting up the Committee on Civil Rights.

The proposed exhibit also emphasized the right of all Americans to economic security. An entire exhibit case devoted to "Economic Rights" was to contain, among other things, a blank form of a "yellow-dog" agreement, the contract once used by companies to force prospective workers to waive their rights to a union; a draft of the Committee on Economic Security's 1934 report proposing a national system of old-age and survivor's insurance; and a Justice Department circular illustrating enforcement of the Wagner Act, the 1935 act that threw the weight of government behind the right of labor to bargain collectively. A booklet drafted to accompany the exhibit noted that President Roosevelt had called for an "Economic Bill of Rights" to counter the economic inequalities that resulted from expanding industrialism. "Without the right of personal economic security and independence," the book editorialized, "the right to life, liberty and the pursuit of happiness was a…meaningless phrase."[32]

Such messages did not survive the first month of private control. The entire section on economic rights, together with the handbill for the 1917 mass meeting, was dropped immediately. So was an 1863 Senate resolution condemning General Ulysses S. Grant's order expelling Jews from Tennessee. (Novins, an active member of B'nai B'rith's Anti-Defamation League, "vigorously opposed" all items relating to Jews on the grounds that the train shouldn't become "a matter of controversy.") Novins also vetoed the pictures of immigrants because "we would get into all kinds of difficulty if we showed two or three pictures of foreign-born Americans who have made outstanding contributions and didn't represent all foreign groups."[33]

Most galling to some of the National Archives staffers was the steady inclusion in the exhibit of material that seemed unrelated to the civil liberties theme—for instance, the account book kept by George Washington during the Revolution or the letter from Joseph Warren appointing Paul Revere a messenger of Massachusetts' Committee of Safety. "I protested in advance that [Washington's account book] was not germane," complained Elizabeth Hamer, who often represented Solon Buck on the committee. "Actually, however, it is not too out of place in the general exhibit our civil liberties exhibit has become."[34]

Such changes notwithstanding, the second version of the exhibit still bore a passing resemblance to the original proposal. Much of the exhibit still focused explicitly on civil rights and liberties, even if those rights no longer included economic security. Contemporary documents such as the executive orders by presidents Roosevelt and Truman remained intact. And the exhibit concluded with displays exuberantly entitled "Democracy Triumphs" and "One World." On February 10, Hamer noted with a paper sigh, "What we hope was a final selection [of documents] was made."[35]

Hamer had written the epitaph for the process too soon. In early June 1947, the *New York Sun* obtained and published a copy of the original list of documents that Hamer and her staff had compiled in 1946. Furor erupted over the inclusion of some of the economic documents, and American Heritage Foundation officials scrambled to assure readers that the list "was compiled by persons having no connection" with the foundation. "Clearly, no document will be carried on this train that is controversial in any political sense," Novins wrote Gardner Osborne, the president of the New York chapter of the Sons of the American Revolution. "Every document would have to pass the test of universal acceptance by the great majority of the American people as a significant landmark of the American heritage."[36]

But who was to determine which documents passed this test? Not Osborne or his fellow members of the Sons of the American Revolution, as Novins made clear in his letter. Rather, in the wake of the uproar, the American Heritage Foundation's ruling triumvirate appointed a new committee to pass final muster on all Freedom Train documents. This new committee included neither the National Archivist nor the Librarian of Congress. Instead, final selection of "the documents upon which all Americans agree" was placed in the hands of four men: John Foster Dulles, the Wall Street lawyer who would later become Dwight Eisenhower's Secretary of State; Winthrop Aldrich; Edwin Weisl, Barney Balaban and Tom Clark's mutual friend; and John W. Davis, the corporate lawyer and prominent southern

Democrat who had been his party's candidate for president in 1924. During the Depression, Davis had been a member of the anti-New Deal Liberty League, and he would go on to defend segregation as the defense counsel in *Brown v. Board of Education*.[37]

Over the next three months, these four men remade the exhibit. Advised by Frank Monaghan, a former Yale historian who had worked on DuPont's "Cavalcade of America" program, they added a score of famous documents to the train. Some, such as the Bay Psalm Book and Thomas Paine's pamphlet *Common Sense*, arguably illustrated the general development of democracy and civil liberties in America. Other documents added to the exhibit weren't clearly related to this theme: Francis Scott Key's draft of "The Star-Spangled Banner," Benjamin Franklin's self-written epitaph, and a letter from the King of Siam to President Lincoln offering the United States a gift of elephants. These were linked only by their place in U.S. history textbooks.[38]

Some of the additions clearly had a conservative cast. The committee devoted an entire display case to Alexander Hamilton, the nation's first Treasury Secretary and the favorite founding father of economic conservatives. Documents by Thomas Jefferson, a hero of liberal New Dealers, were scattered throughout the train, but Jefferson himself was not similarly hailed. When the men entitled one display case "Bonds of Freedom," they were being quite literal: the case contained eleven U.S. Treasury bonds issued between 1779 and 1947. For those who might overlook the significance of financing national projects through bonds rather than higher tax rates, the display provided careful instruction: "Since 1779, Americans have been buying shares in America."[39] Here was a lesson in both economic individualism and consensus.

Much of the committee's influence was more subtle—the result of eliminating "controversial" documents rather than adding new ones. Copies of the Fourteenth and Fifteenth amendments were dropped, and William Lloyd Garrison's abolitionist paper, *The Liberator*, was excised from the large display "Freedom of the Press." Lincoln's Gettysburg Address survived the inspection but was paired with an 1865 address by General Robert E. Lee in which Lee declared it the duty of every American to heal the wounds of the Civil War. The committee vetoed Woodrow Wilson's inaugural address because it contained too many references to "Democratic victory." And Aldrich, a British sympathizer who favored early intervention in World War II, rejected one of Franklin Roosevelt's most famous "fireside chats": "It happens to be my opinion," Aldrich wrote Novins, "that on December 29th, 1940, the United States should have been participating in the battle for freedom on some basis other than 'the great arsenal of democracy.'"[40]

Despite sustained lobbying by civil rights activists, both black and white, the committee dropped entirely the display on wartime protection of civil rights and liberties. "No document issued during recent years has so aroused the interest and enthusiasm for the democratic process among minorities" as President Roosevelt's executive order establishing the FEPC, NAACP executive secretary Walter White wrote to Aldrich in July 1947. But even White's position as a board member didn't help his cause. The Freedom Train, Novins repeatedly explained, was nonpartisan and thus couldn't carry documents that were the subject of current legislative debate.[41]

At least black Americans could point to a few documents—the Emancipation Proclamation and the Thirteenth Amendment abolishing slavery, in particular—that documented their struggle. The same could not be said for labor. In fact, the conspicuous absence of any documents relating to the progress of organized labor drew queries and complaints from congressmen, reporters, and local union officials. The American Heritage Foundation managed to sidestep all such requests by ignoring the issue or arguing that the labor documents available were either "controversial" or insignificant.

When Rep. Adolph J. Sabath (D-Ill.) protested to the Justice Department about the omission in September 1947, he was assured that "the lack was being remedied at once." At the Justice Department's request, a Labor Department librarian quickly suggested several possibilities. Although the contents of one of the documents remains unclear, at least two of the items could hardly have been controversial: the pen used by President Wilson to sign the 1913 act establishing the Department of Labor, and a letter from the President's secretary to a Commerce Department official enclosing the pen. The following month, however, Elizabeth Hamer returned the documents with an apologetic letter: "I am sorry to tell you that [members of the American Heritage Foundation] felt that the language of the documents was a bit too violent for inclusion in an exhibit that has tried very hard to be non-partisan."[42]

The American Heritage Foundation told the Justice Department that they were conferring with two union officials about possible documents. But conveniently those officials were out of town during a foundation board meeting, so the issue wasn't raised. "We are doing nothing about this at the present time," Novins confided to Brophy in December. "The last time I spoke to Mr. Aldrich about the inclusion of labor documents was when the train was in Philadelphia [in September]. If my memory is correct, at that time he discouraged taking any initiative on this matter."[43]

Finally, in March 1948, Novins could evade the issue no longer. Concerned about spiraling costs and eager to show labor's support for the Freedom Train, the American Heritage Foundation began pressuring unions to contribute financially to the campaign. One local labor official included a question with his check: why wasn't the Wagner Act or any other labor-related document on the train? Novins assured George Dizard that the train's organizers had conferred with labor representatives about finding "suitable" documents. But "we were not successful in obtaining documents of comparable stature with others on the Freedom Train," he wrote.[44]

Not everyone was as impressed with the documents on the Freedom Train as Novins apparently was. One week before Novins replied to the union official, Frank Monaghan, the historical consultant to the project, wrote Brophy that the exhibit was "cockeyed in many respects." If the train's run was extended for a second year, he added, about two-fifths of its contents should be replaced. "This 40%," Monaghan wrote, "can easily be replaced by documents that would be vastly better."[45]

Novins offered Dizard a second rationale for the absence of labor documents on the train: "Obviously our program would never have succeeded had we gone beyond the area of fundamental agreement of all Americans into the realm of controversy." If the contents of the Freedom Train were any measure, about the only event of the previous several decades on which all Americans agreed was the waging of World War II itself. Of the thirty post-1920 documents and objects displayed on the train, twenty-seven related directly to the financing and conduct of the war. Two more documented the emergence of the United Nations, but even these had to be properly couched: in the final version of the train, the optimistic "One World" heading used to label this display was changed to "The Nations United."[46]

When the Freedom Train finally got underway in September 1947, it bore almost no resemblance to the exhibit that National Archives staffers had labored on the previous year. The economic message had been removed or reinterpreted. Contemporary documents on civil rights and civil liberties had been excised. And the troublesome word "democracy" had been largely replaced in train exhibits with the concept of "freedom." As Novins wrote Brophy in late 1948, "The Freedom Train program as it is today compared to the concept in Coblenz's mind is not a difference of degree but a difference in kind."[47]

A few groups openly challenged the vision of national unity that the Freedom Train was designed to impart. In late August, a few weeks before the train was scheduled to leave on its journey, the Communist Party's educational department issued a memo warning its district directors of the "demagogic purpose" of the American Heritage campaign's "key backers." "Such sponsors as the N.A.M., the U.S. Chamber of Commerce and Winthrop Aldrich, president of Chase National Bank, are spearheading every reactionary effort to destroy our constitutional liberties," the memo charged. "They are the instigators of the slave labor law, the loyalty orders, the anti-Communist witch-hunt. Their campaign around the FREEDOM TRAIN is a huge propaganda cover-up for the most widespread violation of the Bill of Rights and the Constitution in our history."[48]

The Communist Party memo highlighted the intensifying red scare that increasingly provided both a backdrop and a counterpoint to the Freedom Train's public message of comity and consensus. In March 1947, President Truman had issued an executive order establishing a loyalty-security program for federal employees; and groups around the country began instituting loyalty oaths and background checks. In June, the Republican majority in Congress had passed the Taft-Hartley Act, a sweeping piece of labor legislation that rolled back many of the gains labor had made under the New Deal. When Attorney General Tom Clark addressed a House committee that same month to explain executive branch expenditures on the Freedom Train, he argued that the project would help to "immunize the American body politic against the germs of subversive propaganda."[49]

The Communist memo also showed that nationalist symbols could be bent to either conservative or radical ends. "We cannot go along with the NAM and the Chamber of Commerce in helping to create this illusion of 'national unity,'" the Communists declared. But rather than calling for a halt to the Freedom Train, the Party urged labor unions, church groups, and black and Jewish organizations to organize tours of the train led by "prominent progressives who will point out the significance of the documents in relation to the current struggles of the people." Freedom Train ceremonies, it argued, should be used to expose violations of civil liberties and to fight for labor and civil rights legislation. "We will not surrender to [Big Business] this great opportunity to bring to millions the true meaning of the Bill of Rights, the Constitution, the Emancipation Proclamation, etc.," the memo concluded.

Members of the Fellowship of Reconciliation (FOR), a radical pacifist group, struck a similar note when they picketed the Freedom Train during its stop in New York City in late September. (Among other things, the FOR was demanding the release of World War II draft resisters, some of whom were still imprisoned.) "Is our American Heritage a past to worship? ... Or the challenge of an Unfinished Task," a leaflet distributed by the FOR asked. If the former, "then the documents on the Freedom Train are shrines where we bow, paying our respects to what we might have been," the leaflets declared. "In that case we are stuck with many miserable contradictions of the spirit and meaning of these symbols," including segregation and disfranchisement and "legal" violations of the Bill of Rights. The FOR urged a different interpretation of the train's cargo: The documents "ARE plans for the future," the leaflet declared. "They provide for correcting mistakes in them." The organization urged Americans to "live out the creed set forth in the Freedom Train. Call upon our government to provide full and complete protection of life, liberty and civil rights to all."[50]

Both the Communist Party memo and the FOR leaflet highlighted the gap between two visions of America: one that saw the nation as largely perfected and another that saw it as promising but very much "in process." The leftist magazine *New Masses*, which devoted its September 1947 issue entirely to the Freedom Train, also emphasized the different possible readings of America's past. Which was the American heritage, the heritage of Robert Rogers, "whose 'Rangers' made a record of bloodlust and infamy during the Revolution of '76," or the heritage of the abolitionist radical John Brown? Howard Fast asked. Added A. B. Magil: "Though every American newspaper reader today knows that labor parties are 'alien' to the American tradition, it is a fact that what was probably the first labor party in the world was born in Philadelphia in 1828."[51]

Ultimately, the Communist Party, the FOR, and the leftist contributors to *New Masses* drew a vastly different lesson from America's past than that preached by the Freedom Train's organizers. "If there is any common denominator to democratic Americans," Richard O. Boyer declared in the magazine's lead article, "it is the bed-rock conviction that any man anywhere has the right and duty to express his most fundamental beliefs no matter whom they offend and outrage." Although the American Heritage campaign gave lip service to the First Amendment, it stressed social harmony above all else. Nineteen of those who joined the FOR protest in New York City were arrested, as were two men in Houston caught distributing Communist Party leaflets. The Freedom Train preached unity across all social divides—a message that condemned protest as much as prejudice.[52]

Communists and the FOR were almost alone in denouncing the American Heritage Foundation. Whether because of the stick of red-baiting or the carrot of "tolerance," most other national organizations the party considered potential allies—the AFL, the CIO, the NAACP, B'nai B'rith, and the Urban League, to name a few—gave the Freedom Train project their wholehearted support. Most had been invited to the White House conference and subsequently pledged to organize local chapters in support of the train. In general, the Communist Party's efforts to restate the train's message drowned in a din-ning chorus of acclaim.[53]

Ironically, the Communist Party's actions served mainly to solidify right-wing support for the project. Many Midwestern conservatives had been almost as suspicious of the Freedom Train as their left-wing counterparts. ("Vote Buy-ing Plot Scented in the 'Freedom Train'" read one May newspaper headline.) American Heritage Foundation officials worried particularly about the oppo-sition of Colonel Robert McCormick, the influential publisher of the *Chicago Tribune* whose support they deemed essential to the campaign's success in the Midwest.[54] When news of the Communist Party attacks broke in the press the week before the Freedom Train opened, McCormick and other right-wing holdouts finally climbed on board.[55]

The Freedom Train began its epic journey in Philadelphia on September 17, 1947, the 160th anniversary of the adjournment of the Constitutional Con-vention. The night before the train opened to the public, NBC broadcast a special program of patriotic songs and speeches from Philadelphia's Indepen-dence Hall. At the opening ceremonies at Broad Street Station the following morning, Mrs. Arthur C. Kaufman, a Philadelphia socialite, smashed a bottle of champagne on the red, white, and blue cars, and Supreme Court Justice Owen Roberts led the star-studded crowd of one thousand in a mass recitation of the "Freedom Pledge":[56]

> I am an American. A free American.
> Free to speak—without fear
> Free to worship God in my own way
> Free to stand for what I think right
> Free to oppose what I believe wrong
> Free to choose those who govern my country.
> This heritage of Freedom I pledge to uphold
> For myself and all mankind.

In their welcoming remarks, Senator Edward Martin (R-Pa.) and Attor-ney General Tom Clark sounded the themes of social tolerance and ideological consensus that were to be at the center of the Freedom Train campaign. Martin railed against both Communists and "hooded men," warning that "persecuted Americans will turn in bitterness from Americanism to Communism. Inad-vertently we shall be building a fifth column within our gates." Clark pounded his fist on the podium as he declared, "All of us must be free or none of us are free. No man can have freedom for himself unless he is willing to share it with all, regardless of race, color or religion."

As the train—which had been given the same high track priority as a presidential special—raced north to New York, then wound its way into New England, crowds greeted it at every stop (figure 7.1). In Brooklyn, between fifty thousand and one hundred thousand people besieged the train—five to ten times as many as could be allowed on board during its twelve-hour stop. At Grand Central Station, the *New York Times* reported, "Old women, their heads tied tightly with shawls, and old men, who hobbled with the aid of canes, stood beside wide-eyed school children sucking lollypops." In Boston, the line of people waiting to climb abroad stretched, four abreast, for half a mile.[57]

Many towns staged huge celebrations in the Freedom Train's honor. In Lawrence, Massachusetts, nineteen thousand mill employees joined their managers at a "Freedom Rally" to welcome the train. In Paterson, New Jersey, five aerial bombs burst over the cars as the mayor opened the exhibit to thousands of schoolchildren who had been dismissed from classes for a day. A Freedom Rally in Chester, Pennsylvania, featured prayers by a priest and rabbi, music by the local Elks' Club band, and a group recitation of the Freedom

Figure 7.1. A crowd of ten thousand people gathered at Philadelphia's Broad Street Station to board the red, white, and blue Freedom Train on its opening day. Similar crowds greeted the train in cities across the nation (Time & Life Pictures/Getty Images).

Pledge. Radio stations in Buffalo and Elmira, New York, devoted their Sunday religious programs to the "Heritage" theme.[58]

When the train arrived in Burlington, Vermont, in mid-October, strings of flags and red, white, and blue lights blanketed the city's main streets. Store windows displayed historical scenes, and citizens wore tags proclaiming "Freedom Is Everybody's Job." In the week preceding the train's arrival, schoolchildren took part in a historical quiz and pageant; women's clubs presented a "Freedom Fashion Show" and on-stage naturalization class; veterans led a torchlight procession to the town square; and decorated trucks carried speakers, entertainers, and copies of historical documents to industrial plants around the city.[59]

American Heritage Foundation officials later pointed to such local celebrations as evidence that the Freedom Train campaign was a "grassroots, up-from-the-people movement." In fact, while the crowds testified to Americans' genuine interest in the train's precious cargo, nearly every other aspect of the train's local reception was carefully orchestrated. Organizers realized early on that, because of time and space constraints, only a fraction of those who wished to view the documents—and whom the projects' sponsors hoped to influence—would actually be able to climb on board. Thus, they focused increasingly on using the train to trigger a "patriotic chain reaction" in communities across the country.[60]

At the local level, this "chain reaction" took the form of "Weeks of Rededication." Months before the Freedom Train arrived in a city or town, its mayor received letters from the attorney general and Winthrop Aldrich, urging active local support for the project. In a follow-up letter, the American Heritage Foundation staff asked the mayor to proclaim a week-long celebration to be climaxed by the arrival of the train. "This will consist of a program in which every facet of a community can participate as an expression of rededication to America's traditions of the past and promise of the future," the foundation explained in an early pamphlet. "Each Rededication Week can thus become a week's 'revival meeting' for American democracy."[61]

To organize the celebration, each mayor was urged to appoint a committee of prominent local citizens—a task made easier by the scores of national organizations who urged their local chapters to participate. But the Freedom Train's handlers left little to chance. No sooner was a committee appointed than it received a kit containing all the ingredients of a successful Rededication Week celebration—457 items in all. A thirty-two-page Community Program Booklet suggested appropriate events. A thick publicity package provided stories, editorials, features, and cartoons that could be used by every department of the local newspaper. The foundation sent Freedom Train advertisements to be sponsored by local businesses, scripts and operettas to be used by local broadcasters, and detailed instruction manuals covering everything from store window displays to school pageants. It even supplied speeches for local dignitaries and sermon notes for ministers, priests, and rabbis.[62]

As if that weren't enough, the foundation dispatched an area representative to each city eight weeks before the train was due to work out the details of Rededication Week with the local committee. Implicit in all this coaching was the threat that if a community's planned program wasn't up to code, the train might visit another city or town instead. It is small wonder that these patriotic "revival meetings" looked remarkably similar from Savannah to Spokane.

For those whose communities were not visited by the Freedom Train, Brophy and his staff arranged a deluge of media attention. The American Heritage Foundation's Hollywood committee produced a documentary on Americans' political rights and civic responsibilities (entitled *Our American Heritage*) that was shown in more than fifteen thousand theatres across the country. Newsreels gave the train extensive coverage, and both *Reader's Digest* and *Mademoiselle* devoted full issues to the American Heritage theme. Corporations, labor unions, chambers of commerce, and school districts passed out millions of pamphlets and study guides to employees, members, and students—including four million copies of the comic book *Captain Marvel and the Freedom Train!* Freedom Train messages popped up on radio programs such as *Fibber McGee and Molly*, and Irving Berlin's new song "Freedom Train" (composed in the wake of the White House conference) appeared in jukeboxes across the country.[63]

Tolerance and Consensus

The pageantry and publicity that surrounded the Freedom Train, extended and reinforced its message. American Heritage Foundation officials later estimated that one in every three Americans—roughly fifty million in all—participated in Rededication Week events, while millions more absorbed the campaign's message from radio spots, magazines, and billboards. Even if these figures are severely inflated, there can be little doubt that many more Americans encountered the American Heritage themes through school assemblies, factory rallies, or sermons in church and synagogue than actually viewed the train's contents themselves. What, then, was the message they heard?

The central message of the American Heritage campaign was a call to active citizenship. Newspaper advertisements, car cards, cartoon booklets, and pamphlets distributed in conjunction with the Freedom Train's tour all urged Americans to safeguard their individual liberties by, among other things, voting, serving on juries, paying taxes, obeying the law, supporting schools, and staying informed on public issues. With the encouragement of the American Heritage Foundation, some communities even organized voter registration drives tied to the train's arrival.[64]

If this message appeared to transcend politics, its intent was conservative. In a letter to U.S. Steel chairman Irving S. Olds, Brophy linked citizenship apathy to left-wing infiltration of unions. "Joe Curran of the National Maritime Union said recently that 500 disciplined Communists among the rank and file in his organization of 80,000 members are in a position to elect 107 local union officers out of 150," Brophy wrote. "It is apparent on all sides that people generally are not taking their duties as citizens as seriously as they should." Indeed, Brophy and other foundation officials noted that the train was producing a "better understanding" of American freedoms and responsibilities among workers in industrial cities.[65]

American Heritage Foundation officials may also have hoped to rouse more affluent voters who could offset the political influence of organized labor and a swollen federal workforce. This was the unpublicized goal of the "National Non-Partisan Register and Vote" campaign the Foundation conducted before the 1952 presidential election. When one correspondent charged that the 1952 registration drive would primarily help Democrats, Brophy explained: "Our efforts are directed at the better element of the voting population, and as such should produce a productive, and, I believe, a conservative result." Brophy added that because registered Democrats outnumbered registered Republicans "getting out this vote is the only chance the Republicans have for victory."[66]

But active citizenship, according to the American Heritage Foundation, went beyond merely voting and paying taxes. One of the nine duties of a good citizen, as spelled out repeatedly during the campaign, was "to avoid any group prejudice based on class, race, or religion." "Jew and Gentile, white and Negro, Catholic and Protestant, skilled and unskilled, rich and poor…are all members of this club, the United States of America," the widely distributed pamphlet *Good Citizen* reminded readers. "Do you speak up in defense of anyone who is criticized or ridiculed for his religion or race?" asked one American Heritage newspaper ad entitled "My Country Quiz of Thee." "And if so, do you practice what you preach?"[67]

The American Heritage Foundation devoted particular attention to religious tolerance. The Freedom Train dedicated an entire section to religious freedom: among other things, it contained a 1790 letter from President George Washington to the Hebrew Congregation in Newport, Rhode Island, declaring that the United States gives "to bigotry no sanction, to persecution no assistance." Borrowing a tactic pioneered by the NCCJ, Freedom Train organizers often paired a rabbi, a priest, and a minister in advertisements, on radio talk shows, and on train welcoming committees. Every Rededication Week featured "Freedom of Religion Day" (celebrated by Jews on Saturday and Christians on Sunday) on which preachers were urged to devote their sermons to that topic. In addition, more than one hundred cities on the Freedom Train's route staged interfaith rallies or roundtables, which were often broadcast over local radio stations.[68]

This message of tolerance, however, was simply a corollary of the ideological consensus celebrated by both the Freedom Train and the American Heritage campaign. Borrowing from the interfaith movement, organizers of the project located America's deepest common belief—the sanctity of the individual—in a shared Judeo-Christian consensus. As elaborated in the handbook *Good Citizen*, which was produced by the Jewish advertising executive Leo Burnett:

> The cornerstone of our republic is a religious concept: that *"every human being is endowed with a soul that is sacred in the eyes of a Sovereign God and with the power to distinguish between right and wrong; that the judgment expressed by a majority of such divinely created human beings is likely to be closest to God's will for all of them; and that every mortal soul is endowed by its Creator with certain natural inalienable rights that no human agency whatever can justly invade."*

In its "sermon notes" and elsewhere, the foundation urged both preachers and laymen to stress "how closely related are our religious ideals and the American form of freedom."[69]

This stress on a religious consensus—Judeo-Christian if no longer Protestant—helped set America apart from the atheistic Communist world, a tactic that was used repeatedly by various groups throughout the cold war. In fact, attempts to link America's national ideals to a deep religiosity may help explain the powerful resurgence of "civil religion" in America at mid-century. Organizers of the Freedom Train campaign repeatedly employed religious terminology for nationalist ends: the documents on the Freedom

Train were "American scriptures," the Train itself was a "national shrine," and the Rededication Weeks were "revival meetings for democracy." In a speech delivered at Grand Central Station, Winthrop Aldrich compared the Freedom Train project to a national "pilgrimage":

> It is a different kind of pilgrimage from the ones that took our ancestors to the Holy Land or Chaucer's wayfarers to Canterbury. For this time, because of the vastness of the country, we are taking the shrine to the people, instead of the people to the shrine.
>
> But the spirit and purpose are the same. It is a means of paying our profound respect to the ideas in which all Americans believe. It is a means of renewing our faith.[70]

The contrast with communism also salvaged the "consensus" from cracks that might otherwise have proved irreparable. Like the NCCJ, the American Heritage Foundation argued that a belief in religious freedom and the primacy of the individual was common to all three of the nation's great religious faiths. In fact, parts of this message were at odds with the teachings of the Roman Catholic Church. Catholics emphasized the importance of tradition and the teaching authority of the Church rather than the individual's conscience and unmediated relationship with God. Moreover, although some Catholic laymen and clergy endorsed the interfaith movement as early as the 1930s, much of the Church hierarchy remained lukewarm toward the movement or openly criticized it because of the religious relativism it implied. Ultimately, many Catholic bishops and archbishops did endorse the Freedom Train; but in doing so they often stressed the nation's "faith" and "freedom" in contrast to atheistic Communism, rather than America's "freedom of faith."[71]

The American Heritage Foundation's embrace of the interfaith message stemmed in part from the influence of Louis Novins and Barney Balaban. More generally, it reflected growing support among key segments of the business community for the interfaith movement after World War II. In the late 1940s and 1950s, America's business community poured sizeable sums into the NCCJ and other groups advocating social harmony and tolerance within the context of ideological consensus. The growing number of Jewish and Catholic executives fueled this alliance, as did the close identification of the interfaith movement with America's cold war interests. But the alliance also pointed up a convenient ideological conjunction: the same message of "tolerance" used to condemn religious prejudice could be used to castigate labor militancy.

Indeed, the American Heritage Foundation's handling of class issues in many ways mirrored its approach to religious ones. When the foundation urged Americans to avoid "class prejudice," it was condemning labor-industry conflict, not disrespect for the poor. In print advertisements, speeches, and countless radio spots, the foundation stressed the basic agreement of labor and business leaders on America's fundamental values. (The precise values in question were often left vague.) Most cities and towns on the Freedom Train's route celebrated "Labor and Management Day," staging joint luncheons, parades, roundtables, and mass rallies in which managers and workers pledged allegiance to common American goals. Many of these techniques were adopted directly from the interfaith movement.[72]

The concept of "class tolerance" legitimized organized labor, but it subtly undermined the legitimacy of the strike, labor's most potent weapon. In speeches and published material, the American Heritage Foundation repeatedly defined the American worker's principal freedom as "the right to work where he wants," a freedom that echoed eerily of the open shop. Other materials painted both business and profits as quintessentially American: one advertisement, for instance, defined both voting in unions and voting in stockholder meetings as forms of good citizenship. The American Heritage program and the Advertising Council's "American Economic System" campaign, said Brophy, are "reverse sides of the same coin."[73]

But just as the notion of interfaith consensus concealed buried tensions, so, too, did the concept of business-labor agreement. At times, such tensions rose to the surface, momentarily marring what American Heritage Foundation organizers had hoped would be a seamless salute to freedom and unity. This happened at a management-labor luncheon in December 1948, held to celebrate the Freedom Train's return to New York City. Paramount's Barney Balaban spoke for management at the luncheon, while A. F. Whitney, president of the Brotherhood of Railroad Trainmen, represented labor.[74]

Balaban began by praising the American Heritage Foundation for arranging a "family reunion" at which business and labor could "pay our respects to our common parentage—the American way of life." Balaban went on to define that parentage, stressing the indivisibility of the nation's political, religious, and economic freedoms. "The record of history discloses that [the relinquishment of profits] have been the inevitable prelude to the relinquishment of other human rights," he declared. "Profits make jobs!...Profits create the gravy for which labor can bargain....The profit system is as American as hot dogs and baseball." Balaban urged labor to "*act* its age!" before concluding with his own Horatio Alger story.

Whitney's speech was in many ways an inverse of that made by Balaban. While Balaban hailed business's contribution to the "American way of life,"

Whitney not surprisingly praised labor's contribution. Balaban implicitly contrasted American freedoms to Communism; Whitney compared them to the fascism of Mussolini and Hitler, leaders who he noted had moved quickly to destroy organized labor. Whitney acknowledged the role of "legitimate management" in the American economy but took pointed jabs at "industrial labor-baiters" and "industrialists who reaped millions of dollars during the two world wars" while labor rolled up its sleeves. It is small wonder that a move to publish the luncheon's speeches was stymied at least temporarily by a debate over whether to distribute Whitney's speech.[75]

Such clear fracture points, however, were relatively rare. In part, this reflected the abstract nature of words such as "freedom" and the degree of control the American Heritage Foundation exercised over the media campaign. But it also reflected the growing willingness of many national labor leaders to suppress their differences with management in the face of expanding global Communism, domestic red-baiting, and an American economic boom. By September 1947, when the Freedom Train got underway, the militancy American labor had displayed just one year earlier had largely disappeared. And many American workers were for the first time beginning to enjoy a lifestyle that could fairly be called middle class.

"A Shame Beyond Description": Race and the Freedom Train

For the Freedom Train's organizers, the issue of race proved far trickier than that of religion or class, for here common ground was harder to define. In the late nineteenth and early twentieth centuries, "national unity" generally meant a healing of Civil War wounds, a union of northern and southern whites that explicitly relegated black Americans to second-class status. In the wake of World War II, however, such a resolution to the race issue was no longer acceptable. If the American Heritage Foundation sided with blacks in their struggle for equality and inclusion, it was sure to alienate southern whites. But if it sided with white segregationists, it threatened to undermine its own message of inclusive consensus. Initially, Foundation officials tried to finesse the issue by defining segregation as a local, rather than a national, issue or denouncing it in tones so soft they could barely be heard. Ultimately, however, in a development that foreshadowed the civil rights struggles of the 1950s and 1960s, pressure from southern blacks and their white allies forced the Foundation to take a tougher stance. In so doing, the American Heritage Foundation became one of the first national organizations since Reconstruction to impose desegregation—however limited—on the South.

The issue of segregation first came to the fore in June 1947 when Lester Granger, executive secretary of the Urban League, addressed a letter to American Heritage Foundation president Thomas Brophy. Noting that the Urban League was among the Freedom Train's many sponsors, Granger wrote, "For me, it would be a monumental travesty upon our democratic concept, if the Emancipation Proclamation were to be exhibited to an American audience rigidly segregated according to race" (figure 7.2). Granger urged American

Figure 7.2. An ex-slave reads the Emancipation Proclamation aboard the Freedom Train. The issue of race derailed the efforts of train organizers to present the nation as unified, inclusive, and consensual. Civil rights activists repeatedly noted the irony of allowing the Emancipation Proclamation to be displayed to audiences rigidly segregated by race (Time & Life Pictures/Getty Images).

Heritage Foundation officials to insist on desegregated viewing below the Mason-Dixon Line or to cancel the train's southern stops.[76]

Brophy's response shows that he clearly recognized the explosive potential of the race issue but had no intention of using the Freedom Train to promote social change. He immediately forwarded Granger's letter to Louis Novins, noting that it "calls for a skillful reply." Brophy's own inclination was to sidestep the issue by telling the black leader that the American Heritage Foundation merely supplied the train to communities across the nation but took no responsibility for local viewing arrangements. He added to Novins, however, "I am not sure such forthrightness is wise."[77]

At roughly the same time that Granger was writing to Brophy, pressure on the race issue was developing on another front. In December 1946, President Truman had responded to rising racial tensions in the U.S. by appointing a presidential Committee on Civil Rights; he charged the committee with recommending actions that the federal government could take to better protect the civil rights of all Americans. By early June 1947, some members of the committee, led by Lever Brothers President Charles Luckman, were arguing that "an educational civil rights campaign should be launched on a national scale." The committee's chairman, General Electric President Charles E. Wilson, resisted this approach, arguing instead for wrapping the civil rights message into the Freedom Train campaign. Wilson, who also served on the board of the American Heritage Foundation, soon won over Attorney General Clark, who told President Truman that he believed this approach was "quite sufficient."[78]

Although Wilson, like Clark, generally supported civil rights, he may have hoped to blunt the critical edge of a civil rights educational campaign by burying it in the Freedom Train's more general celebration of American values. There is no evidence that either the American Heritage Foundation or the Advertising Council altered publicity materials to highlight the civil rights message. Still, in early July, Wilson presented a resolution to the American Heritage Foundation declaring that "no segregation of any individuals or groups of any kind on the basis of race or religion be allowed at any exhibition of the Freedom Train held anywhere." The executive committee of the Board of Trustees unanimously adopted the resolution.[79]

American Heritage Foundation officials later argued that "any other course was unthinkable. It is our firm determination that the American Heritage program shall be an instrumentality for strengthening the freedoms and liberties of all Americans regardless of race, creed or color." At the time, however, many of those associated with the American Heritage Foundation were clearly skittish about taking a public stand on segregation; some executive committee members undoubtedly hoped the resolution could be used to quiet Granger and Luckman without stirring public outcry in the South. In any case, rather than announcing the desegregation decision, they voted unanimously to have the Attorney General stipulate in his letter to mayors that there would be no segregation on the train. Committee members seem to have hoped that the issue would go away or could be handled quietly behind the scenes.[80]

But if Tom Clark had been reluctant to back an independent civil rights campaign, he was equally disinclined to raise the issue explicitly in a letter. "The feeling here…is that such a statement would be out of place in this letter, both because it might tend to point up the issue where it does not exist, and because it might become, quite easily, a political football," the Attorney General's liaison to the American Heritage Foundation wrote. "That, of course, is what we all wish to avoid, in every respect." Ultimately, Clark's office and the Freedom Train organizers settled on subtler phrasing. In describing the train's contents, Clark would note that the documents "in their spirit and meaning belong to all Americans equally."[81]

Lester Granger and NAACP officials were privately informed of the executive committee's resolution, then were sworn to secrecy. But to other blacks, who lacked the benefit of such inside information, the American Heritage Foundation appeared to have said nothing at all. Thus, in mid-September, the black picture magazine *Our World* devoted a two-page spread to a poem entitled "Freedom Train" by the acclaimed black poet Langston Hughes. In introducing the poem, the editors claimed that the American Heritage Foundation had taken the name for its train from a famous slave spiritual about rebellion against slave masters. "It is unthinkable that so vital a project should have been clouded by questions of whether Negro Americans will be permitted to view these documents in the South on the same basis as all citizens," the editors wrote. "It is a shame beyond description to plan for exhibition of the Emancipation Proclamation for 'whites only' and 'colored only.'"[82]

Langston Hughes's poem, which also appeared in the *New Republic*, struck a far darker note than Irving Berlin's flag-waving rhapsody of the same name. Berlin's "Freedom Train" celebrated established American liberties, hailing "the Documents that made us great." Hughes's poem, by contrast, explicitly questioned the reach of those freedoms:

> …The Birmingham station's marked COLORED and WHITE.
> The white folks go left, the colored go right—
> They even got a segregated lane.

Is that the way to get aboard the Freedom Train?
I got to know about this
Freedom Train!
If my children ask me, *Daddy, please explain*
Why There's Jim Crow stations for the Freedom Train,
What shall I tell my children? ... *You* tell me –
'Cause freedom ain't freedom when a man ain't free.
But maybe they explains it on the
Freedom Train ...

Our World publisher John Davis mailed the poem to every member of the American Heritage Foundation's board along with a letter challenging each, "as one of our fellow Americans," to take the "necessary effective steps" to ensure that there would be no discrimination in connection with the Freedom Train.[83]

Brophy's outraged response to Davis's letter stated that the Freedom Train would be open to all without segregation or discrimination "insofar as it is in the power of the Board of Trustees of the American Heritage Foundation to control this." But in Davis's eyes this did not go far enough. "Our American democracy is a living thing," the editor replied. "Your Board of Trustees may be satisfied with the status quo as it affects Negro Americans in the South, but millions of Negro Americans and millions more of their white fellow Americans are not. These true American patriots say to you very simply that it *is* within the power of the American Heritage Foundation to guarantee absolutely no segregation in regard to the Freedom Train project." Davis suggested that the train bypass southern railroad stations and instead use ramps from railroad sidings, which would allow all Americans to enter the train together. Building such ramps "may cost money—but there are millions of Americans whose nickels and dimes will be devoted to such a cause," he added.[84]

Langston Hughes's poem, Davis's letter, and a newspaper column by Paul Robeson criticizing the Freedom Train served warning to the American Heritage Foundation that it would not be able to suppress the segregation issue much longer.[85] In September, the foundation responded to growing pressure from blacks by adding F. D. Patterson, president of the Tuskegee Institute, to its board of trustees. When he accepted the position, Patterson asked Freedom Train organizers to make public their position on segregation before or at the same time as their announcement of his election to the board. On September 26, nine days after the Freedom Train left Philadelphia's Broad Street Station, Winthrop Aldrich did just that.[86]

But announcing the decision was not the same as publicizing it. When one American Heritage Foundation staffer urged that the ban on segregation be broadcast through national channels, Louis Novins hit the roof. John Fitzgerald had argued that widely publicizing the policy would take pressure off members of the foundation's advance team (known as "area representatives"), who were responsible for finalizing local arrangements. "I am completely in disagreement with all suggestions listed," Novins wrote. "If we followed them, we should be going out of our way to stir up difficulties and dissension." Rather, Novins argued, the area representatives should confer privately with southern mayors and mayors' committees to determine the attitude in each town. "Our purpose is not to stimulate public discussion on the subject but to take only the necessary steps of determining the official policy," Novins added.[87]

Novins clearly hoped to avoid a showdown in the South. But he also recognized that the American Heritage Foundation would have to enforce its policy once it crossed the Mason-Dixon Line. This realization provoked the first in a series of behind-the-scenes discussions about the nature of segregation and the foundation's jurisdiction. Novins argued that Freedom Train officials should make hourly inspections of southern railroad stations during the train's stop to ensure that there was no discrimination in the lines leading to the train. But this interpretation was too broad for some members of the foundation's board. Although the full board upheld the executive committee's ban on segregation, it voted that the organization's responsibility did not extend beyond the doors of the train.[88]

Margaret Patterson, the wife of former Secretary of War Robert P. Patterson, led the move to curb the foundation's jurisdiction. Her reasoning underscores the dangers of arguing for tolerance and inclusion on the grounds of national unity. For a decade, opponents of nativism, racism, anti-Catholicism, and anti-Semitism had been arguing that intolerance played into the hands of Nazis and Communists who were trying to divide America against itself. But Patterson, with an eye to the South, turned this argument on its head:

> Funds for the Foundation have come from all sections of the country, and from all races and creeds. This support was given with the hope that greater understanding of our American Heritage would help to cement all factions.
>
> If instead we allow the Train to become a spearhead for a minority, or even for a majority, we betray the trust of America as a whole, no matter how deeply sympathetic we are.

To highlight any minority rouses its fighting spirit and focuses the prejudice against it,—and this leads to disunity.

"Divide and Conquer" is the most effective slogan of Communism and our strength depends on our solidarity as Americans,...

In my opinion, it is important that we do not stir one group of Americans against another.

As Patterson clearly recognized, banning segregation favored interracial unity over interregional harmony.[89]

Memphis

As the Freedom Train pushed south, the American Heritage Foundation redoubled its efforts to head off a conflict. The organization's area representatives cajoled and threatened local mayor's committees into dropping discriminatory viewing plans. Meanwhile, the Freedom Train's national handlers stopped supplying the NAACP with advance information on the train's stops. For all these precautions, rumors of trouble filtered out of the South. In mid-October, syndicated columnist Walter Winchell reported that some southern cities were setting up separate viewing times for blacks and whites—a plan that Novins, Brophy, and Aldrich all agreed constituted segregation. The American Heritage Foundation officials told reporters they knew nothing of such plans, even as they pressured southern communities to drop them.[90]

The issue finally came to a head in Memphis. As Novins was well aware from his work in the movie industry, Memphis had one of the strictest racial codes in the South: the city even required that movie scenes showing a commingling of blacks and whites be sliced before films could be shown within city limits. Since World War I, Memphis politics had been tightly controlled by Edward H. Crump, whom one historian has described as "one of the toughest political bosses ever to emerge in the U.S." Crump and his political protégé, Memphis mayor Jim Pleasants, argued that integrated viewing of the Freedom Train would "poison the minds of the people" and spark race riots. On November 18, after two weeks of fruitless negotiations with the American Heritage Foundation, Pleasants announced the city's policy to the press: when the train arrived in Memphis on January 7, 1948, it would be open to whites and blacks for 6.5 hours each.[91]

Reached for comment by Memphis newspapers, Louis Novins called off the stop. In so doing, he appears to have pushed his authority to the limit. Although

Brophy, Aldrich, and Novins all agreed that the American Heritage Foundation should not tolerate separate viewing hours for whites and blacks, the full board remained divided on the issue. Margaret Patterson immediately fired off a letter to Brophy protesting the cancellation of the stop and arguing that "people, both white and colored, who are denied the privilege of standing together in person, may still stand together in reverent belief in Freedom." Novins warned Aldrich not to circulate Patterson's letter to other board members as it might "invite unnecessary discussion." Indeed, another trustee—while not challenging the Memphis cancellation directly—urged caution, adding, "the Freedom Train is not coming out of the South unscathed."[92]

The cancellation of the Memphis stop drew immediate applause from American blacks and liberal whites. The Muncie, Indiana, branch of the NAACP sent a telegram congratulating Novins and the American Heritage Foundation for "showing hope you will stand by your democratic convictions." Board member and Tuskegee Institute President F. D. Patterson also applauded Novins's "courageous" action. The Vancouver, Washington, branch of Progressive Citizens of America wrote: "Through the foggy atmosphere of witch hunts in the Capitol, Senate Committees wielding the blackjack for the monopolies and trusts and the Un-American Committee crusading against freedom of speech and civil liberties, our members beheld your edict…as rays of the rising sun on the horizon."[93]

In Memphis, a coalition that included both city newspapers, many businessmen, and some civic organizations lobbied Mayor Pleasants to change his mind. But the mayor—backed by Crump—only dug in more deeply: the Sunday after he issued his original decision, Pleasants took to the radio to warn of bloodshed if whites and blacks boarded the train together. The mayor's speech so inflamed the issue that the coalition called off the campaign, arguing that now the train's appearance might indeed spark violence. "The Freedom Train has actually come to Memphis already insofar as its ideals are concerned," one veterans' organization said in withdrawing its request. The physical appearance of the train now "would be a mockery. Any artificially-planned week of rededication, in view of what has occurred, would be meaningless."[94]

Newspapers scattered across the South also praised the American Heritage Foundation's move, and dozens of communities scrambled to replace Memphis on the Freedom Train's itinerary. Many cities already on the train's southern swing hastily issued public assurances that they would waive Jim Crow at their stations for the Freedom Train's visit. Atlanta's mayor William Hartsfield was widely quoted as saying he was "willing to stand beside any American citizen, regardless of race or creed, in mutual admiration and respect for those great historical charters of American freedom." Such reactions prompted Novins to speculate, "Perhaps the cancellation of the Memphis visit has had a better educational effect than the appearance of the train itself."[95]

Not all southerners accepted the decision so quiescently. Particularly in Memphis and the Deep South, many saw the cancellation as a power grab on the part of the North. "It is just another opportunity of you northerners to ram the negroes down the throats of southerners of the white race, when if the truth were admitted you would not give our negroes a crust of bread if they were hungry," a Mrs. Harry Jay wrote Novins. Memphis papers were filled with angry letters to the editor—many from neighboring states—backing the mayor's stance. One writer decried "northern dictators," while another warned that "if this concession is granted…other requests of similar nature will be made by trouble makers from other states." A third redefined "segregation" in geographic terms: "The Freedom Train will practice 'segregation' too, and bar Memphis."[96]

Just how far the racial issue skewed traditional political lines can be seen in a letter from one Sylvanus Polk to a Memphis paper. "It may be that this whole program is essentially political; that the spiritual political successors of Mrs. Eleanor Roosevelt and Mr. Henry Wallace have prepared this program to exploit these sacred documents," Mr. Polk wrote. Aldrich, Brophy, and Novins, staunch Republicans and Wallace-haters all, would undoubtedly have been startled by the comparison. But it did underscore one central irony: the consensus philosophy that these men embraced partly for conservative economic reasons could have radical implications when applied to issues of race.

"Problem D"

Overnight the cancellation of the Memphis stop turned the Freedom Train into an explosive issue throughout the Deep South. In Vicksburg, Mississippi, the town's "Old Guard" agitated against the American Heritage Foundation, charging that the organization was trying to trigger a black revolt. The mayor of Meridian, Mississippi, warned that the train might have to bypass his town because the Chamber of Commerce had refused to organize Rededication Week ceremonies there; the stop was rescued only after Meridian's Junior Chamber of Commerce, church groups, and school officials stepped forward to promote the train. The segregation issue became so hot that the American Heritage Foundation's national director worried about the fallout if messages were intercepted in southern telegraph offices; he instructed advance workers to refer to the issue in telegrams simply as "Problem D."[97]

The sudden explosiveness of the race issue also forced the American Heritage Foundation to reconsider its definition of segregation. On November 17, the day the Memphis stop was cancelled, Brophy had recommended a solution to this "difficult and delicate" problem in a memo to Aldrich. "Assuming that whites and negroes will assemble in different waiting rooms in some southern railroad stations, it is inevitable that two lines will develop," Brophy wrote. These lines would have to be merged before they reached the train door, but in determining how this would be done "the basic premise is that…all must be treated alike." Thus, if the black line was held up for an extended period—or if blacks and whites were admitted by hours—this would constitute segregation. But if blacks and whites were admitted to the train alternately in groups of one hundred or so, "we would consider that regulation."[98]

Aldrich agreed to the plan, and Freedom Train workers were instructed accordingly. But four days later, Novins urged a revision of the policy. The mayor of Hattiesburg, Mississippi, had just announced that foundation representatives had agreed to allow two different lines to feed the train. Novins told Aldrich that he had been flooded with calls from southern reporters, and—while he had thus far denied knowledge of the Hattiesburg plan—he would not be able to avoid a direct statement much longer. "I do not see how the Foundation can state publicly that dividing the people into segregated blocks of 100 whites and 100 colored people does not violate the spirit of our resolution," Novins said. "There is no doubt from my conversations with newspaper people that they consider this to be the same type of segregation as that suggested by the Mayor of Memphis, only varying in degree."[99]

There is no record of Aldrich's response to Novins. The Hattiesburg situation was resolved quietly—the exact details aren't clear—and the American Heritage Foundation again ducked a public statement on the issue. Unofficially, Novins and his coworkers appear to have adopted the advice of Walter White, who suggested that at southern stops, a single line be brought through a side entrance to the depot, avoiding waiting rooms altogether. Two Georgia cities, Savannah and Brunswick, merged separate black and white lines at the entrance to the railroad yard—apparently without protest. American Heritage Foundation officials undoubtedly hoped that the segregation issue had been put to rest.[100]

They had not counted on Birmingham, Alabama. In the wake of World War II, the steel town's black population was as politically active as any in the South. In the months before the scheduled arrival of the Freedom Train, the city's black ministers had boycotted a segregated "festival of faith" sponsored by white Protestants; the black newspaper, the *Birmingham World*, had fought the traditionally Jim Crow Armistice Day parade; and protests from the Negro Business League had convinced the Junior Chamber of Commerce to integrate black "features" into the Christmas Carnival parade. All this sparked a strong counterreaction from local white supremacists.[101]

Hoping to head off a showdown during the Freedom Train's visit, the American Heritage Foundation's area representative and the head of Birmingham's local arrangements committee decided on a policy similar to that proposed by Hattiesburg: black and white lines would feed the train, with viewers let into the cars in blocks of twenty each. White newspaper reporters were informed of the "Birmingham Plan" but observed a voluntary gag order to prevent trouble.

One newspaper was not invited to the meeting. But on December 4, Emory Jackson, publisher of the *Birmingham World* and president of the local NAACP chapter, learned of the plan. He immediately called Novins, who told him that the American Heritage Foundation was still reviewing the Birmingham policy and advised against making a public ruckus. Jackson ignored Novins's advice and presented the plan to the Birmingham NAACP that evening. The group agreed not only to oppose the segregationist policy but also to "carry the message of freedom's protest to every corner of the world." Some even wanted to declare the day of the train's arrival "Freedom Protest Day."[102]

Over the next two weeks, Birmingham blacks deluged the national offices of the American Heritage Foundation and the NAACP (which had remained surprisingly mum on the issue) with telegrams and letters urging the cancellation of the stop. Meanwhile, a local NAACP committee told the three-man Birmingham City Commission that the plan was contrary to local practice because black and white citizens could already stand in single lines in banks, post offices, and supermarkets. In a telling addition that suggests the ways in which the train's initial message of social harmony could be subverted, the NAACP committee also argued that the Birmingham Plan "defeats the purpose for which the Freedom Train was organized." Not only did the train's sponsors "seek to exhibit freedom undivided," the Birmingham blacks argued, but also they "[hoped] to explore new frontiers in progressive race relations."[103]

Still, the American Heritage Foundation stalled. At a special meeting held December 8 to discuss the line-up outside the train, the foundation's board accepted Aldrich's advice that it issue no public statement on the issue. On the day local NAACP members presented their case to the Birmingham City Commission, Brophy sent a telegram to the commission's president "respectfully reaffirm[ing]" the segregation ban, but offering no further definition of that word. This allowed Commission President Cooper Green to respond that "without deviating from that understandable policy" the city would, as a police precaution, maintain separate lines to the train "merged continuously, fairly and with equal opportunity to all."[104]

The American Heritage Foundation was not alone in its reluctance to speak up. The public silence of Walter White and the NAACP's national office prompted Emory Jackson to complain "that no word has come lately from you as we fight with hope fading." The most charitable explanation for the hesitation of both national organizations is the fact that Birmingham officials and the foundation's area representative could point to several black citizens who, in one fashion or another, had endorsed the Birmingham Plan. Among them was Dr. E. W. Taggert, a local dentist who also sat on the NAACP's national board. Dr. Taggert later explained that he had approved the plan, despite his "unalterable" opposition to segregation, because it seemed the only way to bring the Freedom Train to Birmingham and avoid besmirching the city's image.[105]

Finally, on December 22, just a week before the Freedom Train was due to arrive, Emory Jackson had had enough. While the Birmingham NAACP formulated boycott plans, Jackson wrote Aldrich directly asking whether the foundation had changed its policy on segregation and, more important, how the foundation defined the word. "The American Heritage Foundation is represented as saying [the Birmingham Plan] is not 'segregation,'" Jackson wrote. "Birmingham Commissioner Eugene Connor says that [it] is 'segregation' and he should know."[106]

The following day, Brophy finally responded to the telegram Cooper Green had sent nearly a week earlier. Birmingham, the American Heritage Foundation's president insisted, had to have a single integrated line that extended the length of the Freedom Train and through the entire exhibit area. Two of the city's three commissioners immediately rejected Brophy's demand, telegramming that "our segregation law...is not a mantle to be laid aside at the instance of either this or that visitor to the city." On December 24, Brophy finally called off the Birmingham stop.[107]

Walter White immediately hailed the decision as "the greatest Christmas gift to the cause of democracy which can be given." In a syndicated column published a few days later, he added: "The courage of the American Heritage Foundation in sticking to its principles...has done more to make sharp and clear the issue of bigotry versus democracy than any other episode in recent years." The NAACP gave the foundation its highest honor, and the curator of the New York Public Library's Schomburg collection included the organization on his 1947 honor roll of race relations. Even the *Daily Worker* called the Freedom Train's southern journey "a spectacular victory over the Jimcrow system."[108]

In Memphis, the cancellation of the Freedom Train helped trigger the downhill slide of political boss Edward Crump. Crump had long relied on the support of Memphis' business community, as well as on his ability to manipulate the black vote by paying poll taxes and recruiting black leaders through calculated paternalism. But the Freedom Train incident embarrassed and alienated a handful of the city's "forward-thinking" business owners, and this group—with the strong support of the *Memphis Press-Scimitar*—formed a citizen's committee to counter the Crump machine. At the same time, the blatant racism revealed by the episode so outraged many of the city's black citizens that they turned against those leaders who cooperated with Crump. In the fall of 1948, black laborers, liberal business owners, and civic reformers joined forces to defeat Crump's handpicked candidate for the U.S. Senate, handing the boss his first major political setback. One black activist called the Freedom Train standoff "the beginning of the end" for Crump.[109]

Elsewhere, the train's legacy on racial issues was murkier. The Freedom Train could not erase decades of accumulated racial prejudice in either the North or the South. But it did do more than perhaps any other event of the early postwar period to bring Gunnar Myrdal's "American Dilemma" sharply to the attention of a national audience.[110] Although the train's impact was primarily symbolic, it had some practical effect as well. The American Heritage Foundation pressured mayors in Montgomery and other southern cities to include blacks on their Rededication Week planning committees; these committees provided an early forum for southern blacks and whites to work together on civic issues. More important, the Freedom Train episode gave southern blacks a trial run at a tactic they would perfect during the civil rights movement of the 1950s and early 1960s: embarrassing national power brokers into forcing the South to live up to stated "American" ideals.

On January 16, 1949, the Freedom Train returned to Washington D.C. for a week-long celebration of President Truman's inauguration. Then it officially closed its doors. Organizers had considered extending the train's run for another year but worried about their ability to raise the necessary funds. In addition, the National Archives, which was responsible for ensuring the safe return of the documents, had raised questions about their condition. From the beginning, preservationists had noted problems maintaining the proper temperature and humidity on the train. Then on March 4, 1948, as the train sat on a siding in San Bernardino, California, a fire broke out in one of the cars. The fire was extinguished without damaging any of the priceless documents—and the episode was miraculously kept out of the press—but the National Archives hardly felt reassured.[111]

Thus on January 22, 1949, sixteen months and thirty-seven thousand miles after it began, America's great festival of "rededication" came to an end. But, although the Freedom Train itself was dismantled, its legacy lived on in America's political landscape and patriotic lexicon. The Freedom Train's slogan—"Freedom Is Everybody's Job"—showed up in speeches, advertising campaigns, and even on the stationery used by Voice of America in the early 1950s. The American Heritage Foundation survived into the late 1960s and carried many of the themes of the Freedom Train campaign into subsequent projects on behalf of national holidays, voter registration, and Radio Free Europe.

By promoting a shared American Way, the Freedom Train campaign helped open a door for those on the fringes of the nation's "mainstream" culture. The train and the accompanying media campaign helped popularize the vision of the interfaith movement and call attention to the national disgrace of segregation. It also provided a cultural language and symbolic lever that could be used by those fighting for integration, tolerance, and civil rights. At the same time, the tolerance and inclusion the Freedom Train project promoted tended to downplay class divides and rested ultimately on the assumption that Americans shared a common ideology: although the elements of this consensus were sometimes disputed, they emphatically did not include Communism. Thus, the Freedom Train episode helped pave the way for a new form of repression: in the years that followed, as many Catholics and Jews and even some black Americans moved toward the American "mainstream," charges of "communism" were used to bludgeon those who asked for too much, too fast.

CHAPTER 8

Crusading for Freedom at Home and Abroad

On April 18, 1948, Italy held its first postwar elections. In the months leading up to the vote, many U.S. leaders watched developments in Europe with mounting alarm. In 1947, the Soviets had rigged Hungary's elections and purged left-wing anticommunist political leaders. In February 1948, communists seized power in Czechoslovakia, toppling leaders greatly admired in the West. In March, the Soviet delegation walked out of four-power discussions in Berlin, and the U.S. commander in Germany warned that a Soviet attack might occur within days. Against this backdrop, Italy's well-organized and well-financed Communist Party, allied with the militant Italian Socialist Party, threatened to exploit widespread economic discontent and sweep to power in free elections. U.S. government leaders saw the elections as "an apocalyptic test of strength between communism and democracy"—a test that might well determine the fate of democracy on the continent.[1] The Italian election, Senator Arthur Vandenberg declared, was "the most important election in the next one hundred years."[2]

Italian Americans rushed to the aid of their country. Galvanized by Italian-language newspapers and radio stations, the Catholic Church, fraternal organizations, and community leaders, Italian Americans launched a massive letter-writing campaign to inform their overseas kinsmen of the dangers of voting Communist and the virtues of the "American way." In the early months of 1948, thousands of Italian Americans lined up at post offices around the country to mail letters to family and friends abroad. Italian-American newspapers from New York to San Francisco suggested topics for letters, provided writing help, or printed messages that could be clipped and signed. The New

England Marshall Plan Committee organized "Freedom Flights" to carry letters from Boston-area Italian Americans overseas. Catholic priests passed out pre-printed letters after mass. And radio stations offered free recording time to those who wished to send phonograph records instead: at radio station WOV in New York, which devoted half its time to Italian-language programming, more than four hundred war brides turned up to record phonographs, which were airmailed to friends and relatives in the Old Country. On March 23, the *New York Times* reported that "the volume of airmail letters to Italy had doubled in the last few days"; by April, a million extra Italy-bound letters a week were passing through the New York post office.[3]

Commentators later hailed the "Letters to Italy" campaign as a "spontaneous uprising," prompted by Italian Americans' "sentimental attachment" to Italy, their "horror of the Godlessness [sic] of Communism," and their "deep love for America and...fervent belief in a political system based on the dignity and importance of the individual."[4] The campaign did tap deep sentiment within the Italian-American community, but it was hardly a grassroots effort. Drew Pearson, the muckraking columnist and liberal anticommunist, inspired the letter-writing campaign. It was orchestrated by Italian-American leaders, many of whom had once supported Mussolini and now seized the opportunity both to defeat Old Country leftists and to redeem themselves in American eyes. The campaign also drew strong backing from public officials both within and outside of the Truman administration, who saw personal letters from friends and relatives as a particularly effective form of propaganda.

The "Letters to Italy" campaign was an early example of a technique used extensively by the U.S. during the cold war: popular or public diplomacy.[5] From the late 1940s on, both government officials and private elites worked to enlist civil society in general—and immigrants and their children, in particular—in a defense of the American Way overseas. The Letters to Italy campaign grew out of an earlier foray into public diplomacy, the Friendship Train of 1947, and it in turn inspired another: the ambitious "Letters from America" campaign of the 1950s. In addition to these efforts, scores of private groups, working closely with the State Department, the Central Intelligence Agency (CIA), and the U.S. Information Agency (USIA), recruited millions of Americans into student exchanges, pen pal programs, trade group meetings, cultural congresses, sister city affiliations, and a massive "Crusade for Freedom" to raise money for Radio Free Europe and Radio Free Asia. In the 1950s, the USIA billed various "People-to-People" programs as among its most important initiatives, on a par with better remembered projects such as the "Family of Man" exhibit and the "Atoms for Peace" campaign.[6]

Such efforts should be understood not simply as weapons in the cold war but as part of the complex and ongoing process of constructing a domestic consensus on America's core values. During both the Letters to Italy and the Letters from America campaigns, millions of ethnic Americans were bombarded by—or, quite literally, handed—the language with which to describe their American blessings. In churches, community halls, foreign-language newspapers, street rallies, and radio broadcasts, first- and second-generation Americans were repeatedly reminded that the U.S. was a land of freedom and plenty, a bastion against godlessness, and the only steadfast ally of their respective homelands. Organizers of both campaigns clearly hoped to counter leftist propaganda in Europe and to spread American values through a "campaign of truth" far more personal—and thus more effective—than Voice of America broadcasts. At the same time, by recruiting U.S. ethnics into the effort to "sell" American values to the world, campaign organizers hoped to solidify the allegiance of these thirty-five million Americans to a particular vision of the American Way. The "Crusade for Freedom" was aimed at a far broader audience—the entire American public—but it too had a reflexive quality. Crusade organizers encouraged millions of Americans to sign "Freedom scrolls," send "Freedom-grams" to Eastern Europe and make small contributions to the campaign. In so doing, they sought to "develop" in Americans a "greater awareness" of their own blessings, to reinforce an anticommunist consensus, and to "persuade each and every American—man, woman, and child"—that he or she stood on the front lines of battle against that "Evil Force."[7]

The elites who spearheaded such efforts were for the most part drawn from the ranks of moderate and liberal cold warriors in both parties. Hardcore red-baiters such as Sen. Joseph McCarthy and the leaders of the House Un-American Activities Committee were generally less concerned with fostering social harmony and building broad public support for anticommunist internationalism than with exposing "enemies" at home. Embracing a rightwing populism that was at odds with the very notions of civility and consensus, they nevertheless cast a long shadow over many cold war campaigns.[8] Those elites who sought to shape a cold war consensus in the late 1940s and 1950s never abandoned the notion that the U.S. was a Judeo-Christian or tri-faith nation, but increasingly they shifted their emphasis from religious pluralism to ecumenical religiosity—to the notion that the U.S. was a God-fearing nation in contrast to its atheist enemy. (This shift in emphasis tended to elide differences with the rhetoric offered by Sen. McCarthy and his allies on the Christian right.[9]) Ads encouraging Americans to enlist in the "Crusade for Freedom" hailed efforts to unmask communist villains behind the Iron

Curtain; while such ads focused on Eastern Europe, they implicitly justified and reinforced a domestic culture of informing. Most important, the intensifying red scare marginalized many on the liberal left who had once used the language of shared values to argue for a more egalitarian society.

Finally, efforts like those described here suggest both the dangers and possibilities that the cold war—and America's newfound internationalism—opened for ethnic Americans. Those first- and second-generation Americans who questioned the equation of freedom and plenty with the U.S. status quo—those who challenged the nation's tactics or doubted that communism was inherently antithetical to America's "democratic" values—risked being labeled "un-American." At the same time, cold war anticommunism allowed many ethnics to reconcile their religious and Old World allegiances with their new American identities and to incorporate themselves more fully into the American "mainstream." Cold war popular diplomacy allowed some immigrants and their children to position themselves, not as members of threatening and alien minorities, but as U.S. ambassadors and the staunchest of American patriots.

"The Hour Is Striking for Lafayette's Return..."

The idea of using American citizens—and particularly Americans of comparatively recent foreign descent—to spread U.S. values and burnish the nation's image abroad was hardly a cold war brainstorm. Americans had long realized that immigrants and their children provided the nation's strongest link to the Old World. In the nineteenth century, western land speculators sometimes planted glowing "letters from America" in European newspapers to encourage immigrants to migrate to the American West. During World War I, George Creel's Committee on Public Information encouraged General Pershing to send wounded Italian-American soldiers to Italy to convalesce. These ethnic troops, Creel reported, spread the Wilsonian gospel and "turned out to be our best propagandists."[10]

During World War II, commentators across the political spectrum had again seen a special role for immigrants and their children in projecting an "American way" overseas. In the face of fratricidal fighting in Europe, both U.S. and refugee intellectuals found in America what Gunnar and Alva Myrdal called "a living system of expressed ideals for human cooperation."[11] Liberal commentators argued that America's ethnic citizens had been steeped in a creed of democratic freedom and ethnic coexistence that uniquely qualified them to help their European kindred rebuild after the war. At the same time, opinion molders ranging from Louis Adamic to the editors of *Fortune* had argued that mobilizing first- and second-generation Americans in a foreign crusade would curb disunity at home. "The hour is striking for Lafayette's return and Kosciusko's too," declared columnist Samuel Grafton in the *New York Post*. "We need to develop among our own tumbling millions of foreign origin, the new leaders for whom Europe waits."[12]

The federal government made limited use of this approach during the war. After Pearl Harbor, most Americans supported the war effort, even if they disagreed on the precise nature of the enemy. And while the U.S. certainly engaged in psychological warfare, the outcome of the conflict hinged more on manpower and munitions than on winning hearts and minds. Officials in the Treasury Department used war bond campaigns to channel ethnic loyalties into national allegiance, and the Voice of America recruited refugee intellectuals and prominent Americans of European descent to broadcast speeches and commentaries overseas. For the most part, however, wartime efforts to shape America's political culture were unrelated to efforts to reach publics abroad.

This changed dramatically in the decade following World War II. By 1947, the hot war against the Axis powers had been replaced by a long cold war against the Soviet Union and its allies. The power of the Red Army and, after 1949, Soviet possession of the atomic bomb made the risks associated with direct military engagement great indeed. Moreover, if many liberals and leftists had seen the war against the Axis as a global struggle against fascism—a "fight to the death between the free world and the slave world," in the words of Henry Wallace[13]—most cold warriors applied the same logic to communism: they saw the rise of powerful Communist Parties in democratic countries like France and Italy not as an example of partisan politics but as an extension of the threat posed by the Soviet Union. In this context, the U.S. used a combination of economic pressure, covert action, psychological warfare, and limited military engagement with "proxy" states to contain communism around the globe. As the effort to win hearts and minds abroad moved to center stage, U.S. cold warriors in both the public and private sectors increasingly came to see the American public as an important weapon in their arsenal.

Even as cold warriors both within and outside of the Truman administration looked to the American people, many worried that the public and its representatives in Congress were not sufficiently aware of the threat that communism posed to them. The national consensus that had supported U.S. involvement in World War II had quickly unraveled after V-J Day, undone by both the war weariness of the American public and by partisan politics. (Some Republicans feared taking any steps that might strengthen the hand of the

Democratic president.) While cold warriors in both parties hoped to awaken Americans to what they saw as a serious foreign threat, many conservatives sought to convince Americans of the dangers of encroaching "state socialism" at home. Thus, even some who were wary of expanding the powers of the federal government supported private efforts to mobilize Americans into the cold war.

All this came together to produce one of the earliest efforts at cold war public diplomacy: the Friendship Train. In the fall of 1947, Europe was in the grips of a terrible food crisis. Meanwhile, the Soviet Union was consolidating its grip on Eastern Europe, and U.S. foreign policy remained stalled on several fronts. In Congress, Republican isolationists blocked the efforts of a bipartisan coalition of internationalists to pass the Marshall Plan. In Europe, the powerful French and Italian Communist Parties, urged on by the newly formed Communist Information Bureau (Cominform), led mounting opposition to "imperialist" U.S. aid. While American politicians bickered over how to counter the Communist propaganda onslaught, the Republican-controlled Congress slashed funding for U.S. propaganda agencies.[14]

This scenario frustrated and appalled anticommunist internationalists, both within and outside of the Truman administration. Among them was Drew Pearson, the muckraking journalist whose "Washington Merry-Go-Round" column appeared in some seven hundred daily newspapers and as a commentary on two hundred radio stations. In the fall of 1947, Pearson called for a Friendship Train to circle the nation, collecting private donations of food and medicine for the famished millions of Europe. A private committee headed by Hollywood producer Harry Warner answered the call; in November 1947, a flag-bedecked Friendship Train slowly made its way from Los Angeles to New York. The original Friendship Train spawned a series of additional trains, as well as "Friendship Caravans" and "Friend Ships" from parts of the country bypassed by the original convoy.[15]

A private scaled-down version of the Marshall Plan, the Friendship Train was designed to stave off Communism abroad and strengthen a cold war consensus at home by mobilizing American citizens into an international humanitarian effort. Most of Europe was suffering in the fall of 1947: one private relief agency estimated that, without massive food aid, every other child born in Berlin would die before its first birthday.[16] Still, the Friendship Train collected foodstuffs only for Italy and France, the two countries in Western Europe with the largest and most active Communist Parties. Organizers engineered a meeting of the Friendship Train and the Freedom Train in Harrisburg, Pennsylvania, in November 1947, a meeting that underscored the political nature of the first train. At an elaborate send-off ceremony in New York, the U.S. delegate to the United Nations stressed the train's "peacemongering" mission and added that it "should leave no doubt that the policy of the [United States] Government is the policy of the people." When the donated food arrived in Europe, it was not simply distributed. Rather, more than ten "Friendship Trains," decorated with American flags and messages in French and Italian, crossed the two countries, stopping regularly for speeches and ceremonies staged by Americans and local officials. (When the Paris offices of several U.S. relief agencies voted to drop the "Pearson ballyhoo," the U.S. Embassy quietly intervened to reinstate the ceremonies.) The European trains, Drew Pearson explained, had been arranged "so [that] the people of those two countries can see them and know where the food came from."[17]

If the Friendship Train attempted to pressure Congress and reassure Europeans by mobilizing the American public, it also suggested the new, if carefully circumscribed, role that the cold war opened for ethnic Americans. Americans with ancestral ties to other lands had long attempted to aid their homelands or to intervene in Old World politics; but in an era of American isolationism, such efforts rarely received the sanction of U.S. officials and other elites. In the context of cold war internationalism, however, organizers of the Friendship Train cast immigrants and their children as American ambassadors. California Governor Earl Warren signed a proclamation about the Friendship Train, flanked by young girls in traditional French and Italian dress. When the train stopped in Ogden, Utah, a local newspaper pictured "three Ogden misses, colorfully costumed in French and Italian dress, present[ing] symbolic cans of milk" to representatives of the two governments. At send-off ceremonies in New York City, French and Italian Americans in national dress paraded down Broadway alongside trucks carrying sacks of flour and macaroni. A waterborne parade through New York Harbor carried thirty-three boxcars on railroad floats past the Statue of Liberty.[18]

The "Letters to Italy" Campaign

Similar themes were soon reflected in the Letters to Italy campaign, which grew out of the Friendship Train episode. According to one account, Toledo's mayor Michael V. DeSalle first broached the idea of an ethnic letter-writing campaign when a section of the Friendship Train stopped in his city. Talking to Drew Pearson, DeSalle suggested that letters from America would provide a perfect complement to the donated foodstuffs: Americans of all ethnicities should write letters to friends and family in Europe telling "how [they were] faring in America and what opportunities were open to [them] here." Pearson liked the idea and plugged it on a December episode of his Sunday night radio show. Broadcasting from Italy, where he was both overseeing and covering the distribution of Friendship Train supplies, Pearson "urged that Americans with friends or relatives in Europe write them personal letters correcting distorted Communist propaganda about the United States."[19]

Pearson's broadcast coincided with growing fears on the part of American officials about electoral developments in Italy. Italian Communists and left-wing Socialists had reacted to their expulsion from the government in May 1947 and to the announcement of the Marshall Plan a month later by staging a series of violent strikes, mass rallies, factory occupations, and assaults on police stations. In the fall of 1947, such actions—together with inflammatory statements by Italian Communist leaders—had convinced American diplomats and military officials that a coup or civil war was imminent. By late December the violence had abated, and all parties had turned their attention to the national elections slated for the following spring. But the focus on free elections proved small consolation to American officials worried about a Communist takeover. In late January, the U.S. ambassador to Italy, James C. Dunn, predicted a sweeping electoral victory for the left.[20]

A week after Dunn made this prediction, the U.S. chargé in Italy wrote Secretary of State James Byrnes proposing a plan very similar to that advocated by Pearson. "We have been told that Italian language daily newspapers in America have devoted a good deal of space" to America's "tremendous" efforts "to help Italy rehabilitate herself," chargé Homer Byington Jr. wrote. "The stories in these papers are described as being full, factual, and pregnant with good will toward Italy and with appreciation of America's unselfish motives." Byington urged the State Department to contact the editors of those papers and ask them "to recommend to their readers the practice of clipping stories describing American aid to Italy and sending them to their friends and relatives in Italy." The chargé enclosed a list of newspapers that should be contacted, together with a warning: "Some weekly papers have editorial policies which are critical of American policy of aid to Europe and therefore should not be approached with any plan such as this."[21]

One Italian-American publisher had already taken action. Generoso Pope, the millionaire president of the Colonial Sand & Cement Co., controlled a media empire that included New York's Italian-language radio station WHOM and America's largest and most influential Italian-language daily, the New York-based *Il Progresso Italo-Americano*. Pope's media holdings and his close ties to Tammany Hall made him one of Italo-America's most powerful leaders, as well as an influential force within the Democratic Party. In late January 1948, a few days before Byington sent his telegram, *Il Progresso* announced that it was launching a "chain letter plan" to inform Italians of the dangers of communism and of the U.S.'s contribution to world peace, global prosperity, and the Italian nation. *Il Progresso* urged readers to join a "Committee of 100,000" by pledging to write letters to friends and family in Italy and persuading ten other Italian Americans to do the same. To guide readers unsure of what to write, *Il Progresso* printed sample letters daily. It also encouraged readers to enclose copies of *Il Progresso* in the packages they sent to their "far-away loved ones."[22]

How direct a role Drew Pearson or the Truman administration played in inspiring Pope's action may never be known. Certainly, the publisher had close ties to the Democratic Party, and Pope knew Pearson well through their common involvement with the Friendship Train. In late 1947 and early 1948, Pearson contributed a regular column to *Il Progresso* and was named a "special correspondent" of the newspaper.[23] In any case, the Letters to Italy campaign also served Pope's political and personal interests. An outspoken supporter and client of Mussolini throughout the 1920s and 1930s, Pope had officially recanted in 1941 and during the war joined moderate liberals in an American Committee for Italian Democracy.[24] Pope's public *volte face* helped him survive wartime attacks by ardent antifascists in the Italian émigré community and the OWI.[25] (Indeed, he was the man tapped by the Treasury Department—over the objections of OWI officials—to head an Italian-American war bond committee.) Still, Pope never abandoned his fundamental conservatism, and he emerged from the war a strong supporter of Italy's Christian Democratic prime minister Alcide De Gasperi. The Letters to Italy campaign thus offered Pope a chance to atone for his past political sins, while remaining true to his conservative political beliefs.

If Pope catalyzed the Letters to Italy campaign within the Italian-American community, he soon had ample aid. In March and early April of 1948, Italian-American newspapers, radio stations, fraternal organizations, and community leaders threw their support behind the campaign. In Italian Harlem, the St. Luke Council of the Knights of Columbus distributed mimeographed fliers exhorting citizens to write their friends and relatives in Italy: "tell them that the Victory of [the Christian Democrats] in Italy will be a Moral Victory for us in the U.S.A. and for the future good of the Italian people" (sic).[26] *Il Voce del Popolo* of Detroit urged readers to join the anticommunist crusade, as did chapters of the Italian American War Veterans and the Order of the Sons of Italy. In San Francisco, home of the West Coast's largest Italian-American community, the

Columbus Civic Club launched a campaign to send one hundred thousand letters overseas. Italian-American dignitaries promoted the "valanga di lettere" (avalanche of letters) at a rally in North Beach, and a car toured the Italian district broadcasting details of the campaign over a loudspeaker. Those unsure of what to write could turn for instructions to the Bay Area's Italian-language daily, *L'Italia*, or pick up sample letters distributed by the women's auxiliary of the Italian Welfare Agency and through Bank of America branches.[27]

Italian-American leaders weren't alone in promoting the Letters to Italy campaign,[28] and in many Italian-American neighborhoods, the Catholic church became a central conduit of information and support. Urged on by U.S. diplomats, the Vatican in early 1948 "suggested" that the American Catholic hierarchy strongly support private efforts to combat Italian Communism, a charge that many dioceses took seriously.[29] In Elmira, New York, parishioners at the Italian "national church," St. Anthony's, heard weekly announcements about the campaign at Sunday mass and found writing instructions and sample letters in their parish newsletters; researchers found that the vast majority of Elmira's Italian Americans first learned of the campaign through the church.[30] Meanwhile, priests in Utica, New York, passed out eight thousand prepared letters warning that a Communist victory would ruin Italy and would trigger world war. A ready-to-sign letter distributed throughout the Brooklyn Diocese on Easter Sunday warned that if Italy embraced communism, it would become simply "another vassal state of Russia."[31]

As these sample letters suggest, campaign promoters both within and outside of the Italian-American community repeatedly urged letter writers to stress the threat a Communist victory would pose to Italy's peace and security. Postcards distributed by the New York-based Committee to Aid Democracy in Italy (which needed only to be addressed and signed) stressed that if Italians embraced Communism at the polls, they would betray both their ancestors and their long heritage of independence. One postcard reminded Italians—and perforce Italian Americans—that 1948 was the centennial of the revolution that freed Italy from foreign oppressors and created a "free, independent, democratic" nation. A second postcard featured the rising of the dead: "We are the martyrs of Italy's independence," intoned one skeleton. "We are going to remind the forgetful that we have not died in vain."[32] A model letter published in *Il Progresso* similarly mixed patriotic appeals with religious imagery. Calling the anticommunist campaign "this blessed crusade of resistance," the letter called on all Italians "who truly love *la Patria*" to commemorate the anniversary of 1948 by "annihilat[ing] the communist snakes that poison with their fatal bites the nation and render her easier prey for her crucifiers."[33] Whatever the effect on Italians, such letters clearly played to Italian Americans' romantic patriotism.

Sample letters and writing instructions also highlighted the dangers to faith and family of a Communist takeover in Italy—and implicitly in the U.S. as well. A cut-and-sign letter published in *Il Progresso* warned of the "lies and the perfidious maneuvers of the Russian tyrants and their hangman's underlings. These [people] do not want your salvation, but want your ruin, the destruction of your blessed, beloved family, the banning of your religious beliefs, the renunciation of your faith and of your devotions."[34] A form letter passed out to parishioners in Jersey City, New Jersey, went further still. Italians who voted for the Communists, the letter declared, would drive the Pope from Rome and bring "the malediction of God" down upon themselves and their families. "Your churches and your homes would be destroyed, your lands devastated, the Priests and Sisters would be massacred, and your dear ones would be dragged away as slaves in Russia to be bound to infamous work and to die of cold and hunger." The Monsignor E. Monteleone instructed his parishioners to sign and address the letters, then return them to the church to be stamped and mailed.[35]

Those guiding the letter-writing campaign did not focus solely on the horrors of a Communist victory in Italy. Many sample letters and writing instructions responded to Soviet propaganda by coupling denunciations of communism with depictions of its implicit alternative: the American Way. Both Italian- and English-language newspapers printed sample letters extolling U.S. political and religious freedoms and pointing out that these were guaranteed by the nation's Bill of Rights. In Elmira, New York, St. Anthony's parish newsletter, *The Antonian*, told parishioners to write friends and family in Italy about the blessings of democracy and the rights and privileges Americans enjoyed under a representative government. The ready-to-sign letter attorney Victor Anfuso distributed in Brooklyn on Easter Sunday opened with a joyous picture of American church bells ringing and "people of every race and creed" living together in "peace and prosperity." The letter contrasted this American vision with Italy's likely fate under communism, closing with "the hope that the Resurrection of Our Lord may always be celebrated in the land that is the center of Catholicism." *L'Italia* urged readers to note that education in the U.S. was free and that magazines and newspapers were not censored.[36]

Such letters and instructions presented a whitewashed view of America that belied the temper of the times. Although Americans were free to worship, they did so in churches that were almost entirely segregated by race. Americans prized their political freedoms, but many remained disenfranchised, particularly in the South. And although U.S. magazines and newspapers were not officially censored, domestic anticommunism was in early 1948 already exerting a powerful coercive influence on individuals and organizations. The previous March, President Truman had issued an executive order establishing a loyalty-security program for federal employees and instructing the Attorney General to compile a list of organizations that posed a threat to national security. Three months later, a Republican Congress passed the Taft-Hartley Act, an effort both to drive Communists out of leadership roles in labor unions and to curtail the power of the union movement. In October 1947, the House Un-American Activities Committee subpoenaed the Hollywood Ten, launching a series of hearings that rejuvenated the committee and ultimately helped to consolidate its power. By the end of the year, state and local governments, school systems, and many private employers were beginning to institute loyalty oaths and background checks and were using the Attorney General's list to screen potential employees.

No aspect of the American Way received more attention than America's material plenty. Newspapers ranging from San Francisco's *L'Italia* to the Order of the Sons of Italy's *OSIA News* urged readers to stress that consumer goods were not rationed in America and that the U.S. had no clothing shortage. The *New York World-Telegram* reprinted the letter of a young man in the publishing business to his brother, an Italian civil engineer. The American warned his brother against voting Communist, then described conditions in the United States: "We have plenty of everything in this country and, while everything is expensive, wages are high and everyone has a job." Underscoring this prosperity, the American sent canned food and money to pay for a mass for an uncle who had died during the war. The *World-Telegram* also hailed Anthony D'Angelo, a luncheonette owner who reportedly included twelve pounds of English-language newspapers in every package he sent to his family in Italy. "Even Italians who can't read English can recognize the space devoted to amusements and department store advertising and realize that these things are for sale or they wouldn't be spending money advertising them," the newspaper enthused.[37]

Such comments implied that Italians, too, could enjoy new clothes and washing machines if only they rejected communism at the polls. To some degree, this may have been true, but not simply because of the superiority of America's free enterprise system. Alone among major powers, the U.S. had reaped an economic bonanza from the war, emerging with the largest share of global GNP in world history. Through the Friendship Train and private care packages, Italians had already profited from American largesse. They stood to gain far more from the Marshall Plan, which the U.S. Congress finally approved in March 1948.

Writing instructions and sample letters stressed this fact, suggesting that the United States, not the Soviet Union, offered Italy true friendship. "From America, money, medicine, packages join you, while Russia asks tributes of war, boats and machinery, and imposes its veto to the damage of Italy in the United Nations," one letter declared.[38] Another ran through a more detailed recounting of America's good deeds and urged Italians to "have faith in America's proven friendship."[39] The same point was vividly captured in a cartoon, which appeared in *L'Italia* just days before the Italian election. Two men stood on a dock next to a huge American freighter and watched a Russian warship steam toward port. The freighter, they noted, was loaded with grain, while the battleship carried the Italian Communist leader Palmiro Togliatti.[40]

In the intellectual framework of the campaign, America's blood ties to Italy clinched this friendship. Italian-American newspapers reminded readers that their letters would carry special weight in the Old Country because they were kin. A sample letter published in *Il Progresso* attacked the Communal Council of Taranto (which the paper said was dominated by Socialists and Communists) for refusing to welcome an American squadron on the "pretext" that the Americans threatened Italian independence. "The American boats in the Mediterranean have the blessed and civil mission of protecting the liberty and the independence of the people from Russian aggressions," the letter declared. "Among the marines who are in Taranto, there are sons of Italians and youths who heroically fought in order to liberate Italy from its odious enemy." The letter not only stressed the kin links between the U.S. and Italy, but also recast Italy as a victim, rather than a perpetrator, of the recent war.[41]

But even American friendship had its limits—as government officials, Italian-American leaders, and sample letters were quick to point out. Truman himself had declared that the Marshall Plan and the Truman Doctrine were "two halves of the same walnut," and U.S. officials made it clear that no aid would flow to an Italy under Communist control. State Department officials and private promoters of the campaign encouraged letter-writers to stress this point and to cast it in personal terms. A ready-to-send postcard distributed by the Committee to Aid Democracy in Italy showed an "iron curtain" separating Italian Americans and their aid from relatives in the Old Country. When staffers at *La Tribuna Italiana* in Milwaukee penned letters for readers who could not write, they drove the message home: "if the forces of true democracy should lose in the Italian election, the American Government will not send any more money to Italy and we won't send any more money to you, our relatives."[42]

It is impossible to determine how many Italian Americans participated in the Letters to Italy campaign or followed the formulas offered in published instructions and sample letters, but evidence suggests that participation rates were substantial. Certainly, the campaign was heavily promoted by Italian-American leaders, and U.S. postmasters reported an explosion of Italy-bound mail in the spring of 1948. Some of this can undoubtedly be attributed to bulk mailings by Italian-American individuals and groups to unrelated "kin."[43] But many letters were sent by and to individuals. When Cornell sociologists interviewed Italian-American families in Elmira, New York, in August 1948, more than 40 percent said one or more family members had mailed letters as part of the effort.[44]

What accounted for this apparent outpouring of support for the Letters to Italy campaign? In part, it reflected the fierce anticommunism shared by many Italian-American leaders in the postwar period, an anticommunism that was fueled in part by the Catholic Church. Unlike many Catholic immigrant groups, Italian Americans had sustained a strong radical tradition in the late nineteenth and early twentieth centuries, but this radical strain largely disappeared in the postwar period. Many of the community's *prominenti* were, like Pope, former philofascists who had emerged from the war chastened, but with their conservative Italian nationalism intact. And under the twin shadows of communism and anticommunism, even many liberals and former leftists edged to the right. Luigi Antonini, for instance, the first vice president of the International Ladies Garment Workers Union (ILGWU) and president of Italian Dressmakers Local 89, was the dominant figure in Italian-American labor. A reform socialist and staunch antifascist, Antonini had collaborated before and during the war with both liberal New Dealers and leftists. But Antonini was a pragmatist and, like many American social democrats, he was no friend to communism. In 1943, he joined Generoso Pope in forming the American Committee for Italian Democracy. That same year, Antonini created the Italian-American Labor Council, which in the postwar period funneled ILGWU and AFL funds to anticommunists in the Italian labor movement.[45]

The Letters to Italy campaign thus played to religious and political allegiances deeply rooted in Italian Americans' ethnic past. At the same time, it gave Italian Americans a dramatic way of displaying their loyalty to their adopted land. When many in the community supported Mussolini in the late 1930s, they did so primarily as Italian emigrants and alienated Americans. But the Letters to Italy campaign drew strong support from federal officials, business and civic groups outside of Italian areas, and prominent Americans ranging from New York Mayor William O'Dwyer to Hollywood producer James Nasser. "If all the people in the United States of foreign birth or extraction will start movements in each group to write letters to their friends and relatives in their homelands telling how much better freedom and Americanism are than despotism...we can win the cold war," declared House Speaker Joseph Martin (R.-Mass.) in a speech in Toledo. "Millions of lives can be saved....rivers of blood can be prevented...if we go at it with the earnestness and intensity with which we go to battle."[46]

Such words—which virtually equated letter-writing to military service during the war—underscored the fact that active anticommunism increasingly served both as a loyalty test and as a path to full inclusion in American society. For the many Italian-American leaders such as Generoso Pope whose Americanism was clouded by former association with Mussolini, the Letters to Italy campaign offered a chance to make amends for past transgressions. Addressing one Italian-American group, Pope stressed his *American* motives for launching the campaign: "I did what I considered to be my duty as an American citizen," Pope declared. "And with us were millions of Americans, regardless of race, color or creed."[47]

Such reasoning probably had a powerful appeal even to many Italian Americans who did not need to seek political absolution. After decades of alienation and discrimination, Italian Americans in the immediate postwar years were poised to enter the American mainstream. The Letters to Italy campaign seemed to offer a way to hasten this process. "The thousands of Italian Americans who responded to the appeal were less interested in the Italian political situation *per se* than they were in achieving status and integration in the American community," argued a University of Illinois sociologist in 1949. "What better demonstration of that desire than to join the anti-Communist crusade at a time when anti-communism was the supreme test of loyalty!"[48]

But if the equation of Americanism with anticommunism offered Italian Americans a shortcut into mainstream American society, it was a path paved with dangers. The most obvious was the prospect of being cut off from their homeland. The U.S. government announced that, not only would it would slash aid to Italy if the Communist coalition won, it also would expel Communist Party members in the U.S. and refuse immigration visas to any Italian who voted red. With an "iron curtain" falling fast across Eastern Europe, many Italian Americans probably feared Italy would be next. Luigi Antonini, the labor leader, made this point a few days before the election. "Some of our Italian-Americans may have exaggerated in their appeals to the Italian voters," Antonini conceded, "but this was mainly due to their justified fears that their relatives in Italy could have been separated from them by a Communist iron curtain between Italy and America."[49]

Finally, many Italian Americans may have feared for their own status in American society should the Italian Communists triumph—or should they not display sufficient anticommunism. A *nota bene* attached to the bottom of sample letters published in *Il Progresso* noted that the specific words writers used didn't matter. "What matters are the intentions," the postscript read. "What matters is the determination to distance from our head the terrible spectre of a monster, that—if it were unfortunately to triumph—would be the destruction of our liberties, the profanation of our families, the eradication of our religious faith, the perversion of our society."[50] The author of this postscript was likely referring to the evils that would befall Italy under Communism, but the wording is sufficiently ambiguous to suggest another reading. If Communists triumphed in the Italian elections, then Italian Americans could be tarred by association. Only by wholeheartedly participating in the letter-writing campaign could Italian Americans distance themselves from Communist forces in their homeland and prove their loyalty to their adopted country.

Not all Americans agreed with the U.S.'s heavy-handed tactics in Italy or believed that America should stand for anti-communism at any cost. Supporters of Henry Wallace, the Progressive Party's presidential candidate in 1948, denounced U.S. intervention in the Italian campaign. And some eighty prominent liberals and leftists—including Louis Adamic, composer Leonard Bernstein, playwright Arthur Miller, and Senator Glen Taylor—sent a telegram to President Truman calling for "an end to all outside interference with democratic electoral procedure in Italy.[51] Much of the outcry over U.S. actions came from liberals and leftists outside of the Italian-American community, but some Italian Americans also braved possible reprisals to voice their opposition to the letter-writing campaign and related U.S. efforts to influence the election outcome. On the Wednesday before the election, some two hundred protesters turned out for a rally at Manhattan Center sponsored by the Committee for Free Elections in Italy. Rep. Vito Marcantonio, a New York leftist with close ties to the Communist Party, condemned U.S. intervention in a speech read to the rally. "The action of our State Department, our former Fascists, and of the former lick-spittles of Mussolini in the City of New York is more evidence that our foreign policy is one of aid to anti-democratic elements throughout the world," Marcantonio declared. "This must be stopped. It must be stopped by free Americans." Committee chairman Fileno de Novellis echoed these sentiments in explaining the event to reporters: "Thousands of Americans of Italian origin feel deeply humiliated by the continuous flow of suggestions, advice and pressure put on the Italians, as though they were unable to decide for themselves whom to elect," Novellis said. "The rally [voiced] the protests of all decent and truly democratic Americans against the interference of any country in the Italian elections of April 18."[52]

Novellis's reference to "truly democratic Americans"—as well as Marcantonio's role in the rally—hinted at the way anticommunism had redrawn America's political map. Many of the liberals and leftists who now protested U.S. intervention in Italy had, in the late 1930s and early 1940s, argued for staunch U.S. opposition to fascism overseas. Their previous support for U.S. involvement abroad had reflected their belief that New Deal America embodied "democratic" values they held dear: for liberals, those values included ethnic tolerance and freedoms of speech, press, and religion; for most leftists, "democracy" also implied a redistribution of economic power. The Left's appropriation of "democracy" in the late 1930s made many industrialists and other conservatives wary of the term, but they could not afford to reject it during World War II. Rather, conservatives stressed "representative democracy," tying political freedom to religious and economic freedoms under the banner of the "American Way."

During the war, the united front against Nazism partially concealed *democracy*'s multiple meanings. But as the wartime coalition broke apart, the term's internal fractures became clear. Communist and Socialist parties across Europe—including many partisans who had been in the front ranks of the Continent's anti-Nazi brigades—invoked "democracy" in the postwar period, as did embattled American leftists. Meanwhile, U.S. political, business, and intellectual leaders continued to portray America as the "democratic" norm, even as the nation slid to the right. During the Letters to Italy campaign, some observers worried that this semantic tug-of-war would cause confusion. Some Italian Americans "may have used expressions and methods which could be misunderstood," two observers reflected in a campaign postmortem. "Saying 'Vote democratic', might mean to an unlettered Italian the Democratic Popular Front, the Communist-extreme-left socialist coalition."[53]

Such confusion ultimately proved inconsequential, for on election day, Italy's Christian Democrats stunned all observers, winning 48.5 percent of the vote and an absolute majority in Parliament. Some observers claimed that the Letters to Italy campaign had a substantial impact on this outcome.[54] Whether or not the letter-writing campaign actually influenced the Italian election, it was an important signpost in Italian-Americans' efforts to locate themselves within the national community. Politicians of both parties commended the group for their patriotic efforts, and House Speaker Joseph Martin publicly thanked Italian Americans for "helping materially" to stall the "westward march of the iron curtain."[55] The campaign provided former fascists with an opportunity to redeem themselves, offered a litmus test of "Americanism" that excluded radicals, and provided a large group of first- and second-generation Americans with a ready language with which to describe the concrete characteristics of the American Way. In the process, it allowed many Italian Americans to reconcile their religious and Old World allegiances with their new "American" identity.

The "Letters from America" Campaign

The electoral victory of Italy's Christian Democrats eased only temporarily the concerns of U.S. government and business leaders, for across Europe, tensions continued to mount. West European communists, guided by the Cominform, staged a series of violent and disruptive strikes in the spring and summer of 1948. In June, after the U.S., France, and England moved to unify Germany's western zones, the Soviets abruptly cut off all electricity and overland routes to West Berlin. At about the same time, the Soviets began testing a new strategy—rallying war-weary Europeans into a broad-based movement on behalf of "peace."

Working through the Cominform and an umbrella front organization called the "Partisans for Peace," the Soviets attempted to harness the feelings of intellectuals, mothers, workers, and other Europeans who were tired of war, economically pressed and unhappy with their nations' new second-rate status. At rallies and congresses and in petition drives across Europe, Peace Partisan spokesmen equated the struggle for "peace" with the struggle against American "warmongers" and "economic imperialists." They condemned U.S. possession of the atomic bomb, charged that Western defense expenditures were draining money from workers' wages, and attacked the Marshall Plan as a vast "dumping operation" designed to "conquer and subordinate" the European market. Although the movement never attracted the six hundred million people worldwide that the Cominform claimed, it attracted enough attention for one historian to dub it a "world crusade."[56]

The "peace" movement was just getting off the ground in September 1948, when Charles Edgar Shaw, an executive at Esso Standard Oil Co., traveled to Germany to advise the U.S. military government on labor relations in German plants. Dismayed by the rising anti-American sentiment he found in Europe, Shaw conveyed his alarm to Winthrop Rockefeller, the future governor of Arkansas and at that point a consultant to Socony-Vacuum Oil Company. Late in 1948 Rockefeller and Shaw began conferring informally with several associates about ways to counter Soviet propaganda and correct European "misconceptions" about the U.S. Other members of the group included pollster Elmo Roper; Noel Sargent, a top public relations executive at the National Association of Manufacturers; and Anna Rosenberg, a labor consultant and manpower expert who in 1951 would be appointed assistant secretary of defense. These individuals ranged from staunch economic conservatives to moderate New Dealers, but all were interested in safeguarding the "American economic system" and promoting business-labor harmony both in the U.S. and abroad.[57]

All saw the possibilities suggested by the Letters to Italy campaign of the previous spring. "One of our greatest assets in telling the American story abroad is the vast potential influence of the 35 million first and second generation Americans," Rockefeller explained in a subsequent fund-raising letter to business associates. Each year these ethnic Americans wrote 250 million letters to friends and family abroad—letters that were "not discounted as propaganda." "If rightly directed," Rockefeller concluded, these letters "could be a decisive factor in the cold war." Charles Shaw underscored this point in a letter to Paul Hoffman, administrator of the Marshall Plan: "Letters from friends and relatives," Shaw wrote, "will certainly be more convincing than the ordinary newspaper or radio propaganda."[58]

In early 1949, Rockefeller and his associates began exploring the possibility of mobilizing American immigrants and their children in a vast letter-writing campaign to burnish America's image abroad. To coordinate the project, they hired Henry Lee Munson, a public relations expert and former executive with the World Wide Broadcasting Foundation, which had beamed shortwave broadcasts from Italian Americans into Italy the previous spring. Mr. Munson quickly conducted a survey of European "misconceptions" about the U.S., which would serve as a guide for the future "Letters from America" campaign. As Rockefeller explained, "A barrage of letters might do as much harm as good unless the approach were right."[59]

Munson distributed some 10,000 questionnaires to key European and American observers, then tabulated the 1702 responses he received. This approach gave the project a scientific veneer. But while the survey may have revealed much about European attitudes, it was Munson and his backers who decided which "beliefs" qualified as "misconceptions." The report on the survey was vetted not only by members of the Rockefeller group but also by State Department officials; the Common Council for American Unity in whose offices Munson was housed; and the Carnegie Endowment for International Peace, which supplied some funding.[60]

Published in the summer of 1949, the report detailed European beliefs judged to be "most seriously hampering understanding of the United States." Although these "erroneous" beliefs varied slightly from nation to nation, several reappeared frequently: "Most Americans are too materialistic"; "Most Americans are guilty of persecuting the Negro"; "American foreign policy is too changeable"; "American national policy is primarily determined by Wall Street"; and "American channels of information are controlled by Big Business for selfish purposes." "It is only by knowing [about these misconceptions] that you can act intelligently!" an ad for the published report declared. "You should know these FACTS for VICTORY in the COLD WAR."[61]

The fact that not all Americans would have seen these views as misconceptions points to a second motive of the Letters from America campaign—one that was never far below the surface. Rockefeller and his associates clearly hoped to shape the message that immigrants carried abroad, but they also hoped a letter-writing campaign would have a salutary impact at home. During the 1930s, millions of first- and second-generation Americans had helped build the left-leaning Congress of Industrial Organizations into a potent political force. And in the postwar period, secular Southern and Eastern European ethnics remained in the forefront of leftist political groups. But immigrants and their children, like other Americans, had profited from the wartime and postwar economic boom, and many from central and Eastern Europe had seen their ancestral lands drawn into the Soviet sphere. By encouraging these newer Americans to compare their freedoms and living standards to those of friends and family abroad, Munson and his sponsors hoped to get them "to think more seriously about the advantages they receive themselves." As Charles Shaw wrote to a fellow oil company executive, "The indirect education which these participants will get in the American way of life and our economic system may be of more value than the effect these letters may have on European thinking."[62]

Rockefeller stressed this aspect of the letter-writing campaign when he approached the American Heritage Foundation (AHF) early in 1949 about sponsoring the project. The Freedom Train, which the foundation had just sponsored, "reminded all Americans of the basic freedoms that are too often taken for granted," Winthrop Rockefeller wrote his uncle and namesake, AHF chairman Winthrop Aldrich. "Reminding Europeans of the values of these freedoms is not an illogical follow-up to the Freedom Train. Asking Americans to implement them by helping to tell the story to Europe follows naturally also."[63]

The zeal with which Truman administration officials backed the project can be seen in letters they wrote urging the American Heritage Foundation to take up the campaign. "I am exceedingly interested to say the least," wrote White House assistant Charles W. Jackson in March 1949. "Personally, I consider this one of the most important phases in the battle for peace." The State Department also lobbied the foundation with increasing urgency as the year wore on. The burgeoning European peace movement alarmed U.S. officials, as did Soviet acquisition of the atomic bomb in August and the "loss" of China to Mao's communist troops in the final month of the year. On February 1, 1950, Secretary of State Dean Acheson wrote AHF president Thomas D'Arcy Brophy that he considered the proposed letter-writing campaign and similar efforts to mobilize private citizens "of paramount importance."[64]

Despite such high-powered lobbying, the American Heritage Foundation delayed taking up the Letters project. When Munson warned that further delays would dim ethnic leaders' enthusiasm for the project, Rockefeller and his associates turned to another organization with extensive ties to America's foreign-language communities. That organization, which had earlier agreed to take Munson under its wing and formally to sponsor his "misconceptions" survey, was the Common Council for American Unity (CCAU).[65]

That the CCAU would take on the Letters project underscores the link between Americanization, anti-Nazism, and postwar anticommunism and highlights the rightward migration of many American liberals after World War II. Before and during the war, the CCAU and its "little magazine" *Common Ground* had worked to combat ethnic and racial prejudice by encouraging mutual understanding among Americans of all backgrounds within the context of shared civic ideals. The magazine's multiethnic and strongly antifascist staff attacked racial segregation and the internment of Japanese Americans during the war, but most of its poems, essays, fiction, and photo essays were upbeat. Rather than dwelling on America's failings, *Common Ground*'s editors and contributors described a harmonious, multiethnic America that they hoped to expand. In 1946, the Baltimore *Afro-American* recommended the quarterly to its readers as "a practical expression of the belief that common ideals commonly held, rather than common blood or color or origin, are the basis upon which the good life must rest."[66]

By the mid-1940s, however, both the CCAU and its "little magazine" began to reflect cracks emerging in America's liberal community. *Common Ground* initially focused on healing divisions between white ethnic and "old-stock" Americans by highlighting the ideals and experiences they shared and encouraging cultural appreciation of different nationality groups. But after the race riots of 1943—when European ethnics joined old-stock Americans in attacks on blacks and Mexican Americans—*Common Ground* made race relations a central theme. The magazine's militantly egalitarian stance alienated many readers, who favored a more gradualist approach.[67]

Ultimately, however, the fateful divide both within the CCAU and American liberalism generally developed around communism. CCAU leaders first confronted the issue in the fall of 1944, when *Common Ground* sponsored a high school speaking tour by the esteemed black poet Langston Hughes. In the midst of the tour, New York *Sun* columnist George Sokolsky, an archconservative who had been on the payroll of the National Association of Manufacturers, named Hughes as America's quintessential fellow traveler. Sokolsky's charge prompted two schools to cancel Hughes's appearance and led others to investigate. Hughes offered to cancel the tour rather than embarrass *Common Ground*, but CCAU executive director Read Lewis and the magazine's managing editor, Margaret Anderson, insisted he continue.[68]

By 1948, much had changed. That summer Lewis encouraged Anderson to accept a glowing article on the anticommunist Letters to Italy campaign coauthored by Sylvan Gotshal, an international business lawyer and CCAU board member who had collaborated with the State Department on election-related propaganda. On Gotshal's advice, Lewis nixed a companion article criticizing the letter-writing campaign, which Anderson had solicited for balance. When a piece critical of the effort finally appeared the following year, Lewis appended a lengthy postscript distancing both *Common Ground* and the CCAU from its views. By then, the CCAU had already agreed to take Henry Munson under its wing and to publish his report on European "misconceptions" of the U.S.[69]

The CCAU's move to the right in part reflected the organization's growing funding problems in a climate of intensifying anticommunism. The CCAU's major financial supporter, the Carnegie Corporation, announced it would not fund the agency beyond 1947, and other foundations also rejected the CCAU's appeals. The reasons for this are not entirely clear, but many donors may have been wary of backing an organization perceived to have Communist ties. (Although the CCAU was not on the Attorney General's list, many of the organization's former stalwarts—Louis Adamic, Carey McWilliams, Langston Hughes, and others—fell victim to red-baiting.) In any case, Lewis urged Anderson to accept Gotshal's piece because he believed the well-connected lawyer would then be more willing to raise funds for the Council. Similarly, Lewis and the CCAU board could hardly overlook the fact that Henry Munson—and eventually the Letters from America campaign—came with Winthrop Rockefeller's blessing and financial support.[70]

Attributing the CCAU's rightward slide solely to a changed funding climate and coercive anticommunism is too simplistic, however, for by 1948, many American liberals saw a growing totalitarian menace in the East. Before and during World War II, many liberals and leftists in the CCAU and elsewhere had decried Nazism for quashing individual freedom and cultural difference; they celebrated America's "unity within diversity," defining "Americanism" largely through contrast with this coercively homogeneous "other." The ease with which communism replaced Nazism in this mental map can be seen in the illustration that adorns the cover of a CCAU brochure publicizing Munson's survey report. The Statue of Liberty towers on the edge of the American continent as freighters steam for Europe, undoubtedly loaded with medicine and grain. From Spain to Turkey and Norway to Greece, the European continent is dotted with recognizable monuments and people in traditional national garb. Eastern Europe, including Yugoslavia, is walled off and colored a dismal gray. Tanks, war planes, gun batteries, and goose-stepping soldiers inhabit this realm. The only familiar landmarks are the onion turrets of the Kremlin.[71]

As communism increasingly supplanted fascism in the minds of American liberals, many came to see it as a threat at home as well as abroad. A fundraising plea that Read Lewis sent to CCAU members in May 1950 eerily echoed the "divide-and-conquer" arguments the organization had once deployed to unite ethnic and old-stock Americans in the face of fascism. "We Americans are faced with a threat not only to our country, but to the civilization in which we live," Lewis wrote. "The attempt of the forces against us to confuse and divide the American people makes doubly important what the Council is doing to unite Americans, to make the belief of every newcomer in American institutions a fighting faith, to overcome the prejudices and discriminations which make for disunity."[72]

Not all American liberals—either within the CCAU or outside of it— passed smoothly from antifascism to anticommunism. Louis Adamic, whose ideas had done so much to shape the CCAU's approach in the late 1930s and early 1940s, emerged as a strong supporter of his homeland hero, Josef Broz Tito. Disillusioned with America's failure to live up to its promises, Adamic applauded Tito's leftist economic views, as well as his break with Stalin in 1948. That Adamic could see Tito as the true standard-bearer of Yugoslavian nationalism reveals a blind spot in the CCAU's picture of undifferentiated communism. But Adamic had broken abruptly with the CCAU in 1944 and, like other lingering leftists, was fast losing his influence. He was shunned by many liberals because of his pro-Tito stance and his support for Henry Wallace's presidential bid in 1948. Denounced by Serbian royalists and church-going Slovenes, and hounded by both the House Un-American Activities Committee and the Federal Bureau of Investigation, Adamic died under mysterious circumstances on his New Jersey farm in 1951.[73]

Some members of the CCAU rank-and-file also questioned the organization's new tack. The Council's publication of Munson's survey report—together with its salute to that report as a critical weapon in the cold war—alienated some longtime supporters. In the fall of 1949, several wrote to reduce or end their contributions. "The schizophrenia to be observed among many American 'liberals' is a constant source of wonderment to me," wrote H. David Hammond of the University of Pennsylvania. "How you can publish articles such as on the Mexican American and Negro problems...and how you speak of 'our heritage of freedom and opportunity,' etc., and yet fall hook, line and sinker for the eyewash, the fine-sounding balderdash put out by our government about the benefits of American 'democracy'...is beyond me." "You reveal that your organization has prostituted itself to the low level of cheap propaganda agency for the State Department."[74]

Mrs. George M. Krall of Morrisville, Pennsylvania, blamed cold war rhetoric for riots in Peekskill, New York, in 1948, in which supporters of Progressive Party presidential candidate Henry Wallace were beaten. Explaining why she had cancelled her subscription to both the CCAU and its "little magazine," Mrs. Krall wrote, "I am as ever interested in proving that all men can live together in freedom and equality, and I am against all kinds of discrimination on grounds of race, religion, sex—and also political opinion. But I am not in favor of pursuing war, whether cold or hot." The Peekskill riots, she concluded, "are the opposite of what Common Ground is supposedly working for."[75]

At one time, such protests might have prompted soul-searching on the part of CCAU board members, but by the fall of 1949, much had changed. Henry Wallace's unsuccessful presidential bid the previous year had confirmed a deep rift between those American liberals who counted themselves as "progressives" and those who saw progressives as "sentimental" and "soft."[76] Two events in the summer of 1949—the victory of Mao's communist forces in China and the Soviet detonation of an atomic bomb—left many Americans feeling a sense of frustration and impotence that paved the way for Sen. Joseph McCarthy's political rise. In this context, the CCAU board dismissed letters from the likes of Hammond and Krall as representing "the general communist, fellow traveler, or Wallace line." Strapped for funds, the organization in April 1950 halved its translations for the foreign-language press and suspended publication of

Common Ground. The following month, with separate funding, it launched the Letters from America campaign.[77]

On April 20, 1950, in a speech to the American Society of Newspaper Editors, President Truman called for a "great campaign of truth" to combat Soviet "deceit, distortion and lies."[78] Truman's speech signaled the opening of a new and more aggressive phase in the U.S.'s postwar efforts to preach the American way abroad. It also provided the perfect fanfare for the Letters from America campaign. In early May, with funding provided by Winthrop Rockefeller, the CCAU mailed letters and brochures announcing the campaign to 320 ethnic organizations and the editors of 900 foreign-language newspapers. The CCAU focused on ethnics from Central, Eastern and Southern Europe, although it eventually distributed newspaper columns filled with writing tips in twenty-five languages ranging from Arabic to Chinese.[79]

In suggesting wording for the brochure announcing the campaign, two CCAU staffers had tried to use the effort not only to burnish America's image abroad but—in the tradition of Adamic, Hughes, and other progressives—to bolster egalitarian values at home. The draft proposed by *Common Ground* editor Margaret Anderson and Florence Widutie called on letter-writers to detail their newfound political, educational, and economic opportunities; but it also urged them to think critically about those areas where America still fell short of its ideals. "What problems in your town are preventing the realization of full freedom and democracy for everyone?" the two women wrote. "Are housing and health adequate?...Are Negroes and orientals badly treated? Are members of your own group sometimes treated as second class citizens?"[80]

All critical self-reflection vanished in the final brochure. Rather than hailing Americans' ability to "join organizations working for better housing, better education [and] civil rights," the pamphlet urged letter-writers to help "win the fight for freedom" by combating "untruths about America that are being spread abroad." Lest anyone doubt the nature of those untruths, the brochure detailed seven:

1. America is plotting to make war...
2. America is exploited by big business...
3. America is headed for a depression...
4. America is grossly materialistic...
5. America is preyed upon by gangsters...
6. America is persecuting the Negro...
7. America is a land of divorce and broken homes...

These themes would provide the backbone of the Letters from America campaign.[81]

Weekly columns distributed by the CCAU to the foreign-language press further reinforced the campaign's sunny-side-up approach. The unsigned columns instructed immigrants and their children on how to paint "truthful" pictures of the nation using the fabric of their daily lives. Correspondents were urged to avoid topics that would simply reinforce Soviet propaganda—"cases of boys getting into trouble, of crime or divorce"—and to focus instead on weddings, religious pageants, and civic activities. A letter mentioning a summer band concert would show Europeans that Americans were not materialists, "insensitive to the pleasures of the spirit." A discussion of June weddings would counteract the image spread by Hollywood movies that America was a land of broken homes. And a description of a Sunday drive in the country would tell "the far-off reader…that his American friend has a car, that he drives about over the countryside as he pleases, and [that he] returns at evening to his own small house on the edge of town."[82]

August Heckscher, an editorial writer for the *New York Herald Tribune*, penned these anonymous columns, but he was not alone in urging letter-writers to accentuate the positive in American life. The CCAU also solicited bylined articles from "outstanding Americans" ranging from General George C. Marshall to Urban League president Lester Granger, from the chairman of U.S. Steel to the secretary-treasurer of the CIO. Occasionally, these articles hinted that life in America was still imperfect: Eleanor Roosevelt, for instance, noted that America's treatment of Negroes was "one of the best propaganda points [the Soviets] have." Still, both Eleanor Roosevelt and Walter White, the executive secretary of the NAACP, urged letter-writers to stress "the favorable changes [in race relations] that have come about." The former president of the General Federation of Women's Clubs agreed: "I have found that one of the greatest misconceptions about the United States is that we persecute the Negro," Mrs. J. L. Blair Buck wrote. "While there are some very bad blots on our record, the whole picture shows an amazing advancement of a race only 90 years away from slavery."[83]

Both the weekly columns and the bylined articles constructed an American Way built around the notions of "freedom" and plenty. Scores of columns urged readers to write about their short work weeks, their high wages, their paid vacations, and the "long procession of automobiles and washing machines" pouring forth from American factories. These benefits, the columns reminded readers, resulted from the American free enterprise system under which "big business" and "free labor" cooperated. General Motors and the United Auto

Workers negotiated wage increases, pensions, and health insurance; Soviet workers had their wages and working conditions "set arbitrarily by the government." Free enterprise meant "freedom from want": when American workers went on strike, it was not because of "desperation or festering grievances," but "to gain a pension or a paid vacation!"[84]

If free enterprise was one critical component of America's package of freedoms, freedom from fear and freedom to worship were others. A Fourth of July column urged letter-writers to reflect on the meaning of the day: Americans could go anywhere, say what they liked, worship God as they chose, and "go to sleep at night knowing that all the family is safe from sudden arrest, imprisonment and deportation." Each Christmas and Easter, the CCAU urged ethnics to flood Europe with holiday cards, which—though seemingly apolitical—would remind foreign skeptics of America's religious and spiritual values. In the context of the cold war, even sending a Christmas card could be an act of patriotism.[85]

While some columns spoke of religious freedom, free labor, and free enterprise, others—particularly those published after the outbreak of the Korean War—urged letter-writers to focus on America's role as head of the "free world." "America, which declared its own independence in 1776, has always wanted other countries to find their own freedom," the Fourth of July column proclaimed. "In risking the lives of her sons [in Korea] to halt aggression and uphold the United Nations, the United States has taken the most significant step ever made toward world peace," another column declared without a trace of irony. Letter-writers were encouraged to remember this context when discussing the draft or wartime shortages. One column suggested appropriate lines: "The country is set to do a job not only in Korea, but wherever aggressors begin their work. I guess we can take whatever hardships or inconvenience result here at home without much grumbling."[86]

Such columns seemed designed as much to solidify an American domestic consensus as to influence opinions overseas. Immigrants from Southern and Eastern Europe had been at the forefront of the radical labor movement of the 1930s; many still suffered from vestiges of discrimination and worried that their working-class sons would be drafted to serve in Korea. Yet, like all American workers, they had also profited from the nation's postwar economic boom, and those from Eastern Europe generally resented the Sovietization of their native lands. By contrasting the American status quo to Stalinism, the Letters from America columns and articles encouraged immigrants to think of their glasses as half full, to remember how much worse things could be.

Such thinking certainly underlay a series of Letters from America discussion groups, which the CCAU set up in ethnic communities in 1951 and 1952. Although the program's columns and bylined articles were being widely reprinted by the foreign-language press, "more direct and personal contacts seemed important...if the campaign was to be developed to maximum effectiveness, *and its domestic potentialities fully realized,*" a CCAU report concluded. Working through church, civic, and cultural organizations in various ethnic communities, CCAU organizers set up a series of discussion groups to which they supplied group leaders. In 1951, the organization arranged twenty-six such talkfests among Finnish Americans in New York City. The following year it expanded the program to seven other ethnic groups in several northeastern cities.[87]

The CCAU billed such discussion groups as "an essential part of the democratic process." "From the old town meeting to current Senate debates, our democracy has evolved through 'talking things over,'" a report on the program explained. But for all this talk of "democracy," the report also made clear that the program had an educational agenda. Using the letter-writing campaign as a starting point, discussion leaders would help participants "clarify their ideas and acquire a fuller and more accurate understanding of our basic institutions and the significance of American democracy." Discussion groups, coupled with the Letters from America campaign, the report concluded, "could make an important contribution not only to the fight for freedom but to the day by day task of Americanization and citizen education." In other words, the discussion groups, like the letter-writing campaign they complemented, were designed to "fix the public meaning of Americanism."[88]

This domestic agenda may explain the support the letter-writing campaign received from America's business community. Most of the direct funding for the effort came from Winthrop Rockefeller and eventually the Ford Foundation, but many corporations enthusiastically plugged the campaign in in-house newsletters. ("Thousands of our workers are foreign born. Please send us material," wrote one.) At least a dozen organized letter-writing drives among their employees. Republic Steel went a step further, urging workers to give letters to their managers to be mailed.[89] Goodyear Tire & Rubber Co. produced a half-hour film entitled *A Letter from America*, which featured an immigrant rubber worker (Karl) writing to his sister (Frieda) behind the Iron Curtain. The film, narrated through a series of flashbacks, incorporated several themes that had been emphasized by corporate America since the NAM campaign of the late 1930s. A conversation between Karl and "Cousin Rudy," who also worked in the rubber plant, underscored the inextricable connection between America's political and economic freedoms: "You understand don't you," Rudy told Karl, "that anytime you start to fool around with any one of our freedoms, you're liable to mess up the whole works." Karl wrote of the productivity made possible by American-style free enterprise—a productivity that produced both new jobs and promotions. Scenes showing Frieda and her children reading the letter allowed a sharp contrast between Rudy's comfortable middle-class home in Goodyear Heights and Frieda's austere quarters in the old country. One of the final scenes showed Karl and Rudy discussing "shareholder democracy" at Rudy's kitchen table. When Karl asked who owned the company, Rudy replied that they did—as well as Goodyear's tire inspector, stock boy, stenographer, and receptionist, and many residents in the surrounding community. "Rudy, that makes us sound like capitalists," Karl gasped. "We are," Rudy replied. "Capitalists American style." "Then what is the difference between capital and labor?" Karl asked. "Oh," responded Rudy, "there isn't any really."[90]

By 1954, the CCAU estimated that over four hundred foreign-language newspapers were publishing some or all of its Letters from America columns, and scores of nationality organizations were plugging the campaign. The letter-writing effort also garnered national press attention. MGM produced a film short entitled *The Million-dollar Nickel*, "dramatically pointing out how much can be accomplished with a 5-cent postage stamp"; the short included appeals by Leslie Caron in French, Eva Gabor in Hungarian, and Ricardo Montalban in Spanish. NBC televised the film nationally, and dozens of radio stations ran appeals by Bing Crosby, Kate Smith, Bob Hope, and other stars calling on Americans to participate. More than thirty governors issued proclamations hailing Letters from America week.[91]

Clearly, the Letters from America campaign was a publicity success. But how was it received in America's ethnic communities? Limited evidence makes this question difficult to answer, but some tentative conclusions are possible. Letters sent to the Common Council suggest that at least some ethnics responded to the call. Immigrants told of writing friends in Greece, Italy, Germany, or Eastern Europe, while others provided copies of letters sent abroad. A Midwestern housewife wrote relatives in Poland about her husband's paid vacation, while an Italian immigrant exuded about California's "little wooden houses" and good schools. "When Soviet tanks were shooting at striking workers in Eastern Germany in 1953, I sent my friends several pictures of an American strike," wrote one man. "Pickets in front of big hotels, in peaceful conversation and laughter with the policemen. Those pictures made an unusual impression."[92]

Detailed reports on the discussion groups launched in 1951 and 1952 suggest that such enthusiasm was not the rule. Some immigrants—particularly those with friends and family still behind the Iron Curtain—resented a campaign that they felt would endanger friends and family abroad. Most continued to correspond with relatives in Central and Eastern Europe, but many kept their letters "simple, non-political and family-focused." Some felt they would not be believed if they spoke too highly of their standard of living in America; others worried that friends abroad would ask for money.[93]

Indeed, these discussion group reports suggest that the successes the Letters from America campaign achieved came primarily on the home front from keeping immigrants focused on conditions abroad. Many complained bitterly about aspects of American life: the lack of respect for the elderly, the freedom of American youth, the difficulty educated immigrants had finding suitable jobs. When discussion leaders turned attention to conditions behind the Iron Curtain, however, the tone of the conversations changed markedly. Viewed in isolation, the American Way seemed flawed at best. Viewed as the only viable alternative to communism or socialism, the American Way seemed laudable indeed.

The "Crusade for Freedom"

Even as the Letters from America campaign was getting off the ground in the spring of 1950, a small group of prominent Americans unveiled a much broader effort designed, in the words of University of Pennsylvania president Harold Stassen, to "arouse private citizens of the United States to take the offensive in the cold war against Communism."[94] The "Crusade for Freedom," as the project was eventually dubbed, called on Americans to take "personal responsibility" for countering Soviet "lies" by signing "freedom scrolls," sending "freedom-grams" abroad, and contributing small amounts to Radio Free Europe and Radio Free Asia.[95] Drawing on the services of the Advertising Council—and run between 1953 and 1955 by the American Heritage Foundation—the Crusade attracted the enthusiastic support of a broad range of moderate and liberal cold warriors drawn from both parties, the Truman and Eisenhower administrations, the business community, the foreign policy and defense establishments, and the national media. By the mid-1950s, one scholar has written, the Crusade for Freedom was "as familiar to the American people as Ivory soap or Ford automobiles."[96]

The origins of the Crusade can be found in 1949 and 1950, when several prominent architects of the cold war—Allen Dulles, General Lucius Clay, C. D. Jackson, and a handful of others—came together to form the National Committee for a Free Europe (known after 1953 as the Free Europe Committee).[97] These men shared a belief that the conflict with the Soviet bloc "would eventually be fought by political rather than military means." The Committee was designed to supplement official U.S. policy by doing things that the State Department could not do because of its need to maintain diplomatic relations with the Soviet Union and Eastern bloc countries. The group sought to organize European exiles into unified national councils that could, in the words of committee chairman Joseph Grew, "stand as symbols of democratic hope for their countrymen in Eastern Europe." This effort met with limited success, but the Committee's foray into broadcasting proved more fruitful. On July 4, 1950, it launched Radio Free Europe, which sought to undermine communist governments by beaming "a muscular brand of political warfare" into five Soviet satellites.[98] Ostensibly private, Radio Free Europe allowed cold warriors in both parties to circumvent Republican isolationists in Congress who were reluctant to fund a federal broadcasting operation overseas, particularly one that would be run by the Truman administration. The service could also engage in more combative programming than would have been possible for an official government agency. Broadcasting, however, was a costly business. Thus, from its launch in 1950 through the early 1970s, the majority of Radio Free Europe's funding came covertly from the CIA.

The Crusade for Freedom was designed in part to obscure this funding mechanism. Still, as historians of Radio Free Europe have noted, a similar result could have been obtained far more easily by relying on large corporate and foundation gifts. This was the approach taken by many other CIA-funded initiatives during the cold war and even by the Free Europe Committee itself in the late 1950s. In the early years of the decade, however, organizers clearly hoped to use a massive grassroots Crusade in much the same way that Treasury Secretary Henry Morgenthau had used war bond drives during World War II: to build broad public support for the basic assumptions underlying U.S. involvement in the cold war.[99] In ads, speeches, and other materials, Crusade organizers and supporters repeatedly stressed that the U.S. was "confronted by a determined and ruthless Enemy…bent on world conquest."[100] Only by "enrolling" personally in the Crusade—by exhibiting, in General Dwight Eisenhower's words, "simple courage and unshakable unity"—could Americans help preserve their "system of government" and their "birthright" of freedom.[101] This emphasis on personal involvement and national unity discouraged both apathy and dissent.

Organizers of the Crusade for Freedom used many techniques that had been employed in the war bond campaigns of World War II. They enlisted the support of the Advertising Council, which developed and distributed advertising mats, car cards, outdoor billboards, and radio and television spots to media outlets across the country. The Advertising Council also worked the Crusade into its radio and television allocation plans.[102] Meanwhile, Crusade organizers set up and maintained "an elaborate volunteer infrastructure which reached to the local community level": some sixty state chairmen and cochairmen oversaw more than one thousand volunteers.[103] These local crusaders in turn mobilized hundreds of community groups. In New York City, for instance, Boy Scouts, newspaper boys, and members of the Civil Air Patrol solicited signatures and donations, while members of the Brotherhood of Railroad Trainmen left "subscription kits" on the seats of New York-bound commuter trains. In 1950, city residents could also enroll in the campaign at police stations, fire houses, Broadway theatres, churches and synagogues, and more than two hundred Western Union offices. This grassroots organization clearly had an effect: General Clay, the campaign's first national chairman, announced that in its first three months, the Crusade had collected 15,507,877 signatures on Freedom Scrolls and some $1.3 million, mostly in contributions of under one dollar.[104]

Like the Treasury Department during World War II, Crusade organizers made heavy use of parades, mass rallies, and other public spectacles—including balloon launches and air drops of "freedom-grams" in many cities.[105] Organizers launched the Crusade in 1950 by commissioning a replica of Philadelphia's Liberty Bell, which was designed to be hung in West Berlin. Cast in England, the "Freedom Bell" was shipped to New York City, paraded up Broadway, displayed before City Hall, and then sent on a tour of twenty-six other cities across the country. When the Freedom Bell finally left New York Harbor bound for Europe, Crusade organizers launched one thousand red, white, and blue balloons—each bearing an individualized "freedom scroll" and a return envelope—from the top of the Empire State Building. The Freedom Bell was installed in Berlin's Rathaus Schöneberg on October 24, 1950, United Nations Day. At precisely 12:03 p.m. E.S.T., its first peals were broadcast by Radio Free Europe and all four U.S. radio networks. Churches and schools across the U.S. tolled their bells at the same moment.[106]

As both the tolling of the church bells and the very name of the Crusade for Freedom suggested, religion played a central role in the campaign. Those orchestrating the effort argued that individual freedom was a right derived "from God" and called the campaign itself "a great moral crusade."[107] Beginning in 1952, the Crusade urged Americans to record or sign Freedom-grams, which were to be beamed into Eastern Europe or wafted over the Iron Curtain by balloon (figure 8.1). Pre-printed Freedom-grams emphasized the binding power of faith: "In America millions regularly pray for an understanding between our peoples. Please add your prayers to ours. Surely our common faith in God is the place where hope for freedom begins."[108]

The Crusade's emphasis on Americans' shared religiosity can be seen as part of a broader effort by various elites in the 1950s to reshape America's

Figure 8.1. New York Governor Thomas Dewey records a "Freedom-gram" to be broadcast into Eastern Europe during the "Crusade for Freedom" campaign. Crusade organizers sought to mobilize millions of Americans into the cold war in order to "develop" in them a "greater awareness" of their own blessings and to reinforce an anticommunist consensus (Getty Images).

national identity. Before and during World War II, federal officials and many private groups had emphasized the nation's shared religious values, arguing that faith in God both united Americans and distinguished them from their fascist foes. In the late 1930s and early 1940s, this religious framework competed with—and sometimes complemented—an alternative message that emphasized the nation's ethnoracial diversity and its secular Enlightenment values. By the 1950s, however, religion had moved to center stage. In early 1954, President Eisenhower attended a Lincoln Day service at a Presbyterian Church in Washington, D.C., accompanied by Barney Balaban, the Jewish Hollywood magnate who had helped transform the Freedom Train. The two men listened to a sermon in which the Rev. George M. Docherty argued that the words "under God" should be added to the Pledge of Allegiance. Without these words, the pastor suggested, the pledge was missing something vital—"the characteristic and definitive factor in the American way of life." Without these words, he declared, "I could hear little Muscovites repeat a similar pledge to their hammer-and-sickle flag in Moscow." Later that day, Eisenhower endorsed the change.[109] It sped through Congress and by mid-June had become law. Two years later, Congress officially adopted "In God We Trust" as the national motto, displacing the long-standing paean to ethnic diversity *E Pluribus Unum*.[110]

Such moves drew support from nonatheists across the political spectrum; but while Catholic conservatives and Protestant fundamentalists generally stressed America's *Christian* roots, the Crusade embraced an interfaith approach. On October 8, 1950—"Freedom Sunday"—General Clay urged ministers, priests, and rabbis across the country to focus their weekend sermons on the movement's "spiritual significance."[111] Crusade rallies and advertisements frequently featured individuals representing the Catholic, Protestant, and Jewish faiths.[112] In March 1952, Crusade organizers asked both Christians and Jews in the U.S. to pray regularly "for unity in spirit on both sides of the Iron Curtain." Such coordinated praying, Crusade organizers contended, would encourage "the victims of communism," while awakening Americans to "a clearer realization of the menace" they faced.[113]

The Crusade for Freedom, like the Treasury Department during World War II, tried both to mobilize and to channel the loyalties of ethnic Americans; but as with the Letters from America campaign—and in contrast to war bond campaigns—efforts to shape views at home and abroad were closely linked. In the fall of 1951, the New York branch of the Crusade set up special committees designed to target twenty-five foreign-language groups, among them Czechs, Greeks, Chinese, Hungarians, Germans, Latvians, and Poles. The Crusade also provided special floats to ethnic celebrations such as the Pulaski Memorial Day Parade and set aside certain days for "national groups from Iron Curtain countries" to record freedom-grams.[114] Ads produced by the Advertising Council for the Crusade frequently reminded newer Americans how lucky they were compared to their kinsmen abroad. One such ad showed an elderly Czech couple holding hands as they listened to a radio presumably broadcasting Radio Free Europe. "Mrs. Novak," the headline read, "your son is safe in Detroit."[115]

Other ads produced by the Advertising Council, and sponsored either by corporations or national media outlets, reminded *all* Americans of their "freedom from fear" by offering chilling depictions of the brutality of Communist regimes. One highlighted a "Hungarian Tragedy!"—"the true story of Mrs. X and the child she was forced to sell to the State." Another told how Radio Free Europe had unmasked a Czech Communist operative, the murderer of a Catholic priest.[116] A third ad, which ran in the *New York Times* and which appears to have been sponsored by the paper, pictured an attractive couple under the heading "MR. AND MRS. MURDERER!" The Margineanus, the ad explained, were aides to the chief of Romania's security police. "Together with other members of the governmental gang, they patronize blood orgies nightly," the text read. "While the torture goes on, the wine bottle is passed around." This couple had been "distinguished citizens of Blaj, respected and admired by the entire community." Now, however, Radio Free Europe was "telling all of Romania about this bloodthirsty couple and their secret torture chamber!"[117]

Such ads focused on Eastern Europe; but by celebrating the naming of names, they reinforced a culture of informing in the U.S. as well. As Stephen J. Whitfield has noted, the West historically "has not allocated a high status to the informer": Judas is the central villain of Christianity, and in both the U.S. and Europe cultural productions have generally portrayed "stoolies" and "squealers" as "especially loathsome." This changed dramatically during the early cold war. Congressional investigating committees subpoenaed actors and screenwriters, labor leaders, foreign policy specialists, and refugee intellectuals, granting clemency for past political indiscretions to those who named names. Films such as the Oscar-winning *On the Waterfront* hailed the righteous informer. Even an American history textbook, coauthored by the founder of Yale's American Studies program, urged readers to report to the FBI suspicions "about Communist activity on the part of their fellow Americans." In doing so, the book suggested, "they are acting in line with American traditions."[118] This red-baiting culture helped to marginalize those Americans who had once used the rhetoric of shared values to further egalitarian ends.

Even in its early years—when organizers aimed at mobilizing Americans at the grass roots—the Crusade for Freedom attracted substantial corporate support. In 1951, both Chevrolet and Ford donated scores of cars and trucks for motorcades designed to cross the country drumming up support for the Crusade; they and other car dealers also turned their showrooms into "enrollment centers."[119] Corporations also sponsored Crusade advertisements produced by the Advertising Council or devoted space in in-house magazines to the campaign. Most of the Crusade's one thousand local volunteers were businessmen, as were many top officials. In 1952, for instance, Crusade officers included Henry Ford II, president of Ford Motor Company; Charles E. Wilson, former president of General Electric; and Winthrop Aldrich, chairman of Chase National Bank.[120]

Despite this array of corporate backers, the Crusade almost never focused on economic issues: advertisements and other campaign materials portrayed communists as godless and aggressive tyrants, not as socialists. Still, the Crusade contributed in more indirect ways to a political culture that was conducive to corporate interests. One of the principle themes of the campaign, repeatedly stressed, was "the efficacy of private initiative...over reliance on government."[121] While this message referred to the Crusade itself, it could easily be translated to other arenas of American society. Moreover, by keeping Americans focused on the cold war—by reminding them of their need to defend individual liberties—the Crusade underscored a point that business groups had been making since the late 1930s. Eugene Holman, chairman of Standard Oil of New Jersey, recognized this when he took over as national chairman of the Crusade in early 1956: "The cold war is still on in earnest," he declared. "Freedom to show individual enterprise is at stake. When Communism marches in, all the freedoms we take for granted disappear."[122]

The massive public campaigns that characterized the Crusade for Freedom in its early years ended abruptly after the failed Hungarian Revolution in the fall of 1956. Many U.S. liberals blamed Radio Free Europe for goading the rebels and for leading them to believe that the West would intervene on their behalf; instead, Soviet troops crushed the rebellion while the U.S. and its allies looked on. The resulting firestorm of criticism destroyed the comparatively broad base of elite support that the Crusade had previously enjoyed. Radio and television spots produced by the Advertising Council continued to give the Crusade some public visibility, but the organization dismantled much of its volunteer infrastructure. After 1956, it relied almost entirely on corporate contributions.[123]

For seven years in the early to mid-1950s, the Crusade for Freedom inundated the airwaves, marked the landscape, and plastered the print media with its message. The Crusade fueled fevered anticommunism, while suggesting that Americans were bound by their shared belief in "the sacredness and dignity of the individual" and in "the God-given 'right to freedom.'"[124] While it is hard to gauge the impact of the Crusade on individual Americans, its impact on public discourse is more readily apparent. Long after discussions of the fund-raising effort on behalf of Radio Free Europe had retreated from the public eye, the phrase "crusade for freedom"—with its connotations of shared faith, belief in individual dignity, and the right of individuals to be free from fear—lingered on in the public vocabulary. Increasingly, however, it was associated with a domestic campaign: the "crusade" of black Americans for civil rights.[125] When blacks in Memphis attempted to win political power in 1959, the Negro Volunteer Ticket adopted the slogan, "This Is a Crusade for Freedom." When New York mayor Robert Wagner addressed a gathering of black clergy in September 1963, he referred to their civil rights work as a "crusade for freedom."[126] And a few days later when Martin Luther King Jr., delivered the eulogy for three young girls who had been killed in the bombing of Birmingham's 16th Street Baptist Church, he used the phrase again. "They are the martyred heroines of a holy crusade for freedom and human dignity," he declared.

> They say to each of us that we must substitute courage for caution. They say to us that we must be concerned not merely about who murdered them, but about the system, the way of life, the philosophy which produced the murderers. Their death says to us that we must work passionately and unrelentingly for the realization of the American dream.[127]

King's eulogy hinted both at the possibilities opened by efforts to define an American consensus over the previous quarter century and at the limitations of that debate.

Conclusion: The Limits of Consensus

Between 1956 and 1960, the Rockefeller Brothers Fund (RBF) convened more than one hundred prominent Americans—industrialists, government officials, academics, labor leaders, editors, philanthropists, generals, and theologians—to "clarify the national purposes and objectives." Organized into a series of working panels, these elites hammered out reports on topics ranging from foreign policy and economics to education, social challenges, and "The Power of the Democratic Idea." Behind the scenes, the discussions sometimes devolved into rancorous debate.[1] The Special Studies Project's final report, however, gave no hint of such disagreement. Issued in 1961 under the title *Prospect for America*, the report hailed American-style free enterprise; decried religious, ethnic, racial, and class tensions; and warned in stern language of the Communist threat. For a democracy to survive in the face of such a threat, indeed, for a democracy to function at all, required not only "shared allegiance to the rules of the game," but a "practical working consensus," the report's authors maintained. This working consensus defined "what is and what is not a significant matter for public debate" and set "the effective limits of the political dialogue." The panel had no doubt what lay at the core of America's consensus: "It is our belief in the individual as the supreme fact of life."[2]

A similar report issued by President Eisenhower's "nonpartisan" Commission on National Goals in 1960—and subsequently publicized by the Advertising Council—struck much the same tone. "Democracy, to be viable, requires a large measure of consensus," one chapter of *Goals for Americans* declared. The presidential commission hinted at incipient dissent, saying it hoped the report itself would help provide "the path to a national consensus." It too, however, warned of the need to defend the Free World from the Communist threat, decried "religious prejudice" and "discrimination on the basis of race," and claimed that Americans were approaching a "classless society." Like the

RBF panelists, the commission repeatedly put the individual at the center of American life: "The paramount goal of the United States was set long ago," the report's opening sentence declared. "It is to guard the rights of the individual, to ensure his development, and to enlarge his opportunity."[3]

Taken together, these two reports testified to the continuing urgency of a question that had preoccupied influential Americans for a quarter of a century: What values and beliefs did Americans of diverse backgrounds share? The reports also outlined the principal elements of agreement that had emerged in the public arena by the beginning of the 1960s: confidence in the democratic abundance of American-style capitalism; distaste for class conflict, religious intolerance, and other forms of social disunity; a conviction that communism represented the principle threat to the U.S. at home and abroad; and, underlying all of these, an emphasis on *individual* freedoms and rights. Finally, the two reports suggested the tenuous and contingent nature of that public accord. Had consensus been pervasive, even among elites, neither report would have had to "clarify" its content or stress its importance to the nation. As R. W. B. Lewis suggested about an earlier period of intense national self-definition, what ultimately unified Americans between the mid-1930s and the mid-1960s was less an answer than a question.[4]

Americans had wrestled with questions of national identity and cohesion since the earliest days of the republic; but in the late 1930s, domestic and international pressures converged to give such questions unusual saliency. The Depression intensified social divisions in the U.S. and called into question many of the verities that had long guided American society and policymaking. The New Deal united millions of Americans in a sweeping reform coalition, but it also triggered intense ideological debates about the proper contours of the nation's political economy. Strains or open hostility between the ancestral homes of millions of American citizens amplified group tensions in the U.S. as well. Finally, the challenge posed by the "alien" ideologies of fascism and communism intensified Americans' sense of unease. Many liberals and leftists saw in rising nativism, red-baiting, union busting, and particularly anti-Semitism the seeds of a domestic fascism. Economic conservatives, meanwhile, worried that the New Deal and the amorphous left-wing movement that supported it foretold the arrival in the U.S. of "state socialism." Subsequent studies have shown that both fears were greatly exaggerated; but to many at the time, they seemed real indeed. Driven by such concerns, public intellectuals, government officials, and organizations across the political spectrum redoubled their efforts to define for Americans their common ground.

Such efforts also drew urgency from another source that cut across ideological divides: the need to defend America against fascism and communism without succumbing to the evils of those "totalitarian" states. Enforced uniformity was widely considered a hallmark of totalitarianism, so American writers and speakers repeatedly emphasized the diversity that distinguished U.S. society. But diversity alone, many opinion molders believed, could breed chaos and intolerance, as it apparently had in much of the rest of the world. (The fall of France, in particular, was read by many as foreshadowing the fate of nations that remained internally divided.) To be an attribute, rather than a danger, diversity needed to be circumscribed and solidly embedded in common ground. Thus, celebrations of American pluralism in the late 1930s and early 1940s were almost always linked to invocations of consensus. At the same time, many of the paeans to America's unifying ideals in this period were intended, not simply as descriptions of the nation, but as prescriptions for the U.S. and the world. By *declaring* that Americans of diverse ethnic, religious, regional, racial, and class backgrounds shared deeply rooted civic values, American intellectuals, government officials, business groups, and other civic leaders sought to call such a consensus into being—to create a nation that was at once diverse and harmonious.

Ultimately, three broad groups played central roles in the effort to shape a public consensus on national values between the mid-1930s and the mid-1950s. Many government officials and cultural elites—individuals ranging from Margaret Mead to the organizers of cold war letter-writing campaigns and the Crusade for Freedom—sought to unify Americans and steel them to withstand first the Fascist and then the Communist threat. Meanwhile, industry, public relations, and advertising executives worked to reassert the authority of business, to halt or roll back the New Deal, and to restore a political culture conducive to the exercise of corporate power with minimal government control. Finally, a loose coalition of individuals and organizations sought to defuse "intergroup" tensions and to promote a more religiously, ethnically, and racially tolerant society. This last group included individuals such as Newton Baker and some of his colleagues in the National Conference of Christians and Jews (NCCJ), who sought to hold American society together but had little interest in transforming the economic and political status quo. It also included many liberals and leftists—Louis Adamic, Gunnar and Alva Myrdal, E. Franklin Frazier, those affiliated with the Council Against Intolerance, and many others—who ultimately hoped to promote greater equality.

Diverse as they were, all of these individuals and groups invoked national unity and shared values, largely rejecting the language of progressive struggle that had propelled social movements for decades. For divergent reasons, they also emphasized individual freedoms rather than majoritarian democracy. Business groups stressed individual rights in order to shore up free enterprise, while many intergroup liberals did so to protect religious and ethnic minorities from the kind of "ghettoization" and scapegoating seen in Europe. Government officials could be found in both categories. Most also saw in "the dignity of the individual" the issue that most clearly set the U.S. off from the totalitarian states.

One other conviction unified almost all of those engaged in promoting a national consensus during these years: the belief that America had a message for the globe. The United States had a long history of racism, nativism, class conflict, and religious intolerance, and those vices did not suddenly disappear. Still, viewed alongside the Spanish Civil War, Central European anti-Semitism, Soviet purges, and Japanese atrocities, America looked—even to many liberals and leftists—tolerant and inclusive indeed. In the late 1930s and early 1940s, Louis Adamic argued that the U.S. contained the seeds of a "pan-human" culture, and scholars ranging from Margaret Mead to the Swedish economist Gunnar Myrdal agreed.[5] During the first decade of the cold war, government officials, business groups, and even intergroup liberals such as those in the Common Council for American Unity sought to mobilize Americans to export the "American Way"; in the process, they hoped to solidify a consensus at home. This cold war vision of the American Way generally emphasized free enterprise, teamwork, and a shared religious faith. Still, even in the postwar years, left liberals, too, believed that America stood for something potentially universal. Carlos Bulosan, a Filipino immigrant laborer whose 1946 memoir is a wrenching indictment of America's continuing racism, found hope in the *idea* for which he believed America stood. "America is in the heart," he wrote. Like Adamic and Myrdal, he believed that U.S. society was deeply flawed, but remained an "unfinished dream."[6]

If those who preached and appealed to a unifying set of American values thus shared common ground, they were also split by a chasmal divide. Some Americans—economic conservatives, many cold warriors, and those intergroup liberals who hoped only to create or preserve social harmony—presented the U.S. as comparatively perfected. In their eyes, America was an intact model of political, religious, and economic freedom, blessed by nearly universal affluence. All that Americans needed to do in order to enjoy their many blessings was to learn to pull together, to get along. In preaching consensus, these groups denied or minimized power imbalances and emphasized *civility* across class, religious, and other lines. By marginalizing dissenters—by casting those who disrupted national unity as somehow un-American—they shored up the social, economic, and political status quo.

This vision of America benefited from the deep pockets of its supporters, but it was never unrivalled. As Bulosan's comment suggests, many of those who celebrated a unifying American idea or way in the late 1930s and 1940s believed that it remained an "unfinished dream." Individuals such as Louis Adamic, Gunnar Myrdal, and the left-liberal writers and artists in the Office of War Information deployed the language of consensus, not to quell dissent or shore up the status quo, but to unite Americans around a set of values that they believed would lead to greater equality. By positing shared ideals and then highlighting the difference between those ideals and an imperfect reality, they created a powerful—if ultimately limited—cultural lever that could be used by those who remained outside of the American dream.[7]

The competition between these two visions of the American Way—as well as the ground they shared—structured national debates in powerful ways well into the 1960s. Corporate America reaped particular benefits from the emphasis on teamwork and consensus. Through most of the 1930s, New Dealers believed that "something was wrong with American capitalism and that government should find a way to repair it."[8] Industrial unionists and leftists frequently went further, calling for organized labor to play a role in managerial decision-making or even for the dismantling of the entire capitalist system. During and after World War II, such views faded rapidly from American political discourse. This can be attributed in part to a shift toward Keynesianism after 1937 by many New Dealers and in part to the booming economy of the war and postwar years.[9] But civic education campaigns that underscored the natural harmony of interests between groups in American society and that posited "teamwork" as a core American value are another piece of this story. Books and media coverage, public pageants, radio and television shows, educational materials, and advertising campaigns carried these messages into schools, churches, homes, and union halls across the nation. Even campaigns launched by "intergroup" organizations such as the NCCJ, the American Jewish Committee, or ultimately the Common Council for American Unity frequently framed issues in ways that shored up the corporate order.[10] If laborers could be convinced of the value of "pulling together" and tolerating others (including those in management), they would be less likely to embrace militant tactics. If working-class immigrants could be reminded of the terrors wrought by Communists in their countries of origin, they would more likely appreciate the virtues of capitalism at home. If Americans of all backgrounds and faiths could be convinced that they stood shoulder to shoulder in the fight for freedom, they would be less likely to turn on their allies in that battle.

The rehabilitation of capitalism also required a change in perspective on the part of large segments of the business community. Increasingly business moderates realized that the best way to regain cultural authority was to convince Americans that they had seen the light—that the "new" form of American capitalism was different from the "robber baron" version practiced in the past; that businessmen were now model civic citizens; that a high-production, high-consumption model of capitalism had revolutionary potential for producing social justice. This view—promoted by such men as Chamber of Commerce president Eric Johnston and advertising executive Thomas D'Arcy Brophy during the war—increasingly gained adherents in the postwar period. It called on industrialists to recognize organized labor's right to exist—even labor's right to bargain collectively—and allowed for a limited federal role in the economy. At the same time, it largely restored the authority and autonomy of business, protecting corporate decision makers from intrusions by labor or unwanted government control. In the postwar period, business groups employed "nonpartisan" institutions such as the Advertising Council and the American Heritage Foundation to funnel these ideas to the national media and other elites, as well as to the public at large.

In repositioning themselves as responsible corporate citizens—and as part of their effort to preach social harmony—business executives and their allies in advertising and public relations increasingly threw their weight behind campaigns that promoted tolerance across ethnic, religious, and even racial lines. This was the message behind corporate-sponsored programs such as *The Adventures of Superman* and the Advertising Council's "United America" campaign. It also helps to explain the ample business support received by groups such as the NCCJ in the postwar period. As two social scientists noted in the mid-1950s, "in many sections of the country intergroup relations has become a good 'cause' for conservatives to be liberal about. It is not basically threatening to their own economic or social status in the community."[11]

The interfaith movement benefited particularly from this alliance and from the broader cultural conversation on consensus. Throughout the nineteenth and early twentieth centuries, no form of nativism was more widespread or virulent in the U.S. than anti-Catholicism. Anti-Semitism, too, surged after the turn of the century, peaking in 1945. Yet during and after World War II, the long-standing equation in public discourse of "Americanism" with "Protestantism" gave way rapidly, if incompletely, to the notion that the U.S. was a "Judeo-Christian" or "tri-faith" nation. Countless public forums in the 1940s and 1950s featured a priest, a minister, and a rabbi, or secular representatives of the three faiths; this tri-faith formulation also appeared in cultural artifacts and events ranging from the "Four Chaplains" stamp and the Freedom Train to the Crusade for Freedom and People's Capitalism campaigns. At the same time, religion increasingly supplanted national origin—and occasionally even race—in discussions of both prejudice and diversity in American life.[12]

Writing in 1955, Will Herberg attributed this development to a demographic transformation: More and more Americans, he argued, were intermarrying across ethnic but within broad religious lines.[13] In fact, Herberg's evidence for the "triple melting pot" was thin, and subsequent sociological studies have cast doubt on his conclusions.[14] Moreover, the shift in the public arena occurred too rapidly to be explained entirely by demographic change. Ideological considerations also played a major role. By casting pluralism in religious terms, public intellectuals, government officials, and others could stress America's democratic diversity without reinforcing potentially divisive loyalties to foreign homelands. At the same time, the notion that Protestantism, Catholicism, and Judaism were "the religions of democracy"—that they were diverse representations of spiritual ideals and moral values that all Americans shared—reinforced the underlying cohesiveness of American society.[15] In the face of irreligion—either the Nazi or Japanese "religion of the state" or the atheism of the Soviet Union—belief in *any* of what Herberg called America's "three great faiths" could provide a basis for cultural unity.[16] Assimilated American Jews, many of whom viewed Judaism solely as a religious affiliation, helped promote the idea. So too did many in the business community, who argued that all three faiths highlighted a core American value: the "sanctity of the individual." By the late 1940s, the "interfaith idea" had emerged in the public arena as a powerful symbol of both American pluralism and American consensus.[17]

If religion was particularly useful to those who sought to portray the U.S. as both unified and inclusive, race proved time and again to be more of a stumbling block. On the one hand, public service advertising and other civic education campaigns often condemned racial animosity in the same sentence as religious prejudice and class hatred. This undoubtedly contributed in the 1940s and 1950s to the delegitimization of white supremacy, particularly in its ugliest forms.[18] At the same time, the issue of race proved particularly explosive and frequently threatened to disrupt the image of the U.S. as a consensual nation. The Advertising Council briefly pulled its United America campaign in the fall of 1948, when civil rights became a hotly contested issue in the presidential election. In the 1950s, the Chicago Commission on Human Relations persuaded major newspapers not to cover racial confrontations in city housing projects, because it worried such coverage would only inflame racial tensions. When black Americans loudly deplored the fact that many southern cities planned segregated viewing of the Freedom Train, the train's organizers initially tried to quiet the protesters and finesse the issue.

Efforts to "contain" the race issue and maintain the appearance of harmonious consensus did not always succeed, however, as the story of the Freedom Train attests. Some Americans had always accepted the argument made by E. Franklin Frazier at the end of World War II: that the only way to achieve true national unity was to repudiate the racial caste system and integrate blacks fully into American life. Gunnar Myrdal's *An American Dilemma*, which posited an internalized consensus, established a liberal orthodoxy on black-white relations that guided policymaking and Supreme Court decisions for more than twenty years. Even campaigns launched by economic conservatives and cold warriors—the Freedom Train, the Crusade for Freedom, and others—sometimes opened doors they hadn't foreseen. The same language of individual rights, faith and freedom used to shore up free enterprise and cement an anticommunist consensus could be appropriated and redeployed by those arguing for civil rights.

Civil rights activists increasingly made use of this cultural lever. They worked to achieve legal and political equality for black individuals by calling on Americans to live up to their "common ideals." Martin Luther King Jr., and other movement activists made powerful use of the jeremiad, a rhetorical form that both presupposes and reinforces a social and political consensus.[19] While King often spoke of equality, he also invoked values that were being promoted in many other quarters: individual freedom, shared faith, and the need for "brotherhood" among "all God's children." In his oft-quoted "I Have a Dream" speech, King used biblical language to describe a faith that would transform "the jangling discords of our nation into a beautiful symphony of brotherhood."[20] Given the political climate of the time—with its public emphasis on comity and "pulling together"—it is perhaps not surprising that the movement made its greatest gains in places such as Birmingham and Selma, where it was able to provoke a violent backlash. In cities where "civility" reigned— Greensboro, North Carolina, for instance—the civil rights movement took far longer to achieve its goals.[21]

Powerful as it was, the language of national consensus also had profound limits. In adopting this rhetoric, King and others were forced to abandon other languages—international socialism, black nationalism, and perhaps most important, human rights—that had propelled movements for equality in earlier decades.[22] As David Howard-Pitney has observed, "To the extent that black intellectual leaders have employed a rhetoric anchored in social consensus, they have had to frame and keep their goals within its nonrevolutionary terms and bounds."[23] The language of consensus—a consensus built around individual freedom—could be deployed to extend civil rights to individual black Americans. It was much less successful at reversing the economic and cultural legacies of a form of group-based oppression: white supremacy.

In 1965, William Morrow and Co. published a new and expanded edition of *And Keep Your Powder Dry*, Margaret Mead's classic 1942 study of the American character. In her preface and introduction to the new volume, Mead noted that the book was in some ways a period piece—a social scientist's "frankly and completely partisan" contribution to winning the war and "establishing a just and lasting peace." Intervening developments, she added, most notably the dropping of the atomic bombs at Hiroshima and Nagasaki, meant that the gulf separating 1942 from 1965 was "as deep as the gulf that separated the men who became builders of cities from Stone Age men."[24]

Mead's other revisions indicated that in one crucial respect, the gap between the two publication dates was not as great as she suggested. Writing in March 1965, as civil rights activists marched on Selma and President Lyndon Johnson's Great Society legislation sped through Congress, Mead declared that Americans were "entering a period of new hope." They were "shaking [themselves] free of the apprehension and apathy of the dismal 1950's" and readying themselves for the kind of effort "they achieved in the past only in response to the desperation of the Great Depression or the exigencies of war." Hoping to further this effort, Mead added a final chapter designed to give Americans an updated sense "of their particular strengths as a people and of the part they may play in the world." To release Americans' energy "for new purposes we must take stock of ourselves," she explained. "Do we still have the character structure we had twenty years ago? Or have changing conditions also affected who and what we are?"[25]

Mead's euphoria was not limited to the domestic arena. Immediately after hailing the Great Society, Mead quoted from a recent address by President Lyndon Johnson on Vietnam:

> For most of history, men have hated and killed one another in
> battle. But we dream of an end to war. We will try to make it so.

For all existence, most men have lived in poverty, threatened by hunger. But we dream of a world where all are fed and charged with hope. And we will help to make it so.

"We have not yet acted on the implications of these words," Mead wrote. "Yet it will not avail us to answer the needs or to right the injustices within the United States as long as we are unwilling to act with full responsibility in the wider world." If Americans did not aid in Vietnam and elsewhere, she argued, they would see themselves "in the likeness of a man who sits calmly on his own doorstep nursing a minor injury, while outside his fence his neighbors are engaged in a desperate battle where every man is needed."[26]

That Mead could still write of a singular character structure—that politicians and civil rights activists still appealed frequently to unifying American values—testified to the lingering strength of a concept that had shaped U.S. political culture for roughly three decades. For most of that time, the majority of Americans—whether they viewed the nation as "in progress" or virtually perfected—had also shared Mead's confidence that America embodied a message for the world. But even as the anthropologist wrote, the notion that "America" symbolized an idea worth fighting for was losing support, particularly among liberals and those on the left. The same month that Mead finished her new preface, President Johnson dispatched the first U.S. combat troops to Vietnam, escalating American involvement in what would soon seem to many an endless and pointless war. The political culture of consensus had always depended on the existence of a strong external "other," whether fascism or communism. When the fight against communism came to seem both unreal and untenable—in Vietnam—the politics of consensus unraveled.

Even as Americans bogged down in Vietnam, developments on the home front challenged one of the basic tenets of postwar consensus culture: the notion that Americans could achieve social justice by continually expanding the economy and "guard[ing] the rights of the individual."[27] On August 11, 1965, five days after President Johnson signed the Voting Rights Act into law, the Watts neighborhood of Los Angeles exploded into flames. The Watts riot—followed in subsequent summers by riots in Newark, Detroit, and other cities—called attention to America's continuing economic and racial inequalities. The civil rights movement had triumphed in part because it could appeal to the notion of individual freedom, but individual opportunity alone could not quickly overcome centuries of group-based oppression. President Johnson recognized this fact when he issued an executive order in September 1965 introducing the notion of affirmative action. "Freedom is not enough," he declared in a speech at Howard University justifying the decision. "You do not wipe away the scars of centuries by saying: Now you are free to go where you want, and do as you desire.... You do not take a person who, for years, has been hobbled by chains and liberate him, bring him up to the starting line of a race and then say, 'you are free to compete with all the others,' and still justly believe that you have been completely fair."[28] Many others far more radical than Johnson—including King near the end of his life—also concluded that economic growth and individual freedom were inadequate tools with which to address the poverty that still plagued many parts of the United States.

Social and cultural trends fueled shifts in the political culture as well. The very affluence that in the 1950s was often equated with the American Way helped produce a youth culture that attacked materialism. White ethnics, black nationalists, Chicano activists, and young Native Americans shunned the unifying language of "Americanism" that had been embraced by their parents, calling instead for a revival of ethnic, Black, Brown, or Red pride. In the late 1930s, such group fragmentation alarmed even left liberals, prompting many to turn to the question of America's common ground. But in the late 1960s, Fascism had been vanquished and Communism seemed to most Americans a greatly diminished threat. The question that had unified Americans for decades—"Are we a nation...with a continuing national ideal?"—no longer seemed terribly relevant.

These trends reverberated through the culture, leaving their mark on institutions and frameworks of thought established over the previous thirty years. The long-running Letters from America campaign was called off, and American Studies programs—founded in the 1940s and 1950s as part of a movement toward citizenship education—suffered an identity crisis. The ethnic revival that began in the late 1960s directly challenged the tri-faith model of America, and the "ethno-racial pentagon"—which divided Americans into categories that roughly corresponded to "black, yellow, white, red, and brown"—increasingly replaced religion as the preferred method for discussing difference in American society.[29] Gunnar Myrdal's *An American Dilemma*, which had established the postwar orthodoxy on race, increasingly fell out of favor, attacked by social scientists and African American leaders alike.[30]

In 1965, the trustees of the American Heritage Foundation considered organizing a new Freedom Train for a national two-year tour. The train, they hoped, "would again serve as a dramatic symbol to spark programs at the national and local levels for more active and responsible citizenship." The endeavor would "emphasize the common heritage of all Americans, stimulate a greater appreciation for our free institutions and encourage national unity." But when pollster George Gallup, a member of the foundation's executive committee, surveyed two dozen media executives to gauge their enthusiasm for the project, their answers testified to the changing times. Some enthusiastically backed the idea, suggesting that the train be directed toward universities or "routed into areas of unrest wherein our peoples have become the pawns of troublemakers." Many others, however, expressed reservations. Some questioned whether a second Freedom Train would have the same impact as the first, which had been launched when "the patriotic fervor and climate" of World War II still prevailed. Others noted that more Americans were visiting Washington and that the spread of television was likely to "diminish interest in a show which originally had as one of its virtues that it could be carried to the people." Two worried that the demolition or deterioration of the country's train terminals might make them unsuitable venues for the viewing of national treasures. The general manager of KRON-TV in San Francisco had a more fundamental concern. "I am afraid," he wrote, "the modern generation needs a totally different approach."[31]

Such comments—and the image of the nation's deteriorating passenger rail system—hinted at a broader fragmentation of American society. In the late 1940s, a train running on continuous tracks was able to link the entire nation, large cities and small towns alike, both physically and psychologically. By 1965, this was harder to do. The unifying experience of World War II was fast fading, and even the cold war's ideological jousting had lost much of its fevered pitch. Such trends only accelerated in subsequent decades. Cable channels and satellite radio, the Internet, niche marketing, retirement communities and gated suburbs were only a few of the developments that increasingly divided Americans by age, income, race, and interest. The Immigration Act of 1965 opened the door to new waves of immigrants, and millions were propelled to the U.S. by a changing global economy. While such developments reinforced internal subcultures, America's sense of national identity was challenged from without by the spread of the Internet and CNN, an international culture of consumption, and a heightened awareness of the global dimensions of labor and particularly environmental problems. Although nearly all U.S. citizens still called themselves Americans at the close of the twentieth century, the importance of that label to many had faded considerably.

If the political culture that inspired national character studies and the Freedom Train faded, however, its legacy survives. Phrases coined or popularized between the mid-1930s and the mid-1950s—including "free enterprise," the "Judeo-Christianity tradition" and the "American Way"—remain staples of U.S. political and cultural discourse. Critics of affirmative action and proponents of welfare reform cast their positions not in the racialist phrases of the past but in the language of individual freedom and opportunity. So too do Americans on both sides of the abortion and immigration debates and those arguing for and against "the right to die." American Studies programs still attract thousands of students each year, while the Advertising Council combats drug use and promotes prenatal care. The American Assembly, a nonpartisan forum charged by Dwight Eisenhower with administering his *Goals for America* report, continues to meet, bringing together diverse elites for "consensus-building" sessions.[32]

Since the mid-1990s, and particularly since 2001, there has been a resurgent interest in the kinds of questions that preoccupied Americans between the mid-1930s and the early 1960s. During the Clinton years, debates over multiculturalism and the eruption of racial tensions on the streets of Los Angeles and Cincinnati spurred widespread discussion of America's common ground and public values. Questions of national unity and identity took on additional urgency after the controversial 2000 presidential election and the terrorist attacks of September 11, 2001. In the wake of those attacks, the nonprofit Advertising Council launched an "I am an American" campaign, which depicted individuals of many ages, races, and religions. Still, a December 2001 cover story in the *Atlantic Monthly* on "red" and "blue" America asked, "Are We Really One Country?"[33]

Behind much of this ongoing national dialogue lurks nostalgia for an earlier age—roughly the period from the New Deal through the key legislative victories of the civil rights movement. Authors with politically divergent agendas see these years as a period of "common citizenship" and "common dreams," a time when Americans were united, "not only by a common purpose, but also by common values."[34] This book suggests that the story is a bit more complex—that Americans of that era were indeed united, but above all by a *quest* for common ground. They too asked the question "Are We Really One Country?" and they worked assiduously to shape the answer.

Abbreviations Used in Notes

ACNS Microfilm	*Records of the American Council for Nationalities Service, 1921–1971,* microfilmed from the holdings of the Immigration History Research Center (Frederick, Maryland: University Publications of America, 1989)
ACNS Records	Records of the American Council for Nationalities Service, ImmigrationHistory Research Center, University of Minnesota, Minneapolis, Minnesota
Advertising Council Archives	Advertising Council Archives, University of Illinois, Urbana, Illinois 13/2/201 Meeting Minutes, 1942–98 13/2/202 Annual Reports, 1943–2000 13/2/207 Historical File, 1941–97 13/2/225 Campaign Review Committee File 13/2/305 Washington Office Subject File, 1942–81
AHF Records	Records of the American Heritage Foundation, National Archives and Records Administration II, College Park, Maryland
AHR	*American Historical Review*
AJC Records	American Jewish Committee Records, RG 347, YIVO Institute for Jewish Research, New York, New York
Aldrich Collection	Winthrop W. Aldrich Collection, Baker Library, Harvard Business School, Boston, Massachusetts

Brophy Papers	Thomas D'Arcy Brophy Papers, Wisconsin State Historical Society, Archives, Madison, Wisconsin
CSAA Records	Child Study Association of America Records, Social Welfare History Archives, University of Minnesota, Minneapolis, Minnesota
Hearings	Congress, Senate, Subcommittee of the Committee on Education and Labor, *Violations of Free Speech and Rights of Labor: Hearings Pursuant to S. Res. 266*, 74th–76th Congs., 1936–1940, Part 35
HML	Hagley Museum and Library, Wilmington, Delaware
HSTL	Harry S. Truman Library, Independence, Missouri
JAH	*Journal of American History*
Jackson Files	Charles W. Jackson Files, Harry S. Truman Papers, Harry S. Truman Presidential Library, Independence, Missouri
NAACP Records	National Association for the Advancement of Colored People Records, Library of Congress, Washington, D.C.
NAM Records	Records of the National Association of Manufacturers, Accession 1411, Hagley Museum and Library, Wilmington, Delaware.
NARA-II	National Archives and Record Administration II, College Park, Maryland
NARS Freedom Train Records	Materials relating to the Freedom Train (1946–53), Educational Program Division, Records of the National Archives and Record Service, RG 64, National Archives, Washington, D.C.
Nash Papers	Philleo Nash Papers, Harry S. Truman Presidential Library, Independence, Missouri
NCCJ Records	National Conference of Christians and Jews Records, Social Welfare History Archives, University of Minnesota, Minneapolis, Minnesota.
NR	*New Republic*

NYPL	New York Public Library, Manuscripts and Archives Division
NYT	*New York Times*
NYTM	*New York Times Magazine*
NYWF Records	Records of the New York World's Fair, 1939–1940, New York Public Library, Manuscripts and Archives Division, New York, New York.
PPA	Franklin D. Roosevelt, *The Public Papers and Addresses of Franklin D. Roosevelt*, 13 vols. (New York: Random House, Macmillan Co., Harper Bros., 1938–1950)
SEP	*Saturday Evening Post*
VSD	*Vital Speeches of the Day*
Waldman Papers	Morris Waldman Papers, RG 347, American Jewish Committee Records, YIVO Institute for Jewish Research, New York, New York
WP	*Washington Post*

Notes

Introduction

1. For a complete recounting of the story of the Freedom Train, see chapter 7.
2. "Address by Honorable Tom C. Clark, Attorney General of the United States, at Bill of Rights Luncheon," NARS Freedom Train Records, Box 2, "746–E7, Tour of the Freedom Train (Pt. 1), From 5/1/46–1/29/47" folder.
3. Barney Balaban to Leon Lowenstein, 31 October 1947, AHF Records, Box 208, "Contributions–American Heritage Foundation" folder.
4. "A Program to Re-Sell Americanism to Americans," 15 November 1946, Brophy Papers, Box 35, Folder 8.
5. Winthrop Aldrich to [Philadelphia mayor] Bernard Samuel, 11 July 1947, in Aldrich Collection, Box 19, "American Heritage Foundation, July 1947" folder.
6. *Oxford English Dictionary*, 2nd ed., s.v. "consensus."
7. Arthur M. Schlesinger, Jr., *The Vital Center: The Politics of Freedom* (Boston: Houghton Mifflin Co., 1949; Cambridge, Mass.: Riverside, 1962), 190, x.
8. Clinton Rossiter, "The Democratic Process," in U.S. President's Commission on National Goals, *Goals for Americans: Programs for Action in the Sixties, Comprising the Report of the President's Commission on National Goals and Chapters Submitted for the Consideration of the Commission* (Englewood Cliffs, N.J.: Prentice-Hall, 1960), 61.
9. The best overview of the postwar consensus is offered in Godfrey Hodgson, *America in Our Time: From World War II to Nixon, What Happened and Why* (Garden City, N.Y.: Doubleday, 1976; New York: Vintage Books, 1978), 67–98. See also John Higham, "The Cult of the 'American Consensus': Homogenizing Our History," *Commentary* 27 (January 1959): 93–100; Geoffrey Perrett, *A Dream of Greatness: The American People, 1945–1963* (New York: Coward, McCann & Geoghegan, 1979); William L. O'Neill, *American High: The Years of Confidence, 1945–1960* (New York: Free Press, 1986); J. Ronald Oakley, *God's Country: America in the Fifties* (New York: Dembner Books, 1986; distributed by W. W. Norton); William H. Chafe, *The Unfinished Journey: America Since World War II* (New York: Oxford University Press, 1986); David Halberstam, *The Fifties* (New York: Villard Books, 1993); and James T. Patterson, *Grand Expectations: The United States, 1945–1974*

(New York: Oxford University Press, 1996). For a more nuanced discussion of "the rise and fall of the cold war consensus" (7) focused on intellectuals, see Daniel Horowitz, *The Anxieties of Affluence: Critiques of American Consumer Culture, 1939–1979* (Amherst: University of Massachusetts Press, 2004).

10. For an early overview of the literature stressing grassroots resistance on the left, see Thomas Sugrue, "Reassessing the History of Postwar America," *Prospects* 20 (Fall 1995): 493–509. For examples that stress conservative resistance to the liberal consensus, see Gary Gerstle, "Race and the Myth of the Liberal Consensus," *JAH* (September 1995): 579–86; Thomas Sugrue, *The Origins of the Urban Crisis: Race and Inequality in Postwar Detroit* (Princeton: Princeton University Press, 1996); and Lisa McGirr, *Suburban Warriors: The Origins of the New American Right* (Princeton: Princeton University Press, 2001).

11. Sugrue, *Origins of the Urban Crisis*, 7. In "Reassessing the History of Postwar America," Sugrue warned that much of the recent revisionist historiography "romanticize[s] the struggles of the oppressed," "overlooks the limitations of resistance," and "underestimates the power of cultural elites, big business, and the media in shaping popular tastes and restricting grassroots." He called for the "unmask[ing of] the mechanisms by which the powerful so successfully maintained their power" (504). A few works take important steps in that direction. Robert Griffith ["Forging America's Postwar Order: Domestic Politics and the Political Economy in the Age of Truman," in *The Truman Presidency*, ed. Michael J. Lacey (Washington, D.C.: Woodrow Wilson International Center for Scholars; Cambridge: Cambridge University Press, 1989), 57–88] and Elizabeth Fones-Wolf [*Selling Free Enterprise: The Business Assault on Labor and Liberalism, 1945–1960* (Urbana: University of Illinois Press, 1994)] examine the role of the business community in shaping U.S. political culture after 1945. Lary May explores Hollywood's role in forging a postwar consensus in his insightful study *The Big Tomorrow: Hollywood and the Politics of the American Way* (Chicago: University of Chicago Press, 2000).

12. Martin Marty uses the phrase "centripetal impulse" in *Under God, Indivisible, 1941–1960*, vol. 3, *Modern American Religion* (Chicago: University of Chicago Press, 1996), 3.

13. I have borrowed the term "cultural conversation" from R. W. B. Lewis, who first applied it to an intense discussion of what he called the "American Adam" among U.S. artists and intellectuals between roughly 1820 and 1860. "A culture," Lewis wrote, "achieves identity not so much through the ascendancy of one particular set of convictions as through the emergence of its peculiar and distinctive dialogue." Although I do not believe that a culture—or a nation like the U.S.—is necessarily defined by a *single* "cultural conversation," I find Lewis's stress on a defining dialogue useful. R. W. B. Lewis, *The American Adam: Innocence, Tragedy and Tradition in the Nineteenth Century* (Chicago: University of Chicago Press, 1955), 2–3.

14. "Address by Roger W. Straus," NCCJ Records, Box 9, "Roger W. Straus, 1936–37" folder; "Freedom to Progress," speech by H. W. Prentis Jr., before a regional meeting sponsored by the NAM and the Virginia Manufacturers Association in Richmond, 9 April 1940, NAM Records, Series I, Box 2, "Freedom, General" folder.

15. I have borrowed this phrase from Barbara Dianne Savage, *Broadcasting Freedom: Radio, War, and the Politics of Race, 1938–1948* (Chapel Hill, N.C.: University of North Carolina Press, 1999), 22.

16. Daniel Geary, "Carey McWilliams and Antifascism, 1934–1943," *JAH* 90 (December 2003): 912–934.

17. My formulation in this paragraph—and particularly my use of the word "civility"—was inspired in part by William H. Chafe's *Civilities and Civil Rights: Greensboro, North Carolina, and the Black Struggle for Freedom* (New York: Oxford University Press, 1980).

18. For other discussions of this shift, see Alan Brinkley, *The End of Reform: New Deal Liberalism in Recession and War* (New York: Knopf, 1995), 164–74; and Gary Gerstle, "The Working Class Goes to War" in *The War in American Culture: Society and Consciousness during World War II*, ed. Lewis A. Erenberg and Susan E. Hirsch (Chicago: University of Chicago Press, 1996), 105–27.

19. *U.S. Macintosh*, 283 U.S. 605 (1931).

20. To be sure, the interfaith concept was not embraced by everyone. It drew opposition from the Catholic hierarchy, from Protestant fundamentalists and evangelicals, and from some Jewish theologians. Many liberal intellectuals in the late 1940s and early 1950s also drew parallels between Catholicism and Communism, arguing that both threatened American democracy.

21. David Hollinger, "American Intellectual History: Some Issues for the 1980s," in *In the American Province: Studies in the History and Historiography of Ideas* (Bloomington,Ind.: Indiana University Press, 1985; Baltimore: Johns Hopkins University Press, 1985), 184.

22. Daniel T. Rodgers, *Contested Truths: Keywords in American Politics Since Independence* (New York: Basic Books, 1987), 8. For a masterful study of a single American "keyword," see Eric Foner, *The Story of American Freedom* (New York: W. W. Norton, 1998).

23. There were other reasons for this as well, including the rising standard of living experienced by many Americans as a result of the postwar economic boom and the G.I. bill. However, the rediscovery of poverty as a political issue in the mid-1960s suggests that affluence alone cannot account for this shift in the parameters of political debate.

24. For further discussion of this issue—particularly the failure of this rhetoric to adequately address the "economic consequences and cultural legacies of white supremacy" (3)—see Nikhil Pal Singh, *Black Is a Country: Race and the Unfinished Struggle for Democracy* (Cambridge: Harvard University Press, 2004).

25. President Clinton began talking about the "vital center" after his reelection in November 1996 and hailed it in his final State of the Union address. Other Democratic and Republican politicians and pundits, including President Bush, embraced the concept in the late 1990s. Although the war in Iraq and other policies of the Bush administration have helped to discredit this view in liberal circles, it has by no means disappeared. Rep. Rahm Emanuel, a key tactician behind the Democratic Party's victory in the 2006 Congressional elections, called for governing from the "vital center" five times in his first press conference

following the election. For recent examples of such calls, see Ted Halstead and Michael Lind, *The Radical Center: The Future of American Politics* (New York: Doubleday, 2001); Mark Satin, *Radical Middle: The Politics We Need Now* (Boulder, Colo.: Westview Press, 1994); John P. Avlon, *Independent Nation: How Centrism Is Changing the Face of American Politics* (New York: Harmony Books, 2004); Peter Beinart, "A Fighting Faith: An Argument for a New Liberalism," *NR*, 13 December 2004, 17–29; David S. Broder, "Freshmen in the Vital Center," *Washington Post*, 9 January 2005, Sec. B; and Silla Brush, "We Won! Now What the Heck Do We Do?", *U.S. News & World Report*, 20 November 2006.

Chapter 1

1. These results came from a phrase search of the historical *New York Times* (using the ProQuest database) and of the Library of Congress's online catalogue. A phrase search of the Reader's Guide Retrospective database offers similar results. The books published before 1933 are Jennie K. Durkes, *The American Way of Playing Ukulele Solos* (Chicago: Lyon & Healy, 1919?) and Gifford K. Simonds and John G. Thompson, *The American Way to Prosperity* (Chicago: A. W. Shaw Co., 1928). By contrast, the years between 1933 and 1939 brought Earle Looker, *The American Way* (New York: The John Day Co., 1933); John Ward Studebaker, *The American Way: A Democracy at Work in the Des Moines Forums* (New York: McGraw-Hill Book Co., Inc., 1935); Newton Diehl Baker et al., *The American Way: A Study of Human Relations Among Protestants, Catholics, and Jews* (Chicago: Willett, Clark & Co., 1936); David Cushman Coyle, *The American Way; Together with Three Additional Discussions by Carl Dreher, Carl Landauer, Gerald W. Johnson* (New York: Harper, 1938); George S. Kaufman and Moss Hart, *The American Way* (New York: Random House, 1939); and George E. Sokolsky, *The American Way of Life* (New York: Farrar & Rinehart, Inc., 1939).
2. In addition to the books listed above, see Henry A. Wallace, "The Search for an American Way," *Scribner's Magazine*, July 1936, 22–27; and Elmer Davis, "On the American Way of Life," *Harper's*, February 1937, 329–32.
3. *Harper's*, April 1937, 556.
4. Coyle, *American Way*, vii.
5. David Cushman Coyle, "The American Way," *Harper's*, February 1938, 225; Carl Dreher, "The American Way: A Voice from the Left," *Harper's*, March 1938, 400; Carl Landauer, "The American Way As It Looks to an Émigré from Germany," *Harper's*, May 1938, 633; Gerald W. Johnson, "The American Way: The Two Fundamentals," *Harper's*, April 1938, 487; Bernard DeVoto, "The Easy Chair: Notes on the American Way," *Harper's*, May 1938, 669.
6. R. W. B. Lewis, *The American Adam: Innocence, Tragedy and Tradition in the Nineteenth Century* (Chicago: University of Chicago Press, 1955), 2–3.
7. James Truslow Adams, *The Epic of America* (Boston: Little, Brown and Co., 1931), 404. The words "American" and "dream" appeared side by side only eight times in the *New York Times* between 1851 and the end of 1930. Often, the second word was plural. The phrase "American dream" appeared in the newspaper 216 times between 1931 and 1939.

8. Warren Susman first noted the popularization of the term "American Way" in the mid-1930s in *Culture as History: The Transformation of American Society in the Twentieth Century* (New York: Pantheon Books, 1984), He attributed it to the widespread "discovery" during that decade of the anthropological concept of culture. According to Susman, the term reflected an emerging notion that Americans shared common patterns of "behavior and belief, values and lifestyles, symbols and meanings" (153–54). Susman's analysis highlights one key facet of the term, but it—like the "culture concept" itself—tends to obscure differences and exaggerate similarities. The content of the American Way was intensely debated in the 1930s, and the term was frequently used prescriptively rather than descriptively.

9. James Truslow Adams, "The Ideas That Make Us a Nation," *NYTM*, 24 November 1940, 3.

10. I have borrowed the phrase "crisis of Americanism" from Michael Denning, *The Cultural Front: The Laboring of American Culture in the Twentieth Century* (London; New York: Verso, 1996), 129.

11. T. H. Watkins, *The Great Depression: America in the 1930s* (Boston: Little, Brown, 1993), 39–40, 51, 54–55; Morton Keller, *Regulating a New Economy: Public Policy and Economic Change in America, 1900–1933* (Cambridge: Harvard University Press, 1990), 15–16; John Kenneth Galbraith, *The Great Crash: 1929* (Boston: Houghton Mifflin, 1955; rev. ed. with a new introduction by the author, 1997), 127; William E. Leuchtenburg, *Franklin D. Roosevelt and the New Deal: 1932–1940* (New York: Harper & Row, 1963), 1.

12. David M. Kennedy, *Freedom from Fear: The American People in Depression and War, 1929–1945* (New York: Oxford University Press, 1999), 11, 20–23.

13. Studs Terkel, *Hard Times: An Oral History of the Great Depression* (New York: Pantheon Books, 1970), 19–21.

14. Leuchtenberg, *Franklin D. Roosevelt*, 3, 21; Watkins, *Great Depression*, 57.

15. Robert S. McElvaine, ed., *Down and Out in the Great Depression: Letters from the Forgotten Man* (Chapel Hill: University of North Carolina Press, 1983), 48.

16. Quoted in Stuart Ewen, *PR! A Social History of Spin* (New York: Basic Books 1996), 237. Eric Hobsbawm argues in *The Age of Extremes: A History of the World, 1914–1991* (New York: Pantheon Books, 1994) that the Depression of the late 1920s and 1930s endangered the world capitalist system "probably for the first, and so far the only, time" in history (87). Although other scholars disagree, there can be little doubt that many contemporary observers worried about this danger.

17. Watkins, *Great Depression*, 98–103.

18. Malcolm Cowley, "The Flight of the Bonus Army," *NR*, 17 August 1932, 14–15.

19. Quoted in Watkins, *Great Depression*, 76.

20. Gerald W. Johnson, "The Average American and the Depression," *Current History*, February 1932, 672.

21. I owe this phrase to David. A. Hollinger, who used it in a letter. Hollinger has called attention to the significance of this interregnum for the development of American national identity in "National Solidarity at the End of the Twentieth

Century: Reflections on the United States and Liberal Nationalism," *JAH* 84 (September, 1997), 561.

22. Leonard Dinnerstein and David M. Reimers, *Ethnic Americans: A History of Immigration*, 3rd ed. (New York: Harper & Row, 1988), 43.

23. The emergence of social or "grassroots" history in the late 1920s and the rise of academics with comparatively recent ties to the Old World also fueled this interest. In the 1930s, scholars such as George Stephenson, Carl Wittke, Marcus Lee Hansen, Theodore Blegen, and Oscar Handlin produced some of the first important works in immigrant and ethnic history.

24. Kennedy, *Freedom from Fear*, 18; Lynn Dumenil, *The Modern Temper: American Culture and Society in the 1920s* (New York: Hill and Wang, 1995), 284–87.

25. John R. Commons, *Races and Immigrants in America*, 2nd ed. (New York: Macmillan, 1920), 11.

26. Lawrence Glickman, "Inventing the 'American Standard of Living': Gender, Race and Working-Class Identity, 1880–1925," *Labor History* 34 (Spring/Summer 1993): 221–35.

27. Daniel J. Kevles, *In the Name of Eugenics: Genetics and the Uses of Human Heredity* (New York: Knopf, 1985), 59–62.

28. Carl N. Degler, *In Search of Human Nature: The Decline and Revival of Darwinism in American Social Thought* (New York: Oxford University Press, 1991), 53.

29. George Sánchez, *Becoming Mexican American: Ethnicity, Culture and Identity in Chicano Los Angeles, 1900–1945* (New York: Oxford University Press, 1993), 225.

30. Lizabeth Cohen, *Making a New Deal: Industrial Workers in Chicago, 1919–1939* (Cambridge: Cambridge University Press, 1990), 253–58.

31. On Hollywood, see Neil Gabler, *An Empire of Their Own: How the Jews Invented Hollywood* (New York: Crown Publishers, 1988); and Lary May, *The Big Tomorrow: Hollywood and the Politics of the American Way* (Chicago: University of Chicago Press, 2000), 57–65. See also Daniel Pope and William Toll, "We Tried Harder: Jews in American Advertising," *American Jewish History* 72 (1982): 26–51; and Ewen, *PR!*. For a general discussion of this point and its relationship to left-wing politics, see Denning, *Cultural Front*.

32. Kennedy, *Freedom from Fear*, 18–19.

33. Dumenil, *Modern Temper*, 160–65, 283–300.

34. Particularly in the case of blacks, such efforts were far from perfect. For criticisms of the New Deal's evenhandedness, see Barton J. Bernstein, "The New Deal: The Conservative Achievements of Liberal Reform," in *Towards a New Past: Dissenting Essays in American History* (New York: Pantheon Books, 1968), 263–88.

35. Cohen, *Making a New Deal*, 333–49.

36. In his seminal book *American Crucible: Race and Nation in the Twentieth Century* (Princeton, NJ: Princeton University Press, 2001), Gary Gerstle traces a racist strain in American nationalism throughout the twentieth century, but he pays scant attention to virulent anti-Semitism and rising ethnic tensions in the late 1930s. David Kennedy's monumental treatment of the Depression era in *Freedom from Fear* discusses anti-Semitism only in the context of European refugees

and gives virtually no treatment to other tensions between ethnic groups. Many other surveys of the period pay even less attention to such issues. This contrasts with the tremendous attention such tensions received in the late 1930s from intellectuals, civic leaders, and others.

37. Louis Adamic, *From Many Lands*, 9th ed. (New York: Harper & Brothers, 1940), 294.

38. Leonard Dinnerstein, Roger L. Nichols, and David M. Reimers, *Natives and Strangers: Ethnic Groups and the Building of America* (New York: Oxford University Press, 1979), 244.

39. McElvaine, *Down and Out in the Great Depression*, 151–54.

40. Ronald Takaki, *Strangers from a Different Shore: A History of Asian Americans* (Boston: Little, Brown, 1989), 326.

41. Sánchez, *Becoming Mexican American*, chap. 10.

42. "Black Legion's Spread Surprising to Midwest," *NYT*, 31 May 1936, Sec. E. The *New York Times* alone contained over two hundred references to the Black Legion in 1936. Those who missed the press accounts could catch the Humphrey Bogart film *Black Legion*, which appeared in theaters the following year.

43. Many American Catholics, following the lead of church leaders, supported Franco and believed that the forces who opposed him were dominated by Jews. In the late 1930s, diocesan newspapers in cities such as Boston, New York, Hartford, and Cincinnati were filled with anti-Semitic venom. Leonard Dinnerstein, *Antisemitism in America* (New York: Oxford University Press, 1994), 111–14.

44. Philip Perlmutter, *Divided We Fall: A History of Ethnic, Religious, and Racial Prejudice in America* (Ames: Iowa State University Press, 1992), 231–32; Adamic, *From Many Lands*, 296–97.

45. As Benjamin Alpers has pointed out, in the early years of the Great Depression, "dictatorship [whether fascist or communist] was an important political fantasy for a heterogeneous group of Americans." Only in the second half of the 1930s did fascist and communist dictatorships become "the evil against which nearly everyone in American political life struggled." Benjamin L. Alpers, *Dictators, Democracy & American Public Culture: Envisioning the Totalitarian Enemy, 1920s–1950s* (Chapel Hill: University of North Carolina Press, 2003), 3.

46. Ellen Schrecker, *Many Are the Crimes: McCarthyism in America* (Boston: Little, Brown, 1998), 14–15.

47. Denning, *Cultural Front*, xv.

48. See, for example, Carey McWilliams, "Fascism in American Law," *American Mercury*, June 1934, 182–88; Reinhold Niebuhr, "Pawns for Fascism, Our Lower Middle Class," *American Scholar* 6 (1937): 145–52; Paul Y. Anderson, "Fascism, American Style," *Nation,* 26 March 1938, 347–48; "American Fascists," *NR,* 8 March 1939, 117–18; "Churches and American Fascism," *Christian Century,* 13 March 1935, 327–29; Stanley High, "Star-Spangled Fascists," *Saturday Evening Post,* 27 May 1939, 5–7; and Sinclair Lewis, *It Can't Happen Here: A Novel* (Garden City, NY: Doubleday, Doran & Co., 1935).

49. Daniel Geary, "Carey McWilliams and Antifascism, 1934–1943," *JAH* 90 (December 2003): 912.

50. Dinnerstein, *Antisemitism in America*, 112. Perlmutter puts the number at roughly 120 in *Divided We Fall*, 234.

51. Watkins, *Great Depression*, 317, 321; "Nazi Letters Link Consuls and Clubs," *NYT*, 7 June 1934; "New German Group Outlines Policy Here," *NYT*, 18 April 1936; "25,000 Hear Critics of Nazis Assailed," *NYT*, 30 August 1937; "9,000 at Bund Fete Mark 'Independence'," *NYT*, 4 July 1938; "22,000 Nazis Hold Rally in Garden; Police Check Foes," *NYT*, 21 February 1939. The final quote is from a Bund poster advertising the mass rally; the poster is now held by the National Museum of American Jewish Military History in Washington D.C.

52. Alan Brinkley, *Voices of Protest: Huey Long, Father Coughlin and the Great Depression* (New York: Knopf, 1982), particularly 266–67. Brinkley argues that Coughlin lost much of his following in the later 1930s as he increasingly distanced himself from FDR. While this may have been true, the number of references to him in speeches, articles, and the internal memos of diverse groups suggest many elites and cultural producers remained deeply worried about both his influence and the broader phenomenon he represented.

53. "Minutes of the NCCJ Board of Trustees, Wednesday, October 7, 1942," NCCJ Records, Box 2, "Board of Trustees, 1941–45" folder.

54. Howard Mumford Jones, "American Scholarship and American Literature," reprinted in *Ideas in America* (Cambridge: Harvard University Press, 1944), 10.

55. Archibald MacLeish, "The Irresponsibles," *Nation*, 18 May 1940, 619–23.

56. Quoted in Richard H. Pells, *Radical Visions and American Dreams: Culture and Social Thought in the Depression Years* (New York: Harper & Row, 1973; reprint, Middletown, Conn.: Wesleyan University Press, 1984), 314, 316.

57. Lewis Mumford is quoted in Pells, *Radical Visions*, 360; George S. Counts, "The Social Record," *American Issues*, ed. Willard Thorp, Merle Curti, and Carlos Baker (Philadelphia: J. P. Lippincott Co., 1941), 1:1017–22.

58. Howard Mumford Jones, "Patriotism—But How?" *Atlantic* 162, November 1938, 585–92.

59. Harvard launched a Ph. D. program in American Civilization and began assigning graduate student "counselors" to residential houses to stimulate interest in U.S. culture among students. It also formed a radio workshop that broadcast student-written productions on American history over WRUL in Boston and various stations of the World Wide Broadcasting Foundation. Material on these and other initiatives can be found in the Records of the Committee on Extra-Curricular Reading, American Civilization Program, Harvard University Archives.

60. "Harvard Reading List in American History, June 1937," Harvard University Archives, Pusey Library, Harvard University, Cambridge, Mass.

Chapter 2

1. "Salvos of Cheers Greet President," *NYT*, 28 June 1936.

2. *PPA* (1936), 231.

3. "Roosevelt Barred a 'Fighting Speech'," *NYT*, 28 June 1936.

4. *PPA* (1936), 231.

5. *PPA* (1933), 14–15.

6. *PPA* (1935), 137.

7. *PPA* (1935), 132.

8. *PPA* (1934), 372.

9. *PPA* (1934), 123.

10. *PPA* (1935), 403.

11. See, for instance, *PPA* (1936), 334.

12. John B. Kirby, *Black Americans in the Roosevelt Era: Liberalism and Race* (Knoxville, TN: University of Tennessee Press, 1980), 23.

13. *PPA* (1935), 191, 193. The bill was passed the following year over Roosevelt's veto.

14. *PPA* (1936), 231.

15. *PPA* (1934), 422. As David Kennedy notes on p. 246 of *Freedom from Fear: The American People in Depression and War 1929–1945*, FDR's use of the word "right" in this speech represented "a significant escalation of the rhetoric of political claims" (New York: Oxford University Press, 1999).

16. FDR's "Four Freedoms" address is available at http://www.fdrlibrary.marist. edu/4free.html [accessed 23 January 2006].

17. *PPA* (1934), 288, 291.

18. Members of the archconservative Liberty League tended to liken New Deal policies to communism, but some economic conservatives argued that the New Deal was in fact ushering in National Socialism. For an example, see *Smoke-Screen* (New York: Southern Publishers Inc., 1940) by the Democratic congressman-turned-newspaper columnist Samuel Pettengill.

19. *PPA* (1934), 317.

20. *PPA* (1935), 405.

21. *PPA* (1933), 340. See also *PPA* (1937), 363.

22. *PPA* (1934), 317–18.

23. *PPA* (1936), 232–33.

24. *PPA* (1936), 233.

25. *PPA* (1936). 233–34.

26. David W. Noble, "The Reconstruction of Progress: Charles Beard, Richard Hofstadter, and Postwar Historical Thought," in *Recasting America: Culture and Politics in the Age of the Cold War,* ed. Lary May (Chicago: University of Chicago Press, 1989), 62.

27. Lary May, "Introduction," in *Recasting America*, p. 2, 4.

28. *PPA* (1938), 38.

29. *PPA* (1937), 366.

30. Gary Gerstle, "The Politics of Patriotism: Americanization and the Formation of the CIO," *Dissent* 33 (Winter 1986): 84–92; John L. Lewis, *The Miners' Fight for American Standards* (Indianapolis: Bell Publishing Co., 1925), 179–80.

31. Quoted in Gerstle, "Politics of Patriotism," 89.

32. Quoted in Kennedy, *Freedom from Fear*, 220.

33. The leader of the American Communist Party, Early Browder, offered this famous quote. Ellen Schrecker, *Many Are the Crimes: McCarthyism in America* (Boston: Little, Brown, 1998), 15.

34. Henry A. Wallace, "The Search for an American Way," *Scribner's*, July 1936, 26–27.
35. Gary Gerstle first called attention to the use of "Americanist" language by the industrial labor movement in "The Politics of Patriotism" and *Working-Class Americanism: The Politics of Labor in a Textile City, 1914–1960* (Cambridge; New York: Cambridge University Press, 1989). Gerstle's nuanced discussion of "the language of Americanism" in the latter work focused largely on the tensions between two groups within one union: radical organizers and ethnic traditionalists. I am primarily interested in juxtaposing the vision of "Americanism" offered by the CIO's national leaders to those put forth by the president and business groups.
36. The quote is from Steven Fraser, *Labor Will Rule: Sidney Hillman and the Rise of American Labor* (New York: Free Press, 1991), 127. For additional discussions of the various meanings of "industrial democracy" in the early part of the century, see Nelson Lichtenstein and Howell John Harris, eds., *Industrial Democracy in America: The Ambiguous Promise* (Washington, DC: Woodrow Wilson Center Press; Cambridge; New York: Cambridge University Press, 1993), 2, and Gerstle, "Politics of Patriotism," 88–89.
37. Robert H. Zieger, *John L. Lewis: Labor Leader* (Boston: Twayne Publishers, 1988), 53.
38. Melvyn Dubofsky and Warren Van Tine, *John L. Lewis: A Biography*, abridged ed. (Urbana: University of Illinois Press, 1986), 211, 132.
39. W. Jett Lauck, *Political and Industrial Democracy, 1776–1926* (New York: Funk & Wagnalls Co., 1926), 1, 3.
40. Robert H. Zieger quotes from a 1935 memo Lauck wrote to Lewis in *The CIO, 1935–1955* (Chapel Hill: University of North Carolina Press, 1995), 25.
41. Kennedy, *Freedom from Fear*, 296–97.
42. Gerstle, "Politics of Patriotism," 88.
43. For a thorough discussion of these debates within one CIO union, see Gerstle, *Working-Class Americanism*, 182–87 and 219–29.
44. Quoted in Zieger, *CIO*, 26.
45. Speech by CIO attorney A. J. Isserman, reprinted in the *CIO News*, 23 July 1938; "Unity Keynotes CIO State Convention in New York," *CIO News*, 24 September 1938.
46. Len De Caux, "Wanted, More Paul Reveres!" *CIO News*, 5 June 1939.
47. "Labor Facts," *CIO News*, 13 October 1941; "Labor Facts," *CIO News*, 14 October 1940.
48. Box describing the *Right to Strike* pamphlet, *CIO News*, 28 April 1941; "Labor Facts," *CIO News*, 16 September 1940; "What Is This CIO?" *CIO News*, 27 February 1939; "Lewis Scores Nazi Barbarism; Sees Labor Unions as Bulwark of Democracy," *CIO News*, 21 November 1938; Len De Caux, "Looking Ahead" column, *CIO News*, 21 October 1940.
49. Excerpts from speech by J. Warren Madden to the American Political Science Association meeting, *CIO News*, 2 January 1939; "Chain of Democracy" cartoon, *CIO News*, 17 April 1939.

50. John L. Lewis, "The CIO—A Mighty Force for Freedom," *CIO News*, 14 November 1938; Len De Caux, "Looking Ahead" column, *CIO News*, 30 September 1940.

51. Cartoon and "Looking Ahead" column by Len De Caux, *CIO News,* 30 September 1940.

52. Excerpts from speech by John T. Jones, *CIO News*, 25 August 1941.

53. For more on the CIO's "culture of unity," see Lizabeth Cohen, *Making a New Deal: Industrial Workers in Chicago, 1919–1939* (Cambridge; New York: Cambridge University Press, 1990), 333–49.

54. "Keeping the Wolf from the Door" cartoon, *CIO News*, 28 November 1938; "Lewis Scores Nazi Barbarism; Sees Labor Unions as Bulwark of Democracy," *CIO News*, 21 November 1938. The CIO generally used the term "minority" much as we do today to refer to racial, ethnic, and religious minorities. By contrast, the National Association of Manufacturers charged that the CIO was trampling on the rights of numerical "minorities" by demanding a closed shop.

55. "Fifth Column," *CIO News*, 3 June 1940; photo of picketers, *CIO News*, 3 June 1940; "Storm Troopers," *CIO News*, 6 October 1941.

56. An 1859 notice announcing a sermon, for instance, urged readers to "avail the blessing of this free enterprise," *NYT*, 28 May 1859.

57. Quoted in S. H. Walker and Paul Sklar, "Business Finds Its Voice, Part I," *Harper's,* January 1938, 114.

58. Quoted in Richard S. Tedlow, "The National Association of Manufacturers and Public Relations during the New Deal," *Business History Review* 50 (Spring 1976): 30–31.

59. These individuals are all quoted in Stuart Ewen, *PR! A Social History of Spin* (New York: Basic Books, 1996), 294–95.

60. Quoted in Walker and Sklar, "Business Finds Its Voice, Part I," 115.

61. Thomas C. Boushall, "The American Way: Its Opportunity and Its Challenge," *Vital Speeches of the Day* 5, 15 May 1939, 459.

62. All of these efforts are detailed in the three-part *Harper's* series by Walker and Sklar, "Business Finds Its Voice," which ran in *Fortune* beginning in January 1938.

63. Ewen, *PR!* Ewen quotes Edward L. Bernays's famous article, "The Engineering of Consent" (1947), on p. xiv. He discusses the role of the CPI on p. 104.

64. William L. Bird, Jr., *"Better Living": Advertising, Media, and the New Vocabulary of Business Leadership, 1935–1955* (Evanston, IL: Northwestern University Press, 1999).

65. Press release dated 27 September 1935, in HML, Accession 1410, Records of the E. I. Du Pont de Nemours & Co. Public Affairs Department, History Files, Box 36, "Cavalcade of America" folder.

66. "Tuning in on The Cavalcade of America" and "Cavalcade of America Recordings—Now Available for School Use," both in HML, Accession 1803, E. I. du Pont de Nemours & Co. Advertising Department Records, Box 5, "Cavalcade of America" folder.

67. Press release dated 27 September 1935 in HML, Accession 1410, Records of the E. I. Du Pont de Nemours & Co. Public Affairs Department, History Files, Box 36, "Cavalcade of America" folder.

68. "Jane Addams of Hull House" script in HML, Accession 1803, E. I. du Pont de Nemours & Co. Advertising Department Records, Box 5, "Cavalcade of America" folder.

69. Glenn Griswold, "The McGraw-Hill Public Relations Forum," *Public Opinion Quarterly* 3 (October 1939): 705–6.

70. Tedlow, "National Association of Manufacturers and Public Relations during the New Deal," 28–32. The quoted phrase appears to come from an internal history of the NAM.

71. Ibid., 33.

72. Congress, Senate, Committee on Education and Labor, *Labor Policies of Employers Associations*, report 6, part 6, 76th Congress, 1st sess., 1939, 157, 159–67. The LaFollette Committee, which investigated the NAM in the late 1930s, summarizes the scope of the campaign on the pages cited above. Much of the material created by the NAM's public relations team is reproduced as exhibits in *Hearings*.

    In *Dust Bowl: The Southern Plains in the 1930s* (New York: Oxford University Press, 1979), 137–38, Donald Worster describes the rightward shift of a small newspaper in Cimarron County, Oklahoma. He notes that in 1937, the *Cimarron News* "began to carry, almost every week, nationally syndicated cartoons portraying politicians as thieves and pickpockets, labor union leaders as nasty thugs, and farmers and small businessmen as victims of both." While I have not been able to view a copy of the paper, Worster's description of this material, together with the date, strongly suggests it was disseminated by the NAM.

73. Stuart Ewen makes the link between the Creel Committee and the NAM in *PR!*, 309. The material quoted comes from an internal NAM memo reproduced in Congress, Senate, Committee on Education and Labor, *Labor Policies of Employers Associations*, report 6, part 6, 76th Congress, 1st sess., 1939, 157–59. See also "Memorandum on Community Public Information Programs to Combat Radical Tendencies and Present the Constructive Story of Industry," in NAM Records, Series I, Box 111, "Public Relations–Community Programs, Memo on Public Information, 1938" folder.

74. Walter Weisenburger is quoted in the minutes of the 19 April 1937 meeting of the NAM's Committee on Public Relations. The minutes are reproduced in *Hearings*, 14384. There are countless examples of the NAM appealing to the self-interest of its listeners. The NAM initially courted farmers as part of a strategy to slow the formation of a farmer-worker alliance. A publication aimed at women's groups stressed that mass production had lowered dress prices and made "charm" and beauty products more widely available, while technological advances saved women from household "drudgery" and made it easier to keep in touch with far-flung family members. *Primer for Americans* in NAM Records, Series III, Box 846, "Primer for Americans, 1940–41" folder.

75. Ironically, the NAM itself spent some time groping for the appropriate phrase. In memos and press releases from 1935 and 1936, NAM staffers referred to the "American system" or the "American plan of living." By 1937, they had settled on the more euphonious phrase.

76. "Don't Let Catchwords Catch Us," in NAM Records, Series I, Box 111, "Public Relations–Service for Plant Publications, July 1935–Dec. 1940" folder.

77. "Who Is the Laborer?" in NAM Records, Series I, Box 111, "Public Relations–Service for Plant Publications, July 1935–Dec. 1940" folder.

78. Copies of these ads can be found in NAM Records, Series I, Oversize Box 10.

79. Leaflet entitled *Let George Do It!* reproduced in *Hearings*, 14420.

80. *The American Way*, Booklet no. 1 in the You and Industry Series, reproduced in *Hearings*, 14433.

81. Kennedy, *Freedom from Fear*, 316, 326.

82. "Meeting of 'Advisory Committee,' N.A.M. Committee on Public Relations, March 17, 1939," in NAM Records, Series I, Box 112, "Committee–Public Relations Advisory Committee, General, 1939" folder.

83. Press release issued by Hartford Theological Seminary, 9 January 1939, in NAM Records, Series I, Box 114, "Public Relations, 'Democracy–Religion Stand or Fall Together, Fuller F. Barnes Tells Seminary,' January 9, 1939" folder.

84. "Service for Plant Publications" (January 1939) in NAM Records, Series I, Box 111, "Public Relations–Service for Plant Publications, July 1935–Dec. 1940" folder. A more provocative version of this argument can be found in a billboard put up by the California Merchants and Manufacturers' Association. "What Destroyed France?" it asked. "Our National Safety Demands Stop Labor Rows." A photo of the billboard appeared in the *CIO News* on 2 September 1940.

85. "The Role of the N.A.M. Public Information Program Today," in NAM Records, Series I, Box 112, "Committee–Public Relations, General, 1939" folder.

86. Ibid.

87. Moley is quoted in Ewen, *PR!*, 296.

88. Press release issued by Hartford Theological Seminary on 9 January 1939.

89. Prentis's views on the word "democracy"—and his preference for the term "republic"—are elucidated in a speech he delivered to the Congress on Education for Democracy, which met at Columbia University in August 1939. Excerpts of the speech are reprinted in *CIO News*, 28 August 1939.

90. "Freedom to Progress," speech by H. W. Prentis, Jr., before a regional meeting sponsored by the NAM and the Virginia Manufacturers Association in Richmond, 9 April 1940, NAM Records, Series I, Box 2, "Freedom, General" folder.

91. Ibid.

92. "The People Look at National Defense: Results of a Survey for the National Association of Manufacturers," in NAM Records, Series I, Box 111.

93. "Certain Recommendations in Connection with NAM's Public Information Program in 1941," in NAM Records, Series I, Box 114, "Public Relations–Misc.–Certain Recommendations in Connection with NAM's Public Information Program in 1941" folder.

94. In NAM Records, Series I, see article accompanying picture of "Uncle Sam's hat" billboard in Box 111, "Public Relations, Service for Plant Publications, July '35–Dec. '40" folder; advertising brochure in Box 111, "American Family Robinson (6/40)" folder; and "Tripod of Freedoms" script in Box 113, "Public Relations–Motion Pictures Script, Jan. 1941" folder. See also *Primer*

for Americans in NAM Records, Series III, Box 846, "Primer for Americans, 1940–41" folder.

95. "I'm Glad I'm an American," in NAM Papers, Series I, Box 111, "Public Relations, Service for Plant Publications, July '35–Dec. '40" folder.

Chapter 3

1. George S. Kaufman and Moss Hart, *The American Way* (New York: Random House, 1939), 154; "Opening Tonight of 'American Way,'" *NYT*, 21 January 1939.
2. Carrie Tirado Bramen, *The Uses of Variety: Modern Americanism and the Quest for National Distinctiveness* (Cambridge: Harvard University Press, 2000), 1. Bramen offers a fascinating discussion of the relationship between diversity and national unity in a different period, as well as the divergent political ends that the notion of diversity can support.
3. Louis Adamic, "'America' Is a Magic Name," *Journal of Educational Sociology* 16 (February 1943): 327–28.
4. For an early discussion of some of these efforts, see Richard W. Steele, "The War on Intolerance: The Reformulation of American Nationalism, 1939–1941," *JAH* 9 (Fall 1989): 9–35.
5. Les K. Adler and Thomas G. Paterson, "Red Fascism: The Merger of Nazi Germany and Soviet Russia in the American Image of Totalitarianism, 1930's–1950's," *AHR* 75 (April 1970): 1051; Benjamin L. Alpers, *Dictators, Democracy & American Public Culture: Envisioning the Totalitarian Enemy, 1920s–1950s* (Chapel Hill: University of North Carolina Press, 2003), 150–51; Edward A. Purcell, Jr., *The Crisis of Democratic Theory: Scientific Naturalism and the Problem of Value* (Lexington: University Press of Kentucky, 1973), 205.
6. "Jews Face Crisis in Eastern Europe," *NYT*, 7 February 1937; "Historic Basque Town Wiped Out; Rebel Fliers Machine-Gun Civilians," *NYT*, 28 April 1937; "Soviet 'Cleansing' Sweeps Through All Strata of Life," *NYT*, 13 September 1937; "All Captives Slain; Civilians Also Killed as the Japanese Spread Terror in Nanking," *NYT*, 18 December 1937. On the last episode, see also Iris Chang, *The Rape of Nanking: The Forgotten Holocaust of World War II* (New York: Basic Books, 1997).
7. For a more extended discussion of the reaction of foreign observers, see Wendy Lynn Wall, "The Idea of America: Democracy and the Dilemmas of Difference, 1935–1965" (Ph.D. diss., Stanford University, 1998), 293–98.
8. Louis Adamic, *From Many Lands*, 9th ed. (New York: Harper & Brothers, 1940), 296–97.
9. This observation benefits from Philip Gleason's insightful discussion about World War II in *Speaking of Diversity: Language and Ethnicity in Twentieth-Century America* (Baltimore: Johns Hopkins University Press, 1992), 166–67. Gleason argues that during World War II "cultural pluralism [in the U.S.] was predicated upon, and made possible by, a high degree of consensus" about certain civic beliefs, among them "respect for the principle of equality before the law" and "recognition of…the rights of minorities." Although I would agree that cultural pluralism was predicated on assumptions about consensus, I believe the precise *content* of that consensus was a matter of great debate.

10. A summary of Adamic's lecture is reprinted in Adamic, *From Many Lands*, 291–301. For specific quotes, see 291, 292, and 299.

11. "Louis Adamic (1989–1951): His Life, Work, and Legacy," *Spectrum* 4 (Fall 1982): 1–2; Robert F. Harney, "*E Pluribus Unum*: Louis Adamic and the Meaning of Ethnic History," *Journal of Ethnic Studies* 14 (Spring 1986): 29. For a recent biography of Adamic from a literary perspective, see Dan Shiffman, *Rooting Multiculturalism: The Work of Louis Adamic* (Madison, N.J.: Fairleigh Dickinson University Press, 2003).

12. Nicholas V. Montalto, *A History of the Intercultural Education Movement, 1924–1941* (New York: Garland Publishing Co., 1982).

13. John Higham, *Send These to Me: Immigrants in Urban America*, rev. ed. (Baltimore: Johns Hopkins University Press, 1984), 75.

14. Robert Spiers Benjamin, ed., *I Am an American; By Famous Naturalized Americans* (Chicago: Alliance Book Corp., 1941).

15. "Ballad of All Americans," *Newsweek*, 25 March 1940, 40. For discussions of the song and its impact, see Warren I. Susman, *Culture as History: The Transformation of American Society in the Twentieth Century* (New York: Pantheon Books, 1984), 205; Martin Bauml Duberman, *Paul Robeson* (New York: Knopf, 1988), 236–37; Gleason, *Speaking of Diversity*, 193; and Michael Denning, *The Cultural Front: The Laboring of American Culture in the Twentieth Century* (London: Verso, 1996), 115–18, 128.

16. See, for instance, the press release dated 27 July 1940 in NYWF Records, Box 366, "Negro" folder.

17. Quoted in Robert W. Rydell, *World of Fairs: The Century-of-Progress Expositions* (Chicago: University of Chicago Press, 1993), 186. Although the organizers had hoped each of the thirty-two "major" nationality groups would produce a full week's program, a lack of financial support made this impossible. "Only the Negro and Italian committees produced a full week's program," the organizers reported. *Report of the American Common Program at the World's Fair 1940 in New York,* NYWF Records, Box 366, "Disbursements" folder.

18. Adamic, *From Many Lands*, 296–97.

19. John F. McClymer, "Gender and the 'American Way of Life': Women in the Americanization Movement," *Journal of American Ethnic History* 10 (Spring 1991): 6; William Charles Beyer, "Searching for *Common Ground*, 1940–1949: An American Literary Magazine and Its Related Movements in Education and Politics" (Ph.D. diss., University of Minnesota, 1988), 17–24, 31–50. See also Daniel E. Weinberg, "The Ethnic Technician and the Foreign-Born: Another Look at Americanization Ideology and Goals," *Societas* 7 (1977): 209–27.

20. Bramen, *Uses of Variety*, 78–84.

21. Adamic advocated "organic" Americanization in the third volume of his Nation of Nations series, *What's Your Name?* (New York: Harper & Brothers, 1942), 20–23. He wrote that his own name had evolved from Adamič to Adamic "*organically while I was becoming an American*." The change, he added, "occurred without deliberation on anybody's part. There was no issue. I yielded to no pressure. I was subjected to none. The hook just disappeared. Naturally. Inevitably."

Dan Shiffman describes Adamic as an advocate of "transitory pluralism" in *Rooting Multiculturalism*, 68.

22. Adamic, *From Many Lands*, 298–99.
23. Ibid., 291.
24. "Editorial Aside," *Common Ground* 1 (Autumn 1940): 103.
25. Adamic, *From Many Lands*, 293, 298.
26. Adamic, "'America' Is a Magic Name," 327–28.
27. Louis Adamic, *My America, 1928–1938* (New York: Harper & Brothers, 1938), 337.
28. Adamic, "'America' Is a Magic Name," 328.
29. Quoted in Shiffman, *Rooting Multiculturalism*, 159.
30. For a recent example of this view being attributed to Myrdal, see Nikhil Pal Singh, *Black Is a Country: Race and the Unfinished Struggle for Democracy* (Cambridge: Harvard University Press, 2004), 39. "Myrdal's distinction between theory and practice was a canny one. It has been a powerful intellectual device for shoring up the universal basis of American national norms in the face of contrary evidence ever since," Singh writes. "With it, Myrdal and his collaborators established the framework in which the liberal emphasis on racial reform in the United States has been understood ever since, namely, as something that is paradoxically already accomplished and never quite complete."
31. Adamic, *From Many Lands*, 309. These quotes come from "Special Questionnaire on the Negro," reprinted in the book. In a brief heading, Adamic notes that the article was originally published in the *North Georgia Review* in the fall of 1939 and "later reprinted in numerous Southern newspapers."
32. This anonymous letter is reprinted in Adamic, *From Many Lands*, 339.
33. Ibid., 309.
34. Adamic and some of his correspondents are quoted in Richard Weiss, "Ethnicity and Reform: Minorities and the Ambience of the Depression Years," *JAH* 66 (December 1979): 581.
35. Walter A. Jackson, *Gunnar Myrdal and America's Conscience: Social Engineering and Racial Liberalism, 1938–1987* (Chapel Hill: University of North Carolina Press, 1990), 103. Jackson quotes the phrase "race chauvinism."
36. Various individuals and groups did, however, inflect the story differently. While some emphasized the "common" story of immigration, others put greater stress on the nation's diverse cultural streams.
37. Louis Adamic, *Two-Way Passage* (New York: Harper & Brothers, 1941), 90–101.
38. For details on Bilbo's plan and the impact this had on black intellectuals, see Jackson, *Gunnar Myrdal*, 119, 131.
39. For a fascinating discussion of black Americans' shifting attitudes toward Africa, see James H. Meriwether, *Proudly We Can Be Africans: Black Americans and Africa, 1935–1961* (Chapel Hill: University of North Carolina Press, 2002).
40. Viola Llewellyn to Walter White, 4 November 1940, and Walter White to Viola Llewellyn, 6 November 1940, both in NAACP Records, Box II-A-371, "The Council Against Intolerance in America, 1940–41" folder.
41. Adamic, *Two-Way Passage*, 98.

42. Adamic, "Plymouth Rock and Ellis Island," in *From Many Lands*, 299–300. This same argument was later made by psychologists testifying for the plaintiffs in *Brown vs. Board of Education*. They, however, used it to argue for the dismantling of segregation. Adamic simply called on blacks to overcome their sense of shame.

43. Adamic, *Two-Way Passage*, 98–100.

44. Barbara Dianne Savage, *Broadcasting Freedom: Radio, War and the Politics of Race, 1938–1948* (Chapel Hill: University of North Carolina Press, 1999), 36–45. See also Montalto, *History of the Intercultural Education Movement*, 149–70.

45. Minutes of a 5/21/50 meeting of the Committee on the Program for Negro Week held at the Negro Actors' Guild on 5/21/40, NYWF Records, Box 366, "Negro" folder. In *Cultural Front*, Michael Denning portrays Adamic as embodying the "pan-ethnic Americanism" of the Cultural Front. He argues that "African American culture often became the touchstone for this new 'American' culture." "Indeed," Denning writes, Paul Robeson's concerts were, for his audiences, an embodiment of this Popular Front vision. By singing songs from around the world, he created a symbolic federation of national folk musics anchored in the African American spiritual" (132). Denning sees Paul Robeson's rendition of "Ballad for Americans" as representing the "aesthetic ideology" of the Popular Front. The episodes described here suggest that Denning's celebratory description of the relationship between the Cultural Front's "pan-ethnic Americanism" and African Americans needs to be qualified.

46. Savage, *Broadcasting Freedom*, 22.

47. Rydell, *World of Fairs*, 186.

48. L. D. Reddick, "The Negro in the Building of America," NYWF Records, Box 366, "Negro" folder.

49. "2 Stage Stars Get 'Tolerance' Badge," *NYT*, 28 May 1939, Sec. G

50. Beyer, "Searching for *Common Ground*," 65–66.

51. "2 Stage Stars Get 'Tolerance' Badge."

52. Morris S. Lazaron, *Common Ground: A Plea for Intelligent Americanism* (New York: Liveright Publishing Corp., 1938), ix.

53. "Clergymen to End Amity Tour Jan. 22," *NYT*, 14 January 1934, Sec. N; "Interfaith Group Plans a New Drive," *NYT*, 5 February 1934.

54. Newton Diehl Baker, Carlton J. H. Hayes, and Roger Williams Straus, *The American Way: A Study of Human Relations Among Protestants, Catholics, and Jews* (Chicago: Willett, Clark & Co., 1936).

55. Another organization at the forefront of this effort was the Conference on Science, Philosophy, and Religion in Their Relation to the Democratic Way of Life, which was founded in 1939 at the Jewish Theological Seminary in New York City. For fascinating discussions of this organization from different viewpoints, see James Gilbert, *Redeeming Culture: American Religion in an Age of Science* (Chicago: University of Chicago Press, 1997), 63–93, and Fred W. Beuttler, "Organizing an American Conscience: The Conference on Science, Philosophy and Religion" (Ph.D. diss., University of Chicago, 1995).

56. "Address by Roger W. Straus," NCCJ records, Box 9, "Roger W. Straus, 1936–37" folder.

57. "An Invitation to Observe Brotherhood Week," NCCJ Records, Box 5, "Broth-erhood Week, 1940" folder. For other examples of this view, see the brochure announcing "Brotherhood Week 1941," NAACP Records, Box II-A-387, "NCCJ, General, 1940–45" folder; and Harold E. Stassen, "Brotherhood: The Way to Live as Neighbors," *VSD* 7 (March 1941): 352. The former brochure declared that the conference "urges loyalty to one's own household of faith, knowing well that this Republic can build a political, economic, and social prosperity only if religion undergirds it."

58. "Dialogue of a Protestant, A Catholic, and a Jew," NCCJ Records, Box 1, "The Trio Program" folder.

59. Mark Silk traces the emergence of this tradition on an intellectual level in "Notes on the Judeo-Christian Tradition in America," *American Quarterly* 36 (1984): 65–85.

60. "An Invitation to Observe Brotherhood Week," NCCJ Records, Box 5, "Brother-hood Week, 1940" folder.

61. Quoted in "Significant Goodwill Conference Brings Together Protestants, Catholics and Jews," *The Baptist*, 16 May 1931, found in NCCJ Records, Box 1, "Historical" folder.

62. John T. McGreevy, *Catholicism and American Freedom: A History* (New York: W. W. Norton, 2003), 204.

63. Quoted in Shiffman, *Rooting Multiculturalism*, 159.

64. Lazaron, *Common Ground*, ix.

65. "A Plea for 'More Than Tolerance,'" *NYT*, 22 December 1940.

66. See Denning, *Cultural Front*, especially 123–36.

67. Benny Kraut, "Towards the Establishment of the National Conference of Christians and Jews: The Tenuous Road to Religious Goodwill in the 1920s," *American Jewish History* 77 (1988): 388–412; Lance J. Sussman, "'Toward Better Understanding': The Rise of the Interfaith Movement in America and the Role of Rabbi Isaac Landman," *American Jewish Archives* 34 (1982): 35–51.

68. "Easter and Passover," *NYT*, 16 April 1927.

69. Kraut, "National Conference of Christians and Jews," 409.

70. NCCJ Records, Box 1, "Constitution, By-Laws" folder.

71. Jackson, *Gunnar Myrdal*, 19.

72. "Newton D. Baker Dies in Cleveland," *NYT*, 26 December 1937; Jackson, *Gunnar Myrdal*, 17–20; David Levering Lewis, *W. E. B. Du Bois: The Fight for Equality and the American Century, 1919–1963* (New York: H. Holt, 2000), 435–36.

73. Roger Straus's father, Oscar Straus, was Theodore Roosevelt's secretary of commerce and labor. His son cofounded the publishing house Farrar, Straus & Giroux. "Clergymen to End Amity Tour Jan. 22," *NYT*, 14 January 1934, Sec. N.

74. "Coonley Urges Post–War Study," *NYT*, 26 August 1941. For more on the "Tri-pod of Freedom" campaign, see chapter 2.

75. Columbia University Professor Carlton J. H. Hayes was the organization's first Catholic cochairman. He retired in 1946 and was succeeded by Thomas E. Bra-niff, president of Braniff Airways.

76. For a useful discussion of the founding of the NCCJ, see Kraut, "National Conference of Christians and Jews," and Sussman, "'Toward Better Understanding.'"

77. See the following in Waldman Papers, Box 39: Morris Waldman to Sol M. Stroock, 12 June 1939, in "Survey Committee, 1936–41, 43 MDW" folder; and "Memorandum on Relationship of Survey Committee and Other Subcommittees to the American Jewish Committee," February 1940, in "Survey Committee, Scope and Function, 1940–41" folder. For a useful history of the American Jewish Committee, including the period dealt with here, see Naomi W. Cohen, *Not Free to Desist: The American Jewish Committee, 1906–1966* (Philadelphia: Jewish Publication Society of America, 1972), chaps. 1–9.

78. List of Survey Committee members, Waldman Papers, Box 39, "Survey Committee Membership, 1936–1941" folder. For comment on the makeup of the Survey Committee, see Alfred L. Bernheim to Richard Rothschild and Sidney Wallach, n.d., in the same folder. The Survey Committee was disbanded in 1941 as part of an AJC reorganization, and its responsibilities were assumed by various AJC departments.

79. Morris Waldman to James N. Rosenberg, 5 November 1936, "Survey Committee, 1936–41, 43 MDW" folder; and "Program for 1937," "Survey Committee, Educational Department Survey, 1933–1942" folder; both in Waldman Papers, Box 39.

80. Cyrus Adler to Morris Waldman, 7 April 1938, Waldman Papers, Box 39, "Survey Committee, 1936–41, 43 MDW" folder. Although the AJC and other Jewish individuals and groups were far from alone in calling attention to the Bill of Rights in the late 1930s, they were certainly at the forefront of this effort. In the process, they helped catalyze what Michael Kammen has called the "discovery of the Bill of Rights" between 1939 and 1941. Michael Kammen, *A Machine That Would Go of Itself: The Constitution in American Culture* (New York: Knopf, 1986), 337.

81. As early as 1935, the AJC reported that it was working closely with groups ranging from the NCCJ and the Federal Council of Churches of Christ to the National and Columbia Broadcasting Companies. A partial list of the groups funded by the American Jewish Committee from the late 1930s through World War II includes the NCCJ, the Council Against Intolerance, the Service Bureau for Intercultural Education, the Council for Democracy, the Common Council for American Unity, the Institute for Propaganda Analysis, Friends of Democracy, Mother's Day Declaration, League for Fair Play, Citizenship Educational Service, American Council Against Nazi Propaganda, the Writers War Board, and Labor Education Services. For more on the relationship between Franz Boas and the AJC, see Waldman Papers, Box 5, "Boas, Franz, 1933–35, 83–40,42–43" folder. For an example of Survey Committee activities during one five-month period, see "Survey Committee, Report of Activities, January to May, 1938," Waldman Papers, Box 39, "Survey Committee Reports, 1938–1939, 41" folder. See also "Report of Information and Service Associates," Waldman Papers, Box 39, "Survey Committee, Educational Department Survey, 1933–1942" folder; "Minutes. Meeting of the Domestic Public Relations Committee, November 28, 1944," Waldman Papers, Box 35, "Public Relations Committee, 1943–45" folder; and Steele, "The War on Intolerance," 25–29.

82. Laurel Leff, *Buried by the Times: The Holocaust and America's Most Important Newspaper* (New York: Cambridge University Press, 2005), 13.

83. One AJC member went so far as to propose in late 1939 that Jews "become active proselytizers" so as not to appear to be a "mysterious, exclusive blood-descendent group." "Memo on Misconceptions to Mr. Rothschild from Mr. Cherin," 3 November 1939, Waldman Papers, Box 39, "Survey Committee, Educational Department Survey, 1933–1942" folder.

84. "General Educational Program Against Anti-Semitism in the United States" and "Report of Information and Service Associates, 1 May 1935," both in Waldman Papers, Box 39, "Survey Committee, Educational Department Survey, 1933–1942" folder. See also Kraut, "National Conference of Christians and Jews," 410; and Montalto, *History of the Intercultural Education Movement*, 188–204.

85. "Report of the [NCCJ] Director," 15 May 1939, NCCJ Records, Box 1, "Annual Reports, 1928–1939" folder. The AJC memo quoted in this and the following paragraph is "Memorandum on Basic Strategy," December 1939, Waldman Papers, Box 39, "Survey Committee, Educational Department Survey, 1933–1942" folder.

86. "Memorandum on Basic Strategy," December 1939, Waldman Papers, Box 39, "Survey Committee, Educational Department Survey, 1933–1942" folder.

87. For example, see "Dialogue of a Protestant, a Catholic, and a Jew," NCCJ Records, Box 1, "The Trio Program" folder. In a much-quoted speech to the 1895 Cotton States Exposition in Atlanta, Booker T. Washington declared: "In all things that are purely social we can be as separate as the fingers, yet one as the hand in all things essential to mutual progress." Quoted in Nell Irvin Painter, *Standing at Armageddon: The United States, 1877–1919* (New York: W. W. Norton, 1987), 217.

88. Memo from DB [David Bernstein] to FNT [Frank Trager], 16 October 1939, Waldman Papers, Box 8, "Council Against Intolerance in America" folder.

89. "Religious Leaders Ask Social Reform," *NYT*, 27 March 1933. For an early draft of this document that places more emphasis on the role of government, and less on the cooperation of business and labor leaders, see Stephen S. Wise Papers, Box 51, "NCCJ" folder, American Jewish Historical Society, Waltham, Mass.

90. "Leader Condemn Propaganda Evils," *NYT*, 2 June 1939.

91. "An Invitation to Observe Brotherhood Week, February 18–25, 1940," NCCJ Records, Box 5, "Brotherhood Week, 1940" folder.

92. "15,000 Cheer Hague for Ban on CIO; 'Reds' Are Defied," *NYT*, 7 January 1938.

93. Louis Finkelstein, J. Elliot Ross, and William Adams Brown, *The Religions of Democracy: Judaism, Catholicism and Protestantism in Creed and Life* (New York: Devin-Adair Co., 1941)

94. Will Herberg, *Protestant-Catholic-Jew: An Essay in American Religious Sociology* (Garden City, N.Y.: Doubleday, 1955), 84. The NCCJ's vision preceeded by several decades the "triple melting pot" described by Herberg in this classic work.

95. Margaret Mead's words in a draft of her 1972 memoir *Blackberry Winter* are quoted in Virginia Yans-McLaughlin, "Science, Democracy, and Ethics: Mobilizing Culture and Personality for World War II," in *Malinowski, Rivers, Benedict,*

and Others: Essays on Culture and Personality, ed. George W. Stocking, Jr. (Madison: University of Wisconsin Press, 1986), 193–94.

96. Margaret Mead, *And Keep Your Powder Dry: An Anthropologist Looks at America* (New York: William Morrow and Co., 1942), 3.

97. "The Rake's Progress," *Nation*, 14 February 1942, 181; Gordon Waterfield, *What Happened to France* (London: J. Murray, 1940), 1, 2–3, 10–11. Waterfield's book was reprinted four times in its first four months.

98. Howard Brick, "Talcott Parson's 'Shift Away from Economics,' 1937–1946," *JAH* 87 (September 2000): 501–2.

99. Ibid., 493, 501–2, 504, 506.

100. Lorenz J. Finison, "The Psychological Insurgency: 1936–1945," *Journal of Social Issues* 42 (1986): 21–33, especially p. 32.

101. Carl N. Degler, *In Search of Human Nature: The Decline and Revival of Darwinism in American Social Thought* (New York: Oxford University Press, 1991), 62–64.

102. Fred Matthews, "The Revolt Against Americanism: Cultural Pluralism and Cultural Relativism as an Ideology of Liberation," *Canadian Review of American Studies* 1 (1970): 22.

103. Pioneers of "culture and personality" theory included such prominent social scientists as Margaret Mead, Lawrence Frank, Edward Sapir, Ralph Linton, John Dollard, and Eric Erikson. Margaret Mead, "National Character and the Science of Anthropology," in *Culture and Social Character: The Work of David Riesman Reviewed*, ed. Seymour Martin Lipset and Leo Lowenthal (New York: Free Press of Glencoe, 1961), 17.

104. Margaret Mead, "The Study of National Character," in *The Policy Sciences: Recent Developments in Scope and Method*, ed. Daniel Lerner and Harold D. Lasswell (Stanford, Calif.: Stanford University Press, 1951), 71–73.

105. Douglas Haring, "Aspects of Personal Character in Japan," *Far Eastern Quarterly* 6 (November 1946): 14–15. Not all scholars saw infancy as the moment in which personality was indelibly stamped by culture. But even those who saw the interaction between culture and personality as dynamic and ongoing tended to focus on child-rearing.

106. Matthews, "Revolt Against Americanism," 16–24, especially 18.

107. For an extended discussion of social scientists and social engineering, see William Graebner, *The Engineering of Consent: Democracy and Authority in Twentieth-Century America* (Madison: University of Wisconsin Press, 1987).

108. Mead, *Keep Your Powder Dry*, 17.

109. Yans-McLaughlin, "Science, Democracy, and Ethics," 197. For an extended discussion of the role cultural anthropologists and particularly social psychologists played in the war effort, see Ellen Herman, *The Romance of American Psychology: Political Culture in the Age of Experts* (Berkeley: University of California Press, 1995), chaps. 2–4.

110. Mead, *Keep Your Powder Dry*, 27.

111. D. W. Brogan, *The American Character* (New York: A. A. Knopf, 1944); David Reisman, *The Lonely Crowd: A Study of the Changing American Character* (New

Haven: Yale University Press, 1950); Henry Steele Commager, *The American Mind* (New Haven: Yale University Press, 1950); David M. Potter, *People of Plenty: Economic Abundance and the American Character* (Chicago: University of Chicago Press, 1954); Max Lerner, *America as a Civilization* (New York: Simon & Schuster, 1957); Max Lerner, *The Unfinished Country: A Book of American Symbols* (New York: Simon & Schuster, 1959)

112. Mead, *Keep Your Powder Dry*, 22.

113. Ibid., 27.

114. For instance, in a famous study published in 1911, Boas attacked the cephalic index—the measure most widely used by physical anthropologists to classify racial groups—by showing that the head shapes of children of diverse ethnic backgrounds "approach[ed] a uniform style" after their mothers had been in the U.S. for a period of time. If such a basic physical trait changed, Boas concluded, "we are compelled to conclude that...the bodily and mental make-up of the immigrant may [also] change." Degler, *In Search of Human Nature*, 63–64.

115. Ruth Benedict, *Patterns of Culture* (1934; reprint, with a preface by Margaret Mead, Boston: Houghton Mifflin, 1959), 10–11. Benedict used the word "race" as it was used at the time—to encompass the concepts now called "race" and "ethnicity."

116. Benedict, *Patterns of Culture*, 46, 13, 16.

117. Mead, *Keep Your Powder Dry*, 145–46.

118. Ibid., 24. This analysis suggests a key difference between Mead's and Myrdal's vision of America. Myrdal saw the American Creed as deeply embedded in the psyches of all Americans, south and north. It also foreshadows a growing tendency on the part of U.S. writers in the 1940s and 1950s to ignore the South when generalizing about "America."

119. The following discussion has been shaped in part by my reading of Richard Handler, "Boasian Anthropology and the Critique of American Culture," *American Quarterly* 42 (June 1990): 252–73.

120. Mead, *Keep Your Powder Dry*, 10–11, 127–29.

121. Ibid., 49.

122. Ibid., 120, 202. Not surprising, some readers were dissatisfied with Mead's analysis. Fanny Buford, a black college student who went on to marry Ralph Ellison, read the book in 1943 for a class assignment. She wrote that she was unable to identify with the "average American scene described" but argued that this was not due "entirely to the fact that I am a Negro and not just 'an American.'" She pointed out that there were millions of poor sharecroppers, Okies, and "residents of urban slums." "If I were [one of these]," she wrote, "I would want to know what it was in the American character, or my character that kept me that way." Buford added that "the element of dollar-worship in the American character" had produced a "Frankenstein which...thrives on power, greed and prejudice apart from the host of American people." Fanny Buford, "A Comment on Miss Mead's Book *And Keep Your Powder Dry*," January 25, 1943, is in the Margaret Mead papers at the Library of Congress. Available: http://www.loc.gov/exhibits/mead/oneworld-char.html (accessed June 22, 2006).

123. Mead, *Keep Your Powder Dry*, 120, 194–95, 202–3.

124. Ibid., 204–5, 235, 249, 252–54, 256, 261.

125. Jackson, *Gunnar Myrdal*, 16–22, 25–26, 32–33.

126. Jane Howard, *Margaret Mead: A Life* (New York: Ballantine Books, 1984), 175–76, 199.

127. Jackson, *Gunnar Myrdal*, 151.

128. Ibid., xiv–xv.

129. Ibid., 61–62; Sissela Bok, *Alva Myrdal: A Daughter's Memoir* (Reading, MA: Addison-Wesley Publishing Co., 1991), 91–92; Kimball Young, "William I. Thomas (1863–1947)," *American Sociological Review* 13 (1948): 102–4.

130. Jackson, *Gunnar Myrdal*, 68–69, 79. The Mydrals are quoted on 79.

131. Ibid., 147, 152, 157. The quoted phrases all come from Alva Myrdal and Gunnar Myrdal, *Kontakt med Amerika* (Stockholm: A. Bonnier, 1941). Although I have consulted the Swedish text, I have relied on Jackson for specific translations. See also Gunnar Eidevall, "America in the 1940s, As Seen By Gunnar and Alva Myrdal, Victor Vinde, and Thorsten Jonsson," *Swedish-American Historical Quarterly* 34 (1983): 131–41.

132. Quoted in Jackson, *Gunnar Myrdal*, 67, 62.

133. Jackson, *Gunnar Myrdal*, 132.

134. Ibid., 92 and 137. The quoted phrase is Myrdal's.

135. Quoted in ibid., 139.

136. Ibid., 139.

137. Ibid., 106–8, 114–15.

138. Bok, *Alva Myrdal*, 145–47; Jackson, *Gunnar Myrdal*, 140–46. Myrdal is quoted on p. 145.

139. Myrdal and Myrdal, *Kontakt med Amerika*, 32–33. The book is quoted in Jackson, *Gunnar Myrdal*, 146–49.

140. Quoted in Jackson, *Gunnar Myrdal*, 149.

141. Myrdal and Myrdal, *Kontakt med Amerika*, 34–52; Bok, *Alva Myrdal*, 150.

142. Specific quotes are drawn from Jackson, *Gunnar Myrdal*, 150–52, 399. See also Myrdal and Myrdal, *Kontakt med Amerika*, 52–56.

143. Jackson, *Gunnar Myrdal*, 157, 160–61.

144. Singh, *Black Is a Country*, 134. For an extended discussion of the influence of *An American Dilemma* in many quarters, see David W. Southern, *Gunnar Myrdal and Black-White Relations: The Use and Abuse of* An American Dilemma, *1944–1969* (Baton Rouge: Louisiana State University Press, 1987).

145. Bok, *Alva Myrdal*, 151.

146. Quoted in Jackson, *Gunnar Myrdal*, 399.

147. Ibid., 162–63. Myrdal is quoted on 163.

Chapter 4

1. "Hitler Way/American Way" cartoon, *CIO News*, 8 December 1941.

2. For a thorough discussion of the populist rhetoric employed by both the Coughlinites and the CIO, see Michael Kazin, *The Populist Persuasion: An American History*, rev. ed. (Ithaca, N.Y.: Cornell University Press, 1998), chaps. 5 and 6. For

its use by artists and intellectuals aligned with the Popular Front, see Michael Denning, *The Cultural Front: The Laboring of American Culture in the Twentieth Century* (London; New York: Verso, 1996), especially 123–36. Although Kazin and Denning call the language of popular insurgency used by the CIO and many on the left "populist," other scholars have called it "progressive." For examples, see Lary May, ed., *Recasting America: Culture and Politics in the Age of Cold War* (Chicago: University of Chicago Press, 1989).

3. This argument has benefited from my reading of Lary May, "Making the American Consensus: The Narrative of Conversion and Subversion in World War II Films," in *The War in American Culture: Society and Consciousness during World War II,* ed. Lewis A. Erenberg and Susan E. Hirsch (Chicago: University of Chicago Press, 1996), 71–102.
4. Frank W. Fox, *Madison Avenue Goes to War: The Strange Military Career of American Advertising* (Provo, Utah: Brigham Young University Press, 1975), 56.
5. Robert H. Zieger, *The CIO, 1935–1955* (Chapel Hill: University of North Carolina Press, 1995), 163.
6. John Morton Blum, *V Was for Victory: Politics and American Culture during World War II* (New York: Harcourt, Brace, Jovanovich, 1976), 21–31. MacLeish is quoted on 29.
7. Ibid., 17.
8. For a fascinating, if somewhat celebratory, discussion of the war bond campaigns, see Lawrence R. Samuel, *Pledging Allegiance: American Identity and the Bond Drive of World War II* (Washington, D.C.: Smithsonian Institution Press, 1997). The quoted phrase, attributed to administration officials, appears on p. 14.
9. The pamphlets in the G.I. Roundtable series, along with historical background and analysis, are available at http://www.historians.org/Projects/GIroundtable/index.html (accessed 14 November 2006).
10. Mark H. Leff, "The Politics of Sacrifice on the American Home Front in World War II," *JAH* 77 (March 1991): 1306–13. See also Robert Griffith, "The Selling of America: The Advertising Council and American Politics, 1942–1960," *Business History Review* 57 (Autumn 1983): 389–91.
11. Daniel L. Lykins, *From Total War to Total Diplomacy: The Advertising Council and the Construction of the Cold War Consensus* (Westport, Conn.: Praeger, 2003), 16.
12. See, for instance, "Current Home Front Campaigns: October 20, 1944" in Advertising Council Archives, 13/2/207, Box 107, Folder 7015.
13. Quoted in Clayton R. Koppes and Gregory D. Black, *Hollywood Goes to War: How Politics, Profits and Propaganda Shaped World War II Movies* (New York: Free Press, 1987), 64.
14. Office of War Information, *The War Messages of Franklin D. Roosevelt: December 8, 1941, to April 13, 1945* (Washington, D.C., 1945), 29; "Divide and Conquer," *CIO News,* 20 April 1942; "Divide and Conquer," *Victory* 20 January 1943, 89; Office of War Information, Bureau of Motion Pictures, *A List of U.S. War Information Films* (Washington, D.C., 1943), 8; Office of War Information, Domestic Branch, *Information Guide: The Enemy* (Washington, D.C., April 1943);

"Washington's Information Manual for Hollywood, 1942," reprinted in *Historical Journal of Film, Radio and Television* 3 (1983); *Why We Fight: Divide and Conquer* (U.S. War Department, 1943).

15. Office of War Information, *Radio Background Material; Subject: Rumors* (Washington, D.C.; December 10, 1942); Office of War Information, Domestic Branch, *Information Guide: Rumors* (Washington, D.C., May 1943).

16. Benjamin Leontif Alpers, *Dictators, Democracy, & American Public Culture: Envisioning the Totalitarian Enemy, 1920s–1950s* (Chapel Hill: University of North Carolina Press, 2003), 197–201.

17. "The Screen in Review," *NYT*, 13 January 1944. For another discussion of the film along the same lines, see Erenberg and Hirsch, eds., *The War in American Culture*, 1.

18. May, "Making the American Consensus," 79, 82. May quotes the screenwriter John Howard Lawson.

19. "Service for Plant Publications" (January 1939) in NAM Records, Series I, Box 111, "Public Relations–Service for Plant Publications, July 1935–Dec. 1940" folder.

20. "Dies at Rally Here Warns U.S. to Stop Its 'Aping' of Europe," *NYT*, 30 November 1939; Joseph McBride, *Frank Capra: The Catastrophe of Success* (New York: Simon & Schuster, 1992), 258–59, 455–60.

21. Ibid., 463–64.

22. Alpers, *Dictators, Democracy and American Public Culture*, 202.

23. Daniel Geary, "Carey McWilliams and Antifascism, 1934–1943," *JAH* (December 2003): 912.

24. Henry Agard Wallace, "The Price of Free World Victory," *VSD* 8 (1 June 1942): 482–85. The speech was soon dubbed "The Century of the Common Man."

25. Henry R. Luce, "The American Century," *Life,* 17 February 1941, 65.

26. Eric Foner, *The Story of American Freedom* (New York: W. W. Norton, 1998), 232.

27. Wallace, "Price of Free World Victory," 483.

28. Alpers, *Dictators, Democracy, and American Public Culture,* 241–49.

29. "Washington's Information Manual for Hollywood, 1942," reprinted in *Historical Journal of Film, Radio and Television* 3 (1983): 174–75.

30. Memo from Alan Cranston to Raymond Rich, 6 February 1942, NARA-II, RG 208, Office of War Information Records, Entry 222, Box 1079, "Foreign Language Division (Objectives, etc.)" folder.

31. See for example: Office of War Information, Domestic Branch, *Information Guide: The Enemy* (Washington, D.C., April 1943); and Office of War Information, "'I Am Not Crazy Enough to Want War'... Hitler" (Washington, D.C., 1943).

32. George Zachary to Allen Ducovny, 3 April 1943, and Bob Maxwell to George Zachary, 12 April 1943, both in CSAA Records, Box 24, Folder 240.

33. Hollywood, for instance, produced such films as *Little Tokyo, U.S.A.* (1942), and *Air Force* (1943), which portrayed even Japanese Americans as enemy traitors. The first film was approved by the War Department, and the army cooperated on the filming of both. Koppes and Black, *Hollywood Goes to War,* 72–81.

34. Memo from Alan Cranston to Elmer Davis, 26 January 1943, NARA-II, RG 208, Office of War Information Records, Entry 222, Box 1079, "Foreign Language Division (Objectives, etc.)" folder. For more on Italian Americans' relationship to Mussolini before World War II, and the tensions between federal agencies over how to deal with them, see John Diggins, *Mussolini and Fascism: The View from America* (Princeton: Princeton University Press, 1972), 77–143; and James Miller, "A Question of Loyalty: American Liberals, Propaganda, and the Italian-American Community, 1939–1943," *The Maryland Historian* 9 (1978): 49–71.

35. Allan M. Winkler, *The Politics of Propaganda: The Office of War Information, 1942–1945* (New Haven: Yale University Press, 1978), 56, 67; "Three More Ration Books Coming Says OWI's 'Battle Station' Tract," *NYT,* 30 March 1943; Blum, *V Was for Victory,* 41; *When Radio Writes for War* (Office of War Information, 1943).

36. Fox, *Madison Avenue Goes to War,* 56.

37. Quoted in Sydney Weinberg, "What to Tell America: The Writers' Quarrel in the Office of War Information," *JAH* 55 (June 1968): 86.

38. "Explanation Given on Split in OWI," *NYT,* 14 April 1943.

39. Weinberg, "What to Tell America," 85–87.

40. "Writers Who Quit OWI Charge It Bars 'Full Truth' for 'Ballyhoo'," *NYT,* 16 April 1943.

41. Quoted in Weinberg, "What to Tell America," 88.

42. McBride, *Frank Capra,* 475–77; Winkler, *Politics of Propaganda,* 65–71; Blum, *V Was for Victory,* 39–41.

43. Young & Rubicam ad entitled "Six Useful Ways to Advertise When You Have No Sales Problem," *Fortune,* February 1944, 167.

44. Fox, *Madison Avenue Goes to War,* 50; Lykins, *From Total War to Total Diplomacy,* 22, 47.

45. Leff, "Politics of Sacrifice," 1310–13. See also the numerous war bond advertisements available at http://scriptorium.lib.duke.edu/adaccess/warbonds.html (accessed 15 February 2007).

46. *When Radio Writes for War*

47. *Fortune,* April 1943, back cover.

48. *SEP,* 6 September 1943, 18.

49. Available at http://scriptorium.lib.duke.edu/adaccess/inflation.html (accessed 12 December 2005).

50. *SEP,* 7 October 1944, 43.

51. *Fortune,* July 1944, 205.

52. *Fortune,* May 1943, 147.

53. For a more extended discussion of this issue, see Leff, "The Politics of Sacrifice."

54. *Fortune,* August 1943, 205.

55. *Life,* 25 January 1943, 80.

56. *Fortune,* August 1943, 205.

57. *SEP,* 25 April 1942, 55.

58. Available at http://scriptorium.lib.duke.edu/adaccess/inflation.html (accessed December 12, 2005).

59. *Fortune,* February 1944, 88.

60. These ads ran inside the back cover of *Fortune* in February and March 1944. Ads in this series also appeared in *Life*, the *Saturday Evening Post*, and newspapers across the country.

61. George Seldes, *Facts and Fascism* (New York: In Fact, Inc., 1943), 11–12, 80, 276.

62. Zieger, *CIO*, 164.

63. Ibid., 103–4, 111, 143–44, 186. Zieger argues that even the CIO's Political Action Committee, formed in 1943 to give the union a stronger political voice at the national level, reflected this shift. "The image of the worker as a brawny superman rarely appeared in the PAC literature, while that of the ordinary citizen took center stage," he writes.

64. Clinton S. Golden and Harold J. Ruttenberg, *The Dynamics of Industrial Democracy* (New York: Harper & Brothers, 1942), xxv–xxvi, xv, ix. Davenport did, however, disagree with Golden and Ruttenberg on the union shop, which he saw as a grave violation of individual liberties.

65. Zieger, *CIO*, 163.

66. Ibid., 150–52, 172.

67. William L. O'Neill, *A Democracy at War: America's Fight at Home and Abroad in World War II* (New York: Free Press, 1993), 211.

68. Andrew A. Workman, "Manufacturing Power: The Organizational Revival of the National Association of Manufacturers, 1941–1945," *Business History Review* 72 (Summer 1998): 285.

69. Zieger, *CIO*, 145.

70. Nelson Lichtenstein, *Labor's War at Home: The CIO in World War II* (Cambridge; New York: Cambridge University Press, 1982), 111; Zieger, *CIO*, 175.

71. Zieger, *CIO*, 169–70.

72. David M. Kennedy, *Freedom from Fear: The American People in Depression and War, 1929–1945* (New York: Oxford University Press, 1999), 216.

73. Alan Brinkley, *The End of Reform: New Deal Liberalism in Recession and War* (New York: Knopf, 1995), 212.

74. "Your Day in the Court of Public Opinion," an address delivered by NAM executive vice president Walter Weisenburger before the War Congress of American Industry on 3 December 1942, in NAM Records, Series III, Box 844, "Key Documents–Basic Memos, 1942–45" folder. See also "Worksheet of Specific NIIC Objectives," 6 November 1943, in NAM Records, Series III, Box 843, "Campaigns–Documents, 1943–45" folder; and Workman, "Manufacturing Power," 291.

75. Brophy to Bush, 10 August 1944, in Brophy Papers, Box 57, Folder 9.

76. Elizabeth A. Fones-Wolf, *Selling Free Enterprise: The Business Assault on Labor and Liberalism, 1945–1960* (Urbana: University of Illinois Press, 1994), 22–24.

77. "A 'New' C. of C.," *Business Week,* 8 August 1942, 19–20; Eric Johnston, *America Unlimited* (Garden City, N.Y.: Doubleday, Doran and Co., 1944); Workman, "Manufacturing Power," 293–94.

78. Johnston, *American Unlimited*, especially 40, 14, 84, 75, 28–29, 148, 92–96.

79. "A New Public Relations Policy for NAM," 8 November 1944, in NAM Records, Series III, Box 843, "Campaigns–Documents, 1943–45" folder.

80. "A Business Program for a Better America" (an NIIC document produced in 1944), in Brophy Papers, Box 57, Folder 9.
81. "A Suggested Platform for the National Industrial Information Committee," dated 3 November 1943, in NAM Records, Series III, Box 843, "Campaigns –Documents, 1943–45" folder.
82. "'Worksheet' of Specific NIIC Objectives," dated 6 November 1943, in NAM Records, Series III, Box 843, "Campaigns–Documents, 1943–45" folder.
83. "A Suggested Platform for the National Industrial Information Committee."
84. "Interpreting Free Enterprise to Grassroots America: A Summary of NIIC Activities," in NAM Records, Series I, Box 67, "Free Enterprise, General" folder; "Merchandising the Business Story to Opinion Molders in Education and the Churches," in NAM Records, Series III, Box 844; and "Report and Recommendations to Industry of the N.A.M. Committee on Cooperation with Churches," in NAM Records, Series III, Box 842, "NAM Board Meeting, 2/25/44" folder.
85. "Recommendations Regarding Public Relations Activities of the National Association of Manufacturers and the National Industrial Information Committee," submitted by Kenyon & Eckhardt Inc. on 3 November 1944, Brophy Papers, Box 57, Folder 9.
86. Memo from Edwin Cox to Thomas Brophy, 13 February 1945, Brophy Papers, Box 57, Folder 9.
87. Ad entitled "Guts," *NYT*, 30 December 1944. See also "How Americans Can EARN MORE, BUY MORE, HAVE MORE," *NYT*, 23 December 1944, and "SEZ WHO?" *NYT*, 20 January 1945.
88. Thomas D'Arcy Brophy to Chet Foust, 31 August 1944, in Brophy Papers, Box 57, Folder 9.
89. "Excerpt from 'PLANNING,' January 25, 1945" in NAM Records, Series III, Box 843, "Advertising, January 1945" folder.
90. "Personal Conversation with *B. E. Hutchinson*–1/11/45," and memo of phone conversation with Charles J. Stillwell on 12 January 1945, both in NAM Records, Series III, Box 843, "Advertising, January 1945" folder; "Comparison of Advertising Series and Consumer Booklet," in NAM Records, Series III, Box 843, "Campaigns–Documents, 1943–45" folder. The booklet in question can also be found in the latter folder.
91. Memo from C. E. Harrison, Jr., to the NIIC staff, 29 January 1945 in NAM Records, Series III, Box 843, "Campaign–Documents, 1943–45" folder.
92. Workman, "Manufacturing Power," 296–300, 308, 312–16, 281.

Chapter 5

1. John Morton Blum, *V Was for Victory: Politics and American Culture during World War II* (New York: Harcourt, Brace, Jovanovich, 1976), 217–18. See also Flora Bryant Brown, "NAACP Sponsored Sit-ins by Howard University Students in Washington, D.C., 1943–1944," *Journal of Negro History* 85 (Autumn 2000): 279–80. According to Brown, flyers announcing the sit-in also contrasted "Hitler's way" to the "American way."

2. "Report by Riesenfeld to AJC's 34th annual meeting," January 1941, Waldman Papers, Box 39, "Survey Committee, Educational Department Survey, 1933–42" folder.

3. Wendy L. Wall, "'Our Enemies Within': Nazism, National Unity and America's Wartime Discourse on Tolerance," in *Enemy Images in American History*, eds. Ragnhild Fiebig-von Hase and Ursula Lehmkuhl (Providence, R.I.: Berghahn Books, 1997), 219.

4. National Conference of Christians and Jews, *Bulletin*, July 1941 and March 1942. "Council Against Intolerance" folder, Blaustein Library, American Jewish Committee, New York; Richard W. Steele, "The War on Intolerance: The Reformulation of American Nationalism, 1939–1941," *Journal of American Ethnic History* 9 (Fall 1989): 28.

5. *No Ocean Separates Us from Our Enemies Within* brochure, in NCCJ Records, Box 1, "Annual Reports, 1940–49" folder.

6. David M. Kennedy, *Freedom from Fear: The American People in Depression and War, 1929–1945* (New York: Oxford University Press, 1999), 747.

7. *PPA* (1942), 5–6.

8. Office of War Information, Domestic Radio Bureau, *When Radio Writes for War* (Washington, D.C., 1943).

9. "Memorandum to Nathan Ohrbach from Henry W. Levy," 28 September 1944, Waldman Papers, Box 34, "Program and Policy, 1943–49" folder.

10. The federal government's contacts with the AJC and the NCCJ are mentioned in "Plans for Combating Anti-Semitism in Early 1942," January 1942, Waldman Papers, Box 39, "Survey Committee, Educational Department Survey, 1933–42" folder.

11. *ITU News*, 13 October 1944. Gary Gerstle first called attention to these ads in *Working-Class Americanism: The Politics of Labor in a Textile City, 1914–1960* (Cambridge,: Cambridge University Press, 1989), 295–97. Gerstle suggested that they were produced by officials at the War Advertising Council and the U.S. Treasury Department, but an extensive search of War Advertising Council records—as well as a survey of scores of war- bond advertisements in Duke University's John W. Hartman Center for Sales, Advertising, and Marketing History—have turned up no other ads with similar messages. Both the argument and tone of these ads are very similar to other materials put out by the AJC and the NCCJ, and they coincide with an effort by the staffs of both organizations to step up their efforts to reach working-class immigrants. An image very similar to one of the ads in the *ITU News*—"Invitation to Commit Suicide"—graced the cover of the 14 August 1944 issue of *The Union*, a publication of the CIO-affiliated International Union of Mine, Mill and Smelter Workers. Another cartoon with a similar theme appeared in the 6 November 1944 issue of *The Union*; the artist who signed that cartoon, Eric Godal, also signed cartoons distributed the following year by the American Jewish Committee's National Labor Service. In one regard, these ads parallel many war bond advertisements placed by private corporations during the war: although they contain an appeal to buy bonds, the bulk of the ad is devoted to a different agenda entirely.

12. *ITU News,* 27 October 1994; *ITU News,* 15 September 1944; and *ITU News,* 30 September 1944.

13. Gerstle, *Working-Class Americanism,* 292–98.

14. Ibid., 301.

15. Kennedy *Freedom from Fear,* 761.

16. Benjamin L. Alpers, *Dictators, Democracy, and American Public Culture: Envisioning the Totalitarian Enemy, 1920s–1950s* (Chapel Hill: University of North Carolina Press, 2003), 168–69.

17. Eric Foner, *The Story of American Freedom* (New York: W. W. Norton, 1998), 239.

18. Michael Denning, *The Cultural Front: The Laboring of American Culture in the Twentieth Century* (London; New York: Verso, 1996), 130.

19. For examples of this attitude, see "Minutes of the NCCJ Board of Trustees, Wednesday, October 7, 1942," in NCCJ Records, Box 2, "Board of Trustees, 1941–45" folder; and AJC Records, GEN-10, Box 216, "Educational Materials–Labor" folder.

20. "Steam from the Melting Pot," *Fortune,* (September 1942,): 134.

21. Lorraine M. Lees, "National Security and Ethnicity: Contrasting Views during World War II," *Diplomatic History* 11 (Spring 1987): 113–25. The first quote comes from an in-house history of the OSS's Foreign Nationalities Branch, written in 1945 and cited by Lees.

22. Ibid., 122–24.

23. For part of that time, Nash was actually stationed in the White House and reported to presidential assistant Jonathan Daniels. Oral history interviews with Philleo Nash conducted in Washington, D.C., on June 24 and in August 17, 1966 by Jerry N. Hess. Available at http://www.trumanlibrary.org/oralhist/nash1.htm and http://www.trumanlibrary.org/oralhist/nash2.htm (accessed 9 August 2005).

24. The source for this and the following paragraph is a 3 June 1943 memo entitled "America's Foreign Language Groups" in Nash Papers, Box 19, "Minorities–Info Programs–Nash Proposal and Reports, June–September 1943" folder.

25. Nash conceded that Polish Americans, the third largest foreign-language group among the miners, might not have been the target of foreign propaganda. He also noted that about eighty thousand striking miners were black.

26. Nash's mother's family included several prominent abolitionists, and his paternal uncle served as the first secretary of the National Association for the Advancement of Colored People. During his years with the Roosevelt and Truman administrations, Nash promoted fair employment and housing practices and oversaw both the President's Committee on Civil Rights and the Committee on Equal Opportunity in the Armed Forces. Joseph A. Pika, "Interest Groups and the White House under Roosevelt and Truman," *Political Science Quarterly* 102 (Winter 1987–1988): 663–66; and James Officer, "Philleo Nash (1909–1987)," *American Anthropologist* 90 (December 1988): 952–56.

27. Adamic sent copies of his book to Eleanor Roosevelt and Assistant Secretary of State Adolph Berle and promoted his ideas at a private White House dinner with the Roosevelts and Winston Churchill. Adamic followed up on the dinner with a long memo to Eleanor Roosevelt, which was subsequently circulated within the

administration. Louis Adamic, *Two-Way Passage* (New York: Harper & Brothers, 1941), 266–68, 290; Lorraine M. Lees, "Louis Adamic and American Foreign Policy Makers" (paper presented at the symposium on "Louis Adamic: His Life, Work, and Legacy," St. Paul, Minnesota, 29–30 May 1981), in the author's possession.

28. Adamic, *Two-Way Passage*, 270, 286, 311.

29. "Steam from the Melting Pot," *Fortune*, September 1942, 134, 137.

30. Lawrence R. Samuel, *Pledging Allegiance: American Identity and the Bond Drive of World War II* (Washington, D.C.: Smithsonian Institution Press, 1997), chap. 5. Occasionally, the government used such bond drives for propaganda, broadcasting them to foreign countries over shortwave radio.

31. "MacLeish Attacks Divisionists and Defeatists," FLIS Press Releases, 23 March 1942; and "Address by Alan Cranston, Chief, Foreign Language Division, Office of War Information, Before the Editors and Publishers of Foreign Language Newspapers in New York City, August 25, 1942," both in ACNS Microfilm, Reel 19.

32. Quoted in Dan Shiffman, *Rooting Multiculturalism: The Work of Louis Adamic* (Madison, N.J.: Fairleigh Dickinson University Press, 2003), 87–88.

33. For a history of the magazine, see William Charles Beyer, "Searching for *Common Ground*, 1940–1949: An American Literary Magazine and Its Related Movements in Education and Politics" (Ph.D. diss., University of Minnesota, 1988).

34. *PPA* (1944), 101. See also the president's D-Day Prayer on the Invasion of Normandy, *PPA* (1944), 152.

35. This quote from FDR's 27 October 1941 Navy Day address, reprinted in *Roosevelt's Foreign Policy, 1933–41: Franklin D. Roosevelt's Unedited Speeches and Messages* (New York: W. Funk Inc., 1942), 513–14.

36. U.S. Office of War Information, *Enemy Japan* (Washington, D.C., 1945), 3. For additional federal depictions along the same lines, see two pamphlets put out by the Office of War Information earlier in the war: *Radio Background Material; Subject: The Enemy* (Washington, D.C., 1 July 1942); *Radio Background Material; Subject: Our Enemies, The Nazis* (Washington, D.C., 12 January 1943). For a similar image in the popular press, see "Nazi Marriage Service," *Time*, 5 July 1945, 44.

37. *PPA* (1936), 85.

38. For example, in an undated memo written to colleagues in Washington and Hollywood in the summer of 1943, Philleo Nash noted that the OWI was "not able to get out posters and publications any longer." He recommended that the agency increase contacts with a variety of private organizations—including the AJC, the ADL, and others—and encourage them "to carry out the publications for this program we are unable to continue." Memo entitled "A Minorities program for the Office of War Information, Domestic Branch" from Philleo Nash to Palmer Hoyt and James Allen, n.d., in Nash Papers, "Minorities–Information Programs–Nash Proposal and Reports, June–September 1943" folder.

39. The NCCJ's military camp program is described in the January and May 1943 issues of the organization's *Bulletin*. Also see pamphlets in NCCJ Records, Box 11, "World War II Publications" folder.

40. Gretchen Knapp, "Wartime 'Cultural Democracy': The National Conference of Christians and Jews and the United Service Organizations," unpublished paper

delivered at the 1994 annual meeting of the AHA in San Francisco (copy in the author's possession).

41. Gretchen Knapp, "Experimental Social Policymaking during World War II: The United Service Organizations (USO) and American War-Community Services (AWCS)," *Journal of Policy History* 12 (2000): 321–38.

42. Ibid., 322; "Handbook of Campaign Organization and Operation for United Service Organizations for National Defense, Inc." and "Operation USO, Report of the President, United Service Organizations, Inc., February 4th, 1941–January 9th, 1948," both in Hoover Institution Library, Stanford University.

43. Quoted in Knapp, "Wartime 'Cultural Democracy.'"

44. "The Message as Given at Camp Wallace…by James V. Allred," in NCCJ Records, Box 11, "World War II Publications" folder.

45. "Minutes of the NCCJ Board of Trustees, Wednesday, October 7, 1942," in NCCJ Records, Box 2, "Board of Trustees, 1941–45" folder.

46. For more on the National Labor Service, see AJC Records, GEN-10, Box 216, "Educational Materials–Labor" folder.

47. *Three Pals* comic book, in NCCJ Records, Box 11, "World War II Publications" folder.

48. Extensive documentation on this episode can be found in RG 407, the Records of the Adjutant General (Army), AGG 569.14 and in Record Group 247, The Office of the Chief of Chaplains, Entry 1, 16W3, 3/12B, Box 119, NARA-II. The story of the four chaplains is also told in Henry L. Feingold, *A Time for Searching: Entering the Mainstream, 1920–1945*, vol. 4, *The Jewish People in America* (Baltimore: Johns Hopkins University Press, 1992), 259; and Isidor Kaufman, *American Jews in World War II: The Story of 550,000 Fighters for Freedom* (New York: Dial Press, 1947), 305–9. One of the Protestant chaplains, Clark Poling, was the son of the head of the U.S. Army chaplains' service.

49. "Report and Recommendations to Industry of the N.A.M. Committee on Cooperation with Churches," in NAM Records, Series III, Box 842, "NAM Board Meeting, 2/25/44" folder.

50. Will Herberg uses the term "interfaith idea" in his seminal *Protestant-Catholic-Jew: An Essay in American Religious Sociology*, rev. ed. (New York: Doubleday & Co., 1960), 244.

51. Press release and essay entitled "The Best Example of Teamwork I Know…," in NCCJ Records, Box 9, "Frank Trager" folder. See also "Nisei Boy's Thanks Win Essay Contest," *NYT*, 21 February 1946.

52. Some details of this story, including these locations, come from the author's telephone interview with Nobukazu Oyanagi on 23 September 2005. Notes in the author's possession.

53. "The Best Example of Teamwork I Know…"

54. Ibid.

55. This part of the story was recounted many years later by Noble's older brother Waichi in an article for *Arches*, an alumni magazine of the University of Puget Sound. Available: http://www2.ups.edu/dsa/photoalbum/CherryTrees/JapnInter3.GIF (accessed 16 January 2006).

56. Telephone interview with Nobukazu Oyanagi.

57. Kennedy, *Freedom from Fear*, 768.

58. Robert H. Zieger, *The CIO, 1935–1955* (Chapel Hill: University of North Carolina Press, 1995), 155.

59. Kennedy, *Freedom from Fear*, 345–46.

60. J. Saunders Redding, "A Negro Looks at This War," *American Mercury* 55 (November 1942): 585, 589–90.

61. Horace Mann Bond, "Should the Negro Care Who Wins the War?" *The Annals of the American Academy of Political and Social Science* 223 (September 1942): 82–84.

62. Carey McWilliams, *Brothers Under the Skin*, rev. ed. (Boston: Little, Brown, 1964), 23–24.

63. See Merl E. Reed, *Seedtime for the Modern Civil Rights Movement: The President's Committee on Fair Employment Practice, 1941–1946* (Baton Rouge, La.: Louisiana State University Press, 1991).

64. Zieger, *CIO*, 155–56.

65. "'Mixed' Division Urged on Army," *NYT*, 22 March 1942.

66. For the founding of CORE, see James Tracy, *Direct Action: Radical Pacifism from the Union Eight to the Chicago Seven* (Chicago: University of Chicago Press, 1996), 20–35.

67. The recommendations of the NCCJ staff, and the decision of board, on these matters can be traced through a series of memos and reports contained in NCCJ Records, Box 2, "Board of Trustees, 1941–45" folder.

68. *They Got the Blame: The Story of Scapegoats in History*, in Nash Papers, Box 8, "Domestic Propaganda - Materials re: Discrimination" folder.

69. Zieger, *CIO*, 156–59.

70. Thomas Cripps and David Culbert, "*The Negro Soldier* (1944): Film Propaganda in Black and White," *American Quarterly* 31 (Winter 1979): 625, 637–38. This article also informs the discussion in the next two paragraphs.

71. This fact was not lost on viewers at the time. See the letter to the editor entitled "A Soldier's View," *NYT*, 30 January 1944, Sec. X.

72. Robert C. Weaver, "Whither Northern Race Relations Committees?" *Phylon* 5 (1944): 208.

73. McWilliams, *Brothers Under the Skin*, 17.

74. Howard A. Droker, "Seattle Race Relations During the Second World War," *Pacific Northwest Quarterly* 67 (October 1976): 170.

75. Ibid., 171.

76. "Toledo's Program Eases Racial Bias," *NYT*, 25 December 1951.

77. Droker, "Seattle Race Relations," 171–72.

78. Such episodes were covered extensively in the black press. Arnold R. Hirsch, *Making the Second Ghetto: Race and Housing in Chicago, 1940–1960* (Cambridge, New York: Cambridge University Press, 1983), 40–67.

79. Earl Robinson with Eric A. Gordon, *Ballad of an American: The Autobiography of Earl Robinson* (Lanham, Md.: Scarecrow Press, 1998), 151–52; Brooks Atkinson, "The Play," *NYT*, 6 October 1942.

80. Josh White, *Josh White in Chronological Order, vol. 6, 1944–1945* (Vienna, Austria): Document Records, 1997).

81. This episode is recounted by Allan's son in the documentary *Strange Fruit*, prod. and dir. Joel Katz, 58 min., California Newsreel, 2002, videocassette.

82. Nancy Kovaleff Baker, "Abel Meeropol (a.k.a. Lewis Allan): Political Commentator and Social Conscience," *American Music* 20 (Spring 2002): 54–55.

83. For recent examples, see Michael Denning, *Cultural Front*, 335, and Robert J. Norrell, *The House I Live In: Race in the American Century* (New York: Oxford University Press, 2005), 141–42.

84. *The House I Live In* (RKO, 1945) is available on *Uncle Sam: The Movie Collection*, vol. 1 (The Chudwig Group, 2000).

85. Norrell, *The House I Live In*, 141–42.

86. Baker, "Abel Meeropol," 55.

87. "Film Benefits 10 Groups," *NYT*, 19 June 1946.

88. "Ray Milland Wins First Film 'Oscar,'" *NYT*, 8 March 1946.

Chapter 6

1. Details of the episode, including the Clark Kent quote, are from Seymour Peck, "A Down-to-Earth Superman," *PM*, 15 May 1946 16. For background information, see Les Daniels, *Superman: The Complete History; The Life and Times of the Man of Steel* (San Francisco: Chronicle Books, 1998).

2. Judith Klein, "Addition of Social Conscience Swells Child Serial Popularity," *New York Herald Tribune*, 14 July 1946.

3. Stetson Kennedy, *The Klan Unmasked* (Boca Raton: Florida Atlantic University Press, 1990), 91–94.

4. Harriet Van Horne, "Superman's Message Is for Grownups, Too," *New York World-Telegram*, 10 September 1946.

5. Script outline for show to be broadcast 2/10/47 to 3/10/47 in CSAA Records, Box 38, Folder 391.

6. Klein, "Addition of Social Conscience Swells Child Serial Popularity."

7. This line from an *ADL Bulletin* is quoted in Stuart Svonkin, *Jews Against Prejudice: American Jews and the Fight for Civil Liberties* (New York: Columbia University Press, 1997), 44–45.

8. For materials relating to this effort, see CSAA Records, Box 24.

9. Jack Gould, "On the New Superman," *NYT*, 28 April 1946, Sec. X.

10. Both Mead and the NCCJ recommended against using the terms "Jew" and "Negro" to describe individual characters for fear of engendering hostility. (For this reason, the series writers generally used names to indicate a character's background.) "It is better to say, 'Jews, Catholics and Protestants,'" Mead declared at one meeting. "The Lord gave us three races and if you mention all three in the same sentence you are better off." Mead's comment—which suggests that Catholics and Protestants, as well as Jews, are separate "races"—also highlights the conflation of "race" and "religion" that appears in many documents from this period. See minutes of Radio Committee Meeting, 18 March 1946, in CSAA Records, Box 24, Folder 236.

11. Thomas Whiteside, "Up, Up and Awa-a-y!," *NR*, 3 March 1947, 15–16.

12. Martin Grams, Jr., *Radio Drama: A Comprehensive Chronicle of American Network Programs, 1932–1962* (Jefferson, N.C.: McFarland, 2000), 23.

13. See press materials in CSAA records, Box 24, Folder 240.

14. Whiteside, "Up, Up and Awa-a-y!," 15–16.

15. The reference to the "mass mind" comes from the Robert MacIver's concluding essay in R. M. MacIver, ed., *Unity and Difference in American Life: A Series of Addresses and Discussions* (New York: Institute for Religious & Social Studies, 1947; distributed by Harper & Bros.).

16. Ibid., 4–5, 33.

17. Ibid., 59.

18. Ibid., 5–7. Finkelstein opened his remarks by acknowledging that America's "moral influence" was "indispensable to the establishment of world understanding" and could only be exerted "if America sets its own moral house in order." Most of his remarks, however, focused on the need to encourage Americans to think about their common interests.

19. Americans for Democratic Action (ADA), for instance, actively promoted civil rights in the postwar period. Yet ADA founder Arthur M. Schlesinger, Jr., stressed consensus when discussing the issue in his 1949 call-to-arms *The Vital Center: The Politics of Freedom* (Boston: Houghton Mifflin Co., 1949), 190. Schlesinger argued that most Americans accepted "at least in principle, the obligations spelled out" in the 1947 report issued by the President's Committee on Civil Rights, and he dismissed the "revolt of the southern governors against President Truman's request for civil rights legislation" as "temper tantrums rather than a cry of conscience against civil rights." Schlesinger argued that "the South on the whole accepts the objectives of the civil rights program as legitimate, even though it may have serious and intelligible reservations about timing and method." With the benefit of historical hindsight, this conclusion seems astonishing.

20. For an example of such thinking from the mid-1940s, see Andre Mesnard, "Plans for a New France," *NR*, 11 September 1944, 299–301. "Perhaps the most shocking thing brought to light by the defeat of [France in] 1940 was the bankruptcy of the elite whose task it was to unite the nation morally," Mesnard wrote. "When the crisis came, it was discovered that Frenchmen, in key positions, thought not as citizens of France, but as members of groups."

21. Stuart Chase, *Democracy Under Pressure: Special Interests vs. the Public Welfare* (New York: Twentieth Century Fund, 1945), 20.

22. Arthur M. Schlesinger, Jr., originally excerpted the Yeats poem in "Not Right, Not Left, But a Vital Center," *NYTM*, 4 April 1948. Some two decades later, Joan Didion employed another line from the same poem in *Slouching Towards Bethlehem* (New York: Farrar, Straus & Giroux, 1968), a book depicting the fragmentation of America in the late 1960s.

23. These radical features included public power, progressive taxation, and consumer legislation. Robert Griffith, "The Selling of America: The Advertising Council and American Politics, 1942–1960," *Business History Review* 57 (Autumn 1983): 388.

24. Schlesinger, *Vital Center*, x.
25. Such fears prompted the army's Information and Education Division to launch what became known as the *G.I. Roundtable* series, a group of pamphlets produced by the American Historical Association (AHA) in the final years of the war that were designed to foster discussion of various subjects among GIs and ease their transition to the postwar world. Documents from and analysis of this unusual effort are available at http://www.historians.org/projects/GIRoundtable/index.html (accessed January 29, 2006).
26. I have borrowed this phrase from Barbara Foley, *Spectres of 1919: Class & Nation in the Making of the New Negro* (Urbana: University of Illinois Press, 2003).
27. Nell Irvin Painter, *Standing at Armageddon: The United States, 1877–1919* (New York: W. W. Norton, 1987), 346, 359–60; Lizabeth Cohen, *Making a New Deal: Industrial Workers in Chicago, 1919–1939* (Cambridge: Cambridge University Press, 1990), 12, 36.
28. "Roosevelt Issues Brotherhood Plea," *NYT*, 15 January 1944.
29. William H. Chafe, *The Unfinished Journey: America Since World War II*, 2nd ed. (New York: Oxford University Press, 1991), 93–94; "Police Battle 3,500 Pickets in a New Philadelphia Riot," *NYT*, 1 March 1946.
30. Speech delivered on 1 October 1946 by Advertising Council executive director T. S. Repplier entitled "How the American Enterprise System Is Being Re-Sold to the American People," HSTL, Harry S. Truman Papers, Dallas C. Halverstadt Files, Box 1, "Advertising Council, The – Miscellaneous" folder. A sense of unease also permeates the confidential "Proposal for a 'Production Urgency' Campaign" circulated to Advertising Council board members in October 1946. The proposal is in Brophy Papers, Box 35, Folder 8.
31. The CIO-PAC embraced President Roosevelt's call for an "economic bill of rights," arguing for national health insurance, full employment legislation, and other social programs. In retrospect, business' fear of the organization seems hopelessly misplaced. As James Caldwell Foster points out in *The Union Politic: The CIO Political Action Committee* (Columbia: University of Missouri Press, 1975), the organization's power eroded steadily in 1946 and the November elections ended in disaster.
32. "Disorders Halted in Tennessee City," *NYT*, 27 February 1946; "Outbreak in Tennessee Jail," *NYT*, 1 March 1946; "Killing of Negroes Is Protested Here," *NYT*, 2 March 1946.
33. "Negroes Mobbed in Alabama Town," *NYT*, 11 August 1946.
34. The warning was delivered by Clark H. Foreman, president of the Southern Conference for Human Welfare, in a commencement address at the Hampton Institute. "Southern Leader Warns of 'Fascism'," *NYT*, 17 August 1946.
35. "Philadelphia Riot Ends in One Death," *NYT*, 30 September 1946.
36. "Major Race Riot in Chicago Seen," *NYT*, 11 December 1946. See also Arnold R. Hirsch, *Making the Second Ghetto: Race and Housing in Chicago, 1940–1960* (Cambridge: Cambridge University Press, 1983), 56, 60.
37. The quote is from "The Veterans March On," *NYT*, 13 August 1946. The description of this episode is drawn from "Tennessee Sheriff Is Slain in Primary Day

Violence," *NYT*, 2 August 1946; "Armed Veterans Run Town After Tennessee Bloodshed," *NYT*, 3 August 1946; "Election in Tennessee," *NYT*, 3 August 1946; "Veterans' Direct Action a Minor Post-War Fear," *NYT*, 11 August 1946; Jennings Perry, "Rebellion in Tennessee," *Nation,* 10 August 1946, 147; "GI Revolution," *Commonweal* 44 (16 August 1946): 419; and Theodore H. White, "The Battle of Athens, Tennessee," *Harper's*, January 1947, 54–61.

38. Proposal by Thomas D'Arcy Brophy dated 15 November 1946 and entitled "A Program to Re-Sell Americanism to Americans," Brophy Papers, Box 35, Folder 8.

39. "'Militant' Unity Asked to Fight Bias," *NYT*, 15 December 1945.

40. "Address by Honorable Tom C. Clark, Attorney General of the United States, at Bill of Rights Luncheon" in NARS Freedom Train Records, Box 2, "746-E7, Tour of the Freedom Train (Pt. 1), From 5/1/46–1/29/47" folder.

41. War Advertising Council, *From War to Peace: The New Challenge to Business and Advertising* (New York; Washington: War Advertising Council, 1945).

42. War Advertising Council, *From War to Peace*

43. The Advertising Council's operating budget was provided by six organizations: the Association of National Advertisers, the American Association of Advertising Agencies, the Periodical Publishers Association of America, the Bureau of Newspaper Advertising, the National Association of Broadcasters, and the Outdoor Advertising Association. James W. Young to Judge Joseph M. Proskauer, 12 April 1946, AJC Records, Box 3, "Advertising Council" folder; "The Sixth White House Meeting for the Board of Directors and Committees of the Advertising Council," Jackson Files, Box 17, "Advertising Council–White House Meeting, Feb. 15–16, 1950" folder; Daniel L. Lykins, *From Total War to Total Diplomacy: The Advertising Council and the Construction of the Cold War Consensus* (Westport, Conn.: Praeger, 2003), 46–47.

44. For instance, Charles W. Jackson, the Truman administration's chief liaison to the Advertising Council, was a New York City advertising executive for twenty years before joining the Office of Price Administration and then the Office of War Information. After the war, he was shifted first to the Office of War Mobilization and Reconversion and then to the Office of Government Reports. From 1947 to 1953, he reported directly to the Assistant to the President, John R. Steelman.

45. Griffith, "Selling of America," 392.

46. "The Sixth White House Meeting for the Board of Directors and Committees of the Advertising Council."

47. Jackson Files, Box 12, "White House Meeting–General Correspondence–October 27, 1947" folder, and Box 13, "White House Meeting–Speakers File–October 27, 1947" folder; "Truman 'Seminar' Bolsters Aid Plan," *NYT*, 28 October 1947.

48. David M. Potter, *The American Round Table Discussions on People's Capitalism at Yale University, New Haven, Connecticut, November 16 and 17, 1956* (New York, 1957).

49. "Memorandum on Proposed Advertising Council Round Table," in Brophy Papers, Box 4, Folder 4.

50. "Advertising Council Annual Report, 1954–55," in Advertising Council Archives, 13/2/202, Box 1; Arthur Goodfriend, *What Is America?* (New York:

Simon & Schuster, 1954); Potter, *The American Round Table Discussions on People's Capitalism*, 4.

51. Lykins, *From Total War to Total Diplomacy*, 54.

52. Jackson is quoted in Griffith, "Selling of America," footnote 10. See also "Business Steps Up Its Candle Power: The 5th Year of the Advertising Council, March 1, 1946–March 1, 1947," in Advertising Council Papers, Record Series 13/2/202, Box 1.

53. *From War to Peace*; minutes of the 5 June 1946 meeting of the Public Advisory Committee in Advertising Council Archives, 13/2/201, Box 2, "Advertising Council, Minutes, May–June 1946" folder; Charles G. Mortimer, Jr., to William Randolph Hearst, 13 April 1949, Advertising Council Archives, 13/2/201, Box 4, "March–April 1949" folder. Mortimer noted that the committee "was selected to give representation to all the important elements in our national life –management, labor, religion, banking, education, agriculture, social service, medicine, and law. The three major religions are represented. Negroes are represented by Mr. Charles Houston. Obviously, any representative committee of this sort will include other than the conservative point of view."

54. "Thomas Brophy, Ad Executive, Dies Trying to Save 2 Children," *NYT*, 30 July 1967. Also see the biography included in the finding aid to Brophy's Papers.

55. Brophy, "Program to Re-Sell Americanism to Americans"; memo from W. B. Smith to Ed Cox, 10 June 1946; and "500,000 Mark American Day in Central Park," *New York Herald Tribune*, 20 May 1946; all in Brophy Papers, Box 35, Folder 8.

56. Brophy, "Program to Re-Sell Americanism to Americans"

57. Minutes of the NCCJ Board of Directors meeting on 11/29/45, in NCCJ Records, Box 2, "Board of Directors, Nov. 1945" folder.

58. Minutes of the NCCJ Board of Directors meeting on 11/29/45.

59. "Brotherhood Aims Hailed by Truman," *NYT*, 15 February 1946.

60. "Braniff Takes Religious Post," *NYT*, 27 April 1946; "Benson Ford Takes Interfaith Office," *NYT*, 5 October 1951.

61. "Ford Fund Gives Million for Center for 'World Brotherhood' Near U.N.," *NYT*, 14 February 1951.

62. For example, see the comments of Dwight R. G. Palmer, president of General Cable Corporation, on racial tensions in the company's St. Louis plant during the war in James E. Pitt, *Adventures in Brotherhood* (New York: Farrar, Straus, 1955), 212–13. General Cable was one of the first companies to test an in-plant NCCJ program on tolerance.

63. Memo to Everett R. Clinchy from Frank N. Trager, 27 May 1946, NCCJ Records, Box 9, "Frank Trager" folder. Trager wrote this memo as he was leaving the NCCJ to take a similar role with the Anti-Defamation League of B'nai B'rith.

64. For an overview, see Pitt, *Adventures in Brotherhood*, 213–20. For examples of programs at specific plants, see NCCJ Records, Box 11, "Labor-Management Conferences" folder. *A Handbook on Human Relations* (New York: Farrar, Straus, 1949), written by the NCCJ's president Everett R. Clinchy, offered short essays, questions for discussion, and additional readings for those participating in such programs.

65. "Stassen Cautions on Spread of Bias," *NYT*, 31 January 1946.

66. Memo to Frank Trager from Milton Krents, 27 February 1946, NCCJ Records, Box 9, "Frank Trager" folder.
67. Brochure on "Co-operation with Motion Picture Theatres, Brotherhood Week, 16–24 February 1946," NCCJ Records, Box 9, "Frank Trager" folder.
68. "Request of the National Conference of Christians and Jews" (5 June 1946), Advertising Council Archives, 13-2-305, Box 1, "Christians and Jews, 1946" folder.
69. "Advertising News and Notes," *NYT*, 4 July 1946; Advertising Council's Radio Fact Sheet, No. 31 (12 August 1946), Jackson Files, Box 4, "Group Prejudice—'A Post-War Menace'" folder.
70. The American Jewish Committee had pitched a similar campaign to the Advertising Council five months earlier, but an Advertising Council screening board tried to broaden the proposal to include "industrial and international relations." As a result, it was ultimately rejected by the Council. See proposal accompanying letter from Evans Clark to E. J. Coil, 23 January 1946, and memo to Dr. John Slawson from A. L. Bernheim, 13 September 1946, both in AJC Records, Box 3, "Advertising Council" folder.
71. Quoted in Daniel Pope and William Toll, "We Tried Harder: Jews in American Advertising," *American Jewish History* 72 (1982): 26.
72. Memo from Alfred L. Bernheim to Richard C. Rothschild, 9 January 1947, AJC Records, Box 3, "Advertising Council" folder.
73. Douglas Meldrum to C. L. Whittier, 18 July 1946, Advertising Council Records, 13/2/305, Box 1, "Christians and Jews, 1946" folder; "Advertising News and Notes," *NYT*, 4 July 1946. These individuals were hardly the radicals that scholars such as Michael Denning and Lary May see transforming the culture industry in the 1930s; they were, by and large, staunch supporters of free enterprise. Yet they too favored a more inclusive vision of the nation—one that at the very least included Jews and Catholics.
74. Form letter from Douglas Meldrum to Dr. Samuel Cavert, 22 July 1946, Advertising Council Records, 13/2/305, Box 1, "Christians and Jews, 1946" folder.
75. "Radio Fact Sheet, No. 31" (12 August 1946); "Radio Fact Sheet, No. 31" (27 October 1947); and "Television Fact Sheet, No. 31-A" (undated), all in Jackson Files, Box 16, "Ad Council – Radio – Fact Sheets (1 of 2)" folder.
76. Lincoln's famous quote appears in a radio allocation spot from 31 January 1947 found in AJC Records, Box 3, "Advertising Council" folder.
77. See package of newspaper advertisements released by the campaign in early 1948 and located in AJC Records, Box 3, "Advertising Council" folder.
78. In an internal memo, an American Jewish Committee staffer claimed that the organization had helped persuade the Advertising Council to emphasize self-interest more than brotherhood. Memo from A. L. Bernheim to Dr. John Slawson, 13 September 1946, AJC Records, Box 3, "Advertising Council" folder.
79. In the original version of the ad, the "correct" answer to these two questions was "not the issue." This answer says much about the perceived limits of the United America campaign. The original ad copy is in Brophy Papers, Box 1, Folder 7. The final version, which was released in early 1948, is in AJC Records, Box 3, "Advertising Council" folder.

80. Memo from Douglas Meldrum to T. S. Repplier and Staff re: Meeting at Freedom House, 17 December 1946, Advertising Council Archives, 13/2/305, Box 1, "Christians and Jews, 1946" folder.

81. Minutes of the Campaigns Review Committee Meeting on 30 September 1948, Advertising Council Records, 13/2/225, Box 1, "1948–1969" folder.

82. "What Helps People Helps Business: The Sixth Year of the Advertising Council, March 1947 to March 1948," "…What Helps People Helps Business: The Advertising Council Seventh Year, March 1948 to March 1949," and "How Business Helps Solve Public Problems: A Report on the Eighth Year of the Advertising Council, March 1949 to March 1950," all in Advertising Council Records, 13/2/202, Box 1; Douglas Meldrum to Richard Rothschild, 9 January 1947, AJC Records, Box 3, "Advertising Council" folder; Minutes of the Campaigns Review Committee Meeting on 30 September 1948.

83. For example, see the closing commercial prepared for the radio show *Stars over Hollywood* in May 1947, AJC Records, Box 3, "Advertising Council" folder.

84. Proofsheets of the ads discussed in this and the next paragraph can be found in Advertising Council Archives, 13/2/207, Box 126, File 91105; Box 8, File 528; and Box 9, File 581. In "The Selling of America," Griffith notes that "the spectre of Communism was sometimes explicitly incorporated" into public service ads; he does not link this to wartime rhetoric (p. 409).

85. Minutes of the Campaign Reviews Committee Meeting, 17 December 1952, Advertising Council Records, 13/2/225, Box 1, "1948–1969" folder.

86. The campaign, which continued into the 1960s, was designed to emphasize the nation's spiritual values, to encourage attendance at and financial support for churches and synagogues, and to foster anticommunism at home and abroad. Docket Memo, RBF Executive Committee (11/7/52) in Rockefeller Archives Center, Tarrytown, New York, Rockefeller Brothers Fund Papers, Grants/Series 4, "Religion in American Life" folder. For advertising materials produced in conjunction with this campaign between 1949 and 1955, Advertising Council Archives, 13/2/207.

87. Griffith, "The Selling of America," 392–93; Meg Jacobs, *Pocketbook Politics: Economic Citizenship in Twentieth-Century America* (Princeton: Princeton University Press, 2005), 221–23.

88. Minutes of Meeting of Board of Directors and Sponsor Members, 20 September 1946, Advertising Council Records, 13/2/201, Box 3, "Sept.–Oct. 1946" folder; Confidential memo entitled "Proposal for a 'Production Urgency' Campaign," Brophy Papers, Box 35, Folder 8.

89. In *The End of Reform: New Deal Liberalism in Recession and War* ([New York: Alfred A. Knopf, 1995], 4–5), Alan Brinkley argues that by 1937 New Dealers were already backing away from their belief that "something was wrong with capitalism and that government should find a way to repair it." He argues that thereafter they increasingly adopted a Keynesian model that was "on the whole less challenging to the existing structure of corporate capitalism." While Brinkley's argument is convincing, most in the business community did not perceive this shift.

90. Elizabeth A. Fones-Wolf, *Selling Free Enterprise: The Business Assault on Labor and Liberalism, 1945–60* (Urbana: University of Illinois Press, 1994), 49.

91. Quoted in William H. Whyte Jr., and the editors of *Fortune, Is Anybody Listening? How and Why Business Fumbles When It Talks with Human Beings* (New York: Simon & Schuster, 1952), 4.

92. Ibid., 4.

93. Griffith, "Selling Free Enterprise," 403. For a fascinating discussion of this effort that focuses on the NAM, see Fones-Wolf, *Selling Free Enterprise*.

94. "How Can the American People Be Given a Better Understanding of Our Economic System?" in AHF Records, Box 210, "Economic Campaign" folder.

95. The ANA represented corporate advertisers, while AAAA represented agencies. In fact, the two organizations, in cooperation with the U.S. Chamber of Commerce, conducted a variant of this campaign that focused on industrial plants and the communities in which they were located.

96. "Ad Drive Set to Aid Free Enterprise," *NYT*, 18 April 1947.

97. Minutes of the Meeting of the Board of Directors and Sponsor Members, 17 January 1947 and 14 March 1947, both in Advertising Council Archives 13/2/201, Box 3.

98. With a few exceptions, the meeting minutes summarize the objections raised but don't indicate who raised them. E. Franklin Frazier was not present at either meeting, although he may have submitted comments in writing. Minutes of Public Advisory Committee Meeting, 8 January 1947, Advertising Council Archives, 13/2/201, Box 2.

99. Minutes of Public Advisory Committee Meeting, 8 January 1947 and 9 April 1947, both in Advertising Council Archives, 13/2/201, Box 2.

100. The CIO's general counsel Lee Pressman, a former Communist, was one of those who opposed the campaign on grounds that it would weaken the labor movement. Lykins, *From Total War to Total Diplomacy*, 96.

101. Minutes of Public Advisory Committee Meeting, 8 January 1947.

102. Jacobs, *Pocketbook Politics*, 75–79, 141–45.

103. Griffith, "Selling of America," 396.

104. Chase, *Democracy Under Pressure*, especially pp. 2, 71, 75, and 88. In her influential study *Pocketbook Politics*, Meg Jacobs has suggested that the alliance between organized labor and "purchasing-power progressives" reached its high point during World War II, then unraveled in 1946 and 1947 largely as a result of intense attacks by business interests. I believe this chronology needs some revision. Chase's book suggests that the alliance that had driven "pocketbook politics" since the early 1920s was already badly frayed by the end of the war—and damaged in part by actions like the coal strike of 1943.

105. Jacobs, *Pocketbook Politics*, 145.

106. Chase, *Democracy Under Pressure*, 7.

107. Boris Basil Shishkin, *The Reminiscences of Boris Shishkin* (New York: Oral History Research Office, Columbia University, 1975); "Boris Shishkin Dies; AFL-CIO Ex-Official," *WP*, 14 June 1984, Sec. C; "130 Liberals Form a Group on Right," *NYT*, 5 January 1947; Boris Shishkin, "The Crisis Ahead," *Nation*,

21 October 1944, 495; "Boris Basil Shishkin," *Fortune,* October 1948, 141; Michael J. Hogan, *The Marshall Plan: America, Britain, and the Reconstruction of Western Europe, 1947–1952* (Cambridge: Cambridge University Press, 1987), 142.

108. Minutes of Public Advisory Committee Meeting, 8 January 1947 and 9 April 1947.

109. "How Business Helps Solve Public Problems: A Report on the Eighth Year of the Advertising Council, March 1949 to March 1950," Advertising Council Archives, 13/2/202, Box 1.

110. "…What Helps People Helps Business: The Advertising Council Seventh Year, March 1948–March 1949," Advertising Council Archives, Box 1, Record Series 13/2/202.

111. "The Miracle of America," AHF Records, Box 210, "Economic Campaign–A.H.F." folder.

112. MAT No. R-7 in "A Powerful Retail Merchandising and Public Relations Program to Explain the American System of Free Enterprise," Advertising Council Archives, 13/2/207, Box 69, File 460.

113. Ad No. AES40A in Advertising Council Archives, 13/2/207, Box 69, File 547.

114. For an example of the ad in a publication, see *Time,* 29 November 1948, 109. For more on its circulation, see "…What Helps People Helps Business."

115. April ad mat in "A Campaign to Explain the American Economic System," Brophy Papers, Box 75.

116. For examples of this ad, see *Time,* 3 January 1949, 65, and *Life,* 10 January 1949, 3.

117. Editors of *Fortune* in collaboration with Russell W. Davenport, *U.S.A.: The Permanent Revolution* (New York: Prentice-Hall, 1951), 66–67.

118. Ibid., 77–78.

119. Peter F. Drucker, *The New Society: The Anatomy of the Industrial Order* (New York: Harper, 1950); Frederick Lewis Allen, *The Big Change: America Transforms Itself, 1900–1950* (New York: Harper, 1952). The Advertising Council published and distributed the proceedings of its first roundtable under the title *Basic Elements of a Free, Dynamic Society* (New York: Macmillan, 1951).

120. Frank Adams, "Who, When, What, and All That," *NYT,* 9 January 1949, Sec. BR; "Letter from Stassen to Premier Stalin," *NYT,* 5 October 1950; "Text of Stassen Speech Announcing His Candidacy for President," *NYT,* 28 December 1951.

121. "Advertising Council Annual Report, 1955–56," Advertising Council Archives, 13/2/202, Box 1; "People's Capitalism: The Background–How and Why This Project Was Developed," Advertising Council Archives, 13/2/305, Box 9, "People's Capitalism Exhibit, 1956" folder.

122. Potter, *American Round Table Discussions on People's Capitalism*; David M. Potter, *The American Round Table, People's Capitalism, Part II: An Inquiry into the Social and Cultural Trends in America under Our System of Widely Shared Material Benefits at the Yale Club, New York, New York, May 22, 1957* (New York, 1957); Grant McConnell, *The American Round Table; People's Capitalism, Part III: Major Economic Groups and National Policy, Held at the University of Chicago, October 22, 1958* (New York, 1959).

123. "Copy for People's Capitalism Exhibit" attached to February 1956 exchange between Ted Repplier and Chalmers Roberts, Advertising Council Archives, 13/2/305, Box 9, "People's Capitalism Exhibit–US Reactions, 1956" folder.

124. "Eisenhower Visits Capitalism Show," *NYT*, 14 February 1956; "Ceylonese Like Our Ed Barnes," *NYT*, 27 May 1957.

125. "Eisenhower Visits Capitalism Show"; "'Average Family' as U.S. Emissary," *WP*, 16 February 1956; "U.S. Exhibit Ready to Vie with Reds," *NYT*, 19 August 1956.

126. For an example of both concerns, see memo from Elmer B. Staats, executive officer of the Operations Coordinating Board, to Abbott Washburn, Deputy Director of the USIA, 14 February 1956, Advertising Council Archives, 13/2/305, Box 9, "People's Capitalism Exhibit–U.S. Reactions, 1956" folder. According to "Ceylonese Like Our Ed Barnes," the exhibit remained focused on the Barnes family, and it pictured a slum only to show the housing development that had replaced it.

127. Alma Scurlock to Theodore Streiber, 28 February 1956, Advertising Council Archives, 13/2/305, Box 9, "People's Capitalism Exhibit–U.S. Reactions, 1956" folder. For background information, see "Bucks County Boom Beset by Problems," *NYT*, 26 December 1953.

Chapter 7

1. William A. Coblenz, "The Freedom Train and the Story of Its Origin: Our Civil Liberties on Wheels," *Manuscripts* 10 (Winter 1958): 30–34, 59.

2. "Address by Honorable Tom C. Clark, Attorney General of the United States, at Bill of Rights Luncheon" in NARS Freedom Train Records, Box 2, "746-E7, Tour of the Freedom Train (Pt. 1), From 5/1/46–1/29/47" folder.

3. Truman to Clark, 20 April 1946, and Louis Novins to Thomas D'Arcy Brophy, 19 July 1948, both in AHF Records, Box 212, "General: Jan.–Sept. 1947" folder.

4. For this and the following paragraph, see Coblenz, "Freedom Train and the Story of Its Origin," 34, 59; memo from E. Hamer, 17 September 1946, NARS Freedom Train Records, Box 2, "746-E7, Tour of the Freedom Train (Pt. 1), From 5/1/46–1/29/47" folder; "The Freedom Train: Background of the Program," *Tide*, 30 April 1948, 24–25.

5. Coblenz, "Freedom Train and the Story of Its Origin," 59.

6. Barney Balaban to Leon Lowenstein, 31 October 1947, AHF Papers, Box 208, "Contributions — American Heritage Foundation" folder. For biographical information in this and the previous paragraph, see *Current Biography 1946* (New York: H. W. Wilson Co., 1946), 28; "1,100 Honor Balaban at Movie Dinner Here," *NYT*, 22 November 1946; and James E. Pitt, *Adventures in Brotherhood* (New York: Farrar, Straus and Co., 1955), 65.

7. "Mission of the Movies Abroad," *NYT*, 24 March 1946, Sec. II.

8. Confidential memo entitled "Proposal for a 'Production Urgency' Campaign" and 15 November 1946 proposal by Thomas D'Arcy Brophy entitled "A Program to Re-Sell Americanism to Americans," both in Brophy Papers, Box 35, Folder 8.

9. See Brophy to Aldrich, 26 July 1946; William G. Werner to Brophy, 24 July 1946; Evans Clark to Brophy, 17 July 1946; unsigned memo about discussion with Devereau Josephs, 12 June 1946; Grafton Perkins to Brophy, 29 June 1946; Brophy to Niles Trammel, 25 September 1946; and Tom Clark to Theodore Repplier, 8 November 1946; all in Brophy Papers, Box 35, Folder 8.

10. Memo from Brophy to Winthrop Aldrich, 24 February 1947, Aldrich Collection, Box 19, "American Heritage Foundation: Jan.–Feb. 1947" folder.

11. "Present at luncheon — the 10th in Atty Gen'l Clark's office — 'Bill of Rights'" and "Address by Honorable Tom C. Clark, Attorney General of the United States at Bill of Rights Luncheon," NARS Freedom Train Records, Box 2, "746-E7, Tour of the Freedom Train (Pt. 1), From 5/1/46 to 1/29/47" folder.

12. See note at bottom of "Address by Hon. Tom C. Clark, Attorney General of the United States, at Bill of Rights luncheon in the Office of the Attorney General," and unsigned memo, 11 December 1946, both in NARS Freedom Train Records, Box 2, "746-E7, Tour of the Freedom Train (Pt. 1), From 5/1/46 to 1/29/47" folder.

13. Gilbert Bailey, "Why They Throng to the Freedom Train," *NYTM*, 25 January 1948, 18; "Freedom Train: Background of the Program," 25–26.

14. Aldrich was on the board of a half-dozen major corporations, in addition to serving as president of the International Chamber of Commerce from 1945 to 1947.

15. "The First Two Years: A Progress Report to the Board of Trustees of the American Heritage Foundation," 17, AHF Records, Box 17. For a list of those who attended the January 27 luncheon, as well as records of pledges and donations from attendees, see Aldrich Collection, Box 19, "American Heritage Foundation, January–February 1947" folder. In late May, Aldrich contacted prominent executives in nineteen different industries asking them to take the lead in raising $50,000 each from their respective industries. See Brophy to Aldrich, 23 May 1947, and telegram of the same date sent by Aldrich to the various industry leaders, both in Aldrich Collection, Box 19, "American Heritage Foundation, May–June 1947" folder.

16. "First Two Years," 18–19; contents of folder labeled "American Heritage Foundation 1947," and John D. Rockefeller Jr. to Winthrop Aldrich, 26 September 1947, in "American Heritage Foundation, September 1947" folder, both in Aldrich Collection, Box 19.

17. Samuel F. Pryor to Brophy, 5 June 1947, in "American Heritage Foundation, May–June 1947" folder; form letter sent by Aldrich to various corporate executives, 24 November 1947; memo from Brophy to Aldrich dated 24 February 1947 in "American Heritage Foundation: Jan.–Feb. 1947" folder; all in Aldrich Collection, Box 19. In October 1947, Brophy urged Aldrich to approach banks and insurance companies for sizeable contributions since "the insurance companies in particular have a great stake in combating subversive influences in this country." See memo from Brophy to Aldrich dated 8 October 1947, in Aldrich Collection, Box 19, "American Heritage Foundation, October 1947" folder.

18. "Remarks by Thomas D'Arcy Brophy, President, American Heritage Foundation, at the Exercises at Federal Hall, New York on Sept. 25, 1947," in "American

Heritage Foundation, September 1947" folder; and Aldrich to Bernard Samuel, 11 July 1947, in "American Heritage Foundation, July 1947" folder; both in Aldrich Collection, Box 19.

19. Memo from Brophy to Aldrich, 4 August 1947, Aldrich Collection, Box 19, "American Heritage Foundation, August 1947" folder; Coblenz to Brophy, 28 March 1947, AHF Records, Box 215, "Members of Board and Committees–A.H.F." folder.

20. Coblenz to Brophy, 28 March 1947 in AHF Records, Box 215, "Members of Board and Committees–A.H.F." folder.

21. "Conference at the White House for the Purpose of Organizing the American Heritage Program and Inaugurating the Freedom Train" and "Addresses Delivered at the White House Conference," both in AHF Records, Box 198, "White House Conference" folder.

22. Brophy did note that "it would be very difficult to eliminate…altogether" the use of the word. Aldrich to Brophy, 1 July 1947, in "American Heritage Foundation, May–June 1947" folder, and Brophy to Aldrich, 3 July 1947, in "American Heritage Foundation, July 1947" folder, both in Aldrich Collection, Box 19.

23. I have borrowed the term "democratic revival" from Philip Gleason, *Speaking of Diversity: Language and Ethnicity in Twentieth-Century America* (Baltimore: The Johns Hopkins University Press, 1992), 191.

24. Sidney Hook, "What Exactly Do We Mean by 'Democracy'?" *NYTM*, 16 March 1947, 10; John Foster Dulles, "The Meaning of Freedom," *VSD*, 15 July 1948, 581.

25. In addition to the articles by Sidney Hook and John Foster Dulles above, see: Philip Murray, "The C.I.O. Looks Ahead," *Nation*, 4 November 1944, 554–55; Joseph H. Ball, "Democratic Ideology and Domestic Problems," *VSD*, 15 December 1944, 138–40; Bernard J. Sheil, "The Bishop and the CIO: A Program for Industrial Democracy," *Commonweal*, 5 January 1945, 294–96; "Democracy: Time for a Change?" *Newsweek*, 16 April 1945, 93–94; Brooks Atkinson, "Democracy as Russia Defines It Today," *NYTM*, 4 November 1945, 14; Harold J. Laski, "What Democracy Means in Russia," *NR*, 28 October 1946, 551–52; "Our Form of Government Is 'Republican,'" *SEP*, 14 June 1947, 180; and Arthur M. Schlesinger, Jr., "Democracy: What Does It Mean?" *VSD*, 15 April 1948, 401–2.

26. Friedrich August von Hayek, *The Road to Serfdom* (Chicago: University of Chicago Press, 1945); "Totalitarian Democracy," *Christian Century*, 14 August 1946, 991–92; "Our Form of Government Is 'Republican,'" 180. See also Yves R. Simon, "Democracy and the Purists: Wrecking Democracy from Within," *Commonweal*, 27 October 1944, 32–36; and Henry Steele Commager, "Democracy and Planning," *American Mercury*, January 1946, 113–17.

27. Daniel T. Rodgers, *Contested Truths: Keywords in American Politics Since Independence* (New York: Basic Books, 1987), 215–16. Brophy to Don Belding, 2 June 1947 in AHF Records, Box 212, "A.H.F. General, Jan.–Sept. 1947" folder.

28. For example, a "Radio Fact Sheet" put out in conjunction with the campaign stated: "This campaign…concentrates on that area in which there is the widest agreement—pride in our American heritage of individual freedom." "Radio Fact

Sheet" dated 8 December 1947, Aldrich Collection, Box 19, "American Heritage Foundation, December 1947" folder.

29. Sheldon F. Waldo, "Our American Heritage of Freedom," *VSD*, 15 February 1948, 262. See also a speech by American Heritage Foundation board member Charles Luckman, "Where Freedom Begins," *VSD*, 15 July 1948, 583.

30. Unsigned memo, 8 January 1947, NARS Freedom Train Records, Box 2, "746 - E7, Tour of the Freedom Train (Pt. 1), From 5/1/46–1/29/47" folder.

31. Elizabeth Hamer was chief of the National Archives' Division of Exhibits and Publications. For this and the following two paragraphs, see "Documents Obtained to Date and Set Aside for Justice Department's Proposed Bill of Rights Exhibit Tour," AHF Records, Box 209, "Documents–Re: Freedom Train" folder. See also "Bill of Rights Exhibit," NARS Freedom Train Records, Box 1, "Freedom Train (Early Reference Material)" folder.

32. Draft pages beginning "Franklin Delano Roosevelt was not the first to advocate the expansion of our personal rights to include social and economic rights," NARS Freedom Train Records, Box 1, "Freedom Train (Early Reference Material)" folder.

33. Memo from Elizabeth Hamer to Solon Buck, 29 January 1947, NARS Freedom Train Records, Box 2, "746-E7, Tour of the Freedom Train (Pt. 1), From 5/1/46 to 1/29/47" folder. Also, compare "Documents Obtained to Date and Set Aside for Justice Departments Proposed Bill of Rights Exhibit Tour" (cited above) to the document list compiled by Novins and Hamer on 8 February 1947: "Freedom Train Documents," NARS Freedom Train Records, Box 2, "746-E7, Tour of the Freedom Train (Pt. 2), From 2/1/47 to 4/13/47" folder.

34. Elizabeth Hamer to Solon Buck, 6 March 1947, NARS Freedom Train Records, Box 2, "746-E7, Tour of the Freedom Train (Pt. 2), From 2/1/47 to 4/13/47" folder.

35. Memo from Elizabeth Hamer, 10 February 1947, NARS Freedom Train Records, Box 2, "746-E7, Tour of the Freedom Train (Pt. 2), From 2/1/47 to 4/13/47" folder.

36. Novins to Gardner Osborne, 20 June 1947, AHF Records, Box 209, "Documents–Re: Freedom Train" folder.

37. Memo from Hamer to Buck, 17 July 1947, NARS Freedom Train Records, Box 2, "746-E7, Tour of the Freedom Train (Pt. 3), From 4/14/47 to 7/31/47" folder.

38. The impact of the Document Approval Committee can be traced in part by comparing various lists of documents to be carried on the train. See "Documents Proposed for Exhibit on the Freedom Train," 10 July 1947, in "Documents Loaned and Insurance" folder, and "Documents for Freedom Train," 12 August 1947, in "Documents–Re: Freedom Train" folder; both in AHF Records, Box 209. See also "Supplementary List of Documents for Freedom Train," 4 September 1947, in Aldrich Collection, Box 19, "American Heritage Foundation, September 1947" folder. The final list of documents is presented in "Documents and Memorabilia of Our American Heritage on the Freedom Train," NARS Freedom Train Records, Box 1. The documents that appeared on the train are also listed and explicated in Frank Monaghan, *Heritage of Freedom: The History and Significance*

of the Basic Documents of American Liberty (Princeton: Princeton University Press, 1947).

39. "Bonds of Freedom," NARS Freedom Train Papers, Box 1, "Freedom Train (Early Reference Material)" folder.

40. Novins to John Foster Dulles and other members of the Documents Approval Committee, 22 September 1947, AHF Records, Box 209, "Documents–Re: Freedom Train" folder; Aldrich to Novins, 8 September 1947, Aldrich Collection, Box 19, "American Heritage Foundation, September 1947."

41. Walter White to Winthrop Aldrich, 18 July 1947, AHF Records, Box 209, "Documents–Re: Freedom Train" folder. For Novins's response, see for example, Novins to Louis Wirth, 16 December 1947, in AHF Records, Box 198, "Area Summaries" folder.

42. "Freedom Train to Remedy a Lack," *P.M.*, 19 September 1947, found loose in AHF Records, Box 11; Helen Steele to Elizabeth Hamer, 12 September 1947, and Elizabeth Hamer to Helen Steele, 28 October 1947, both in NARS Freedom Train Records, Box 2, "Tour of the Freedom Train (Pt. 5), From 10/1/47 to 12/15/47" folder.

43. Lyle C. Wilson to Edward Shugrue, 16 October 1947; Edward Shugrue to Lyle C. Wilson, 24 November 1947; and Novins to Brophy, 11 December 1947; all in AHF Records, Box 209, "Documents–Re: Freedom Train" folder.

44. Novins to George E. Dizard, 22 March 1948, AHF Records, Box 209, "Documents–Re: Freedom Train" folder.

45. Frank Monaghan to Brophy, 16 March 1948, AHF Records, Box 209, "Documents–Re: Freedom Train" folder.

46. The thirtieth document was President Truman's 1946 proclamation granting independence to the Philippines.

47. Novins to Brophy, 19 July 1948, AHF Records, Box 212, "General: Jan.–Sept. 1947" folder.

48. For this and the following paragraph, see 29 September 1947 memo from the educational department of the Communist Party to all district educational directors, in Aldrich Collection, Box 19, "American Heritage Foundation, September 1947" folder.

49. "Statement by the AG before the House of Representatives Committee on Expenditures in the Executive Departments concerning the Freedom Train," 18 June 1947, HSTL, Tom C. Clark Papers, Box 37, "Freedom Train (1)" folder.

50. Fellowship of Reconciliation leaflet in HSTL, Dick Dickson Papers, Box 1, Scrapbook Vol. 6; Memo from the FBI Director to the Attorney General, 26 September 1947, in HSTL, Tom C. Clark Papers, Box 37, "Freedom Train (2)" folder.

51. See Howard Fast, "One Man's Heritage," 6; and A. B. Magil, "Unfinished Business," 10, both in *New Masses*, 30 September 1947.

52. Richard O. Boyer, "The Bill of Rights is Bed-Rock," *New Masses*, 30 September 1947, 3; Memo from the FBI Director to the Attorney General, 26 September 1947; "Cops Route Conchies Picketing Freedom Train," *New York Daily News*, 26 September 1947; "Memorandum Report Submitted by Thomas D'A. Brophy to the Board of Trustees, October 6, 1947" in Aldrich Collection, Box 19,

"American Heritage Foundation, Board of Trustees, 1947" folder; Bradsher, "Taking America's Heritage to the People," 238; John Stanford, for the Committee of the Communist Party of Houston, to Mayor Oscar Holcombe, Members of the City Council, and Chief of Police, 9 February 1948, in Brophy Papers, Box 16, Folder 4.

53. A list of all the organizations represented at the White House conference can be found in "The First Two Years: A Progress Report to the Board of Trustees of the American Heritage Foundation," AHF Records, Box 17.

54. McCormick to Aldrich, 8 September 1947, Aldrich Collection, Box 19, "American Heritage Foundation, September 1947" folder.

55. For additional information on the American Heritage Foundation's efforts to woo McCormick and other Midwestern conservatives, see: Brophy to Aldrich, 14 July 1947 and 6 August 1947, in "American Heritage Foundation, July 1947" folder; Robert E. Wilson to Aldrich, 21 August 1947, in "American Heritage Foundation, August 1947" folder; "Commies Admit Plot to 'Smear' Freedom Train," *Chicago Tribune*, 11 September 1947, in "American Heritage Foundation, September 1947" folder; and Aldrich to Robert E. Wilson, 2 October 1947, and "A Vote Buying Plot Scented in 'Freedom Train,'" *Chicago Tribune*, 28 May 1947, both in "American Heritage Foundation, October 1947" folder; all in Aldrich Collection, Box 19. The National Blue Star Mothers of America, another right-wing group, continued to attack the train for promoting the United Nations and for including among its organizers members of B'nai B'rith. See leaflet entitled "Freedom Train Junket Can Lead to the Enslavement of Christendom," in HSTL, Tom C. Clark Papers, Box 38, "Freedom Train (3)" folder.

56. For this and the following paragraph, see various clippings loose in AHF Records, Box 11.

57. "100,000 Besiege Freedom Train in Brooklyn, Only 10,000 Get In," *New York Herald Tribune*, 28 September 1947; "Brooklyn Hails Freedom Train," *NYT*, 28 September 1947; and "'Melting Pot' Sees the Freedom Train," *NYT*, 26 September 1947. Brophy to John R. Steelman, 3 November 1947, Brophy Papers, Box 12, Folder 9.

58. "The First Two Years: A Progress Report to the Board of Trustees of the American Heritage Foundation," 110, 143, AHF Records, Box 17; "Freedom Train In; Opening Tomorrow: 10,000 See Its Exhibits at Stop in Patterson," *New York Herald Tribune*, 24 September 1947; program for the Chester, Pennsylvania, Freedom Rally held 19 November 1947, NAACP Records, Box II-A-359, "American Heritage Foundation, General, 1947–49" folder.

59. Lyman C. Hunt, Burlington Superintendent of Schools, to J. Edward Shugrue, national director of the American Heritage Foundation, 30 September 1947, Aldrich Collection, Box 19, "American Heritage Foundation: Board of Trustees, 1947" folder.

60. Novins to W. K. Hollander, 12 January 1948, AHF Records, Box 208, "Confidential" folder; "The First Two Years," 7, 22.

61. This pamphlet was written before Freedom Train organizers decided to downplay the word "democracy." "Conference at the White House for the Purpose

of Organizing the American Heritage Program and Inaugurating the Freedom Train," AHF Record, Box 198, "White House Conference" folder. For this and the following paragraph, also see "The First Two Years," 7–9.

62. For this and the following paragraph, see "The First Two Years," 7–9.

63. "The First Two Years," 15, 90–106. Also see contents of the following folders in Aldrich Collection, Box 20: "American Heritage Foundation, Feb. 1948," "American Heritage Foundation, June 1948," "American Heritage Foundation, July–August 1948," and "American Heritage Foundation, Nov.–Dec. 1948."

64. The "nine promises of a good citizen" are spelled out in the AHF booklet, *Good Citizen: The Rights and Duties of an American*, which was widely distributed by corporations and schools. This can be found in AHF Records, Box 200. For an example of an advertisement encouraging active citizenship, see "Let *Him* Do It," AHF Records, Box 208, "Confidential" folder. A voter registration drive held in Los Angeles in conjunction with the Freedom Train's visit raised voter registration there to a new high and stimulated similar campaigns in other cities on the train's tour. "The First Two Years," 154.

65. Brophy to Olds, 29 July 1947, in "American Heritage Foundation, July 1947" folder; and Brophy to Aldrich, 19 November 1947, in "American Heritage Foundation, November 1947" folder, both in Aldrich Collection, Box 19.

66. The letter was redrafted after an aide pointed out that that it was "a most dangerous one over the signature of the President of the Foundation." Draft letter from Brophy to James G. Blaine, 29 August 1952; memo from C. M. Vandeburg to Brophy, 5 September 1952; both in Brophy Papers, Box 12, Folder 9.

67. *Good Citizen*, 43; copy for "My Country Quiz of Thee" ad, AHF Records, Box 208, "Confidential" folder.

68. Monaghan, *Heritage of Freedom*, 44; The First Two Years," 139–44.

69. Memo from Brophy to Aldrich, 28 April 1947, Aldrich Collection, Box 19, "American Heritage Foundation, March–April 1947" folder; *Good Citizen*, 61; "The First Two Years," 139. I have slightly modified the formatting of the original quote.

70. "Remarks by Winthrop W. Aldrich in Connection with the Inauguration of the Freedom Train, Grand Central Terminal, New York, Wednesday, September 24, 1947" Aldrich Collection, Box 19, "American Heritage Foundation, September 1947" folder.

71. See for example, the remarks of Boston's Archbishop Cushing, quoted in "The First Two Years," 140.

72. "The First Two Years," 105–14.

73. *Good Citizen*, 5. Louis Novins to Jack P. Cunningham, 28 July 1947, AHF Records, Box 208, "Confidential" folder; "Remarks before the Advertising Club of Boston, Thomas D'A. Brophy, May 14, 1948," Brophy Papers, Box 25, Folder 1.

74. For this and the next two paragraphs, see AHF Records, Box 214, contents of "Labor–Management Luncheon–American Heritage Foundation" folder.

75. It is unclear whether Balaban's speech was ever reprinted. However, Cardinal Spellman, who also addressed the luncheon, worked part of Balaban's address into a later sermon.

76. Granger to Brophy, 27 June 1947, AHF Records, Box 212, "A.H.F. General, Jan.–Sept. 1947" folder.

77. Brophy to Novins, 1 July 1947, AHF Records, Box 212, "A.H.F. General, Jan.–Sept. 1947" folder.

78. Tom Clark to President Truman, 2 June 1947, in HSTL, Tom C. Clark Papers, Box 37, "Freedom Train (1)" folder.

79. Draft of letter by Novins to Walter White and Lester Granger and for release to the press, 29 September 1947, AHF Records, Box 219, "Segregation–A.H.F." folder; Brophy to Charles Luckman, 12 July 1947, Aldrich Collection, Box 19, "American Heritage Foundation, July 1947" folder.

80. Draft of letter by Novins to Walter White and Lester Granger and for release to the press, dated 29 September 1947. Edward Stanley, the liaison between the attorney general's office and the AHF, prefaced a letter to Louis Novins with the comment: "I had a long talk on the telephone with Mr. Brophy, and I gathered that no dramatic action is contemplated in respect to the race problem." Edward Stanley to Novins, 24 July 1947, AHF Records, Box 208, "Confidential" folder.

81. Stanley to Novins, 24 July 1947.

82. "Memorandum to Mr. White from Mr. Wilkins," 15 August 1947, NAACP Records, Box II-A-359, "The American Heritage Foundation, Freedom Train–General, 1947–49" folder; "Freedom Train" spread from October issue of *Our World*, AHF Records, Box 219, "Segregation–A.H.F." folder. (The October issue of *Our World* was released in early September.)

83. In addition to pages from *Our World* cited above, see text of "The Freedom Train" by Irving Berlin, NAACP Papers, Box II-A-359, "AHF Press Releases–Newspaper Clippings, 1947" folder; John P. Davis to Barney Balaban, 5 September 1947, AHF Records, Box 219, "Segregation–A.H.F." folder. Langston Hughes' poem ran in the 15 September 1947 issue of the *New Republic*.

84. Brophy to Davis, 6 September 1947, and Davis to Brophy, 10 September 1947, AHF Records, Box 219, "Segregation–A.H.F." folder.

85. Paul Robeson's column, "Plain Talk," appeared in the 27 September 1947 issue of *People's Voice*, a leftist African-American newspaper that had been founded in 1942 by Adam Clayton Powell, Jr. Robeson began his column "I want freedom itself not a Freedom Train." FBI Director Edgar J. Hoover alerted the attorney general and American Heritage Foundation officials to the column.

86. Telegram from F. D. Patterson to Aldrich, 22 September 1947, in "American Heritage Foundation, September 1947" folder, and "Minutes of the Meeting of the Board of Trustees, October 8, 1947 at 2:30 p.m." in "American Heritage Foundation, Board of Trustees, 1947" folder; both in Aldrich Collection, Box 19.

87. Memo from Fitzgerald to Brophy and Novins, 29 September 1947, and memo from Novins to Fitzgerald, 1 October 1947, both in AHF Records, Box 219, "Segregation–A.H.F." folder.

88. Novins to Fitzgerald, 1 October 1947; "Minutes of the Meeting of the Board of Trustees, October 8, 1947 at 2:30 p.m."

89. Margaret Patterson to Aldrich, 12 January 1948, Aldrich Collection, Box 20, "American Heritage Foundation, Jan. 1948" folder.

90. Gloster B. Current to John M. Rae, 24 November 1947, NAACP Records, Box II-A-359, "American Heritage Foundation, Freedom Train–General, 1947–1949" folder; telegram from Walter White to Aldrich, 15 October 1947; letter from Novins to Walter White, 22 October 1947; and memo from Brophy to Winthrop Aldrich, 17 November 1947, all in AHF Records, Box 219, "Segregation–A.H.F." folder.

91. The Memphis episode is described in some detail in a letter and attachments sent by Louis Novins to *Boston Traveler* managing editor Harold Wheeler on 4 February 1948. See also Louis Novins to Mrs. Robert P. Patterson, 3 December 1947. Both are in AHF Records, Box 219, "Segregation–A.H.F." folder. Michael K. Honey, discusses Crump in *Southern Labor and Black Civil Rights: Organizing Memphis Workers* (Urbana: University of Illinois Press, 1993), 8, 246.

92. In addition to items in the previous footnote, see Margaret Patterson to Brophy, 25 November 1947; and Harry T. Kendall to Louis Novins, 21 November 1947, both in AHF Records, Box 219, "Segregation–A.H.F." folder. Also see Novins to Aldrich, 3 December 1947, Aldrich Collection, Box 19, "American Heritage Foundation, December 1947" folder.

93. See telegram to Novins from the Muncie NAACP, dated 26 November 1947; F. D. Patterson to Novins, 26 November 1947; and Thomas S. Flynn to Novins, 21 November 1947, all in AHF Records, Box 219, "Segregation–A.H.F." folder.

94. See Novins to Harold Wheeler, 4 February 1948, AHF Records, Box 219, "Segregation–A.H.F." folder. Also see a 24 November 1947 editorial in the *Memphis Press-Scimitar*, in Aldrich Collection, Box 19, "American Heritage Foundation, November 1947" folder.

95. Novins to Harold Wheeler, 4 February 1948; Novins to Mrs. Robert P. Patterson, 3 December 1947.

96. Mrs. Harry Jay to Novins, 22 November 1947, AHF Records, Box 219, "Segregation–A.H.F." folder. For this and the following paragraph, see letters to the editor clipped from Memphis papers in the same folder.

97. "Progress Report, Week Ending Nov. 22, 1947" by Eric Friedheim; "Progress Report, Week Ending Nov. 28, 1947," by Eric Friedheim; and "Memo to All Area Directors from J. Edward Shugrue," 24 November 1947, all in AHF Records, Box 207, untitled folders.

98. Memo from Brophy to Aldrich, 17 November 1947, AHF Records, Box 219, "Segregation–A.H.F." folder.

99. Brophy to Novins, 19 November 1947; and Novins to Aldrich, 21 November 1947, both in AHF Records, Box 219, "Segregation–A.H.F." folder.

100. Walter White's suggestion is mentioned in an unsigned, undated note attached to a telegram from Emory O. Jackson to White. The telegram, dated 5 December 1947, is in NAACP Records, Box II-A-359, "American Heritage Foundation, Freedom Train, Alabama, 1947–48" folder. See also "Freedom Train to Skirt 2 Cities; Many in South Lift 'Jim Crowism,'" *NYT*, 25 December 1947.

101. Emory O. Jackson to Walter White, 16 December 1947, NAACP Records, Box II-A-359, "American Heritage Foundation–Freedom Train, Alabama, 1947–1948" folder.

102. Emory O. Jackson's "Freedom Train Report" and attached resolution of the Birmingham NAACP, both in AHF Records, Box 220, "Birmingham (Ala.) Incident" folder. See also Jackson to White, 16 December 1947.

103. "NAACP Citizens Committee's Statement Prepared for Presentation to the Birmingham City Commission Tuesday Morning, December 16, 1947"; and Emory O. Jackson to Walter White, December 29, 1947, both in NAACP Records, Box II-A-359, "American Heritage Foundation–Freedom Train, Alabama, 1947–48" folder. Jackson estimated that black citizens of Birmingham sent more than three hundred telegrams protesting the plan. Many examples can be found in AHF Records, Box 220, "Birmingham (Ala.) Incident" folder.

104. Margaret Patterson to Winthrop Aldrich, 12 January 1948, Aldrich Collection, Box 20, "American Heritage Foundation, January 1948" folder; untitled press release describing Birmingham episode issued 24 December 1947, AHF Records, Box 219, "Segregation–A.H.F." folder.

105. Telegram from Emory O. Jackson to Walter White, 16 December 1947; and E. W. Taggert to Walter White, 30 December 1947; both in NAACP Records, Box II-A-359, "American Heritage Foundation, Freedom Train, Alabama, 1947–48" folder.

106. Jackson to Aldrich, 22 December 1947, AHF Records, Box 220, "Birmingham (Ala.) Incident" folder.

107. Public Safety Commissioner Eugene Bull Connor and Commissioner of Public Improvement J. W. Morgan signed the telegram; Cooper Green did not. Untitled press release concerning events in Birmingham.

108. Telegram from Walter White to Louis Novins, 24 December 1947, AHF Records, Box 220, "Birmingham (Ala.) Incident" folder; typescript of Graphic Syndicates column by Walter White for release 1 January 1948, NAACP Records, Box II-A-359, "American Heritage Foundation–Freedom Train, Alabama, 1947–48" folder; "Racial Honor Roll Lists 19 Winners," *NYT*, 9 February 1948; "Freedom Train Visitors Dent New Orleans Jimcrow (stet)," undated clipping from the *Daily Worker* found in NAACP Papers, Box II-A-359, "American Heritage Foundation–Freedom Train, General, 1947–49" folder.

109. Edward J. Meeman, editor of the *Memphis Press-Scimitar,* to Brophy, 2 October 1948, Brophy Papers, Box 16, Folder 6; Honey, *Southern Labor and Black Civil Rights,* 248–49.

110. The *Adventures of Superman* radio show considered airing a program that featured Superman, the Freedom Train, and a black youth working together to help a southern city overcome its "un-American" hatreds. A five-page story outline of this *Superman* program is included in the papers of a consultant who worked on the series, however it is not clear whether the show was ever aired. See CSAA Records, Box 24, Folder 240.

111. See memos dated March 4 and 5, 1948, NARS Freedom Train Records, Box 2, "746-E7, Tour of the Freedom Train (Pt. 6), From 1/5/48 to 6/9/48" folder.

Chapter 8

1. James E. Miller, "Taking Off the Gloves: The United States and the Italian Elections of 1948," *Diplomatic History* 7 (1983): 35–36.

2. Quoted in Richard Robbins, "Letters to Italy–A Reconsideration," *Common Ground* 10 (Autumn 1949): 40.

3. "Italian 'Freedom Flight'," *NYT*, 27 March 1948; "One Thing and Another," *NYT*, 28 March 1948, Sec. II; "Italians Warned of Red 'Slavery'," *NYT*, 23 March 1948.

4. Sylvan Gotshal and Halsey Munson, "Letters to Italy," *Common Ground* 9 (Autumn 1948): 4, 6, 11.

5. Such efforts at public diplomacy have received relatively little attention from diplomatic historians; they have been all but ignored by historians of the domestic U.S.

6. For a brief overview of some of these projects, see Scott Lucas, *Freedom's War: The American Crusade Against the Soviet Union* (New York: New York University Press, 1999), 107–27.

7. "Preliminary Outline of Program for a Crusade for Freedom: A Project of the American Heritage Foundation," AHF Records, Box 17, "Crusade for Freedom Releases" folder.

8. For an extended discussion of right-wing populism during the early Cold War, see Michael Kazin, *The Populist Persuasion: An American History*, rev. ed. (Ithaca, N.Y.: Cornell University Press, 1998), 165–93.

9. For instance, in his famous Wheeling, West Virginia, speech delivered on 9 February 1950, Sen. McCarthy described Alger Hiss as "the man who sold out the Christian world to the atheistic world." Ellen Schrecker, ed., *The Age of McCarthyism: A Brief History with Documents*, 2nd ed. (Boston: Bedford/St. Martin's, 2002), 241.

10. David M. Kennedy, *Over Here: The First World War and American Society* (New York: Oxford University Press, 1980), 65.

11. Quoted in Walter A. Jackson, *Gunnar Myrdal and America's Conscience: Social Engineering and Racial Liberalism, 1938–1987* (Chapel Hill: North Carolina University Press, 1990), 149.

12. Quoted in Louis Adamic, *Two-Way Passage* (New York: Harper & Brothers, 1941), 260–61.

13. Henry Agard Wallace, "The Price of Free World Victory," *VSD* 8 (1 June 1942): 482.

14. Many Republicans feared that a peacetime propaganda agency would be used to help reelect President Truman or to spread New Deal tenets around the globe.

15. "Pearson Go-Round," *Newsweek*, 22 November 1948, 58; Drew Pearson, "The Washington Merry-Go-Round" column, *WP*, 20 December 1947, Sec. B; "Friendship on Wheels," *Newsweek*, 1 December 1947, 22; Edward J. Nickel, "Generosity: An American Tradition," *Parade*, 21 December 1947, 5.

16. Theodore A. Wilson and Richard D. McKinzie, "Save the Wheat, Save the Meat, Save the Peace: The Food Crusade of 1947," *Prologue* 3 (Winter 1971): 136.

17. "City Hails Friendship Train; Food Total Is Put at 270 Cars," *NYT*, 19 November 1947; Drew Pearson, "Washington Merry-Go-Round" column, *WP*, 12 December 1947, Sec. C, and 30 December 1947, Sec. B; "Trains of Friendship and Freedom Meet," *NYT*, 18 November 1947; scrapbooks five and six in Dick Dickson Papers, HSTL. The hoopla surrounding the train's passage across the United

States—and the coverage given the distribution of food in Europe—suggests that its intended audience was not simply foreign.

18. Scrapbook five, Drew Dickson Papers; "City Hails Friendship Train."
19. Gotshal and Munson, "Letters to Italy," 6; Robbins, "Letters to Italy – A Reconsideration," 43; Drew Pearson, "Washington Merry-Go-Round" column, *WP*, 30 March 1948 and 24 April 1948, Sec. B.
20. Miller, "Taking Off the Gloves," 40–45.
21. Byington's confidential dispatch of 28 January 1948 is printed in U.S. Department of State, *Foreign Relations of the United States, 1948*, vol. 3 (Washington, D.C., 1974), 822–23. Although Byington did not cite Pearson specifically, he did note that the idea was "suggested by several Americans in Italy who are not connected with the Government." Most news organizations credited the columnist with launching the Letters to Italy campaign, and Pearson covered it extensively in his columns.
22. John P. Diggins, *Mussolini and Fascism The View from America* (Princeton: Princeton University Press, 1972), 84; "Il Progresso Propone L'Invio D'Un Milione Di Lettere In Italia Per Combattere La Manaccia Del Comunismo," *Il Progresso Italo-Americano*, 19 January 1948; "To Tell Italians of Gifts," *NYT*, 24 January 1948. *Il Progresso* regularly ran articles on the campaign, as well as sample letters and writing instructions.
23. "Friendship Train Gets Pledges Here," *NYT*, 15 November 1947.
24. Italian Fascist authorities helped Pope acquire his newspaper empire, and he accepted free telegraph service and other special privileges from them throughout the 1930s. Pope, in turn, hailed Mussolini in the pages of his papers and raised vast sums for Italy during the Ethiopian War. Only after President Roosevelt warned Pope personally in 1941 did the publisher repudiate Mussolini. During the war, Pope endorsed the Italian-American Labor Council's call for a national conference to unify Italian-American groups. John Diggins calls the resulting committee "an expedient fusion of ex-Fascist sympathizers and anti-Fascist fighters: the former seeking new democratic respectability, the latter trying to organize for a coming showdown with the Stalinists." Diggins, *Mussolini and Fascism*, 84–86, 109, 303, 347–48, 401, 404–5.
25. Miller, "A Question of Loyalty," 57–59.
26. Undated flier addressed to "Citizens of Harlem," Vito Marcantonio Papers, NYPL, Box 51, "International Relations; Italy, Assistance To" folder.
27. Gotshal and Munson, "Letters to Italy," 6–8; "Italian 'Freedom Flight'" *NYT*, 27 March 1948; "La Campagna Delle Lettere All'Italia," *L'Italia*, 2 March 1948; "100.000 Lettere All'Italia," *L'Italia*, 26 March 1948; "L'Inizio Della Campagna Per L'Invio Di Lettere In Italia," *L'Italia*, 30 March 1948.
28. For instance, the *Denver Post* and a local Denver theater paid the cost of cablegrams sent to Italy, as did the Chamber of Commerce in St. Petersburg, Florida. Alexander Smith and Sons Carpet Co. of Yonkers, New York, offered to send airmail letters to Italy. And in Syracuse, New York, form letters were circulated by the Republican Club in cooperation with the Catholic Church. Gotshal and Munson, "Letters to Italy," 10; "Pleas to Italy Ask Vote Against Reds," *NYT*,

8 April 1948; E. Edda Martinez and Edward A. Suchman, "Letters from America and the 1948 Elections in Italy," *Public Opinion Quarterly* 14 (Spring 1950): 113.

29. James Edward Miller, *The United States and Italy, 1940–1950: The Politics and Diplomacy of Stabilization* (Chapel Hill: University of North Carolina Press, 1986), 244. In "Taking Off the Gloves" (44), Miller notes that the Vatican—though firmly anticommunist—was initially "ambivalent about Italy's nascent democracy." With American encouragement, however, "the Church edged toward full participation in the anti-Communist coalition."

30. Martinez and Suchman, "Letters from America," 121–23.

31. "Group to Aid Italians to Fight Communists," *NYT*, 17 March 1948; "Lawyer Here Fights Communism in Italy," *NYT*, 28 March 1948.

32. Martinez and Suchman, "Letters from America," 117–18.

33. *Il Progresso Italo-Americano*, 24 January 1948.

34. *Il Progresso Italo-Americano*, 21 January 1948.

35. Martinez and Suchman, "Letters from America," 113, 115. The widespread use of form and sample letters during the campaign suggests that organizers were not sure individual Italian Americans could be counted on to send the "right" message. It also suggests that the intended audience for the campaign was as much domestic as foreign: U.S. officials, Catholic priests, and conservative Italian-American leaders may have hoped to convert the majority of Italian Americans to active anticommunism. At the same time, Italian-American *prominenti* probably hoped to prove the loyalty of their community.

36. Martinez and Suchman, "Letters from America," 114–15, 122; "La campagna delle lettere all'Italia," *L'Italia*, 2 March 1948.

37. "La campagna della lettere all'Italia"; Gotshal and Munson, "Letters to Italy," 5, 7–8.

38. *Il Progresso Italo-Americano*, 19 January 1948.

39. Martinez and Suchman, "Letters from America," 114.

40. *L'Italia*, 14 April 1948.

41. *Il Progresso Italo-Americano*, 23 January 1948.

42. In early March, Ambassador Dunn sent a telegram to the State Department suggesting that American letter-writers tell their friends and relatives that they would no longer be able to send gift and food packages if the Italians voted the Democratic Front into power. Stephen Ambrose, *Rise to Globalism: American Foreign Policy Since 1938* (Baltimore: Penguin Books, 1971), 90; U.S. Department of State, *Foreign Relations of the United States, 1948*, vol. 3 (Washington, D.C., 1974), 842; Martinez and Suchman, "Letters from America," 115, 118; "Letters to Be Sent to Italy," *NYT*, 22 March 1948.

43. For instance, Monsignor Monteleone, the same priest who passed out form letters to his parishioners, sent an additional five thousand form letters to friends in Rome, Naples, Turin, Milan, and Genoa to be distributed in factories there. Martinez and Suchman, "Letters from America," 113.

44. Martinez and Suchman, "Letters from America," 123.

45. Ronald L. Filippelli, *American Labor and Postwar Italy, 1943–1953: A Study in Cold War Politics* (Stanford: Stanford University Press, 1989), 21–26.

46. Martinez and Suchman, "Letters from America," 113; Robbins, "Letters to Italy–A Reconsideration," 43.

47. Pope's address to the Citizen's Committee of the Columbus Scholarship Fund is quoted in Martinez and Suchman, "Letters from America," 112.

48. Robbins, "Letters to Italy – A Reconsideration," 41.

49. Miller, "Taking Off the Gloves," 48; "Pleas to Italy Ask Vote Against Reds, *NYT*, 8 April 1948; "Salvemini Denies Protest on Italy," *NYT*, 16 April 1948.

50. See, for instance, *Il Progresso Italo-Americano*, 21 January 1948.

51. The fact that Louis Adamic joined this appeal suggests the ways in which the shift from antifascism to anticommunism altered America's political landscape. "Sets Founding Day of Wallace Party," *NYT*, 12 April 1948; "Appeal to Voters in Italy Assailed," *NYT*, 15 April 1948; "Salvemini Denies Protest on Italy," *NYT*, 16 April 1948.

52. Some news accounts referred to the committee sponsoring the rally as the *Italian American* Committee for Free Elections in Italy (emphasis added). "Appeal to Voters in Italy Assailed," *NYT*, 15 April 1948; undated typescript, Vito Marcantonio Papers, NYPL, Box 68, "Speeches and Press Releases, Misc." folder; "Pleas to Italy Ask Vote Against Reds," *NYT*, 8 April 1940.

53. Gotshal and Munson, "Letters to Italy," 11.

54. The letter-writing campaign—and particularly its role in publicizing the threat of a U.S. aid cutoff—may have proved particularly important in villages in Southern Italy and Sicily, where leftists had made inroads with talk of land redistribution. In such areas, where inhabitants relied heavily on "gift packages from uncles and cousins in the United States," one Christian Democratic official wrote, the letters from America "struck home…with the force of lightening." "U.S. Letters Anger Leftists," *NYT*, 1 April 1948; "I Comunisti Italiani Protestano Per La Valanga Di Lettere Dall'America," *L'Italia*, 2 April 1948; "Letter Campaign Denounced," *NYT*, 9 April 1948; Martinez and Suchman, "Letters from America," 120; Miller, "Taking Off the Gloves," 51. A letter reprinted in the *New York Times* in late April suggests that some Italians may have resented American advice, even as they followed it: "Following your suggestion, most of my neighbors and my family have agreed not to vote the Communist ticket," Conolato Luvera wrote his brother Paul of Anacortes, Washington. "I understand you people will be having an election soon. We all hope that you and your neighbors don't mind if we tell you how you should vote."

55. Martinez and Suchman, "Letters from America," 120.

56. In historical accounts, the Berlin blockade and subsequent military and diplomatic milestones of the Cold War have consistently overshadowed discussions of the postwar "peace" movement in Europe. In the late 1940s and early 1950s, however, this Soviet effort at "public diplomacy" stirred deep concern among U.S. political, intellectual, and business leaders and prompted a rapid rebuilding of the U.S.'s information arsenal. The most sustained treatment of the postwar peace movement in Europe can be found in Marshall Shulman, *Stalin's Foreign Policy Reappraised* (Cambridge: Harvard University Press, 1963). David Caute

describes the peace movement as a "world crusade" in *The Fellow-Travellers: A Postscript to the Enlightenment* (New York: Macmillan, 1973), 289.

57. Memo from Winthrop Rockefeller to Winthrop Aldrich, n.d., in "Letters from America–Rockefeller Correspondence" folder; and unsigned letter to Mrs. De-Witt Stetten, 19 January 1949, in "Letters from America - Winthrop Rockefeller Memorandum on Future Plans and Correspondence" folder; both in ACNS Records, Shipment 5, Box 2 (hereafter S5/B2).

58. Draft letter from Winthrop Rockefeller dated 31 March 1950 in ACNS Records, S5/B2, "Letters from America–Rockefeller Correspondence, ca. 1949–1953" folder; E. C. Shaw to Paul G. Hoffman, 20 January 1949, ACNS Records, S6/B17, "CCAU Letters to Europe Project" folder.

59. Memo from Winthrop Rockefeller to Winthrop Aldrich, n.d.

60. *What Do Europeans Think About the United States?* brochure, ACNS Records, S5/B2, "Letters from America–Rockefeller Correspondence" folder; William Charles Beyer, "Searching for *Common Ground*, 1940–1949: An American Literary Magazine and Its Related Movements in Education and Politics" (Ph.D. diss., University of Minnesota, 1988), 346; Henry Lee Munson to Thomas D'Arcy Brophy, 24 May 1949, Brophy Papers, Box 26, Folder 3.

61. "Beliefs Most Seriously Hampering Understanding of the United States," n.d., ACNS Records, S5/B2, "Letters from America–Rockefeller Correspondence" folder. *What Do Europeans Think About the United States?* brochure.

62. Henry Lee Munson to William Sylvan, 27 March 1951, ACNS Records, S5/B2, "Letters from America–Rockefeller Correspondence, ca. 1949–53" folder; memo from C. E. Shaw to C. L. Alexander, 28 October 1949, ACNS Records, S6/B17, "CCAU Letters to Europe Project" folder.

63. Winthrop Rockefeller to Winthrop Aldrich, n.d., Aldrich Collection, Box 21, "American Heritage Foundation, January–February 1949" folder.

64. Charles W. Jackson to American Heritage Foundation president Thomas D'Arcy Brophy, 16 March 1949, Brophy Papers, Box 20, Folder 6; Dean Acheson to Brophy, 1 February 1950, in Aldrich Collection, Box 21, "American Heritage Foundation, January–June 1950" folder.

65. Henry Munson to Charles Shaw, 12 September 1949, ACNS Records, S6/B17, "CCAU Letters to Europe Project" folder.

66. Beyer, "Searching for *Common Ground*" provides an excellent history of the magazine. The Baltimore *Afro-American* is quoted on 257.

67. Ibid., 194, 201–5, 278–82, 336–38, 421.

68. Ibid., 223–27.

69. Ibid., 345–46, 350.

70. The biographical note appended to Gotshal's "Letters to Italy" piece noted that he was "active in the business, financial, and philanthropic world" and was chairman of the Board of the United Jewish Appeal of Greater New York. Gotshal and Munson, "Letters to Italy," 12; Beyer, "Searching for *Common Ground*," 301–3, 347–48, 351–53, 357.

71. *What Do Europeans Think About the United States?* brochure.

72. Form letter from Read Lewis to CCAU members, 17 May 1950, ACNS Records, S6/B5, "CCAU Board of Directors–Notices and Agenda, 1950" folder.

73. Adamic died of a gunshot wound. Historians still debate whether this was a murder or suicide. "Louis Adamic (1989–1951): His Life, Work, and Legacy," 2; Lees, "Louis Adamic and American Foreign Policy Makers"; Jeffrey Robert Ryan, "The Conspiracy That Never Was: United States Government Surveillance of Eastern European American Leftists, 1942–1959" (Ph.D. diss., Boston College, 1990), 198–202; Beyer, "The Search for *Common Ground*," 215–19.

74. Letter from H. David Hammond, 7 November 1949, ACNS Records, S6/B17, "CCAU Letters to Europe Project" folder.

75. Letter from Mrs. George M. Krall, 13 October 1949, ACNS Records, S6/B17, "CCAU Letters to Europe Project" folder.

76. Arthur M. Schlesinger, Jr., *The Vital Center: The Politics of Freedom* (Boston: Houghton Mifflin Co., Riverside Press Cambridge, 1949), 36.

77. "Minutes of Board of Directors' Meeting," 14 November 1949, ACNS Records, S5/B2, "Letters from America–Advisory Committee, Minutes and Correspondence (3)" folder; form letter from Read Lewis to Board Members, 24 April 1950, ACNS Records, S6-B5, "CCAU Board of Directors–Notices and Agenda, 1950" folder.

78. "Truman Proclaims World-Wide Fight to Crush Red Lies," *NYT*, 21 April 1950.

79. The "Letters from America" releases were initially translated into twenty-two languages, but eventually that figure rose to twenty-five. Between May and August, 1950, most "Letters from America" columns and articles were translated into Chinese; but after China entered the Korean War, this tapered off dramatically. See "Letters from America, Chinese releases," ACNS Records, Reel 16, Frame 715 (hereafter R16/F715). Merely issuing a press release in a particular language did not insure that the article would be reprinted, but when the Common Council ran a "Letters from America" contest in 1954, it received copies of letters sent abroad in twenty-three languages. "Letters from America Contest," ACNS Records, S5/B2, "Letters from America–Advisory Committee (1)" folder.

80. "Suggestions from Margaret Anderson and Florence Widutie," n.d., ACNS Records, S6/B17, "CCAU–Letters to Europe Project" folder.

81. "Will *You* Take Part in the *Campaign of Truth?*" brochure, ACNS Records, S6/B5, "CCAU Letters from American Committee–Agenda, Minutes, Papers" folder.

82. See the following on ACNS Microfilm: "Campaign of Truth" (R21/F250); "The Strength of America" (R21/F258); "June Is the Time of Weddings" (R21/F274; and "Culture in America" (R21/F295).

83. "Letters from America Committee Meeting," 14 November 1951, in "Letters from America–Advisory Committee, Minutes and Correspondence (2)" folder; and "A Short Summary of the Articles and Columns Released to the Foreign Language Press," 31 January 1952, in "Letters from America–Advisory Committee (2)" folder; both in ACNS Records, S5/B2; "Digests of Sample Weekly Columns and Feature Articles," 31 December 1953, ACNS Records, S5/B1, "Letters from America–Advisory Committee (1)" folder. On ACNS Microfilm, see: "As Others See Us" by Mrs. Franklin Delano Roosevelt (R21/F271); "American

Women Do Their Part" by Mrs. J. L. Blair Buck (R21/F283); "On Guard for America" by General George C. Marshall (R21/F316).

84. ACNS Microfilm: "The Pen of America" (R21/F254); "Speaking of Big Business" (R21/F260); "A Far-Reaching Accomplishment" (R21/F270).

85. "After the Fourth of July," ACNS Microfilm (R21/F277). For examples of the call for Christmas and Easter cards, see press releases dated 14 March 1951 and 7 December 1951, ACNS Records, S5/B2, "Letters from America–Projects, ca. 1951" folder.

86. ACNS Microfilm: "Culture in America" (R21/F295); "The Home Front" (R21/F301).

87. For an interesting discussion of the use of "democratic discussion groups" as tools of social engineering, see William Graebner, *The Engineering of Consent: Democracy and Authority in the Twentieth-Century America* (Madison: University of Wisconsin Press, 1987). The philosophy behind the discussion groups and other details of the program can be found in ACNS Records, S6/B17: "Discussion Groups: A Report and a Program," 31 July 1951, in "CCAU Discussion Groups–Fund Raising Reports, Programs, 1951" folder; and "Discussion Program with Nationality-Group Organizations: Report of the Director," n.d., in "CCAU Discussion Groups–Program and Material, 1953" folder.

88. "Discussion Groups: A Report and a Program." In "Gender and the 'American Way of Life': Women in the Americanization Movement," *Journal of American Ethnic History* 10 (Spring 1991): 3–20, John McClymer notes that the Americanization movement that burgeoned during World War I "was not so much a way of transforming immigrants and their children into real Americans as a campaign to fix the public meaning of Americanism."

89. In ACNS Records, S5/B2, see: "Letters from America: The Story of a Bold Campaign to Help Win the War of Ideas," 4, in "Letters from America–Advisory Committee (3)" folder; and "Let's Write Truth Letters to Europe," a reprint from *Fafnir News*, in "Odell, Robert H., Director, Letters from America, Correspondence and Publicity" folder.

90. The film is discussed and quoted in William L. Bird, Jr., *"Better Living": Advertising, Media, and the New Vocabulary of Business Leadership, 1935–1955* (Evanston, Ill.: Northwestern University Press, 1999), 168–70.

91. "An American Story," ACNS Records, S6/B5, "CCAU Letters from America Committee–Agenda, Minutes, Papers" folder; Scott Lucas, *Freedom's War: The American Crusade Against the Soviet Union* (New York: New York University Press, 1999), 112.

92. On ACNS Microfilm: "An Example–And an Offer!" (21/F312), and "This Is What Men Write!" (R 21/F331); "The Effect of Letters from America in Combating Communist Propaganda," ACNS Records, S6/B35, "CCAU Letters from America–Guide Materials Collected by R.H. Odell, director" folder.

93. For an overview of the discussion groups, see "Discussion Program with Nationality–Group Organizations"; Report of the Director. For detailed reports on some individual meetings, see ACNS S6/B17, "CCAU Discussion Groups–Reports, 1951–52" folder.

94. Free Europe Committee, *The Story of the World Freedom Bell* (Minneapolis: Nate L. Crabtree Co., 1951), 6.

95. General Lucius Clay, the Crusade's first national chairman, called for Americans to take "personal responsibility" in "Gen. Clay to Help Free-Europe Drive," *NYT*, 27 April 1950. The phrase "crusade for freedom" appears to have first received widespread public attention in news coverage of Herbert Hoover's speech to the 1936 Republican National Convention. Hoover compared the New Deal with the "march of socialism and dictatorships" in Europe and called upon the American people to enter upon a "holy crusade for liberty." Many news organizations, however, changed "liberty" to "freedom." See, for example, "Hoover Assails 'Socialist March,' *NYT*, 11 June 1936. The phrase was occasionally used during the war to describe the battle against the Axis powers.

96. Arch Puddington, *Broadcasting Freedom: The Cold War Triumph of Radio Free Europe and Radio Liberty* (Lexington: University Press of Kentucky, 2000), 22.

97. Dulles served in the Office of Strategic Services (OSS) during World War II and became director of the CIA in 1953. As Military Governor of Germany from March 1947 to May 1949, Clay engineered the Berlin airlift. C. D. Jackson has been described by Blanche Wiesen Cook as "the chief architect of America's psychological warfare effort during and after World War II." He worked for Time-Life, established the Council for Democracy in 1940, and worked in several psychological warfare positions during World War II. He became publisher of *Fortune* in 1949 and four years later was named special assistant to President Eisenhower. According to Cook, Jackson's "chief contribution to the American Century was his notion of 'Enterprise America': the need to achieve a partnership between business and government in the interests of economic expansion worldwide." Blanche Wiesen Cook, "First Comes the Lie: C. D. Jackson and Political Warfare," *Radical History Review* 31 (1984): 42–70, esp. 44 and 46.

98. Puddington, *Broadcasting Freedom*, 7, 12–13, 15. As Puddington explains, the effort to organize émigrés ultimately proved "daunting…due to the divisions and rivalries—personal and political—that separated even the most democratic-minded Poles, Czechoslovaks, and Hungarians."

99. Puddington, *Broadcasting Freedom*, 22–23; Collins, "The Free Europe Committee," 257–65.

100. "Preliminary Outline of Program for a Crusade for Freedom: A Project of the American Heritage Foundation," 14 May 1953, AHF Records, Box 17, "Crusade for Freedom Releases" folder.

101. "Text of Eisenhower Call for Crusade," *NYT*, 5 September 1950.

102. For an overview of the Advertising Council's work on behalf of the Crusade for Freedom, see the Council's annual reports beginning in 1950–51, Advertising Council Archives, 13/2/202.

103. Larry D. Collins, "The Free Europe Committee: American Weapons in the Cold War" (Ph.D. diss., Carlton University, 1973), 276.

104. "Scouts Aiding in 1951 Crusade for Freedom Campaign," *NYT*, 27 August 1951; "20,000 Newsies Raise $90,000," *NYT*, 4 April 1955; "Parades to Mark Washington Fete," *NYT*, 20 February 1955; "Commuter Gifts Asked," *NYT*, 23 October 1951;

"Crusade Drive Spurred," *NYT*, 17 October 1950; "'Crusade' Week Set by Theatre World," *NYT*, 14 October 1950; "Sermons to Stress Religious Liberty," *NYT*, 8 October 1950; "15,507,877 Signed Freedom Scroll," *NYT*, 21 December 1950. For more on the range of organizations supporting the effort, see "1954 Crusade for Freedom: An Interim Report to Friends and Contributors," AHF Records, Box 201.

105. Such public spectacles continued through at least 1954. That year the Crusade raised money by displaying the "Freedom Tank," a homemade armored car used by eight Czechs "to crash through the Iron Curtain." New York mayor Robert Wagner also dedicated a seventy-three-foot model of a radio tower that had been erected in the Time Square to dramatize the campaign, temporarily renaming the square Freedom Square. Such pageantry began to taper off in 1955. "To Show Freedom Tank," *NYT*, January 19 1950; "Tower Dramatizes Radio Fund Appeal," *NYT*, 20 February 1954.

106. *The Story of the World Freedom Bell.*

107. "Text of Eisenhower Call for Crusade," *NYT*, 5 September 1950; "The Freedom Crusade," *NYT*, 4 September 1950; "Crusade for Freedom" display ad sponsored by Bloomingdale's, *NYT*, 10 October 1950.

108. Ad entitled "A Plea to All Americans of All Faiths!" in Advertising Council Archives, 13/2/207, Box 69, File 636.

109. "Nation Needs 'Positive Acts' of Faith, Eisenhower Says," *NYT*, 8 February 1954; "Big Issue in D.C.: The Oath of Allegiance," *NYT*, 23 May 1954.

110. Mark Silk, *Spiritual Politics: Religion and America Since World War II* (New York: Simon and Schuster, 1988), 97–99.

111. "Sermons to Stress Religious Liberty," *NYT*, 8 October 1950; "Freedom Sunday Observed in City," *NYT*, 9 October 1950.

112. See, for instance, ad entitled "A Plea to All Americans of All Faiths!" in Advertising Council Archives, 13/2/207, Box 69, File 636.

113. "Freedom Crusade Calls for Prayers," *NYT*, 22 March 1952.

114. "Freedom Crusade Aided," *NYT*, 22 October 1951; "Rain Cuts Parade of Polish Groups," *NYT*, 8 October 1951; "Crusade Is Slated by 'Freedomgram,'" *NYT*, 21 September 1952.

115. Advertising Council Archives, 13/2/207, Box 69, File 636.

116. Advertising Council Archives, 13/2/207, Box 69, Files 636 and 551.

117. *NYT*, 5 December 1952.

118. Stephen J. Whitfield, *The Culture of the Cold War* (Baltimore: The Johns Hopkins University Press, 1991), chap. 5. For quotes from Whitfield and the textbook, see pp. 101–2.

119. "Freedom Crusade Is 'Rolling in High,'" *NYT*, 19 September 1951, Sec. F; also see Advertising Council Archives, 13/2/207, Box 69, File 598.

120. Collins, "The Free Europe Committee," 276; "Aids Freedom Crusade," *NYT*, June 1952; "Named National Chairman by Crusade for Freedom," *NYT*, 4 August 1952; "Heads Freedom Crusade," *NYT*, 4 September 1952.

121. Collins, "Free Europe Committee," 259.

122. Quoted in ibid., 333; "Tell U.S. Story Holman Pleads," *NYT*, 22 January 1956.

123. Collins, "The Free Europe Committee," 278; Puddington, *Broadcasting Freedom*, 23.

124. These phrases, taken from a *New York Times* editorial endorsing the campaign, appeared repeatedly in Crusade materials. "The Freedom Crusade," *NYT*, 4 September 1950.

125. Americans across the political spectrum sometimes used the term "crusade" to describe the Allied effort during World War II; but a phrase search of the historical *New York Times* (using the ProQuest database) suggests that "crusade for freedom" only came into widespread use in the 1950s. By the 1960s, the phrase was increasingly applied to both the civil rights movement and (retrospectively) to the antislavery movement. For example, see Dwight Lowell Dumond, *Antislavery: The Crusade for Freedom in America* (Ann Arbor: University of Michigan Press, 1961); and Alma Lutz, *Crusade for Freedom: Women of the Antislavery Movement* (Boston: Beacon, 1968). In 1991, African-American scholar Cornel West used the phrase in diagnosing the problems faced by the movement. "The power of the civil rights movement under Martin Luther King was its universalism," he said. "Now, instead of the civil rights movement being viewed as a *moral crusade for freedom*, it's become an expression of a particular interest group." "Rights Movement in Struggle for an Image as Well as a Bill," *NYT*, 3 April 1991, Sec. A, emphasis added.

126. "Five-Negro Slate Fails in Memphis," *NYT*, 22 August 1959; "Kennedy Relies on Negro Clergy," *NYT*, 14 September 1963.

127. "Eulogy for the Young Victims of the Sixteenth Street Baptist Church Bombing," delivered by Martin Luther King, Jr., at the Sixth Avenue Baptist Church in Birmingham, Alabama, on 18 September 1963. Available: http://www.stanford.edu/group/King/speeches/pub/Eulogy_for_the_martyred_children.html. (accessed 13 June 2006).

Conclusion

1. For instance, the report "The Power of the Democratic Idea" grew out of the work of two separate panels, one charged with focusing on the "U.S. Democratic Process" and the other on "The Moral Framework of National Purpose." Both panels were eventually discharged, and a third group was asked to write the final report. The papers of all three group panels can be found in Rockefeller Brothers Fund Archives, Special Studies Project Records, 1956–1960, Series 4, Rockefeller Archives Center, Tarrytown, New York.

2. Rockefeller Brothers Fund, *Prospect for America: The Rockefeller Panel Reports* (Garden City, N.Y.: Doubleday, 1961), xv, xx, 415.

3. U.S. President's Commission on National Goals, *Goals for Americans: Programs for Action in the Sixties, Comprising the Report of the President's Commission on National Goals and Chapters Submitted for the Consideration of the Commission* (Englewood Cliffs, N.J.: Prentice-Hall, 1960), xi, 3–23, 45.

4. R. W. B. Lewis, *The American Adam: Innocence, Tragedy and Tradition in the Nineteenth Century* (Chicago: University of Chicago Press, 1955), 1–2.

5. Louis Adamic, *From Many Lands*, 9th ed. (New York: Harper & Brothers, 1940), 298.

6. Carlos Bulosan, *America Is in the Heart: A Personal History* (1946; repr., Seattle: University of Washington Press, 1973), 310–12. For another example of left-ists seeking to export American values, see my discussion of the origins of the Salzburg Seminar in American Civilization in Wendy L. Wall, "The Idea of America: Democracy and the Dilemmas of Difference, 1935–1965" (Ph.D. diss., Stanford University, 1998), 290–339.

7. In *Black Is a Country: Race and the Unfinished Struggle for Democracy* ([Cambridge: Harvard University Press, 2004], 39), Nikhil Pal Singh argues that Myrdal's "distinction between theory and practice" was a "canny one," a "power-ful intellectual device for shoring up the universal basis of American national norms in the face of contrary evidence ever since." Singh is certainly right that the "American Creed" is far less universal than Myrdal suggested, but I believe he misinterprets the motives of Myrdal and many other liberal intellectuals of the time. I believe they were trying to "shore up" America's national norms largely to provide a tool with which to hold Americans accountable.

8. Alan Brinkley, *The End of Reform: New Deal Liberalism in Recession and War* (New York: Knopf, 1995), 5.

9. Brinkley describes the shift towards Keynesianism in *The End of Reform.*

10. In the postwar period, as anti-Semitism increasingly came to be seen as the archetypal prejudice, many liberals who might once have decried economic exploitation came to see heated economic conflict as every bit as dangerous to American society as religious and racial conflict.

11. John P. Dean and Alex Rosen, *A Manual of Intergroup Relations* (Chicago: University of Chicago Press, 1955), 125.

12. To be sure, not all Americans in the 1940s and 1950s subscribed to the notion of a "Judeo-Christian" tradition or agreed with Will Herberg's 1955 assertion that Protestantism, Catholicism, and Judaism were "equally and authentically American." The interfaith concept drew opposition from the Catholic hierarchy, from Protestant fundamentalists and evangelicals, and from some Jewish theologians. Many liberal intellectuals in the late 1940s and early 1950s also drew parallels between Catholicism and Communism, arguing that both threatened American democracy. The best examples of such thinking are two books by Paul Blanshard: *American Freedom and Catholic Power* (Boston: Beacon, 1949) and *Communism, Democracy, and Catholic Power* (Boston: Beacon, 1951). For an extended discussion of this phenomenon, see John T. McGreevy, "Thinking on One's Own: Catholicism in the American Intellectual Imagination, 1928–1960," *JAH* 84(1) (1997): 97–131.

13. Will Herberg, *Protestant-Catholic-Jew: An Essay in American Religious Sociology,* rev. ed. (New York: Doubleday & Co., 1960).

14. See, for instance, Samuel A. Mueller, "The New Triple Melting Pot: Herberg Revisited," *Review of Religious Research* 13 (Fall 1971): 18–33, and Ceri Peach, "Which Triple Melting Pot? A Re-examination of Ethnic Intermarriage in New Haven, 1900–1950," *Ethnic and Racial Studies* 3 (January 1980): 1–16.

15. Louis Finkelstein, J. Elliot Ross, and William Adams Brown, *The Religions of Democracy: Judaism, Catholicism and Protestantism in Creed and Life* (New York: Devin-Adair Co., 1941)

16. Herberg, *Protestant-Catholic-Jew*, 84.

17. Despite the significance of this development for American civic culture, it has received remarkably little attention from U.S. historians. Scholars have devoted some attention to the mid-century decline in anti-Catholicism and anti-Semitism and to the rise of religiosity in the U.S. during the Cold War. However, the emergence of Judeo-Christianity and the interfaith movement during and after WWII—and their relationship to discussions of American nationalism, pluralism, and consensus—have been largely neglected. This failure reflects a more general blind spot shared by many historians of the twentieth-century United States As John T. McGreevy concludes in "Faith and Morals in the United States, 1865–Present," *Reviews in American History* 26 (1998), "historians of the most religious nation in the industrial world understand their country's immediate past with little reference to religion." McGreevy attributes this neglect to two factors. He argues that the primary narratives used to organize twentieth-century U.S history have either been political or organizational, frameworks not clearly related to religious experience. In addition, "the institutions central to most accounts of twentieth century America—the federal government, corporations, and the professions—are precisely where religion seems least visible" (240). Although I suspect McGreevy is right, his observation is indeed ironic. During the early decades of the Cold War, both politicians and federal agencies (not to mention the mass media and many corporations) were deeply involved in promoting an adhesional religious faith. The contrast with atheist communism meant that the connection between American nationalism and American religion during the 1940s and 1950s was likely greater than it had been in decades.

    Two important exceptions to the general neglect described above are Mark Silk, *Spiritual Politics: Religion and America Since World War II* (New York: Simon & Schuster, 1988), 40–53; and Deborah Dash Moore, "Jewish GIs and the Creation of the Judeo-Christian Tradition," *Religion and American Culture* 8 (Winter 1998): 31-53. While Silk focuses heavily on intellectuals, particularly theologians, Moore focuses on Jews who served in the military during World War II.

18. For instance, racial lynching had long been a public spectacle in the South, attracting crowds that often included women and children. Lynching certainly continued after World War II, but increasingly it went underground.

19. Sacvan Bercovitch, *The American Jeremiad* (Madison: University of Wisconsin Press, 1978); David Howard-Pitney, "The Enduring Black Jeremiad: The American Jeremiad and Black Protest Rhetoric from Frederick Douglass to W. E. B. DuBois, 1841–1919," *American Quarterly* 38 (1986): 490–91.

20. King's "I Have a Dream" speech is available at http://www.stanford.edu/group/King/publications/speeches/address_at_march_on_washington.pdf (accessed 15 November 2006).

21. William H. Chafe, *Civilities and Civil Rights: Greensboro, North Carolina, and the Black Struggle for Freedom* (New York: Oxford University Press, 1980).

22. Carol Anderson, *Eyes Off the Prize: The United Nations and the African American Struggle for Human Rights, 1944–1955* (Cambridge: Cambridge University Press, 2003); Mary L. Dudziak, *Cold War Civil Rights: Race and the Image of American Democracy* (Princeton: Princeton University Press, 2000), especially. 11–13. In *Black Is a Country*, Nikhil Pal Singh shows that not all black intellectuals and activists abandoned these alternative rhetorics.

23. Howard-Pitney, "Enduring Black Jeremiad," 490.

24. Margaret Mead, *And Keep Your Powder Dry: An Anthropologist Looks at America*, new expanded ed. (New York: Morrow, 1965), xi, xxx.

25. Ibid., xii, xxx, 281.

26. Ibid., 309–10.

27. *Goals for Americans*, 3.

28. "To Fulfill These Rights," President Johnson's 1965 Commencement Address at Howard University, is available at http://www.lbjlib.utexas.edu/johnson/archives.hom/speeches.hom/650604.asp (accessed 24 June 2006).

29. I have drawn the term "ethno-racial pentagon" from David A. Hollinger, *Postethnic America: Beyond Multiculturalism* (New York: Basic Books, 1995), 8–9.

30. David W. Southern, *Gunnar Myrdal and Black-White Relations: The Use and Abuse of* An American Dilemma, *1944–1969* (Baton Rouge: Louisiana State University Press, 1987), 261–92.

31. The trustees' goals for a new Freedom Train are outlined in George Gallup to George Healy, Jr., 13 July 1965, AHF Records, Box 202, "Gallup Inquiry re: Freedom Train to Magazine Executives" folder. Excerpts from the executives' responses are in the folder labeled "Comments re: New Freedom Train" in the same box. The American Heritage Foundation decided not to revive the Freedom Train in the late 1960s, although a more modest version circled the U.S. in 1976.

32. Information on the American Assembly, together with copies of its various reports, is available at http://www.americanassembly.org/index.php (accessed 15 November 2006).

33. David Books, "Are We Really One Country?" *Atlantic Monthly,* December 2001, 53–65.

34. Robert Hughes refers to the dissolution of Americans' sense of "common citizenship" in *The Culture of Complaint: The Fraying of America* (New York: Oxford University Press, 1993). See also Todd Gitlin, *The Twilight of Common Dreams: Why America Is Wracked by Culture Wars* (New York: Metropolitan Books, 1995); and Robert D. Putnam, *Bowling Alone: The Collapse and Revival of American Community* (New York: Simon & Schuster, 2000), 18. The last quote comes from the cover of Tom Brokaw's bestseller, *The Greatest Generation* (New York: Random House, 1998).

Index

African-Americans, 26, 84, 92–93, 107, 111, 116, 277. *See also* Louis Adamic, *An American Dilemma*, Freedom Train; *The House I Live In*, Great Migration; National Association for the Advancement of Colored People; segregation
 acceptance in armed services, 150
 in civic unity movement and, 154–55
 within consensus culture, 11, 284–86
 consumer boycotts by, 26
 Great Migration and, 7, 17, 22–23
 Harlem Renaissance for, 25
 "hate strikes" against, 150–51, 180
 in labor organizations, 25
 NAACP and, 25
 cultural pluralism and, 67, 73–76
 "Negro Week" at the New York World's Fair (1940), 76
 in New Deal coalition, 25
 political participation of, 25
 postwar interracial conflict with, 170–71
 in St. Paul "Festival of Nations," 74–76
 sit-ins by, 132
 support of Roosevelt by, 25
 in theatrical films, 110, 153–54
 voting rights for, 171
 war veterans, treatment of, 170–71
 during WWII, 132, 150–55
AJC. *See* American Jewish Committee
Aldrich, Winthrop, 130, 207, 213, 216–17, 225, 231, 260, 276
Alinsky, Saul, 171
Allan, Lewis, 156–158
Allen, Frederick Lewis, 197
Allport, Gordon, 88
Alpers, Benjamin L., 301 *n.* 45
American Association of Advertising Agencies (AAAA), 191–92
American Bankers Association, 207
American Brotherhood, 145
American Committee for Italian Democracy, 254
"American Common," 69
American Creed, 180–81
"American creed," 17
 for Myrdals, Alva and Gunnar, 98–99
An American Dilemma (Myrdal), 72, 95, 97, 100, 239, 285, 288
"American dream," 17, 68, 70–72, 76, 94, 277
"American Economic System" campaign, 190–97, *196,* 211
 labor organizations' support for, 194–95
American Family Robinson (radio show), 54, 59, 61

American Federation of Labor, 23
American Federation of Teachers, 32
"American Heritage" campaign, 201, 207, 209, 211, 223–25. See *also* American Heritage Foundation; Freedom Train.
 Advertising Council and, 207
American Heritage Foundation, 207–9, 211, 213–16, 218–26, 229, 231–33, 235–38, 240, 283, 288. *See also* Freedom Train
 "class tolerance," promotion of, 225–26
 Communist Party criticism of, 218–19
 "Letters from America" campaign and, 260–61
 religious tolerance, promotion of, 224–26
 segregation policy reconsiderations by, 236–39
"American idea," 17
American Indians. *See* Native Americans
"Americanism"
 as anticommunism, 185, 255
 as antifascism *v.,* 112–22
 capitalism, 21
 for CIO, 42–48
 communism *v.,* 210
 "crisis of Americanism," 17–18
 fascism *v.,* 112–16, 122–23, 185
 "Judeo-Christianity" and, 9–10, 243, 283–84
 selling of, 178
 as industrial democracy, 42
 as universalism, 79
 during WWII, in U.S., 112–22
American Jewish Committee (AJC), 82–85, 282
 Advertising Council and, 181, 184
 American Jewish Congress *v.,* 82
 Council Against Intolerance funded by, 85
 "divide and conquer" and, 135
 Nazism in U.S. and, discrediting of, 83
 religious tolerance and, during WWII, 133–38, 144
American Jewish Congress, AJC *v.,* 82
American Labor Party (U.S.), 28
American Liberty League, 49
American Mercury, 29, 151
American Nationalist Federation, 29
American Newspaper Guild, 165
Americans All-Immigrants All (radio show), 75
Americans for Democratic Action (ADA), 329 *n.* 19
American Scholar, 29
American Society of Newspaper Editors, 265
American Studies, 32, 275, 288, 290, 302 *n.* 59
The American Way (book), 15